. . . .

EXCHANGING OUR COUNTRY MARKS

. . . .

D1489750

EXCHANGING OUR COUNTRY MARKS

THE TRANSFORMATION OF AFRICAN IDENTITIES IN
THE COLONIAL AND ANTEBELLUM SOUTH

MICHAEL A. GOMEZ

THE UNIVERSITY OF NORTH CAROLINA PRESS

CHAPEL HILL AND LONDON

Designed by April Leidig-Higgins

Set in Monotype Garamond by Keystone Typesetting, Inc.

Manufactured in the United States of America

The paper in this book meets the guidelines for permanence and
durability of the Committee on Production Guidelines for Book
Longevity of the Council on Library Resources.

Library of Congress Cataloging-in-Publication Data

Gomez, Michael Angelo, 1955–

Exchanging our country marks : the transformation of
African identities in the colonial and antebellum South /
by Michael A. Gomez.

p. cm. Includes bibliographical references and index.

ISBN-13: 978-0-8078-2387-3 (cloth : alk. paper)

ISBN-10: 0-8078-2387-2 (cloth : alk. paper)

ISBN-13: 978-0-8078-4694-0 (pbk. : alk. paper)

ISBN-10: 0-8078-4694-5 (pbk. : alk. paper)

1. Afro-Americans—Southern States—Ethnic identity.

2. Afro-Americans—Southern States—Race identity.

3. Slaves—Southern States—Social life and customs.

4. Southern States—History—Colonial period, ca. 1600–1775.

5. Southern States—History—1775–1865. I. Title.

E185.15.G18 1998   97-21476

305.896'073075—dc21   CIP

Chapter 4 appeared earlier, in somewhat different form,
as "Muslims in Early America," *Journal of Southern History* 60
(November 1994): 671–710, and is reprinted here with permission
of the *Journal of Southern History*.

cloth   05 04 03 02 01   5 4 3 2 1

paper   10 09 08 07 06   10 9 8 7 6

For our son Nathan Manuel, born and died in 1976.

II Samuel 12:22–23

CONTENTS

. . . .

TABLES AND MAPS

. . . .

. . . .

ACKNOWLEDGMENTS

. . . .

I am grateful to a number of individuals for their help and support in bring-ing this work to fruition. In particular, I am indebted to Sterling Stuckey, Gwendolyn Midlo Hall, Colin Palmer, John Thornton, Patrick Manning, and Rosalyn Terborg-Penn for critiquing various drafts of the manuscript. Their input was invaluable; all shortcomings are entirely my own.

Lewis Bateman is to be credited for initially seeing promise in the project and working assiduously to bring it along. I should also like to thank Barbara Hanrahan, who was involved in the project from early on.

Many extended their assistance in archives and libraries throughout the South. I am particularly grateful to the staffs of the state archives at Georgia, Florida, Tennessee, North and South Carolina, Alabama, Mississippi, and Louisiana. The staffs of the Southern Historical Collection at the University of North Carolina at Chapel Hill, the South Caroliniana Library at the University of South Carolina, and the P. K. Yonge Library of Florida History at the University of Florida in Gainesville are also to be commended for their professionalism.

I began this project in the fall of 1987. Each summer since has been devoted to gathering information from the various repositories. Several of these summer excursions were funded through the Bush Research Grant of Spelman College. I am indebted to my entire Spelman family, and especially to the following persons for their unwavering and enthusiastic support for my work: Lois B. Moreland, James Gates, Johnnetta B. Cole, Ruth Simmons, Freddye Hill, and Glenda Price. Thanks to Cynthia Cooke for technical assistance.

Finally, but most important, I extend my utmost appreciation to my wife, Mary, and our daughters, Sonya, Candace, and Jamila, for their companion-ship and understanding. Above all, I thank God.

· · · · · · · · · · · · · · · · ·

EXCHANGING OUR COUNTRY MARKS

· · · · · · · · · · · · · · · · ·

1

· · · · · · · · · · · · · ·

VESEY'S CHALLENGE

· · · · · · · · · · · · · ·

In 1822 a most remarkable experiment was undertaken in and around Charleston, South Carolina. A fifty-five-year-old seafarer, born in either Africa or the West Indies, attempted to destroy the very foundations of American slaveocracy. An examination of Denmark Vesey's insurrection is instructive in that it not only speaks to the capacity of slaves to engage in the ultimate form of resistance but also reveals the nature of social relations within the slave community by the first quarter of the nineteenth century. People of African descent, born in either Africa or the Americas, coalesced for the purpose of realizing a common objective. Free blacks also chose to cast their lot with those in legal bondage, after sober assessment revealed that their own status was precarious if not illusory. Further, the critical role of the evolving black church as a center of resistance and affirmation is underscored by the observation that most, if not all, of the leaders of the revolt were also class leaders or religious instructors in the African Church in Charleston. It is therefore possible to view this endeavor as an attempt to bridge differences of origin, status, and culture by means of religion. As such, the Vesey movement serves as a model for many such subsequent efforts.[1]

Vesey's plans for insurrection were uncovered and those suspected of involvement eventually apprehended. Following legal proceedings, some thirty-five blacks were hanged, at least forty-three were deported to either Africa or the Caribbean, and another fifty-three were released. The trial of

Denmark Vesey and his colleagues is particularly enlightening in that it reveals important insights into his organization and perspective. A number of prosecution witnesses, the majority of whom were either slaves or free blacks, testified to Vesey's unique vision of deliverance from bondage, a vision that involved blacks not only from North America but also from Africa and the Caribbean. One witness, testifying specifically against the codefendant, Rolla, was assured by the latter that "Santo Domingo and Africa would come over and cut up the white people if we only made the motion first."[2] Another witness substantiated the diasporic content of Vesey's message: "Vesey told me that a large army from Santo Domingo and Africa were coming to help us, and we must not stand with our hands in our pockets; he was bitter towards the whites."[3] The Haitian revolution of 1791–1804 was a powerful example of the slaves' potential, its implications reverberating throughout the Americas. Vesey's ability to grasp those implications and incorporate them into an unprecedented prescription for insurrection was stunning in its breadth of conceptualization.

Vesey was himself the very embodiment, the quintessential prototype of the African-European cultural confluence: a Bible-teaching Christian who simultaneously embraced the political leadership and spiritual claims of one of his lieutenants, Gullah Jack, a "conjurer" of significance in his day. Rolla's allegedly voluntary confession includes a poignant depiction of Vesey as a man of deep religious conviction who would "read to us from the Bible, how the Children of Israel were delivered out of Egypt from bondage."[4] The prosecution witness, William, testified that Vesey "studied the Bible a great deal and tried to prove from it that slavery and bondage is against the Bible."[5] Notwithstanding his Christian beliefs, however, Vesey apparently subscribed to the efficacy of Gullah Jack's abilities as a conjurer, for he told one Frank that "there was a little man named Jack who could not be killed, and who could furnish them with arms, he had a charm and he would lead them."[6] In the trial of Peter Poyas, another Vesey codefendant, the fame and reputation of Gullah Jack is noted by a witness who echoes Vesey's claim that "the little man who can't be killed, shot, or taken is named Jack, a Gullah Negro."[7] So fearful was the report of Gullah Jack that a witness testifying against him begged the court to "send me away from this place, as I consider my life in great danger from having given testimony. . . . I was afraid of Gullah Jack as a conjurer."[8] With the Bible in his right hand and Gullah Jack to his left, Denmark Vesey prepared to initiate the apocalypse.

In addition to force and faith, Vesey realized that, absent a third element, his insurrection could not succeed. This third component called for the deemphasis of African ethnic ties while fording the free-slave divide. In their stead, Vesey sought to elevate a single status, a lone condition, that of blackness, of descent from Africa. The theme of unity based solely upon common African ancestry became a refrain in Vesey's message. Prosecution witness Frank conveyed Vesey's words that "the Negro's situation was so bad he did not know how they could endure it, and was astonished they did not rise and fend for themselves."[9] Rolla's confession reiterates Vesey's concern that "we must unite together as the Santo Domingo people did, never to betray one another; and to die before we would tell upon one another."[10] The confession of Jesse, another Vesey insider and confidante, confirms that Vesey understood the struggle in racial terms: "He said, we were deprived of our rights and privileges by the white people . . . and that it was high time for us to seek our rights, and that we were fully able to conquer the whites, if we were only unanimous and courageous, as the St. Domingo people were."[11] Given the task ahead, Vesey deemed it essential to transcend all barriers to racial solidarity.

Closer examination of Vesey's insurrection, however, demonstrates weaknesses inherent in its approach and derivative of the circumstances out of which it sought deliverance. Furthermore, the analysis speaks to the problematic process through which an African American identity was forged during the period of legal enslavement. For although the movement attempted to transcend ethnic and social differences in the quest for freedom, it achieved neither its ultimate objective nor the fashioning of a unifying principle. Organized according to ethnicity, the revolt consisted of an Igbo column led by Monday Gell and a Gullah contingent (a reference to the Congolese-Angolan and/or Gola members of the slave community in the Charleston area and their descendants) under Gullah Jack, in addition to other companies. The division of Vesey's forces into such constituent segments was a concession to the social realities of time and place and clearly indicates that although the leaders of the insurrection had reached a level of political awareness whereby they were prepared to work together, their adherents had not. Rather, the principle of mobilization for the latter called for the primacy of ethnicity and attendant culture over race and intercultural relatedness. As separate ethnicities, the followers of Monday Gell and Gullah Jack were willing to assume responsibilities equally shared by others of like status and interests, but not as individuals organized without regard to ethnic considerations.

The segmented nature of Vesey's organization is important but by no means singular evidence that the early-nineteenth-century African American community was halt at various stations between ethnicity and race in the continuum of identity. Yet resolution to the query of identity was critical to the process of response and regeneration. This book seeks to examine the means by which Africans and their descendants attempted to fashion a collective identity in the colonial and antebellum American South. It is a study of their efforts to move from ethnicity to race as the basis for such an identity, a movement best understood when the impact of both internal and external forces upon social relations within this community are examined. The analysis yields the following conclusion: prior to 1830, the movement toward race and away from ethnicity met with varying degrees of success relative to place and period, and in any case was significantly influenced by ethnic antecedents. In some instances, social stratification within the African American community can be related to preceding ethnic differences. But whether related to ethnicity or not, classism emerged as the principal obstacle to a race-based collective concept.

The idea that the African identity underwent certain transformations is by no means novel. Two of the most profound examinations of that transformation are Amiri Baraka's (LeRoi Jones) *Blues People* (1963) and Sterling Stuckey's *Slave Culture* (1987). The former seeks to demonstrate the various stages and contours of this transition by following the evolution of African American music; the latter accomplishes a similar operation through an examination of the ring shout and nationalist ideology. The premise of Baraka's work is that the movement from African-based work songs to sorrow songs to primitive blues to jazz to classical blues to swing to bebop and beyond reflects a changing self-perspective in conjunction with political and socioeconomic developments over time. Stuckey argues that the ring shout was a principal mechanism by which Africans of varying ethnicities were able to span their differences. In either case, the conclusion is that black folk began to see themselves differently.

Both Baraka and Stuckey have successfully demonstrated the possibility of observing critical moments of creativity by way of cultural efflorescence. This study seeks to build upon such models of transformation by examining certain processes through which people of African descent attempted to reconstitute their collective identity. While recognizing the validity and importance of exploring the political and social implications of musical innovation as well as folkloric tradition, this investigation will draw from additional indexes of sociocultural transition to make the case.

In order to understand the process by which the African American identity was formed, and to flesh out the means by which relations within the African American community developed, it is essential to recover the African cultural, political, and social background, recognizing that Africans came to the New World with certain coherent perspectives and beliefs about the universe and their place in it. What were Africans' worldviews? What were their values, ethics, beliefs? What really mattered to them? Once questions such as these are addressed, it becomes possible to investigate how Africans' interpretation of reality changed as a consequence of the enslavement process and how this reorientation was communicated to descendants.

Given advances in the study of Africa, it is possible to push beyond perfunctory discussions of great Sudanic empires (read Ghana, Mali, and Songhay) in the attempt to say something about the African past. We can now discuss with greater accuracy the origins of subject African populations and the specific forms of their cultural and political accoutrements. For although there are striking similarities of culture and social and political organization in the various regions of Africa, there are also important differences. The key to understanding the process by which these diverse groups of immigrants attempted to fashion a sociocultural coherency is an appreciation of the nature of these differences.

This investigation does not proceed beyond 1830, by which time the South assumes a much more militant stance in its apologetic of slavery. By that date, the relative numbers of American-born slaves far outnumber those of the native African, and the general patterns of the emerging African American identity are discernible. At the same time, there is significant diminution of explicit references in the primary sources to activities of African-born individuals (which is consistent with the fact that their numbers are dwindling), thus making it difficult to continue a line of inquiry specifically concerned with their position and role. A translation has taken place by 1830, consistent with the demographic evidence, that delineates the demise of a preponderant African sociocultural matrix and the rise of an African American one in its place. It is the objective of this study to more clearly define and understand this translation.

My sources can be grouped into six categories: secondary literature concerning North American slavery, scholarly appraisals of the transatlantic slave trade, sources that comprise the debate over the degree and implications of African cultural retentions within the North American slave population, the largely anthropological discussion of the acculturative process (which is clearly related to the former category and barely distinguishable from it), the body of historical and anthropological literature that concerns West and West Central Africa, and those primary materials that form the basis of this study.[12] A major part of the primary materials is the corpus of curiously underused runaway slave advertisements in southern newspapers. These are particularly important in assigning ethnic identities to the slave population; that is, many notices for absconded individuals contain references to place of origin, original names, patterns of scarification, and so on. Of course, such information can be ascriptive; where a slave actually originated and where she was believed to have originated could vary greatly. This same problem occurs regarding the origins of the African slave population as a whole. However, it will be argued here that it is possible to match overall patterns of importation with references to specific individuals and communities, thus obtaining a plausible picture of the general ethnic pattern in the South.

Before proceeding, certain terms and concepts require clarification. The word *community* is used here to convey the concept of a collection of individuals and families who share a common and identifiable network of sociocultural communications (for example, kinship, dietary patterns, labor conventions, artistic expressions, language) that have their origin in either a particular geographic area and period of time or a unique system of beliefs and rationalization. The size of the community can be broadly or narrowly defined by either expanding or contracting the area of origin in question or by adjusting the criteria by which a belief system is determined as such. Thus it is possible to speak of both an African and an Igbo community concurrently; it is also permissible to propose the existence of a Muslim community, as the latter refers to a shared tradition of faith. However, the use of the term does not necessarily imply conscious affinities; that is, those members of varying backgrounds who are described as comprising an African community in America or who are subsequently included in the emergent African American community may not have so viewed themselves. Indeed, that they may not have shared such a perspective speaks to the very means by which the African American identity was formed, namely, through a series of related but at times contradictory processes, developing from both within and without the African collective. Those of African descent had to relate to each other not only according to the logic of their shared condition but also in response to the perception of their condition by those outside of it. The various avenues along which these discourses traveled, in addition to their multiple destinations, constitute the focus of this study.

Ethnicity refers to the same network of sociocultural communications and so at times can be used interchangeably with *community*, but it lacks the elasticity of the latter term. It is therefore employed much more restrictively, so that one cannot speak of a Muslim ethnicity; neither can the descriptor *African* satisfy an inquiry into the specific background of an individual. Bound by language, culture, territorial association, and historical derivation, ethnicity's purpose is to dissociate rather than associate, to engage in a reductionist enterprise as opposed to aggregation. Implicit in the concept of ethnicity is the determination of that which is unique about a group of people; it is an attempt to understand the essence of what distinguishes various collections of individuals.

To be sure, more recent Africanist literature calls attention to the uncritical use of ethnic categorization. There are two basic reasons for this trend. First of all, it is possible to view certain ethnic labels as artifacts of the slave trade. Second, colonialist ideology played a role in the criteria used to define particular ethnicities. Vansina's study of populations in southern Gabon, for example, concludes that requirements of colonial administration resulted in novel and artificial groupings, and that absent the further qualification of ethnicity by territorial specificity, the concept is largely useless if not misleading.[13]

The preceding observation cautions that the history of African social formations is enormously complex. A significant number of these formations did not conform to notions of ethnicity, so that the conscious loyalties of considerable numbers did not extend beyond the village, the village group, or the town. Many such relatively small-scale, culturopolitical group identities were family- or kin-based. At the opposite end of the spectrum were large, centralized states and the phenomenon of the empire (the nuclear state and its subject provinces, themselves formerly centralized and independent). Territorially smaller, densely populated villages and territorially larger, sparsely populated states are also found in the historical record.

Genres such as West African Arabic literature reveal, however, that ethnicities clearly existed prior to colonialism or any other contact with Europeans; some of these sources antedate the colonial period by hundreds of years.[14] To cite a few examples, al-Khuwārizmī refers to the Zaghawa (possibly the Kanuri) near Lake Chad as early as the mid-ninth century. Al-Yaʿqūbī, also writing in the ninth century, identifies the "kingdom of Malal," an early reference to Malinke, who would go on to found the Malian empire. Imperial Songhay's ethnic consciousness is reflected in the titles of government officials such as the Barbush-*mondio* (in charge of the Barabish Arabs), the Maghsharen-*koi* (leader of the Tuareg of Azawad), the Dendi-*fari* (governor of the province from which the Songhay people originated), and so on; and the Sorko and the Arbi (a difficult group to identify) are discussed as ethnicities in several sources. Shaykh Aḥmad Bābā (1556–1627) of Songhay specifically listed the Mossi, the Dogon, and the Yoruba, among other groups, as unbelievers eligible for legal enslavement. And the written and oral traditions agree that the Serrakole (or Soninke) trace their ethnic distinctiveness as far back as ancient Ghana itself. In other words, ethnicity can be detected very early in West Africa.

These and other ethnic identities were formed and facilitated by some combination of centralized states, extensive commercial networks, religion, language, and culture long before exportation via the transatlantic slave trade. This study will further argue that the progression of the slave trade from the barracoon to the field created conditions under which the latent potential of ethnicity developed even among those who were not consciously so disposed prior to their capture. Whether fully formed in Africa or America, ethnicity is crucial to an understanding of African American ethnogenesis.

Directly related to the issue of the formation of the African American identity is the question of acculturation. If by acculturation it is meant a process by which two or more previously distinct and dissociated cultures begin to interact and exchange content in a given locale, resulting in a cultural hybrid of some sort, then it is absolutely essential to examine the political and economic context of the exchange to accurately appreciate its dynamics and consequences. Such a transfer rarely took place within a political vacuum; it certainly did not in the colonial and antebellum South.

Mintz and Price have written that "the monopoly of power wielded by the Europeans in slave colonies strongly influenced the ways in which cultural and social continuities from Africa would be maintained as well as the ways in which innovations could occur."[15] If this was true of the West Indies, the context of the comment, it is even more applicable to the American South, where the various European and African cultures by no means enjoyed equal footing. Due to the privileging of the former, it becomes very difficult to evaluate circumstances in which elements of one culture merged with, were subsumed by, succumbed to, or existed in static and creative tension with those of another without taking into consideration the political disequilibria influencing the process.

There were, in fact, at least two realms of acculturation in the American South. First, there was the world of the slaves, in which intra-African and African–African American cultural factors were at play. This was by far the more complicated of the two realms, as differences and affinities among those born in Africa and those of African descent born in America (and even those shipped to North America from elsewhere in the New World) were negotiated synchronously. But there was obviously interaction with the host society—the white world—both slaveholding and nonslaveholding. The dynamics of cultural transfer within this second realm were conditioned by the asymmetry of power between slave and nonslave. Thus the exchange could not have been "fair"; there is no way to determine the relative strengths and weaknesses of the participating cultures under such conditions. To therefore attempt an analysis of acculturation without taking into consideration issues of hegemony and subjugation is to engage in a misinformed and arguably meaningless abstraction.

To be sure, there are other factors involved in the phenomenon of cultural exchange between those of European and African descent. Herskovits, in insisting upon a comparative approach to the question of acculturation in the New World, examined the characteristics of West Indian and Latin American slave societies in an effort to understand the North American counterpart.[16]

He noted that the degree of contact between whites and blacks, the diverging levels of contact between various categories of slaves and whites in the same locale (for example, "house" versus "field" slaves), and the widely divergent range of slave responses to such contact are all important matters to consider when studying cultural exchange. The degree and form of contact, in turn, were dependent upon such factors as ratios between whites and blacks, urban and rural contexts, the climate and topography, and the nature and consequent organization of the plantation in question. After taking all into consideration, he concluded that the United States could be distinguished from the rest of the Western Hemisphere "as a region where departure from African modes of life was greatest, and where such Africanisms as persisted were carried through in generalized form, almost never directly referable to a specific tribe or definite area."[17]

There are two major points to be made in response to the preceding observations (from a work both pioneering and enduring). First, although reference is made to the variable of plantation organization and the related issue of control as factors in acculturation, it escapes appropriate attention that the very context of such exchange immediately introduces a distortion into the process. Second, subsequent research has substantially qualified the question of African cultural continuity in North America to the extent that it is now possible, indeed necessary, to examine this continuity within the framework of ethnicity. A more informed discussion of the role of ethnicity can only further elucidate an examination of acculturation. As a result of these two realms of acculturation, a polycultural African American community would emerge. That is, African Americans would maintain related yet distinguishable life-styles. The first realm of interaction saw the rise of volitive cultures (or set of related cultural forms), the elements of which were voluntarily negotiated and subsequently adopted by the slaves themselves. Such cultures were displayed beyond the gaze of the host society. What the slave really believed, how she actually perceived the world, how interpersonal relations were really conducted, were all issues of life engaged in a manner as freely and as fully as was possible within this first realm, given the slave regime.

At the same time, people of African and European descent were involved in extensive exchange within the second realm, only in this instance the political and economic control of the latter was such that intervention into the acculturative process was unavoidable. The host society enjoyed physical, psychological, and military powers of coercion and could to varying degrees determine the cultural choices of the enslaved. As a consequence, what emerged was not simply the synthesis of an encounter between European and African cultural forms but a system of cultural codes of imposition, a culture of coercion.[18]

The African American therefore engaged in polycultural rather than syncretic life-styles. Both the culture of coercion and the cultures of volition were simultaneously maintained, one in the open arena (around white folk), the others in the slave quarters and anywhere else absent white representation. But even in the company of whites, in face of the coercive experience, the desire of the slave to define his own reality resulted in what Herskovits has called "reinterpretation."[19] That is, while the culture of coercion tended to dominate the forms of expression, the intent and meaning behind the slave's participation was quite another matter. The slaveholder may have commanded conformity in deed; he could not, however, dictate the posture of the inner person. It was precisely as the song says:

Got one mind for white folks to see,
'Nother for what I know is me,
He don't know, he don't know my mind.[20]

A familiar example of the phenomenon of reinterpretation is found in the realm of religion. As practiced in North America, Protestantism tended to be rigid and inflexible, hostile to the kind of association between African deities and Christian saints found in a number of Catholic societies elsewhere in the New World. Under these circumstances, the African convert to Protestantism (such conversion was relatively rare in the colonial period and increased only incrementally during the antebellum) may have very well reinterpreted the dogma and ritual of the Christian church in ways that conformed to preexisting cosmological views. In the presence of the host community, reinterpretation was the lone option available to the slave. Once removed from the gaze, however, the slave was free to Africanize the religion, thus engaging in reinterpretation and true synthesis simultaneously.

It is the synthesis that best characterizes the activity within the volitive realm of acculturation. In music, art, folklore, language, and even social structure, there is sufficient evidence to conclude that people of African descent were carefully selecting elements of various cultures, both African and European, issuing into combinations of creativity and innovation. Such a process is consistent with the nature of viable cultures; that is, they have the capacity to change and adapt when exposed to external stimuli. The African American slave community, within the volitive realm, made deliberate cultural choices. They borrowed what was of interest from the external society, and they improved upon previously existing commonalities of African cultures in such ways that, with regard to music for example, the slaves' "style, with its overriding antiphony, its group nature, its pervasive functionality, its improvisational character, its strong relationship in performance to dance and bodily movements and expression, remained closer to the musical styles and performances of West Africa and the Afro-American music of the West Indies and South America than to the musical style of Western Europe."[21] In fact, the African antecedent would inform every aspect of African American culture, not simply music. The question remains: What were the mechanisms by which syntheses were created, especially regarding the resolution of inter-ethnic differences? The contention here is that, although an exhaustive answer requires more extensive research, it is likely that the solution relates closely to the ways in which the various ethnicities and their progeny interacted and sought to address the fundamental question of identity.

The creation of the African American collective involved a movement in emphasis away from ethnicity and toward race as the primary criterion of inclusion. That is to say, an identity based upon ethnicity was often a practice both very African and very ancient; race, a social construction intimately informed by the political context, was relatively new and without significant meaning in much of Africa at the dawn of the transatlantic slave trade.[22] *Race*, an elusive term resistant to scientific definition, was essentially invented by Europeans in an effort to categorize various populations both in Europe and beyond. It would only acquire a distinct meaning for Africans with the growing frequency of interaction with whites involved in slaving and other commercial activities.

The reference at this juncture to the European factor allows for a related point to be established, namely, that Europeans in the New World also engaged in a process of reidentification. Importantly and especially in what would become the United States, the European-turned-American established his new identity at the expense of people of Native American and African descent. As the white settler community grew in North America, and as successive generations became increasingly distanced from Europe culturally and psychologically, the settlers began to undergo a reevaluation of their collective personality. The American Revolution was the logical consequence of this development, but it did not end there. The American would continue to search for ways in which he could distinguish himself from his European counterpart. The national character, unlike the European's, was formed by the existence of the frontier, by the abundance of land and means of subsistence, by the exaltation of property, by a new and constitutionally defined relationship between the state and the church. But the national character was also determined by the white American's juxtaposition (and transposition) with the Native American, viewed as living in a veritable state of nature. That is, whatever the American was in the process of becoming, it was necessarily opposite that of the character and condition of the Native American.[23]

Recent work by Patterson and Morrison substantiates the point that if such were the case for the Native American, it was doubly true for the

African.[24] Patterson's argument that the concept of freedom is inextricably connected to and derivative of the condition of slavery is particularly germane to this discussion, for people of African descent became the very essence of slavery. Although the reality is that the American national character has been thoroughly influenced by the African presence, and although American culture is distinctive largely because of the African contribution, these consequences were certainly not by design. On the contrary, the American character was constructed to be synonymous with freedom and the American political experiment a guarantor of the property owner's interests. But in order to know the true nature of freedom, in order to comprehend what it meant to possess, indeed, in order to identify those properties consistent with full humanity, it was necessary to have illustrations of that which constituted their antitheses.

The African slave and her progeny fulfilled this need like no other group, occupying that cranial region in which are preserved concretized examples of antonymic content and allowing for the procession of binary oppositional thinking. In this way, the enslaved black man was the personification of the absence of freedom, nobility, virtue, and anything else consistent with what was wholesome and admirable. By definition, the African came to represent all that the American could never be. These properties were deemed inherent, race the explanatory factor.

Enslaved Africans had to learn the significance of race. Accustomed to their own identification processes, they were viewed by the host society as so many variations on the same theme. It has been assumed that people of African descent automatically shed their earlier affinities and began to take on the mantle of race. This movement toward race and away from ethnicity is presumed to have been a function of time and fading memories. Such has been the assumption.

Without question, the evidence is clear that a significant proportion of the African American community made the transition from ethnicity to race. This was a process that contained a fundamental opposition in that the concept of race originated from without, yet the process was Africanized in that a degree of unity was achieved against the interests of the host society. This basic dialectic—the adoption of an identity forged by antithetical forces from both without and within the slave community—is itself emblematic of the contradictory mechanism by which the African American identity was shaped. But beyond this assertion is the more difficult and complex matter of how such unity was achieved. Did Africans simply decide one day to eschew their ancestral heritage and become "new Negroes"; did they simply forget as the years passed by?

This brings the inquiry to the central issue with which it is concerned.

That is, contrary to the foregoing, Africans and their descendants did not simply forget (or elect not to remember) the African background. Rather, that background played a crucial role in determining the African American identity. Put another way, given the importance of African ethnicity, it is inescapable that ethnicity had a direct impact on African Americans' self-perception. The African American represents an amalgam of the ethnic matrix; that is, the African American identity is in fact a composite of identities. In certain areas and periods of time, the composite approached a uniform whole, as the transition from ethnicity to race was more thorough-going. But for other times and locations, the composite was fragmented and incomplete. When incomplete, differences having their origin in ethnic distinctions were in instances carried over into differences of status, thus transforming the original ethnic divide without ever having grappled with an effective reconciliation. But whether fragmented or whole, the means by which these results were achieved have heretofore remained unexamined. Hopefully, this book will cast some light on these matters. What follows is a sketch of the content.

. . . .

A number of principal groups comprised the African presence in America. Arriving at different times and in different volumes, they tended to be concentrated in respective locations; their relative rates of entry, population sizes, and distribution patterns within the South are therefore critical to understanding the consequent African American identity. Of course, they brought with them their culture and worldviews, the blending of which varied from state to state and was dependent upon ethnic configurations specific to the area in question. All, however, passed through certain stages in moving from ethnicity to race.

The barracoon marked the beginning. Twin conditions of bewilderment and disorientation accompanied disease and demise for many at this point, drawn as they were from their several villages and hamlets to holding stations of varying size and structure. With the slaver finally full and the deal finally done, the African left her world just as she entered it.

The Middle Passage was a birth canal, launching a prolonged struggle between slaveholder and enslaved over rights of definition. Both the European and the African would find themselves deeply influenced by the culture and presence of the other; it would not and could not be a one-way street. But the Middle Passage was also a death canal, baptismal waters of a different kind. At the very least, the African died to what was and to what could have been. The experience would leave an indelible impression upon the African's soul, long remembered by sons and daughters. It is the memory of ultimate rupture, a classic expulsion from the garden.

Whoever he was prior to boarding the slaver, something inside began to stir, giving him a glimpse of what he was to become. Moved to indignity over mistreatment aboard the slaver, the captive's inexorable movement toward self-reassessment was further propelled by surviving the ordeal. Deep bonds of affection transcended ethnic ties, forming one foundation for the eventual movement to race, a path chosen by rather than for Africans.

Contemporary reports are consistent that the African feared white cannibalism; such fears were not unfounded. The African was indeed consumed by the rice fields, by the indigo fields, by the cane fields and silver mines, by the hellish reordering of human relations and the human condition for purposes of plunder and profit. Such consumption, however, required a preliminary period of seasoning, a period of adjustment to remove saline qualities from native-born, "salt-water" Africans. Learning the rudiments of a European language was part of the process, but the language was bent and frayed and stretched and refashioned. The tone of the delivery, the lilt of the voice, the cadence of the words, the coordinated body language were employed to communicate the ideas, emotions, and sensibilities of persons of African descent. As such, Africanized English greatly aided collective, interethnic efforts at resistance.

The advent of the "country-born" introduced a new and permanent variable into the equation of identity formation. The African-born, despite the length of time spent away from her homeland, retained a psychic attachment and orientation toward Africa. The birth of American-born children, however, created a crisis for African parents. They could not avoid internal conflict, their loyalties and centers of affection pulled from either side of the Atlantic. They had been torn from their familial ties in their motherland, but the fruit of their own wombs now blossomed in the place of exile. Further complicating matters were marriages and equivalent arrangements between American-born and African-born spouses. Bonds of affection now existed in both America and Africa. Although home remained Africa for the African-born, where was home for their daughters and sons? In the process of answering these and similar queries, the African could not escape the fact that an important aspect of herself had been deposited on foreign soil, and that the blood of the ancestors now ran through children who would never know them. Equally, the country-born experienced faraway places in the appearance and intonations of their parents. Powerful linkages were forever established, linkages whose meaning would constitute the black man's golden fleece, its implications the black woman's holy grail, for generations to come.

In the course of African–African American interaction, there were many items to be negotiated. Day-to-day concerns provided the framework for a great deal of the exchange. Women and men from both sides of the Atlantic would have necessarily discussed what were the best ways to nurse children and instill discipline, the proper care of the aged and infirm, the best fishing methods, and what constituted respectable behavior in the company of elders. Greetings and departures, appropriate and inappropriate subjects for small talk, and all other social conventions were put into place over time. That is, black folk had to re-create their society, their collective inner life, drawing from any number of ethnic paradigms and informed by the present crisis. But in addition to the minutia of daily cares, arguably weightier and more philosophical discourse took place. An issue that often came up, and was resolved in a way that greatly facilitated the formation of the African American corporate identity, was the subject of the slave trade.

Concomitant with the move toward race was the stratification of black society. Most Africans had been taken out of cultures in which divisions of labor had been apportioned to whole families, within which certain skills and economic activities were passed down from generation to generation. This arrangement of structures, somewhat akin to Western guilds, has led some to characterize much of precolonial Africa as a collection of caste societies based upon differentiated economic and labor functions, into which individuals were born rather than selected. Many, then, came to North America already possessed of ironworking skills, or adept at producing leather manufactures, or with considerable experience in animal husbandry. During the colonial period, skills acquired in Africa together with European stereotyping of Africans in America combined to inform labor differentiation, the basis of classism in the black community. As the colonial period merged with that of the antebellum, African importation began to decline while the percentage of American-born blacks began to increase. Labor differentiation could no longer be based upon ethnicity, but upon other factors. As a result, not everyone worked as laborers in the fields—there were skilled and supervisory duties as well. Furthermore, not all lived in the countryside—many dwelled in towns, where ports were constructed, fine homes crafted, streets laid, iron worked, horses shod, and so on. Blacks were to be found performing all of these tasks and many more.

Classism was an important and inevitable development in the history of the black community. Just as important was the conversion to Christianity, which ultimately facilitated the transition to race. This was primarily through those properties that allowed for differences among and between the African and the country-born to be bridged in an effective manner. At the same time, race influenced religious beliefs within the black community and the African antecedent continued to inform, so that whether individuals converted or not, many participated in that most sublime movement of unity and transition, the ring shout. A clear and unmistakable cultural form directly out of the African past, the shout was practiced long before significant numbers converted to Christianity. The new religion could not alter the centrality of the practice, which had become both substance and metaphor of the African experience in America.

By way of the shout and in conjunction with other avenues such as water baptism, funerary rites, and hoodoo, Christianity was Africanized. Although powerful media of simultaneous transformation and continuity, these practices could not, however, effect a thoroughgoing transition to unity and race-based consciousness. A primary impediment was the emergence of class. The black elite by and large rejected the shout. A number of black clergy railed against it. Together, they saw the practice as heathenish, too African. Inspired by visions of inclusion, the elite created distance. Informed by the material conditions of reality, the folk embraced proximity. The schism was nowhere more conspicuously displayed than in the ritual.

2

. . . .

TIME AND SPACE

. . . .

A great deal has been written about the multifaceted Atlantic slave trade. Opposing arguments have been presented on both the trade and its implications. With regard to the latter, the question of the relationship between the trade and the emergence of Western capitalism has been posed, as well as the impact of the trade on the developmental capacities of the African continent.[1]

As for the trade itself, the debate has centered largely on attempts at quantification, resulting in a number of studies that narrow their focus to specific components or agents in the trade.[2] This high expenditure of energy has rendered a composite picture that is increasingly reliable as it is removed from distortions of sentiment and hyperbole. And yet, such inquiries continue to experience a subtle and rather ironic relationship to moral and ethical questions, notwithstanding their vigorous efforts to have it otherwise. Indeed, the preference for statistics will never succeed in fully masking the human dimensions of the tragedy they seek to represent. By its very nature, the relationship between the "business" of the slave trade and attendant moral considerations will continue to constitute a veritable tar baby for the cliometricians of the profession.

Our purpose here is not to reinvent the wheel. Rather, it is to benefit from the existing consensus in order to establish basic parameters upon which subsequent discussion can be premised. To that end, this chapter takes the position that there was a correspondence between the North American and

British slave trades. The various regions of origin differed in their contributions to the North American market, resulting in huge and consistent numbers coming from West Central Africa and the Bight of Biafra. At the same time, the North American market was distinguished by its relatively balanced sex ratios and high importation of children. Certain American ports received far more slaves than others, and enslaved populations tended to be concentrated in specific locations, throughout which substantial networks were established, linking small and large slaveholdings and expanding the boundaries of the slave's physical setting. Such is the overview, now for the details.

Research subsequent to Curtin's early work essentially substantiates his findings.[3] That is, the total number of Africans imported into the Americas is somewhere between 9.6 and 10.8 million, while the total export figure is about 11.9 million. Concerning North America in particular, this investigation estimates the total import figure at 480,930, or 481,000 for the sake of convenience.[4] The total is 5 percent of the 10 million or so brought into the New World.[5]

The Atlantic slave trade spanned some four hundred years, from the fifteenth to the nineteenth century. By 1650 the number of Africans transported through the trade reached 10,000 per year, below which the numbers did not fall until about 1840.[6] The apex for the trade as a whole was between 1700 and 1810, when approximately 6.5 million Africans were exported.[7] In fact, 60 percent of all Africans imported into the Americas made the fateful voyage between 1721 and 1820, and 80 percent of these immigrants traveled to the New World between 1701 and 1850.[8]

Rates of importation and regions of origin are issues fundamental to this inquiry. The rate of and distribution patterns for North American slave imports coincide with the regional and temporal distribution of the overall British trade.[9] This observation has important implications for the formation of the African American identity. At the same time, the period during which varying groups were exported from Africa is also critical in that certain historical developments would affect some but not necessarily others. The spread of Islam and the proliferation of warfare and raiding to feed New World demand for slaves are examples of historical developments that deeply influenced the social, cultural, and political fabric of various African societies. As a result, Africans emanating at different times from the same ethnicity and region did not necessarily share the same sociopolitical milieu.

Using shipping data (as opposed to demographic-based estimates), Richardson has argued that the decadal distribution of African importation rates into British North America was much more even than previously believed. His overall estimates of British slave exports, shown in table 2.1, demonstrate a gradual rise in the importation rate (with the exception of a dramatic

TABLE 2.1 Decadal Exports for the Whole of the British Slave Trade, 1700–1807

1700–1709	150,000	1760–69	391,000
1710–19	201,000	1770–79	340,000
1720–29	269,000	1780–89	349,000
1730–39	276,000	1790–99	417,000
1740–49	195,000	1800–1807	281,000
1750–59	251,000		

Source: David Richardson, "Slave Exports from West and West-Central Africa, 1700–1810: New Estimates of Volume and Distribution," *Journal of African History* 30 (1989): 3, 6–7. © Cambridge University Press 1989. Reprinted with the permission of Cambridge University Press.

increase between 1759 and 1769) that corresponds with a comparable increase in the demand for slaves throughout the eighteenth century. These figures apply to the overall British export trade but suggest a symmetrical increase in North American slave imports as well.[10]

It may be that Africans arrived in post-Columbian North America prior to 1526, by which time they had certainly disembarked. Their numbers remained insignificant, however, until the advent of the British, who in 1619 imported twenty Africans into Virginia. Some were chattel, some servants for fixed periods of time, others attained freedom. By the end of the seventeenth century, Virginia had succeeded in clarifying the legal status of people of African descent, and they were henceforth associated with slavery. Table 2.2 is a compilation of both Curtin's and Rawley's findings for slave imports from 1626 to 1820.[11] A comparison with the demographic record of the African-based population in the colonies from 1630 to 1780 is possible by means of considering table 2.3, which indicates that the population doubled every ten years between 1650 and 1670 and again between 1680 and 1700. From that point until 1780 the black population doubled every twenty years. The increases witnessed between 1720 and 1740, and again between 1740 and 1760, are matched precisely by the import estimates for those years during which approximately 150,000 Africans came to British North America (table 2.2).[12] When compared with the 43,000 import totals of the previous forty-year span (1680–1720), the 1720–60 import totals represent an increase of more than 300 percent. Although the ratio of the African-born to the African-based population decreased from 2 to 3 in the 1680–1720 period to 1 to 3 in 1720–60, a significant percentage of the African-based population were first-generation African Americans (that is, born in America as opposed to Africa) and therefore very close to their African origins. Stated

TABLE 2.2 African Importation into North America, 1626–1810

1626–50	1,600 (.4%)
1651–75	3,900 (1.03%)
1676–1700	23,000 (6.1%)
1701–20	19,800 (5.25%)
1721–40	50,400 (13.38%)
1741–60	100,400 (26.7%)
1761–80	85,800 (22.8%)
1781–1810	91,600 (24.3%)

Sources: Philip D. Curtin, *The Atlantic Slave Trade: A Census* (Madison, 1969), 140; James A. Rawley, *The Transatlantic Slave Trade: A History* (New York, 1981), 167.

differently, this 1760 population was largely a mix of those either African-born or African-reared.

By 1790, the African-based population had increased to about 757,000. Table 2.4 estimates its expansion. Based upon Fogel and Engerman's calculations presented in table 2.5, the African-born hovered around 22 percent from 1790 to 1810. Although the African-born population declined precipitously after 1810, it represented a significant proportion of the black community before then; much of the remaining African-based population was only one or two generations removed from African soil. It is therefore important to argue that in examining the development of African American culture and society, there is more to gain by adopting a premise of proximity rather than distance.

Concerning destinations, Africans imported into North America disembarked all along the eastern seaboard as well as along the Gulf of Mexico. While the overall pattern of distribution was therefore widespread, importations tended to be concentrated in certain areas. During the colonial period, for example, Africans arrived at a number of points stretching from New England to the mid-Atlantic colonies to the Southeast. However, the vast majority of Africans were brought into the South during the colonial and antebellum periods.

Most of the Africans who entered the Southeast did so through Chesapeake Bay and South Carolina, principally Charleston. In fact, one estimate maintains that for 1701–75, some 54 percent of all slaves imported into the Southeast came through the Chesapeake and the remaining 46 percent arrived via South Carolina and Charleston.[13] Regarding Virginia, the slave population accelerated with the chartering of the Royal African Company in 1672, so that a population that grew very slowly at first (23 in 1625; 300 by 1650) was greatly augmented by importations of more than 1,000 Africans

TABLE 2.3 Growth of the Black Population by Region, 1630–1780

Year	New England	Middle Colonies	South	Total
1630	0	10	50	60
1640	195	232	170	597
1650	380	515	705	1,600
1660	562	630	1,728	2,920
1670	375	790	3,370	4,535
1680	470	1,480	5,021	6,971
1690	950	2,472	13,307	16,729
1700	1,680	3,661	26,137	31,478
1710	2,585	6,218	36,063	44,866
1720	3,956	10,825	54,058	68,839
1730	6,118	11,683	73,220	91,021
1740	8,541	16,452	125,031	150,024
1750	10,982	20,736	204,702	236,420
1760	12,717	29,049	284,040	325,806
1770	15,367	34,929	409,526	459,822
1780	14,427	42,365	518,628	575,420

Source: U.S. Department of Commerce, Bureau of the Census, *Historical Statistics of the United States* (Washington, D.C., 1975), 2:1168.

per year by the end of the seventeenth century.[14] As a consequence of this increased rate, the African-based population in Virginia grew from 12,000 in 1708 to 120,156 in 1756, while the white population increased from 18,000 to 173,316 during the same interval.[15]

In Maryland, the slave population also witnessed incremental growth initially, following slavery's introduction into that colony shortly after 1634.[16] Importation laws were enacted in order to encourage the expansion of the slave population, and in 1671 the colonial legislature cleared the moral hurdle by ruling that the Christian conversion of slaves did not alter their legal status. Slaveholders "now felt that they could import African heathens, convert them to Christianity, and thus justify the act of holding them in slavery."[17] As a result, importation began to increase by the end of the seventeenth century, and by 1750 the black population stood at 40,000 (compared to 100,000 whites).

The 1526 arrival of Africans in what would be become South Carolina was part of a Spanish expedition from the Caribbean.[18] Although the expedition met with misfortune and was forced to return to Santo Domingo, the following one hundred years witnessed a series of struggles between Spanish, French, and Native Americans along the northern Florida coast, struggles that involved the use of Africans by European factions. Whatever the precise

TABLE 2.4 Growth of the Black Population, 1790–1860

Year	Slave	Free	Total	% of Total U.S. Population
1790	697,624	59,557	757,181	19.3
1800	893,602	108,435	1,002,037	18.9
1810	1,191,362	186,466	1,377,808	19.0
1820	1,538,022	233,634	1,771,656	18.4
1830	2,009,043	319,599	2,328,642	18.1
1840	2,487,355	386,293	2,873,648	16.8
1860	3,953,760	488,070	4,441,830	14.1

Source: U.S. Department of Commerce, Bureau of the Census, *Negro Population, 1790–1915* (Washington, D.C., 1918), 29, 53.

details of the precolonial circumstances, black settlement in South Carolina antedates its existence as a British possession. In an effort to boost the slave population, British proprietors in 1663 offered settlers twenty acres for every black male and ten acres for every black female brought into the colony in the first year.[19] Some twenty years later, the black population of South Carolina equalled that of whites, and by 1715, blacks outnumbered whites 10,500 to 6,250. By 1720, the slave population had increased to about 12,000 (compared to 6,525 whites), and in 1724, the African-based population was three times that of its white counterpart.[20] Such was the rapid expansion of the black population in South Carolina that by 1711 whites feared the former was "getting out of hand"; revolts in and after 1720 confirmed these fears, only to be followed by the Stono Rebellion in 1739. By 1750 South Carolina's slave population stood at 39,000.

In contrast to the other colonies in British North America, South Carolina's early population grew out of Caribbean rather than European antecedents. It is Wood's estimate that in the very early years, from 25 to 33 percent of the colony's population was black, and that prior to 1700 most of these were from the West Indies. They came mostly by way of Barbados, then St. Kitts, Nevis, Jamaica, the Bahamas, Bermuda, Antigua, Montserrat, and the Leeward Islands. From 1700 to 1775, however, Rawley estimates that of the 83,825 persons imported into South Carolina, some 67,269 originated from Africa, and Washington Creel writes that over 50,000 Africans entered the colony between 1740 and 1776.[21] The vast majority of these people entered South Carolina through the port of Charleston.

Of the five cities that developed in colonial America—Charleston, Newport, Boston, New York, and Philadelphia—Charleston, founded in 1670, emerged as the principal port of entry for slaves. Boston's participation has

TABLE 2.5 Estimates of the Percentage of African-Born, 1620–1860

1620	98%	1760	36%
1640	93%	1780	22%
1660	70%	1800	19%
1680	49%	1810	21%
1700	58%	1820	12%
1720	46%	1840	4%
1740	40%	1860	1%

Source: Robert William Fogel and Stanley L. Engerman, *Time on the Cross* (Boston, 1974), 22–27.

been described as negligible, while Newport's involvement was "similarly small."[22] New York's port was insignificant in the trade, and Philadelphia's role was equally circumscribed. Charleston and smaller neighboring ports, on the other hand, imported nearly 90,000 people of African descent between 1672 and 1775, leading Higgins to contend that one out of every four "Negro ancestors of the current black population of the United States . . . passed through the colonial port of Charleston."[23] Such a proportion is feasible, especially in view of the fact that from 1804 to 1807 some 40,000 more Africans were "rushed to Charleston in anticipation of the prohibition to begin with 1808."[24]

North Carolina maintained a relatively scanty colonial slave population, and although this segment grew dramatically in subsequent years, it satisfied its demand for slave labor almost exclusively through the agency of Charleston.[25] It is with Georgia, however, that a significant slave population is again encountered. Georgia, the only British New World colony of importance established in the eighteenth century (1733), did not legalize slavery until 1750.[26] By 1760, there were 3,000 blacks and 6,000 whites, but by 1773 those numbers had multiplied to 15,000 and 18,000, respectively. Charleston played a critical role in supplying Africans to Georgia, such that during the colonial period the latter relied upon the port for slaves rather than develop a trade of its own. Of the 7,000 Africans imported into adjacent colonies from Charleston between 1717 and 1775, Georgia received the lion's share, with 50 percent going to either Savannah or Sunbury.[27]

Concerning Louisiana, Midlo Hall estimates that some 5,951 Africans were imported between 1719 and 1743.[28] The French, who established Biloxi in 1699, were superseded by the Spanish, who took effective control in 1769.[29] By that time, some 18,928 Africans had been imported into the colony.[30] Outside of the British mainland and Louisiana, Florida was claimed by the Spanish in 1565. By the 1580s, Africans were employed in the vicinity of St. Augustine and the Spanish fort of Saint Mose. Their numbers remained insignificant until the British takeover in 1763, when the territory was divided into two parts. British East Florida languished until the 1770s and was returned to Spain in 1783, whereas British West Florida saw the establishment of a small black population no later than the 1760s, particularly near Pensacola. Florida remained stagnant until its acquisition by the United States in 1821, when slavery and cotton boosted the economy significantly. Its relatively late development, however, places Florida outside the focus of this study.[31]

By 1830, states such as Alabama, Mississippi, Kentucky, Tennessee, and North Carolina all boasted significant slave populations, derivative, in turn, of the five core colonies/states: Virginia, Maryland, South Carolina, Georgia, and Louisiana. It is important to raise a question regarding the spatial arrangements of slave populations within these states: Where, precisely, were the slaves living? That is, were they evenly dispersed throughout, or were they concentrated in certain areas? The reply to this query relates directly to an accurate appreciation of the African American identity.

The location of slave populations was of course determined by the nature of their servitude. In places such as Virginia and South Carolina, where the importance of tobacco, rice, and indigo preceded cotton's emergence toward the end of the eighteenth century, the Tidewater areas provided most of the land for cultivation. Hence, this is precisely where the bulk of the African-based population resided.[32] In the first half of the eighteenth century, 80 to 90 percent of South Carolina's slave population was contained in those parishes closest to Charleston.[33] In eighteenth-century Virginia, the population of the Tidewater was two-thirds black, with the slave populations of other counties ranging from 60 to 70 percent.[34] With the expansion of cotton cultivation into the Gulf Coast area in the early nineteenth century, much of the transported slave population would be contained within the so-called black belts of the South, along riverain and other cultivable areas. In short, the enslaved African-based population in North America was more concentrated than dispersed.

The foregoing observations challenge the conceptual framework of the slave community vis-à-vis both the adjoining white population and slave communities in the Caribbean and South America. The prevailing view has been that under conditions obtaining in the West Indies and South America, where the slave-to-owner ratio was far greater than in North America due to the former's characteristic larger plantations and patterns of absentee ownership, the retentions and transformations of African culture were much more extensive than in North America. Indeed, Herskovits wrote that blacks in the

United States "lived in constant association with whites to a degree not found anywhere else in the New World."[35] The perception of close relations between blacks and whites in North America, combined with the relatively smaller plantations found there, have led many to concur with Herskovits's view of North America as the site of greatest cultural distance between Africa and its descendants.[36]

Studies subsequent to those of Herskovits have led to some modification of this sweeping generalization; however, the issue of spatial demographics has yet to be reexamined in a fashion that calls into question the aforementioned assumptions about the North American slave community's relative size and proximity to whites. Certainly Franklin and Moss tend to emphasize the issue of proximity as they observe that for the 3,953,760 slaves in 1860 there were only 384,884 owners, and that more than 200,000 of these individuals owned 5 or fewer slaves.[37] In fact, some 338,000 owners, or 88 percent of the 1860 total, owned fewer than 20 slaves. Genovese also seeks to draw attention to the estimate that 50 percent of North American slaves lived on farms as opposed to plantations (a plantation consisting of 20 slaves or more in the North American context) and that both owner and slave worked closely together on farms of 10 or fewer slaves.[38] Sobel similarly argues in her study of eighteenth-century Virginia that "blacks and whites lived together in great intimacy," a perspective Mullin supports.[39]

Stampp, on the other hand, almost singlehandedly points out the corresponding implications of the data, namely, that 50 percent of North American slaves lived on plantations of 20 or more slaves, and that 25 percent lived on plantations of 50 or more.[40] By 1860, large slaveholdings were proportionately more frequent in the lower than upper South (12.7 slaves per owner in the former versus 7.7 per owner in the latter), and only 10 percent or less of the slaves in the South lived in urban areas. Further, the large slaveholdings tended to be "clustered" in those areas best suited for staple crops, a crucial point.

It should be clear that it is possible to emphasize the relatively small average size of the North American slaveholding unit to the point of distortion. It is true (and obvious) that a farm of twenty or fewer slaves is, in isolation, considerably smaller than a West Indian plantation of one hundred or more. But when such a unit is considered in conjunction with other farms and larger plantations among which there was regular commerce, the spatial picture of the African-based community expands considerably. Exchange and interaction among slaveholding units was extensive, such that an individual's familial, social, and cultural world was by no means confined to the particular unit on which she or he lived. As such, emphasizing the individual slaveholding unit to draw attention to the "intimacy" of black-white relations misrepresents the larger and more comprehensive context of interplantational relations among slaves (and black nonslaves) in a given locale.

A comparative analysis of the number of blacks and whites within a specific colony or state can be equally misleading. If the purpose of such an analysis is to examine the extent and nature of interracial relations, the fact that a given colony or state contained a certain percentage of black or white inhabitants discloses very little, especially when the black population was clustered in one section of the colony/state and hence oblivious to people living hundreds of kilometers away but in the same state. On the contrary, it can be argued that blacks and whites did not live in the same state, either spatially or figuratively; this observation has ramifications for the formation of an emerging African American identity.

One study demonstrating the validity of the counterargument is Piersen's work on blacks in eighteenth-century New England.[41] Focusing primarily upon Massachusetts, Connecticut, and Rhode Island, Piersen establishes that a vibrant folk culture thoroughly shaped and influenced by the African antecedent flourished in New England during this period. The black New England community resonated with its own cuisine, dance, style of dress, songs, implements of industry, games, funeral rites, and medicinal practices, all based upon African models. It maintained what is clearly an example of continuity in that it elected its own governors and kings annually, after which parades and festivities resembling John Canoe celebrations were held. In these and other ways, black New Englanders successfully achieved a life-style that conformed to the basic contours of African cultural patterns.

Such texturally rich, African-based expressions should not have been possible, however, according to demographically driven arguments. Indeed, New England through 1750 recruited most of its slaves from the West Indies, the vast majority of whom were African-born. New England slaveholders, few of whom held more than one or two slaves, preferred young Africans "in order to train them entirely within their own families."[42] It was common for slaveholder and enslaved to not only work together but also live in the same house. Such was the familiarity in New England that in enough instances the enslaved broke bread at the same table with the enslaver. Furthermore, the black population accounted for only 2 percent of the New England total at the beginning of the eighteenth century and reached only 3 percent by 1750. Given such conditions, the question forcefully presents itself: How could such a tiny, well-enculturated population resist and attain such a remarkable degree of cultural autonomy?

The answer is found in Piersen's discussion of clustering in New England. Though small and proximate to whites, blacks were also highly concentrated in and around coastal urban areas, in riverain locations, and within Rhode Island's Narragansett region. According to Piersen, "this clustering accounts for the development of an Afro-American folk culture in a society otherwise so dominated by its white population."[43] In the pursuit of an African-derived way of life, eighteenth-century black New Englanders proved that plantations boasting of thousands were not always necessary. If black folk could get from one farm to the next on a regular basis and within a reasonable amount of time, they could and did re-create a distinctive culture, their propinquity to whites notwithstanding.

The lesson learned in New England is obviously applicable to the South. Even if one insists upon retaining the artificiality of colonial and/or state borders, the numbers reveal a huge African-based population, thereby lending support to arguments favoring continuity and retention. The percentages of slaves in various states in 1860 were as follows: South Carolina, 57 percent; Mississippi, 55 percent; Louisiana, 47 percent; Alabama and Florida, 45 percent; Georgia, 44 percent; North Carolina, 33 percent; Virginia, 31 percent; Texas, 30 percent; Arkansas, 26 percent; Tennessee, 25 percent; Kentucky, 20 percent; Maryland, 13 percent; Missouri, 10 percent; and Delaware, 1.5 percent.[44] When the clustering of these populations is taken into consideration, there can be no doubt that such concentrations provided an adequate basis for extensive interaction within the African-based community.

· · · · · · ·

Having discussed the importation rates, destinations, and spatial arrangements of Africans, the regions of origin and patterns of importation can be considered. There are seven general regions from which slaves were imported. The first, Senegambia, encompasses that stretch of coast extending from the Senegal River to the Casamance, to which captives from as far away as the upper and middle Niger valleys were transported. The second, Sierra Leone, includes the territory from the Casamance to Assini, or what is now Guinea-Bissau, Guinea, Sierra Leone, Liberia, and the Ivory Coast.[45] Adjoining Sierra Leone is the Gold Coast, occupying what is essentially contemporary Ghana. Further east lay the fourth region, the Bight of Benin, stretching from the Volta to the Benin River and corresponding to what is now Togo, Benin, and southwestern Nigeria. The Bight of Biafra, in turn, comprised contemporary southeastern Nigeria, Cameroon, and Gabon. West Central Africa includes Congo (formerly Zaire) and Angola, and the seventh region, Mozambique-Madagascar, refers to southeastern Africa, including what is now Mozambique, parts of Tanzania, and the island of Madagascar.

The combined findings of Richardson and Curtin, exclusive of Louisiana,

TABLE 2.6 New Estimates of Origins

Region	Richardson and Curtin	Deviation from Curtin's Original Estimates
Senegambia	13.5%	+.2%
Sierra Leone	16.6%	−.3%
Gold Coast	14.1%	−1.8%
Bight of Benin	3.0%	−1.3%
Bight of Biafra	25.6%	+2.3%
West Central Africa	25.3%	+.8%
Total	98.1%	

Sources: Philip D. Curtin, *Atlantic Slave Trade: A Census* (Madison, 1969), 156–58; David Richardson, "Slave Exports from West and West-Central Africa: New Estimates of Volume and Distribution," *Journal of African History* 30 (1989): 12–14.

yield the estimates of the various regions' relative contributions to the North American servile estate found in table 2.6.[46] The figures reflect an important departure from what was previously known about slave imports in two ways. First, the substantially greater contribution from the Bight of Biafra is consistent with Richardson's view that this coastal region played a larger role in the trade and exported substantial numbers from the beginning of the eighteenth century. Second, it is clear that Sierra Leone was of greater importance to the trade than previously recognized.[47]

Inclusion of Louisiana attenuates the calculations. Midlo Hall has calculated the regional percentages for 1720 to 1820,[48] and a final revision of regional contributions yields the results found in table 2.7. The new estimates exhibit relatively minor adjustments for most of the categories. The Bight of Biafra and West Central Africa remain far and above the principal sources for North America. Senegal, Sierra Leone, and the Gold Coast also retain their importance. The Bight of Benin gains, but it remains a minor numerical contributor whose cultural influence will be felt most keenly in the lower Mississippi.

With a more reliable approximation of the relative numerical contributions of each region, the rates of the regional contributions to North America can now be examined. Again, Richardson's discussion of the British export trade from 1700 to 1807, quantified in table 2.8, is instructive. With the exceptions of Senegambia, the Bight of Benin, and the Bight of Biafra, the relative percentages of the various coastal origins for the British export trade displayed in this table do not vary significantly from those reflecting the import trade into North America. It is therefore likely that the decadal pattern of imports into North America was similar to that of the British

TABLE 2.7 Final Revision of Origins and Percentages of
Africans Imported into British North America and Louisiana

Region	Total	Deviation from North American Estimates Exclusive of Louisiana
Senegambia	14.5%	+1.0%
Sierra Leone	15.8%	−0.8%
Gold Coast	13.1%	−1.0%
Bight of Benin	4.3%	+1.3%
Bight of Biafra	24.4%	−1.2%
West Central Africa	26.1%	+0.8%
Total	98.2%	

Note: The estimates are determined as follows: the number of people from each region of origin or supply zone is calculated for the trade to British North America excluding Louisiana, then for the trade to Louisiana. For example, Senegambia's contribution to British North America constituted 13.5 percent of a total of 445,772, or 60,179.22 (see table 2.6), and its contribution to Louisiana was 27.6 percent of a total of 35,158, or 9,703.608. The sums for British North America and Louisiana are then added for each region and divided by 480,930, the total for the whole of the trade to North America. This operation gives Senegambia a percentage of 14.5 percent. The remaining 1.8 percent can be accounted for by both the Mozambique-Madagascar contribution and the unknown factor. The Upper Guinea, Sierra Leone, and Windward Coast estimates for the Louisiana trade are combined under Sierra Leone here.

export trade. To be sure, Charleston and the Chesapeake differed with regard to the precise mix of ethnicities entering those ports, a function of contrasting preferences that will be examined at a later point, but the overall import composite mirrored that of the export counterpart. The following discussion is therefore predicated upon the foregoing's plausibility.

Richardson does not discuss early African arrivals to British North America from Mozambique and Madagascar, but in fact, British colonies imported "large numbers" from southeastern Africa and Madagascar, particularly between 1675 and 1690.[49] Indeed, Donnan makes reference to three ships from Madagascar (totaling seven hundred people) arriving in the British West Indies in 1678, and further states that during this same period the colonies of Massachusetts, New York, and Virginia were all receiving "East African" slaves.[50] However, it would appear that Mozambique-Madagascar's participation in the trade to North America was early and limited relative to the rest of the trade.

Senegambia, by virtue of its proximity to Europe, was also an early contributor to the North American slave community.[51] Curtin estimates the

TABLE 2.8 Decadal British Export Trade by Region, 1700–1807

Decade	Senegambia	Sierra Leone	Gold Coast	Bight of Benin	Bight of Biafra	West Central Africa
1700–1709	18,150 (12.1)	33,900 (22.6)	27,600 (18.4)	17,550 (11.7)	19,350 (12.9)	33,600 (22.4)
1710–19	29,150 (14.5)	5,230 (2.6)	35,180 (17.5)	20,900 (10.4)	44,820 (22.3)	65,730 (32.7)
1720–29	39,000 (14.5)	6,990 (2.6)	47,080 (17.5)	27,980 (10.4)	59,990 (22.3)	87,960 (32.7)
1730–39	39,880 (14.5)	7,150 (2.6)	48,130 (17.5)	28,600 (10.4)	61,330 (22.3)	89,930 (32.7)
1740–49	18,680 (9.6)	7,200 (3.7)	43,200 (22.2)	15,180 (7.8)	75,880 (39.0)	34,240 (17.6)
1750–59	16,590 (6.6)	47,250 (18.8)	27,900 (11.1)	18,350 (7.3)	104,050 (41.4)	36,190 (14.4)
1760–69	16,430 (4.2)	125,590 (32.1)	32,860 (8.4)	35,600 (9.1)	134,980 (34.5)	45,780 (11.7)
1770–79	10,190 (3.0)	103,580 (30.5)	27,850 (8.2)	34,300 (10.1)	151,120 (44.5)	12,230 (3.6)
1780–89	350 (0.1)	53,100 (15.2)	31,090 (8.9)	25,500 (7.3)	211,000 (60.4)	25,150 (7.2)
1790–99	2,920 (0.7)	50,850 (12.2)	57,520 (13.8)	7,090 (1.7)	170,070 (40.8)	128,390 (30.8)
1800–1807	2,250 (0.8)	42,970 (15.3)	30,050 (10.7)	2,250 (0.8)	123,000 (43.8)	80,320 (28.6)
Total	193,590 (6.2)	483,810 (15.5)	408,460 (13.1)	233,300 (7.5)	1,155,590 (37.1)	639,520 (20.5)

Source: David Richardson, "Slave Exports from West and West-Central Africa, 1700–1810: New Estimates of Volume and Distribution," *Journal of African History* 30 (1989): 13. © Cambridge University Press 1989. Reprinted with the permission of Cambridge University Press.

Note: Figures in parentheses are percentages of exports.

combined Senegambian–Sierra Leonian percentage of the British slave trade from 1673 to 1689 at 12 percent.[52] This pattern persisted, based upon Richardson's findings, through the first half of the eighteenth century, when Senegambia's percentages rose slightly to 12.1 percent from 1700 to 1709 and gradually declined to slightly less than 10 percent by 1750; the second half of the eighteenth century witnessed the continued decrease in Senegambia's participation. For Senegambia, then, its contribution was substantial and early.

Sierra Leone's role in the import trade was almost the opposite of Senegambia's. From its shared 12 percent with Senegambia in the final quarter of the seventeenth century, Sierra Leone experienced a brief spurt in the first decade of the eighteenth, only to be followed by relatively small percentages until midcentury. At that point, its representation quintupled, accounted for more than 30 percent from 1760 to 1779, and remained in double digits until 1807. In contrast to Senegambia, therefore, Sierra Leone's role was equally substantial but relatively late.

The participation of the Gold Coast was also early, accounting for some 21 percent of the Royal African Company's exports from 1673 to 1689.[53] However, the contribution from this region flowed fairly steadily from the last quarter of the seventeenth century until 1807. Except for the span of time between 1760 and 1790, the percentage of people from the Gold Coast did not fall below 10 percent, averaging some 15.7 percent from 1700 to 1759 and from 1790 to 1807. It can be said, therefore, that the Gold Coast's numerical contribution was essentially the same as those of Senegambia and Sierra Leone, but that it was evenly distributed from 1673 until the slave trade's end, constituting a constant presence in North America.

Richardson's projections for the Bight of Benin must be adjusted for the distinctive experience in British North America (excluding Louisiana), where its representation was about half that of the British trade as a whole. At 4.3 percent, its numerical contribution to anglophone America was minimal, an observation that will be borne out by subsequent evidence. The Bight of Benin's cultural impact, however, especially in New Orleans and the lower Mississippi, was disproportionately enormous.

The Bight of Biafra, as it turns out, was a major player in the development of the African-based community in North America. Accounting for more than one-quarter of those Africans imported into the mainland, their numbers were substantial from the beginning of the eighteenth century into the nineteenth. In fact, from 1770 to 1800 Africans from the Bight of Biafra accounted for some 48.6 percent of all Africans exported via the British. In other words, the Biafran contribution was not only as steady as that of the Gold Coast, but its volume was nearly twice as large.

MAP 2.1 West Africa in the Eighteenth and Nineteenth Centuries

West Central Africa, except for the twenty-year span between 1770 and 1790, also contributed as consistently and as equally to the African American gene pool as did the Bight of Biafra. Congo-Angola was an early source of slaves for the Royal African Company, supplying 12 percent of its cargoes during the final quarter of the seventeenth century.[54] The evidence suggests

Fezzan

Gao

Niger River

Zinder

Lake Chad

Sokoto

Maradi

Say

Katsina

Ngazargamu

Gwandu

Kuka

Bagirmi

Gaya

Hausa States

Kano

Kanem-Bornu

Zaria

Borgu States

Bussa

Nupe

Yola

Bida

Oyo Ile

Nok

Jukun

bomey

Oyo

Ilorin

Ibadan

Adamawa

Ibaban

Ife

Igala

Dahomey

Abeokuta

Idah

Vhydah

Egba

Benin

Benin City

Onitsha

Igbo-Ukwu

Lagos

Igbo

Arochuku

Badagry

Porto Novo

Ebrohimi

Aboh

Old Calabar

Itsekiri

Bight of Benin

Twon (Brass)

Opobo

Bonny

Elem Kalabari (New Calabar)

Bight of Biafra

Cape Lopez

that this region was also a principal supplier of slaves during the period of illegal activity after 1808. Together with the Bight of Biafra, West Central Africa accounts for more than 50 percent of African imports into British North America.

In sum, the Bight of Biafra, West Central Africa, and the Gold Coast stand

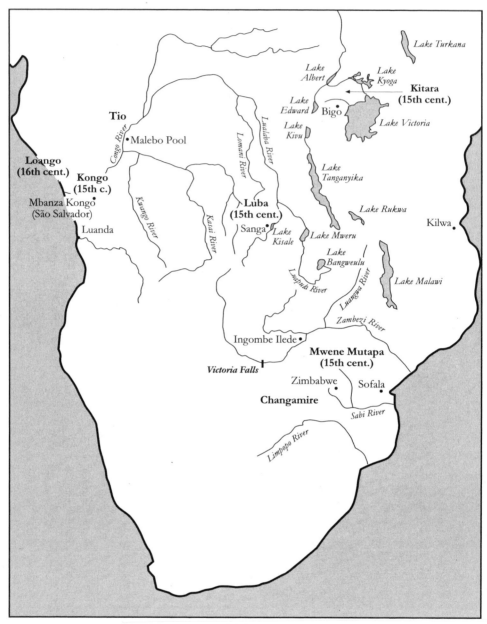

MAP 2.2 West Central Africa, 1400–1600

out as the sources from which Africans were initially and consistently re-cruited into British North America. Although Senegambia and Sierra Leone yielded as many or more individuals as did the Gold Coast, their contributions were not as constant. On the other hand, Benin's representation was minuscule. The relative ebb and flow from these regions played a direct role

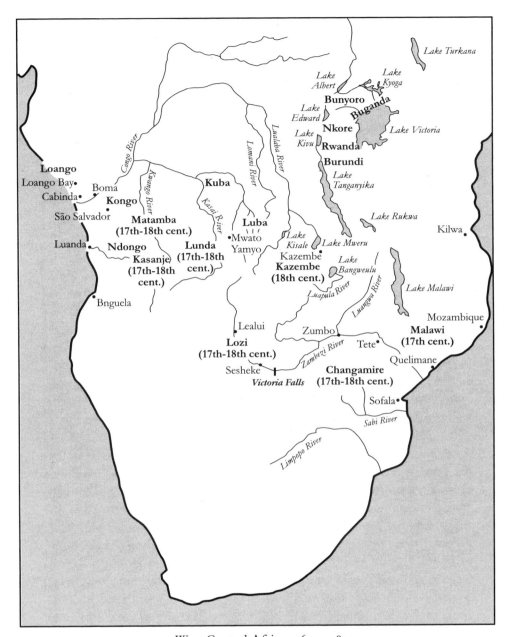

MAP 2.3 West Central Africa, 1600–1800

in both the general direction and more subtle nuances of African American identity and culture.

Considerations of sex, age, and region of origin converge in the North American profile in rather unexpected ways, rendering a composite portrait in which sex ratios are more equally balanced than in most of the Americas and the number of African children imported is relatively high. The composite is informed, first of all, by the data for the whole of the transatlantic trade. Lovejoy and Manning concur that significantly more males than females were exported from the various regions of Africa.[55] Lovejoy's synthesis suggests that the ratio of males to females was on the order of 179 to 100, the consequence of both slave trader demand and internal developments within Africa. Concerning the former, it would appear that slave traders sought to achieve an export ratio of two males to every female. This objective was gradually approached in West Africa during the eighteenth century and more or less approximated in the nineteenth, whereas West Central Africa supplied the desired ratio throughout most of these two centuries. This, in turn, reflected changing attitudes within certain parts of Africa, particularly West Africa, where a preference for the retention of female slaves began to coincide with the external interest in males. In contrast, the seventeenth century saw a relatively balanced export of males and females into the trade.

Correcting the overall trade data, however, are the population estimates specific to North America. Based upon such data, it would appear that for much of the eighteenth century, the North American importation pattern only partially echoed that of other New World plantocracies in that sex ratios tended to be lower than elsewhere, averaging 158 adult males for every 100 adult females.[56] Furthermore, beginning with the 1820 census and progressing decennially until 1860, the ratio of males to females in the United States was as follows: 100 to 95.1, 100 to 98.3, 100 to 99.5, 100 to 99.9, and 100 to 99.3.[57] Although the percentage of African-born by 1820 was only 12 percent (table 2.5), the census data provide some insight and suggest that the end of the eighteenth century may have witnessed a return to the seventeenth-century import pattern in that relatively even numbers of males and females were maintained. Numerical parity is further suggested by information derived from the export record: Until the nineteenth century the shift to a preponderance of males out of West Africa was very gradual, and the Bight of Biafra, a major contributor to the African population in North Africa, maintained the lowest ratios of any supply region, with males accounting for 50 percent of all those exported from the region in the seventeenth century, rising to only 62 percent by 1840. At the same time, the region contributed 53.9 percent of the export total in the eighteenth century (excluding the French participation) and 66.1 percent in the nineteenth.[58] It is therefore reasonable to conclude that the North American import pattern, in contrast to those of neighboring societies, reflected a conscious attempt on the part of slaveholders to maintain a relatively even balance in the sex ratios of the enslaved population.

Concerning the average age of slaves imported to North America, Manning has found that prepubescent children constituted one-fourth of the eighteenth century's overall slave exports, and that their numbers increased to two-fifths of the Africans exported in the nineteenth century.[59] It is probable, however, that the percentage of African children reaching North America was significantly greater than the 25 percent general figure of the eighteenth century. Eltis and Engerman comment that "for much of the eighteenth century, the share of males leaving the Bights of Benin and Biafra was only two-thirds to three-quarters that of their share leaving other African regions, while the share of children leaving Angola and the Bight of Biafra was often double that of other regions."[60] Lovejoy concurs, stating that in the eighteenth century alone about 30.6 percent of the Africans exported from the Bight of Biafra and West Central Africa, and 35 percent taken from Sierra Leone, were children.[61] These percentages would increase in the nineteenth century, especially out of West Central Africa. Further, these three regions supplied some 66.3 percent of the Africans imported into North America. It is therefore likely that at least 33 percent of the African population in North America were children at the point of debarkation.[62]

The foregoing has allowed for a much more complete picture of the overall slave trade, the importation rates of Africans into North America, their geographic origins, sex ratios, and ages, and the patterns of their distribution throughout the South. The way is therefore prepared for a more specific inquiry into the role of ethnicity in the early South, beginning with ethnic groups from Senegambia and the Bight of Benin.

3

. . . .

WARRIORS, CHARMS, AND LOAS

SENEGAMBIA AND THE BIGHT OF BENIN

Mande speakers and others were important components of the Senegambian contingent in North America, recruited and preferred by planters for their unique agricultural experience. The Bambara were a principal group among the Mande, and in Louisiana they played a foundational role. The Bambara hailed from a region in which they shared a number of political, social, and cultural elements with neighboring populations, to whom they were linked in specific ways. Although related to that of the Mande, Bambara culture was nonetheless distinct. This chapter will develop those areas of divergence and argue that the uniqueness of Bambara culture was transferred to North America along with the Bambara themselves. The chapter concludes with a discussion of another early group in Louisiana, the Fon-Ewe-Yoruba.

In the winter of 1738, South Carolinian George Sommer of Beach Hill discovered that two of his slaves were missing. In February of that year he placed a notice in the *South Carolina Gazette*, describing the missing as "two tall Gambia Negro Men, named Prince and Chopco," who spoke very little English and were suspected of hiding on another plantation.[1] George Austin had experienced a similar problem the year before with "a tall Gambia Negro Man, named Carolina, about twenty-five years of age, speaks very bad English."[2] The South Carolinian (and other colonies') newspapers of the period are filled with such references and offer qualitative evidence for the previous chapter's finding that the Senegambian contingent was both early and substantial. In fact, it can be argued that the Senegambian presence provided a significant portion of the foundation for the consequent African American population. It is therefore important to consider the nature of its contribution.

The preceding runaway slave advertisements are similar in that they ascribe a common attribute to the Gambians—their relative height. This association between Gambians and physical stature is fairly constant and repeated in many of the runaway notices. For example, Frederick Grimke of Stono, South Carolina, reported in March 1742 the escape of a "tall Gambia Negro Fellow, nam'd Tony, formerly belonged to Mr. Cheesman of Barbados."[3] That same year Robert Quash searched for a "tall young Gambia Negro Man, named Glasgow." The following year, John Ouldfield of Pedee in Winyaw similarly sought the return of a "lusty tall Gambia Negro Fellow, nam'd Toney, about 35 Years of Age."[4] Although not all Gambians are described as tall, it is clear that physical stature was a quality distinguishing Gambians from other Africans in the minds of slaveholders. This is no minor or trivial detail; slaveholders tended to associate certain undesirable traits with people of shorter stature. Such associations and consequent preferences would also affect interrelations between these groups.

In addition to archetypical height, Gambians were identified by their "country marks," which were commented on with a fair amount of consistency in the runaway slave ads. For example, James Conyers of Black River, South Carolina, remarked in October 1751 that his slave, a "Gambia new negro fellow," was "marked on the forehead with a cross, and had three perpendicular stokes on each cheek."[5] Six years later, Daniel Heyward of Port Royal filed a notice concerning "Junice, a tall slim black Gambia fellow, about forty years of age, with several of his country marks down the sides of his face," and "Cyphax, a well set yellow Gambia fellow . . . 35 years of age, and has several of his country marks down the sides of his face."[6] David Huguenin of Silkhope (on Great Ogechee) was more graphic in 1769 when he reported that one of two absconded Gambians (one described as "yellow," the other "black") bore "his country marks thus))) on each cheek."[7] Within the context of ethnicity and the formation of the African-based community, it is highly significant that not only Africans recognized their differences, but others did as well. The implications of the ability to distinguish were profound, as will be demonstrated.

Not all Africans from Gambia were so designated. A subgroup of Mande speakers, referred to as "Mandingo" or "Mundingo" in many parts of the New World, embarked for the Americas from both Gambia and Sierra Leone. It will therefore be necessary to discuss Mande-speaking populations in the following chapter, but it is appropriate to mention them at this juncture as well. The association between the Gambians and the "Man-dingos" is underscored in the runaway notice printed in July 1771 concerning "a new negro man . . . of the Mandingo or Gambia country, his country name is Jowler."[8] Georgian John Tinkler of Augusta was also concerned in November 1768 that his man Welcome had been missing for three months. Welcome was described as about forty years of age, speaking "very broken English, and says that he's a Mandingo born."[9] Betty, around sixteen years old and "of the Mandingo Country," had escaped from William Ware near the middle of September 1767 and could be further distinguished by the fact that she spoke "indifferent" English.[10] The list of "Mandingo" runaways runs on, including Boatswain's 1762 absence from South Carolinian Samuel Richbourg for nearly six months, Sandy's daring escape from Christopher Holson in 1764, on so on.[11]

The descriptive materials reviewed so far focus on Gambians and tend to emanate from South Carolina and (to a lesser extent) Georgia. In those two colonies, slaveholders expressed a strong preference for Africans from Gambia and the Gold Coast.[12] In fact, Wax argues that Africans from these two regions were more highly valued than others by the colonies as a whole.[13] In addition to the Gambians, planters in South Carolina also prized Africans from the Windward Coast (Sierra Leone).[14] However, it should be observed that a precise division between adjoining regions was not always made, as the following advertisement demonstrates: "Just Arrived from the Island of Goree, on the Windward Coast of Africa . . . 149 Prime Slaves."[15] Planter preference for certain African ethnicities is crucial to understanding the un-folding of African-based society and will be examined in subsequent chapters. At this point it is more important to explain the planter preference itself.

Wood has theorized that Africans from the Sierra Leone region were preferred over others due to their knowledge of rice cultivation.[16] Rice became the principal agricultural commodity during the first fifty years of the Carolina colony, and as it grew to occupy a place of preeminence, the colony began to import greater numbers of Africans to cultivate it. After 1700, South Carolina gradually turned more and more to direct shipments from Africa. The Africans of choice were Sierra Leonians and Gambians; Wood speculates that they were in fact responsible for introducing rice cultivation in South Carolina. Rice was a staple in parts of West Africa, especially along the Windward Coast and in Gambia; it was Jobson's early-seventeenth-century observation that rice was a major part of the Malinke diet along the Gambia. In 1750, Adanson made a similar remark, stating that "rice is almost the only grain sown at Gambia in the lands overflown by the rains of the high season." As far as Sierra Leone is concerned, Durand's early-nineteenth-century report states that "the chief food of the people is rice," a finding echoed by Corry.[17] Consequently, although by no means the only reason, the cultivation of rice was certainly a major factor influencing planter preference.

Joyner provides further insight into the introduction of rice cultivation into North America, arguing that although rice was indeed grown along the West African coast, it was first imported from Madagascar, and that none of the Europeans "had any experience with rice culture at all."[18] His contention is indirectly supported by the early runaway notices, which contain references to Malagasy slaves. For example, in November 1736 Virginian Benjamin Needle of King William County sought the return of an Angolan named "Planter," who had supposedly run away with an older black man whose skin was described as "yellowish" and whose hair was "like a Madagascar's."[19] That the Malagasy were well known in the colonies by this early period is further supported by the notice of P. Lightfoot in March 1737, who was looking for a mulatto slave named Sam who, although he was born in North America, had "the Countenance of a Madagascar."[20] In July 1738 one of three men who had escaped from Coggan's Point on the James River was described as "a Tawny, well made, Madagascar Negro" around thirty years of age.[21] Similarly, Robert Chesley of St. Mary's Courts, Maryland, reported in August 1739 the absence of both a white servant and Robin, a "Madagascar native."[22] Another example of the early Malagasy presence comes from John Ravenscroft of Prince George County, who sought information on three men: Sparks, a Virginia-born seventeen-year-old; the carpenter Gruff, a twenty-six-year-old "short likely Madagascar"; and Tom, a thirty-five-year-old sawyer and "likewise a Madagascar."[23] This early Madagascar presence, though not numerous, was nonetheless long remembered by a few, such that eighty-four-year-old John Barker of Texas would state in the 1930s, "I was born a slave. I'm a Malagasser nigger."[24]

Although Malagasy slaves may have first introduced rice culture into North America, South Carolina soon began directly importing West Africans to provide the bulk of the labor force. The Senegambians very quickly took over the cultivation of the crop because of their own expertise.[25] The West African method of planting by first making a hole in trenches with the heel, dropping in the seeds, and then covering up the hole by foot was maintained. The hoe continued to be used as an "all-purpose implement," as did coiled baskets for winnowing and the mortar and pestle for threshing. Joyner claims that these methods continued as the principal means of preparing the crop until the introduction of the rice mill after 1830.[26]

Of course, South Carolina and Georgia were not the only colonies to import Gambians. They were also present in sufficient numbers in Virginia and Maryland, although rice never assumed the same importance in these two areas. In a description that bears a striking resemblance to the aforementioned 1769 notice of David Huguenin of South Carolina, Margaret Arbuthnott of Hanover ran an ad in 1745 seeking the return of "two new Negroe Men, imported from Gambia." She described one of these Gambians, Jack, as a "yellow Fellow, with 3 small Strokes on each Side of his Face, like this mark (|)."[27] Earlier, in April 1738, "a very black Mundingo Negro man, called Jumper," had escaped from Lewis Burwell.[28] As a final example of Gambians (or Sierra Leonians) in these two areas, there is the case of Pompey, a twenty-four-year-old "Mandingue" who had escaped from his captor in Baltimore.[29]

Donnan is in complete accord with the preceding testimony that Senegambia was a preferred source for Carolinian slaveholders. It is Curtin, however, who was one of the first to specifically identify the Bambara and the Malinke as the chief ethnic groups imported.[30] Although the category of Malinke (or Mande speakers) is general in that it is used to refer to a number of ethnicities speaking closely related languages, the reference to the Bambara, or Bamana, is precise. Curtin's focus on the Bambara partly results from his view that they constituted a major portion of the captives exported from Senegal during the slave trade, a contention supported by Manning and Geggus.[31] It is clear, therefore, that the Bambara faction was significant.

There are certainly references to the Bambara in the runaway slave advertisements of South Carolina and Georgia, but not many. In October 1761, James Parsons of Ashepoo sought the return of "two tall likely new Banbara negro fellows, named Abram and Lymas."[32] John Savage of St. Matthew's Parish similarly filed a notice in December 1774 concerning Buckram and Fortomah, both of whom were about twenty-seven years of age and "of the Bombia country."[33] As another example, Thomas Polhill announced in November 1787 that "an old Negro man, of the Bambra Country" had recently arrived at his plantation.[34] Qualitative, scanty information such as this, however, hardly forms a foundation upon which generalizations can be made.

Louisiana newspapers also contain references to the Bambara. One example is the notice placed in the *Louisiana Gazette* in June 1810 by William Brown, soliciting information about Big Jack, "a native of Bambara, speaking very bad English; he has on his face several notchings."[35] Another example can be found in the 11 October 1806 issue of the *Moniteur de la Louisiane*, in which the owner sought information about "three Negro men, one of the Congo nation and another of the Bambara, and another from a nation whose name I have forgotten."[36] Notwithstanding these notices, the frequency with which the Bambara appear in such ads is surprisingly low. One explanation for the absence of references to the Bambara is the fact that none of the newspapers consulted—*L'Abeille*, *Moniteur de la Louisiane*, *Louisiana Gazette*,

Le Télégraphe, et le commercial advertiser, and so on—began publication before 1802, well after most of the Bambara had been imported into Louisiana.

But in contrast to South Carolina, it is in Louisiana that the Bambara show up in force. Midlo Hall has determined that "large numbers" of Bambara were imported into Louisiana during the French period, and significant numbers were imported under the Spanish.[37] By the time of the latter's reign, it is no longer clear that everyone considered Bambara was in fact Bambara; the term had acquired a generic meaning by the latter quarter of the eighteenth century. Nevertheless, one-quarter of the Sencgambians imported by the Spanish were designated as such; in turn, the Senegambians accounted for 30 percent of the African population in Louisiana between 1760 and 1800.[38]

Manning and Geggus have explained that the terms *Gambia* and *Senegambia* were employed to designate people taken from the Senegambian interior who were mostly Bambara and overwhelmingly male. In contrast, "the Senegal," or Senegalese, were mostly Wolof women taken from the coastal area.[39] This certainly held true for Louisiana, where Bambara males were approximately 93 percent of the Bambara population, Wolof males 60 percent of the Wolof population, and Igbo males 55 percent of the Igbo population. One of the consequences of these importation patterns is that Bambara men necessarily married Wolof, Igbo, and American-born women, whereas Wolof men tended to marry Wolof women. Wolof and Igbo women, in turn, had a much higher ratio of children than did other ethnicities.[40]

The implications for these mixed marriages are unclear, but it would seem that the parents would have found as many points of commonality as possible to raise their children. As will be demonstrated, cultural similarities within Senegambia meant that broad and encompassing conceptualization may have been emphasized over specific form and content without great difficulty—at least for non-Muslims. But some of the Wolof, as well as some of the Fulbe and Malinke from Senegambia, were certainly Muslim. In cases in which the pre-Islamic heritage of the Muslims remained strong, those of nominal standing may have gravitated toward the non-Muslim Bambara worldview and culture. But in those instances in which the Islamic conviction was rooted and vigorous, conflict was likely. Indeed, Saugnier, traveling in Senegal in 1785, claimed that the Wolof and the Bambara were "sworn enemies."[41]

Perhaps such conflict complicated the already problematic circumstance of slavery itself, contributing to the decision by some Wolof women to abscond. Agathe, for one, was a native of Senegal but taken to be American-born ("thought to be creole, having been in the country since her childhood"), and had recently run away from Bayou St. Jean.[42] Then there is the example of Maria, age thirty in June 1819, who had been captured after a one-month hiatus and held in a New Orleans workhouse until claimed.[43] There are a number of other references to such women in the Louisiana papers. Interestingly, almost all of the women were running away alone, unless accompanied by their very young children. If Muslim, could they have been running away from their non-Muslim husbands as well as Louisiana slavery?

Sale notices referring to Wolof women also depict most of them as young; many were mothers. For example, there is the case of a sale in October 1808: "This Negresse is Senegalese, having arrived quite young in the country, around 30 years old, with a 3 year-old little negresse."[44] The previous year the following advertisement appeared: "Negresse for sale. One very attractive Negresse, about 16 years old with her year-old enfant; this negresse is from the Senegal nation, has been in the colony for four years."[45] This means that this woman arrived in Louisiana around the age of twelve, became pregnant at age fourteen, and was sold two years later. Her experience is very similar to "another negresse named Louise, nation Senegal, thirteen to fourteen years old, four years in the country, accustomed to domestic work and useful," who was also placed on the block.[46] Louise was eight when she arrived in Louisiana.

Whether compatible or not, Senegambians were engaged in reordering their private lives because colonial Louisiana's interest was the same as colonial South Carolina's. Rice, which had become important to South Carolina's economy by the last quarter of the seventeenth century, also proved crucial to early Louisiana's survivability. In fact, the first two slave ships to arrive in Louisiana in 1719 carried "several barrels of rice seed and African slaves who knew how to produce the crop."[47] As was true of Carolina, rice cultivation as well as the production of indigo were introduced to Louisiana by Africans. Rice was consumed locally, but tobacco and indigo exports proved unable to compete on the world market.

Although Senegambians were recruited for their agricultural skills, this was not the only type of labor they performed. On the contrary, Senegambians, along with Africans from elsewhere in the continent, were largely responsible for laying the foundations for such ports as Charleston, Savannah, and New Orleans. Indeed, the site that would eventually become New Orleans was so alligator- and mosquito-infested that Frenchmen avoided it, relying heavily upon Africans to build the levees and drainage ditches along the river as well as clear the forests to both plant crops and use the timber in the construction of housing. Paralleling the origins of Cape Town, South Africa, both New Orleans and Natchez, Mississippi, were built in large measure by skilled, enslaved Africans who labored as "brickmakers, joiners, blacksmiths, locksmiths, sculptors, wheelwrights, saddlers, masons, and carpenters."[48] Such was the contribution of the enslaved in Louisiana and elsewhere that Usner states: "Skilled black workers became a significant factor in the growth of colonial cities."[49]

The Senegambians, then, were very important to the launching of economies in Carolina, Georgia, Virginia, Maryland, and Louisiana in every way. But who, in fact, were these Senegambians? What were the major cultural and social markers by which they were identified, and to what extent were these attributes transferred to North America? What is the evidence for such a transfer? What kinds of relationships developed between the Senegambians and other Africans, and what was their role in the formation of the African American identity? It is to questions such as these that the remainder of this chapter will direct its attention.

Senegambia was characterized by both its relative proximity to Europe and its cultural and social affinities. That is, Senegambia, a region noted for the fact that its major population groups participate in similar cultures and maintain closely related societies, constitutes the first subsaharan region with which Europeans established direct commercial contacts in the course of the fifteenth century. As such, it became one of the first important sources of slaves for the Americas as a whole and for North America in particular.

That ethnicity was the principal vehicle of group identification in Senegambia is supported by both historians of the region and contemporary accounts. The secondary literature, used extensively throughout this study, draws heavily upon primary materials of various kinds (that is, oral tradition, official records, shipping data, travel accounts, and so on). Examples of travel literature include Jobson's early-seventeenth-century references to the "Maudingoes" and "Fulbies" of the Gambia, collective terms learned from as opposed to introduced to informants. Later in the seventeenth century, Barbot wrote about the "kingdoms of the Jaloffes [Wolof] and of the Foulles," among others, evidence of ethnic identities transcending political boundaries. "Mundingoes," "Pholeys," and "Jolloiffs" are commented upon by Moore early in the eighteenth century; by 1795, Mungo Park is referring to the same groups as "Mandingoes" and "Foulahs."[50] The fact that similar terms are restated (rather than invented) to describe populations in multiple states is persuasive evidence that ethnicity in Senegambia was current and unambiguous.

As can be discerned from the foregoing, the key ethnic groups included the coastal populations of the Wolof; the Malinke or various groups of Mande speakers; the Sereer; the Fulbe, who occupied the central and upper valleys of the Senegal River, along with the Soninke or Serrakole; and the populations of the far interior, or what is now Mali, where the valley and floodplain of the upper Niger was inhabited by such peoples as the Bambara and the Fulbe.

The history of this section of contemporary Mali is very much related to sahelian, savannah, and forest developments as well, so that the upper Niger is by no means the exclusive property of Senegambia. However, the location of the Atlantic and the emergence of the slave trade led to both extensive and complex relations between the upper Niger and Senegambia proper. Barry has examined the transatlantic trade's impact upon Senegambia.[51]

In addition to their experience with transatlantic trade, many Senegambians were versed in the principles of statecraft. First of all, much of this region constituted the western provinces of the old Malian empire, whose control over the region began to falter toward the end of the fifteenth century and whose central power was completely dissolved during the course of the seventeenth. By that time the slave trade to North America was proceeding in earnest, and Senegambia was composed of several large and well-defined states. Along the coast, the Wolof polities of Jolof, Waalo, Cayor (Kajor), and Baol (Bawol) controlled the flow of commerce between the Atlantic and the interior. The Fulbe of Futa Toro occupied the middle Senegal, site of a number of successive regimes stretching as far back as the eleventh century with the establishment of the state of Takrur. To the south, the Sereer of Salum were established around the same time as an offshoot of the much older coastal polity of Siin. Further south were the much smaller and more numerous Malinke states along the Gambia, such as Kantora, Kabu, and Wuli.

As a consequence of the shift in the trade's focus from the Sahara to the Atlantic, new polities began to emerge in the seventeenth century along caravan routes linking the upper Niger to the coast. Among these states were Bundu, a Fulbe-controlled multiethnic state along the upper Senegal and Faleme Rivers; Khasso, a Fulbe-Malinke kingdom astride both banks of the upper Senegal; Bambuk, a series of Malinke microstates in the goldfields between Bundu and Khasso; and the Serrakole polities of Gajaaga and Guidimakha.[52] These states would also find themselves deeply involved in the transatlantic trade. Whereas Curtin is inclined to minimize their participation, Bathily's research strongly suggests that the number of captives taken from the upper Senegal was much greater and the consequences of their removal far more disruptive than previously believed.[53]

In the far interior, along the upper Niger, the Bambara were themselves no strangers to centralized statecraft.[54] As early as 1625, Fulbe intermarriage with Bambara, Mande, and Berber elements produced the Massassi dynasty of Segu, out of which emerged the leading family of the Kulubali. Under the leadership of Kaladian Kulubali (1652–82) and his successors, Segu raided neighboring villages along the Niger and literally transformed the peasantry into warrior-cultivators, thereby establishing the Bambara reputation for military prowess. The fusion of warrior and cultivator only intensified in the eighteenth century, when Biton Mamari Kulubali (1740–55) fashioned from the free peasantry a large, personal servile army that also served as agricultural labor. The Diara dynasty took over eleven years after Mamari's assassination and led Segu's considerable expansion into the nineteenth century.[55] The experience was similar in Kaarta, Segu's chief rival from the latter quarter of the eighteenth century until the rise of militant Islam in the middle of the nineteenth.[56] The interminable fighting resulted in huge numbers of war captives, many of whom found themselves bound for the Atlantic along with their warrior-cultivator culture, a topic to which we will return shortly.

Of course, the vast majority of the Senegambians were not warriors but cultivators, and therefore owners of skills and experience deftly exploited in the malaria-infested coastal swamps of South Carolina and Louisiana. But they possessed other expertise as well. For example, many of the Fulbe in the Senegal and Niger valleys were pastoralists. Senegambia also contained a number of urban centers, so that a significant number were town-dwellers, not rural peasants. This kind of experience is important in determining who indeed came to North America's shores.

But even though Senegambians of varying ethnic groups came from various polities and pursued several kinds of economic enterprise, there were also regional commonalities. Barry put it this way: "Despite the diversity of such people as the Wolof, Pullo, Tukulor, Manding, Sereer, Soninke, Susu, Juula, Nalu, Baga, Beafada, Bainuk, Basari, etc., Senegambia knows a certain unity of civilization within the framework of this geopolitical space forged by several centuries of life together."[57] To begin, a number of the major ethnic groups spoke languages that belong to the West Atlantic family (with the notable exception of the Mande speakers). Second, Senegambian societies were remarkably similar in structure and usually, with the exception of the pre-Islamic Wolof, characterized by patriliny. Furthermore, as a rule they tended to be stratified into tripartite arrangements consisting of a free population, caste groups, and slaves, within which were numerous substrata not necessarily arranged hierarchically.[58] It was usually the case, therefore, that the upper substrata of both the caste and slave categories enjoyed greater wealth and power than did the lower echelons of the free population. The majority of the free population were, of course, cultivators or herdsmen. The caste category in Senegambia (and throughout much of Africa, for that matter) consisted of endogamous occupational groups such as blacksmiths, *griots*, woodworkers, potters, weavers, and leatherworkers. The castes were, in Curtin's view, not so much below others in the social hierarchy as outside of the hierarchy, whereas Gilbert argues that these categories represented different spheres of power.[59] Such groups were usually prohibited sexually, yet economically and socially essential.

It would of course be interesting to determine if any of these social arrangements were followed in North America. The assumption has been that the new condition of slavery superseded all others, and that individuals so enslaved formed sexual and social partnerships without regard to African conventions. However, one should expect that such preexisting sensibilities, if they could not dictate the process of sexual and social union, could at least inform such.

In addition to speaking (in many instances) related (but not mutually intelligible) languages and maintaining similar social structures, Senegambians tended to be knit together by a wide-ranging system of trade. The Juula (or Jakhanke) merchants, Mande-speaking and Muslim, connected the coast with the interior in ways that facilitated not only the safe passage of commodities but also the transfer of news, formal knowledge, and culture. Senegambians were very much aware of each other, nowhere more so than in the major towns of the region, such as Jenne and Timbuktu, truly cosmopolitan centers where people of varied ethnicity came together for purposes of commerce and/or religion. With the growth of Islam in the region, cultural unity was further enhanced. Finally, climatic and soil conditions reinforced cultural affinities by necessitating an agricultural regimen more or less uniform throughout the region, such that millet and sorghum were the chief cereals of subsistence and rice was grown along the coast and in the interior.[60]

As was true of other Senegambians, the patrilineal, patrilocal, and (for those who could afford it) polygynous Bambara of the upper Niger maintained a tripartite division of society and lived in centralized states.[61] Within the state, people were organized at the village level, or the *dugu*, a collection of which formed the *kafo*, the largest administrative unit in Kaarta and Segu over which was an official named the *fama*.[62]

A coherent discussion of Bambara beliefs is difficult to achieve by way of the contemporary literature alone. Many European travelers mention the Bambara, but the vast majority never reached Bambara lands (or lived to tell about it). The nineteenth-century traveler Raffenel, along with the early-twentieth-century colonial officials Tauxier and Monteil, were the first to provide the kind of detail with which this study is concerned. However, they are all well beyond the period of the slave trade, as are the anthropological data. Extrapolations are therefore unavoidable. Notwithstanding the likelihood of certain accretions, the larger point remains uncontested and reliable: the spiritual realm of the Bambara was of immediate and central concern.[63]

The Bambara, or Bamana, believed in the supreme being Bemba, or Ngala, who in turn created the two principal deities of Faro and Pemba.[64] Faro, master of the spoken word, created the seven heavens along with the spirit of the air, Teliko. Pemba, on the other hand, first assumed the form of a tree, after which he created a woman—the earth—to whom he gave a soul (*ni*) and a double (*dya*). Pemba proceeded to copulate with the earth, and from this union sprang the animals and plants. A period of disorder then ensued, after which order was finally restored by the master of the spoken word. According to Raffenel and Tauxier, lesser gods (*boli* or *bouri* or *silama*) were also created; each Bambara village maintained an area devoted to the service of the principal *boli* of the village. Supplications for health, marital problems, the weather, and so on were made to the *boli*, not Bemba or Faro.[65]

The Bambara view of the soul requires some attention, for it is related not only to other African perspectives on the afterlife but also to the eventual conversion of some to Christianity, and will again be discussed in Chapter 9. As is true of the earth, humans also possess a soul (*ni*) and a double (*dya*), the *ni* being the most important element of human existence.[66] But in addition to these two components, humans and animals as well possess a *tere*, or spiritual force that can be understood as the "character" or personality of the entity. At death, a dissociation takes place among the three elements of the human person such that the *dya* enters the realm of water, the *ni* inhabits an ancestral altar, and the *tere* is transformed into a uninhibited entity called the *nyama*, which "roams about freely."

Bambara belief in reincarnation stems from the view that a newborn child receives spiritual elements from an appropriate, recently deceased relative: the deceased's *ni* becomes the *dya* of the newborn, and the *dya* becomes the *ni*. However, the personality or character of the deceased, having been transformed into the *nyama*, remains dissociated. All life possesses the *tere*-turned-*nyama*, and because humans kill animals, plants, and insects for various reasons, the world is filled with hostile *nyama*. Only the power of Faro keeps the *nyama* of sacrificed animals and birds in check, sacrifices necessary to appease the *nyama* of the ancestors.

For the Bambara, then, there is intimacy among the earth, the spirit world, and human beings.[67] To live safely and productively in such a dangerous and dense spiritual environment required powers capable of negotiating with the realm of the unseen and disembodied. Critical to the negotiations was the amulet, or charm (or talisman), for which the Bambara were noted. Raffenel, in attempting to describe Bambara religion, gives a sense of the amulet's importance: "They [the Bambara] have some fetishist practices which include, among others . . . that of worshiping an enormous earthen vase, known throughout Senegambia under the name of *canari*, which they fill with amulets [gris-gris] of all sorts; they consult it before doing anything of importance."[68] During this first visit to Senegambia, Raffenel may have well confused a focus of worship with a reputed site of intercession and divination. In any event, amulets were critical to the process and constitute an important connection between Bambara life in Africa and subsequent travail in America.

The Bambara came to North America, therefore, out of specific political circumstances bearing certain cultural content. The question becomes, What is the likelihood that either the Bambara worldview or their warrior-cultivator tradition survived the foreign environment of the lower Mississippi? The informed response is that the likelihood was very high, and indeed, the evidence supports the projection. First of all, it must be remembered that the African-based population numerically exceeded its white counterpart throughout most of Louisiana's colonial period. In 1721 the white population was estimated at 1,082, compared with only 533 slaves. By 1732, however, the ratio had reversed itself, so that there were 3,600 slaves and only 1,720 whites. By 1788 the slave population had increased to 20,673 and accounted for 55 percent of the total population of the lower Mississippi.[69] These figures support Midlo Hall's characterization of early colonial Louisiana as "thoroughly Africanized."[70]

The fact that the African-based population was numerically dominant does not, in and of itself, reveal the full picture. When this is coupled with the realization that most of these slaves were on plantations clustered together, it becomes clearer that black-white intercultural contact in Louisiana was minimized by both raw numbers and logistics. Furthermore, white settlers in colonial Louisiana had little of cultural value to offer Africans, Native Americans, or anyone else, as many were the rejects of French society: vagabonds, military deserters, rebellious children, criminals, and the destitute.[71] Under such circumstances, the probability of African retentions was optimal.

In view of the foregoing, it is important to recall the Bambara's profound concern with what is seen and what is not, with the realm of nonphysical entities and that which is perceived by the senses. Amulets were used to effect harmony, equilibrium, and cooperation between the physical and the noumenal; the existence of such instruments in the New World would therefore suggest the continuity of the former worldview. Their employment by a largely African-born population would not have been absent contextual meaning and significance.

There is no doubt that the Bambara continued to manufacture amulets in the New World.[72] For example, the *zinzin*, a charm so-called in Louisiana Creole and used for "support or power," has "the same name and meaning in Bambara." Likewise, the gris-gris, "a harmful charm, comes from the Mande word *gerregerys.*" Another destructive amulet, called the *wanga* in New Orleans, is also of Mande derivation. That such charms were pervasive is further supported by a rash of poisonings in the 1720s directly related to African, and specifically Bambara, production of charms. In the absence of accounts explaining the transfer of Bambara original beliefs, the existence of these media are testimony enough. Surely, the Bambara worldview would be altered over time as a consequence of life in America, but in colonial Louisiana, there is evidence that the Bambara attempted to adhere to their unique understanding of the world.

The successful maintenance of a particular worldview can only be enhanced by the preservation of the language in which such a perspective was originally conceived. In the case of the Bambara in Louisiana, it is Midlo Hall's argument that they "played a preponderant role in the formation of the colony's Afro-Creole culture."[73] Louisiana Creole belongs to "a special language group, the Atlantic Creoles," which are "markedly similar in grammatical structure, in pronunciation, and in literal translations of African idioms."[74] In the case of Louisiana Creole, its vocabulary is "overwhelmingly French in origin, but its grammatical structure is largely African." There is both a retention of specific African words and a syntactical continuity that allows these words to be expressed in an African linguistic context, maximizing the conveyance not only of the sound and meaning of the words themselves but also of the larger worldview and perspective they were created to describe. As such, Louisiana Creole was well developed long before the influx of Haitian slaves into Louisiana following that island's revolution.[75] In that case, it was heavily influenced by the Bambara community and was therefore in all likelihood a major factor in the perpetuation of the Bambara worldview.

A final consideration relating to the matter of the Bambara belief system concerns the question of the preservation of Bambara families. Following Midlo Hall's lead, it would appear that colonial Louisiana pursued a slave policy that provided for some sense of familial security. Thus Midlo Hall writes that "in French Louisiana, creole slave children grew up in tightly knit, nuclear families headed by both African parents. The slave family was scrupulously protected in practice as well as in law. Mother, father, husband, wife, and children under the age of fourteen were not sold separately."[76] She further explains that such a policy was necessitated by the fact that Louisiana received so very few shipments of Africans, as opposed to Haiti, which received the vast majority of those headed for French-controlled lands. Louisiana was therefore constrained to encourage a family life that promoted some stability and produced a self-sustaining slave population. Whatever the rationale of the French, such an arrangement could only enhance the cultural transfer between the African-born and the African-derived. Included in that number were the Bambara who, married to Wolof, Igbo, and American-born women, had to negotiate the specific content of their progeny's cultural heritage. However, they would have found French policy consistent with their own patrilocal and patrilineal systems.

Having addressed the matter of the continuity of the Bambara belief system, the focus can turn to the question of the Bambara as warrior-cultivators. Of course, the slaveholders were much more interested in the cultivator aspect of this hyphenated personality, so that the Bambara and other Senegambians played a key role in the development of agriculture in the lower Mississippi. Is there evidence that the warrior component continued as well?

Clearly, the New World slaveocracy presented serious constraints to the continuation of a warrior tradition among the Bambara (or anyone else). In view of these limitations, it is all the more remarkable to find evidence of the Bambara warrior mentality. The evidence lies in the Bambara reputation for being extremely rebellious.[77] Now, without question, Africans from all ethnic groups displayed varying degrees of defiance; the Bambara had no special claims to such behavior. However, the frequency with which Bambara slaves revolted was such that slaveholders developed a stereotypic image of the Bambara as rebels. What informed such an image?

There were at least three forms of resistance in which the Bambara participated, apparently more so than others. First, there were small-scale revolts— absconding, sabotage, and slaveholder poisonings.[78] It was not uncommon, in fact, for the Bambara and other Africans to abscond together with Native Americans indigenous to the area, some of whom were also enslaved. But individual and corporate acts of escape eventually fed a form of revolt on a larger scale, namely, the creation and maintenance of Maroon communities.[79] These Maroons were located in the cypress swamps, *la ciprière*, in lower Louisiana. In fact, by the end of the American War of Independence, Maroon communities controlled the whole of the Bas du Fleuve, the area between the mouth of the Mississippi River and New Orleans. From the earliest period on, there was a "heavy concentration" of African slaves along the eastern bank of the Mississippi below New Orleans. The Bas du Fleuve witnessed the most rapidly expanding slave population in the area, such that it became the "largest, the oldest, and the most creolized slave population in Louisiana."[80]

The swamps became an important place of refuge for runaways, a place where they lived life on their own terms as best they could: "Slaves and maroons from various plantations met regularly in the *ciprière*. Huts were built, with secret paths leading to them. A network of cabins of runaway slaves arose behind plantations all along the rivers and bayous. Arms and ammunition were stored in the cabins."[81] The Maroons were self-sufficient, engaging in cultivation, gathering (berries, sassafras, palmetto roots, and so on), and maintaining commercial ventures—making baskets and squaring cypress logs for sale outside of the swamps. The Maroons also launched external raids. A very interesting relationship between the Maroons and the outside world developed whereby each was keenly aware of the other; the Maroons "did not distance themselves from the plantations and towns; they surrounded them."[82] The white community was concerned about the Maroons' existence but in no position to do much about it early on. The Maroons were in defensible terrain and well armed, highly suggestive of the continuation of a warrior tradition.

In the second half of the eighteenth century, the Maroon communities became predominantly Creole (slaves born in America, or at least outside of Africa), although the Spanish imported significant numbers of Africans during this period. However, *la ciprière* continued to enjoy strong ties to the Bambara community. In the 1780s, for example, one St. Malo was the leader of the Maroons and was possibly "of Bambara extraction." He controlled the area between the Mississippi and Lake Borne, south of New Orleans, and maintained several permanent settlements there, including Ville Gaillarde and Chef Menteur. During his tenure the Spanish finally decided to take control of the swamps and began raiding the area. St. Malo and many of his entourage were captured and hanged in 1784; by 1788, the slave population of the Bas du Fleuve had decreased by 25 percent. The demise of the Maroons and the warrior tradition did not occur, however, before they were able to teach their successors in the area, the Cajuns and the Canary Islanders, how to survive in the cypress swamps.

In addition to their participation in the Maroons, the Bambara also engaged in another form of large-scale rebellion: open, armed revolt. In the conspiracy of 1731, for example, some four hundred Bambara slaves, all reportedly "speaking the same language," were on the verge of taking up arms.[83] The Bambara did not participate in the Pointe Coupee conspiracy of 1791, as it was largely a "Mina" (Ewe and Fon) affair.[84] The 1795 conspiracy at Pointe Coupee, however, was another matter. In April 1795, a number of slaves were seized at Pointe Coupee and charged with seditious conspiracy. By May of the same year, some fifty-seven slaves and three whites had been convicted; twenty-three of the former were hanged in June, and the remaining thirty-one were flogged and condemned to hard labor in Puerto Rico, Mexico, Florida, and Cuba. The three whites were deported. Midlo Hall has applied a class analysis to the conspiracy, characterizing it as "part of a multiracial abolitionist movement supported by a large segment of the dispossessed of all races in Louisiana and throughout the Caribbean: a manifestation of the most radical phase of the French Revolution, which had spilled over from Europe to the Americas."[85] Although this assessment is certainly plausible, Midlo Hall also writes that the plantations most involved in the conspiracy were those with the largest number of slaves and imbalanced sex ratios, and that the majority of those convicted were from "heavily Africanized estates. The Colin Lacour estate, for example, was heavily Senegambian."[86] This finding, although not conflicting with her thesis, supports my contention that on occasion the Bambara, a significant component of the Senegambian contingent, responded to their enslavement out of their experience as warriors. Their involvement in the 1795 Pointe Coupee conspiracy, as well as in the earlier the conspiracy of 1731, was therefore totally consistent with their previous experience and behavior.

An examination of the role of the Senegambian presence in colonial Louisiana and Carolina-Georgia coincides with the demographic data that the Senegambians came to North America early and in sizable numbers. Their presence laid a foundation for the development of African American culture; the Bambara in particular brought with them certain cultural and social constructs, including the Bambara worldview and the warrior-cultivator tradition. But in Louisiana, the Senegambians were only part of the story (albeit a large part). Populations from the Bight of Benin were also present in the colony from the beginning.

The cultures of the Bight of Benin can be described as a unique blend of Fon, Ewe, and Yoruba elements.[87] There is an ever-growing body of literature on the influence of the Yoruba, Fon, and Ewe cultures on New World societies, with particular emphasis on Haiti, Brazil, and Cuba. The impact of these cultures upon said societies has been nothing less than phenomenal, their continued study clearly warranted. But when it comes to North America, these influences are by no means dominant, with the possible exception of Louisiana. Groups from the Bight of Benin tended to be settled in patterns radiating out from their epicenter in the lower Mississippi.

Ethnicity in the Bight of Benin appears to have been fairly well established among the Ewe (concentrated in present-day Togo, southeastern Ghana).[88] Exhibiting a single language (with different dialects), culture, and claiming descent from the town of Tado, the more than 120 Ewe states (varying in size) were autonomous yet conscious of their affinities during the historical period under review. The Fon of Dahomey (contemporary Benin) also shared a sense of common heritage, although perhaps not to the same degree as the Ewe. Dahomean King Agaja's conquest of Weme (1716), Allada (1724), and Whydah (1727) created a political framework out of which greater cultural unity was possible.[89] It is with the Yoruba, however, that ethnicity was more consciously operative in the Americas than in Africa. In the latter, the Yoruba (a term of possible Hausa derivation and used to refer to the people of the town Oyo Ile) were much more loyal to their respective towns. Within the context of New World enslavement, however, their common language (with dialects), culture, and religion (featuring a shared Oyo Ile, Ife-centered cosmology) combined to erase former boundaries of locality. The Yoruba emerged as a "nation" not only in North America but also in the West Indies and Brazil.[90]

Midlo Hall has determined that some 26.2 percent of the Africans imported into Louisiana from 1760 to 1800 were from the Bight of Benin.[91] What this means is that Fon-Ewe-Yoruba traditions, in place since the beginning of the colony, were reinvigorated during the Spanish period. Ties with the Bight of Benin were further strengthened in the period after 1803, when Louisiana became U.S. property and importation from Haiti became more significant.[92] The cultures of the Fon-Ewe-Yoruba were therefore flourishing alongside and in connection with those of Senegambia.

By way of Haiti primarily, but also via Guadeloupe and Martinique, both slave and free populations accentuated the previously established culture of the Fon-Ewe-Yoruba in the lower Mississippi. These cultural expressions were not so distinct as they were combined, having merged and blended together so creatively as to result in a novel yet relatively coherent metaphysical whole. Under the influence of the Fon-Ewe-Yoruba, other cultural patterns from various parts of West and West Central Africa, in particular from Kongo and Angola, converged in the New World to form what has come to be referred to as the religion of vodu, or vodun or voodoo—the different spellings corresponding more or less to the manifestation of the religion in the specific locations of Dahomey, Haiti, and the lower Mississippi. The terms *vodu* and *vodun* derive from the Dahomean words for "god" and "gods" and are therefore preferred by a number of scholars. For the purposes of our analysis, however, the term *voodoo* will do just fine.

Voodoo should be distinguished to some degree from hoodoo, which will be discussed in subsequent chapters. The bases for this qualified distinction are the varied geographic and experiential origins of the phenomena. Hoodoo, derived initially from West Central Africa, ultimately represents a convergence of African beliefs that took place for the most part in English-speaking North America. In the process of convergence and resistance and, to be sure, acculturation, these systems of belief lost their coherence, so that the practice of hoodoo became primarily associated with procedures designed to change an undesirable condition and not necessarily related to any particular set of deities or system of belief. Voodoo, on the other hand, developed into a highly distinguishable belief system, with its own gods, rituals, and methods of intervention into the human condition. That is to say, though voodoo is itself a synthesis, it is a coherent and specific fusion.

Why the Fon-Ewe-Yoruba influence became more prominent and celebrated than the Bambara is not clear, but there are at least three possible reasons. First, relatively sizable numbers of people originally from the Bight of Benin came to the lower Mississippi simultaneous with and subsequent to the earlier Bambara immigration, suggesting that their cultural ties to Africa were continually renewed. Second, the coherence of the Fon-Ewe-Yoruba belief system as developed in Louisiana, Haiti, and the other French Caribbean colonies may have been greater than that of the Bambara or other groups, as it arguably possessed a larger capacity to be shielded from disruption by its various parallels with Catholicism. And third, the fact that Fon-Ewe-Yoruba beliefs were cultivated in an urban port as important as New Orleans may have given it a distinct advantage over other African belief systems. By virtue of its contact with all who lived and passed through the entrepôt, voodoo necessarily attracted a level of attention that rites centered in remote rural lands and practiced clandestinely could never achieve. Blacks, both slave and free, traversed New Orleans for various reasons and in significant numbers, transferring what they learned in New Orleans to plantations both near and far, thereby assuring voodoo's ascendancy. This ascendancy was by no means the work of blacks alone; many whites also believed in voodoo and solicited aid and succor from its practitioners.[93] The agency of New Orleans itself, therefore, was more than likely pivotal to the growth of Fon-Ewe-Yoruba beliefs.

A great deal has been written about voodoo.[94] A succinct discussion of both the origins and development of these beliefs will therefore suffice. To begin, the Fon and Yoruba exchanged metaphysical views long before the transatlantic slave trade.[95] As a consequence of war, raids, demographic shifts, displacements, diplomatic missions, and trade, these neighboring West African populations succeeded in borrowing aspects of each other's culture. Prior to the emergence of Abomey (in the interior of Dahomey, now the state of Benin) at the dawn of the eighteenth century, the Fon-Ewe had already incorporated and transformed Yoruba gods into their own pantheon. With Abomey's expansion and conquest of southern and coastal Fon-Ewe populations from about 1700 to 1740, there was a reincorporation of previously integrated Yoruba religious elements. Yet another, subsequent process of Fon-Ewe and Yoruba religious fusion took place in the New World, specifically in Martinique, Guadeloupe, and above all Haiti. It was this third synthesis, incorporating West Central African beliefs and practices as well as those from West Africa, that transferred to the lower Mississippi.

The deities of the Fon-Ewe (*loas* in Haiti, *vodun* in Dahomey) and the

Yoruba (*orishas*) are so numerous and their qualities so unique that they are distinctive within the context of West African belief systems. The Fon-Ewe high god, Mawu-Lisa, corresponds to the Yoruba Olorun and is a composite of male and female characteristics that together represent the Fon-Ewe notion of perfect balance. Referred to as Bondieu in Haiti, Mawu-Lisa was joined in the Fon-Ewe pantheon by such *loas* as Gu, the god of iron and warfare who corresponds to Ogun of the Yoruba and is called Papa Ogun or Papa Ogun Feraille in Haiti and Louisiana (and at times Joe Feraille in the latter); and Aziri, a riverain goddess whose Yoruba counterpart is Oshun and who is referred to in Haiti as Erzulie. As is true of Gu and Ogun, the Fon-Ewe god of the crossroads and keeper of the gate, Legba, is another example of a deity originally borrowed from the Yoruba, who referred to him as Eshu-Elegba. Also a trickster, Papa Legba (or Papa Limba) as he is called in Haiti and Louisiana is the principal mediator between humans and deities and is therefore the first to whom supplicants appeal in prayer and ritual. However, it is the serpent god of the sky, Da or Dan Bada of the Fon, who is probably the most recognized representative of voodoo and was identified by both Snelgrave and Isert as the primary deity.[96] Corresponding to Oshumare of the Yoruba, this is none other than the Damballah of Haiti and Louisiana, also known as Li Grand Zombi, whose most common avatar is the rainbow-serpent.

Two traditions developed within voodoo. One, Rada, refers to those rites associated with captives from Allada and others who were defeated by Abomey and sold into the slave trade. Rada is considered the "cool" side of voodoo and is related to tranquil and harmonious pursuits. Petro-Lemba, on the other hand, involves rites concerned with healing and the destruction of evil, and constitutes the "hot" counterpart of voodoo. Petro-Lemba was heavily influenced by the society of Lemba of the northern Kongo area and is associated with the Haitian figure of Don Pedro.[97]

In contrast to Haiti, voodoo as a coherent and comprehensive practice began to dissipate in Louisiana and the lower Mississippi during the course of the nineteenth century. It is true that certain of its practitioners achieved a high level of recognition for their reputed powers, especially Marie Laveau, a free femme de couleur who disappeared mysteriously in 1822 while at the apex of her influence in New Orleans. Notwithstanding its association with spectacular people and spectacular events, voodoo gradually came to be viewed as less a religion and more a particular brand of magic, boasting the efficacy of various potions, charms, and amulets in the lives of its adherents.

Voodoo certainly fulfilled the need for many to identify with the mysterious. To this day, New Orleans and the lower Mississippi enjoy a certain quality of religious mystique and intrigue, so that claims of continuity in this context are undeniable. Because of its origins and development, African-derived culture in Louisiana is unique. However, this culture also came into contact with those beyond the Mississippi. Outside of Louisiana, therefore, voodoo entered planes of intersection with other African-based beliefs operating under somewhat different circumstances. As such, the impact of voodoo progressively weakened as the distance from New Orleans and the lower Mississippi lengthened. Away from the epicenter, voodoo necessarily merged with other African-informed religious practices and consequently lost its distinctiveness.

· · · · · · ·

In this chapter I have examined some of the contributions of the Bambara and the Fon-Ewe-Yoruba to African-derived culture in Louisiana, having begun with a consideration of the Senegambian presence in Carolina and Georgia. But the picture for Carolina, Georgia, and Louisiana is far from complete. Indeed, the discussion of the Senegambian presence along the coast has yet to be fully analyzed. In order to do so, it is necessary to take into account the important question of the role of Islam in Senegambia and, by extension, elsewhere in West Africa. It is to the matter of Islam that the following chapter turns.

4

· · · · · · · · · · · · · · · ·

PRAYIN' ON DUH BEAD

ISLAM IN EARLY AMERICA

It is generally understood that in the course of contact between the Old and New Worlds, Christianity and Judaism were introduced into the latter and indeed facilitated its cultural transformation. For the most part, Europeans were the carriers of these religions, and given their success in colonizing the Americas, religions closely associated with them have received scholarly consideration at the expense of other, non-European (but nonetheless equally Old World) beliefs.

Africans transported via the transatlantic trade also brought with them their own religions. The research into African-based belief systems continues to develop, but it is clear that such transfers took place with varying results, depending upon the spatial peculiarities of the acculturation in question.[1] Among the beliefs introduced into the Americas by Africans was the religion of Islam. Indeed, one of America's most illustrious sons, Frederick Douglass, may have himself been a descendant of Muslims.[2]

In this chapter I will discuss the more pertinent issues surrounding the question of Islam's role within the African-based population in North America. The discussion is placed at this juncture, immediately following an examination of the Senegambian contribution to the African American identity, because many Senegambians were in fact Muslims. Further, I argue here that the nature of the Islamic faith in West Africa was such that, upon transfer to North America, it tended to transcend the specific ethnicities of its adherents. Muslims in America, whether Fulbe or Mandinka or Hausa, had the capacity to relate to one another and to the non-Muslim world as Muslims. It is therefore appropriate to consider the Muslim community within the overall context of ethnicity as constituting a primary means of identification prior to the creation of an African American identity.

Although the emphasis in the preceding chapter was on the non-Muslim Bambara contingent of Senegambia, some of what was discussed anticipates the current chapter in that it essentially concerns such Muslim-controlled or Muslim-influenced phenomena as urban culture and long-distance trading networks. An examination of the "Muslim side" of the Senegambian personality is therefore in order; however, such an examination also provides a means of transition into other African regions, as Islam was by no means confined to Senegambia but was also found in the interiors of Sierra Leone, the Gold Coast, and the Bight of Benin. With the treatment of Islam completed, the study will then be positioned to consider the non-Muslim populations and characteristics of the adjoining regions, beginning with Sierra Leone.

The nature of the data concerning Muslims in North America is such that arguments are necessarily more tentative than conclusive; nonetheless, the consistency of the evidence allows for several statements. First, their numbers were significant, probably reaching into the thousands. Second, Muslims made genuine and persistent efforts to observe their religion; and even though the continuation of their faith took place primarily within their own families, in some cases they may have converted slaves who were not relatives. Third, cultural phenomena found in segments of the African American community, such as ostensibly Christian worship practices and certain artistic expressions, probably reflect the influence of these early Muslims. However, Islam's most lasting and, for the purposes of this inquiry, most salient impact was its role in the process of social stratification within the larger African American society. In ways to be examined, the early Muslim community contributed significantly to the development of the African American identity.

There are essentially two reasons the study of Muslims in the American colonial and antebellum periods has not been taken more seriously. The first has to do with the absence of a satisfactory dialogue between historians of Africa and North America. Suffice it to state here that efforts to address this problem have begun and can be seen in the work of individuals such as Littlefield and Wood.[3] But the second reason concerns the relative dearth of materials on the subject, a scarcity that, in turn, is a function of two factors. First, colonial and antebellum observers failed to accurately record the variegated cultural expressions of African slaves out of ignorance and arrogance, and they were just as ignorant of Islam. The cumulative evidence suggests that such observers could sometimes distinguish the Muslims from among the slave population but had neither the skills nor the interest to record more detailed and careful information about them. The second factor was the reluctance of descendants of these early Muslims to be more forthcoming when discussing Islam. A review of Islam's growth in West Africa serves as a partial remedy to these lacunae.[4]

The evidence for the existence of Muslims in early America comes from both sides of the Atlantic. On the African side, the historical research provides a reasonably clear picture of the political and cultural conditions out of which American-bound captives emerged. On the American side, several types of sources give some insight into the presence and activities of Muslims in the New World: the ethnic and cultural makeup of the African regions of origin, the appearance of Muslim names in the ledgers of slaveholders and in the runaway slave advertisements of newspapers, references to Muslim ancestry in interviews with former slaves and the descendants of Muslims, stated preferences for certain prototypes of Africans by the slaveholding community, recorded observations of instances of Islamic activity, and profiles of notable Muslim figures. Within the last genre are documents written in Arabic by Muslims themselves, a rare phenomenon.

This section is primarily informed by the historical literature concerning the African background. While general statements can be ventured with regard to estimating the Muslim population in America, it must be understood that the data on this subject are almost entirely qualitative in nature; an attempt at quantification can only be speculative.

As a consequence of Berber and Arab commercial activity, Islam had penetrated the savannah below the Sahara by the beginning of the ninth century. Some subsaharan African (or "Sudanese") merchants living in the *sāḥil* (or sahel, literally "shore" or transition zone between the desert and the savannah) and the savannah began to convert, so that Islam became associated with trade, especially long-distance networks of exchange. In some societies, political rulers also converted to the new religion with varying degrees of fidelity, so that Islam became a vehicle by which alliances between commercial and political elites were forged. Islam continued to grow slowly throughout West Africa into the sixteenth century, dramatically increasing its adherents during the nineteenth and early twentieth centuries, as Islam (at times) took on the form of anticolonial cultural resistance. This span of four centuries (beginning with the sixteenth) roughly corresponds to the period of the transatlantic slave trade. A consideration of Islam's historical development in West Africa is therefore essential in trying to formulate an idea of the size and character of the Muslim presence in early America and can be achieved within the previously established schema of regional origins.

The point to be made about the first of these regions, Senegambia, is that this is truly an immense area; if operating in the interior, traffickers in human cargo had several outlets for their trade. They could, for example, sell their captives along the Gambia or Senegal Rivers, direct their caravans to other points along the West African coast, or deal their cargoes into the trans-saharan slave trade. That captives could originate from as far inland as the upper and middle Niger valleys indicates that there were at least three staging areas from which Africans in this region were procured for the Atlantic trade: the coastal area, from the lower Senegal to the lower Casamance valleys; a midrange area, encompassing the middle and upper Senegal and Gambia valleys; and the middle and upper Niger. The presence of Islam within this vast stretch of territory was relative to specific lands and periods of time.

Within the coastal area, the Wolof had for the most part remained unconverted to Islam before the end of the eighteenth century, although Islam had penetrated the Senegal River from the north as early as the tenth.[5] One source, for example, stated in 1455 that the religion of the "Zilofi" (Wolof) kingdom of "Senega" was "Muhammadanism: they are not, however, as are the white Moors, very resolute in this faith, especially the common people."[6] From the sixteenth to the eighteenth century, Islam was confined to the royal courts of such Wolof states as Jolof, Cayor, and Waalo; Muslim advisors served rulers who in turn practiced varying degrees of traditional and/or Islamic religion. By the early nineteenth century, however, Mollien observed that "Mahometanism is making daily progress, and will soon become the only religion of the country of Cayor."[7] The Muslim presence was therefore important and influential.

Along the lower Gambia and the Casamance, the various Mande-speaking populations, along with the Sereer, turned from traditional religions to Islam with the passing of time, facilitated by the presence of Muslim merchants among them.[8] Jobson's early-seventeenth-century description of "Marybuckes" (Muslim clerics) and Islam along the Gambia is echoed by Smith and Moore's early- and Park's late-eighteenth-century observations, demonstrating Islam's growing influence.[9]

It is in the midrange of the Senegambian region, however, that a substantial proportion of the population was Muslim. In the middle Senegal valley a strong Muslim polity was established as early as the eleventh century. Subsequently, a dynasty of fluctuating loyalty to Islam was founded in the early sixteenth century and overthrown in 1776 by a militant Islamic theocracy. Futa Toro, as the state came to be known, was ethnically Fulbe, or Tukulor as the latter term is used to distinguish the Muslim, sedentary, and (in some instances) ethnically mixed portion of the Fulbe from the pastoral, non-Muslim segment. The upper Senegal and Gambia valleys contained proportionately fewer Muslims (and lower population densities), but again, the Islamic factor had been present for several hundred years by the eighteenth century, largely due to the far-reaching Malian empire. In the upper Senegal, Saugnier reported in 1784 that the Serrakole's religion was "nearly allied to Mahometanism, and still more to natural religion"; by 1821 Gray and Dochard essentially said the same: "From a state of Paganism these people are progressively embracing the Mahometan faith."[10] The Islamic factor eventually led to the Muslim-led state of Bundu in 1698, in which the population became predominantly Muslim by the nineteenth century. Thus the mid-range area represents a focus of Muslim power that only increased throughout the duration of the transatlantic trade.

Far into the interior lay the western reaches of the Niger River. The area was a mixture of Muslim and non-Muslim populations from the time of imperial Songhay (1464–1591) to the early nineteenth century, at which point the area known as Maasina fell to the armies of militant Fulbe Muslims. Between the fall of Songhay and the dawn of an islamized Maasina, the area witnessed an intense period of warfare, with the non-Muslim Bambara of Segu establishing control throughout the upper Niger in the eighteenth century. Of great significance is the fact that Muslim and non-Muslim alike were among the numerous war captives, many of whom were eventually traded for transport to the Western Hemisphere.[11]

Based upon the preceding sketch of the Senegambian region, it becomes clear that from the fifteenth through the mid-nineteenth century this area gradually became islamized, more dramatically in the nineteenth than in previous centuries, and that during the nineteenth century the majority of the population became Muslim. But in order to assess the significance of this trend, several factors must be taken into consideration. As previously noted, Senegambia, by virtue of its location vis-à-vis Europe, was a principal supplier of slaves during the early phase of the Atlantic trade.[12] Second, the evidence from a clerically led revolt along the coast in the 1670s, known as the *tubenan* movement, suggests that the Wolof states of the Atlantic coast were deeply affected by the slave trade before the last quarter of the seventeenth century.[13] The Moor Nasir al-Din gained the support of the Wolof peasantry by condemning the participation of the Wolof elite in the slave trade, insisting that "God does not allow kings to plunder, kill or make their people captive."[14] The masses sought asylum in Islam; in 1685 Cultru wrote that the Wolof "are all Mahometans."[15] When the lieutenants of Nasir al-Din in turn betrayed the trust of the peasantry and began selling them into slavery, they were quickly overthrown. Their overthrow suggests the presence of effective opposition to the trade within the coastal area and leads to the conclusion that, beginning in the eighteenth century, the supply of slaves increasingly originated from further inland, in the middle and upper Senegal and Gambia valleys. This shift is indirectly confirmed by the Islamic revolution of Futa Toro, which began in the 1760s and was, in part, the response of the Muslim community to its victimization in the trade.[16] Muslims seeking protection against enslavement created the Islamic polity of Bundu in part as an asylum from the trade, which together with the example of Futa Toro supports the position that the middle and upper Senegal valleys were more severely impacted by the transatlantic trade than previously understood.[17]

Finally, as Raffenel reported that the non-Muslim Bambara of Segu were renowned warriors, "greatly superior to their neighbors in the art of war, the Bambara are truly fearsome," a number of Muslims were necessarily fed into the trade as captives of war.[18] Although the contribution of Senegambia to the trade declined dramatically after 1750, the combined evidence suggests that the bulk of the captives came from the midrange to upper and middle Niger areas, in which Islam was relatively more widespread. After 1750, traders operating in the upper and middle Niger valleys simply redirected the considerable number of war captives to other points along the coast of West Africa.

The next region is Sierra Leone. Late seventeenth and early eighteenth century accounts agree that Mande-speaking Muslim populations were in the numerical minority along the coast: Matthews, for example, wrote of the "Mandingoes," who were "Mahomedans, and as zealous promoters of their religion as even Mahomed himself could wish."[19] From the middle of the sixteenth century through the seventeenth, the region's principal sources for the slave trade were littoral, non-Muslim populations.[20] But for the second half of the eighteenth century, Rodney estimates that 75 percent of the Africans sold into the trade came from the interior.[21] This observation would suggest that for the same period, slaves from this region's hinterland also came to North America in similar proportions.

The interior of present-day Guinea is dominated by the Futa Jallon massif. Originally inhabited by the Jallonke, these Guinea highlands received substantial numbers of Fulbe pastoralists from Maasina in the fifteenth, seventeenth and eighteenth centuries.[22] By the early eighteenth century, tensions between the Fulbe, who were largely Muslim, and the autochthonous, largely non-Muslim Jallonke reached intolerable levels for reasons contested in the scholarly literature.[23] A holy war, or jihād, was launched in the 1720s by an alliance of Fulbe-Jallonke Muslims. After consolidating its power in 1747, the jihād expanded into adjacent lands and became a decidedly Fulbe-controlled operation. Gray and Dochard's emphasis on Futa Jallon's strict observance of Islam is echoed by Callié's depiction of its people as "extremely fanatical," demonstrating the seriousness of the jihād.[24] As a consequence of this movement, large numbers of captives were sold along the coast into the transatlantic trade.

A glance at the jihād suggests that the preponderance of captives sold into the trade were non-Muslims. However, the jihād was not one long, uninterrupted Muslim march to victory. Non-Muslim populations fought back; in particular, the incursions into Muslim-ruled territory by Kundi Burama of Wassulu lasted from the 1760s into the 1780s, wreaking havoc among the Muslim faithful.[25] Lovejoy records that the 1760s through the 1780s was the "most violent" phase of the conflict in Futa Jallon, and resulted in a better than 100 percent per year increase in slave exports from the region.[26] It would appear, therefore, that the Futa Jallon jihād created nearly all of the captives coming from the interior, which in turn accounts for Rodney's estimate of the eighteenth-century trade from the interior. It should be kept in mind, however, that some slaves could have also been procured through the considerable commercial activity of Muslims from Kankan (Guinea) to Kong (the Ivory Coast).

The Gold Coast saw European traders along the Atlantic as early as the fifteenth century. Originally an exporter of gold and a net importer of slaves, the Gold Coast became a net exporter of slaves by the early seventeenth century.[27] In the first decade of the eighteenth, Africans were exported from the region at a rate of 2,500 per year; by the 1740s, the trade peaked at 9,100 per year. The escalation of the trade was a consequence of rising demand and the expansionist behavior of Asante, which pursued an imperialist policy from 1680 (the approximate date of its founding) to 1750.[28] One of the polities defeated by the power of Asante was the province of Gonja, a Muslim territory vitally connected to the middle Niger valley via Muslim commercial networks leading through Kong, Dagomba, Wa, and Mamprussi. In addition, Muslim traders from as far east as Hausaland conducted business on a regular basis in the capital of Kumase.[29] The Islamic presence in the interior "was strong, providing commercial connections with the far interior, so that the Akan states were involved in continental trade on a scale that was at least equal to Oyo, Dahomey, and Benin and was perhaps even greater."[30] All of this suggests that Muslim captives constituted some percentage of the supply from the Gold Coast.

The Bight of Benin saw struggles between Oyo and Dahomey produce a great many captives in the 1780s and 1790s, whose numbers were further augmented by Yoruba resistance to the ultimately successful expansion of Muslims from Ilorin. The latter were inspired by the 1804 jihād and subse-

TABLE 4.1 Percentages of Africans Imported into
North America from Regions Containing Muslim Populations

Senegambia	14.5%
Sierra Leone	15.8%
Gold Coast	13.1%
Bight of Benin	4.3%
Bight of Biafra	24.4%

quent caliphate of Usuman dan Fodio at Sokoto (in northern Nigeria). Again, as was true of the jihād in Futa Jallon, Muslims as well as non-Muslims lost their liberty and found their way into the transatlantic trade. The existence of large numbers of Muslim "Hausas" in Bahia (Brazil) is confirmation of this observation.[31] There are also references to Africans from northern Nigeria in North America, an example of which is the recorded preference by a Mississippi planter for Africans "of the Bornon, Houssa, Zanfara, Zegzeg, Kapina, and Tombootoo tribes."[32] In light of this information, it is reasonable to propose that a significant number of the captives exported from the Bight of Benin were Muslim.

For this discussion, the regions of West Central Africa and Mozambique will not be reviewed, as the Muslim factor was either nonexistent (true of the former) or the total contribution to the North American slave population was negligible (the case with the latter). This leaves the Bight of Biafra, where large numbers of non-Muslim captives were procured via numerous, small-scale raids in a densely populated region. There were some trade relations with Muslims to the north; however, it would appear that the number of Muslims arriving on the coast for export was negligible.[33]

Table 2.7 provides percentages for the various regions of origin. Those relevant to the present investigation are presented in table 4.1. Altogether, the five regions listed in table 4.1 account for 72.1 percent of the slaves exported to North America.[34] If the Bight of Biafra is eliminated from further consideration, it would mean that 47.7 percent of Africans imported to North America came from areas in which Islam was of varying consequence. That means that of the 481,000 Africans who came to British North America during the slave trade, nearly 230,000 came from areas influenced by Islam.[35] It is therefore reasonable to conclude that Muslims may have come to America by the thousands, if not tens of thousands. A more precise assessment is difficult to achieve.[36]

It would be a mistake to simply focus on the Muslim population, however, for Islam's impact in West Africa was not confined to the converted, practicing community. On the contrary, many non-Muslims were acquainted with a number of its tenets through the activities of Muslim traders and clerics. The Muslim trading networks, through which the Juula, Yarse, and Hausa merchants supplied disparate West African communities with goods from as far away as the Mediterranean, also linked the savannah with the forest area, from Senegambia to Lake Chad.[37] Their apolitical, nonproselytizing code of behavior explains the receptivity of many Muslim and non-Muslim communities to their commercial endeavors.

In addition to, and often in conjunction with, the activities of Muslim traders was the role of Muslim clerics throughout West Africa. Far removed from the lofty positions of the erudite in cities such as Kano and Jenne, numerous clerics of a more utilitarian calling were spread across the region's expanse. Literate in Arabic, these men performed religious and diplomatic services for royal courts and commoners alike. In particular, they provided amulets for both Muslims and non-Muslims; in fact, Muslim amulets, often containing Qur'ānic inscriptions encased in sealed pouches, were very popular among non-Muslim populations, as it was believed that writing possessed particular efficacy.[38] Mosques and *madrasas*, or Qur'ānic schools, were invariably established in the Muslim part of town or in the nearby Muslim village. As a result, many West Africans practicing indigenous religions were nonetheless familiar with and influenced by Islam, having been exposed to Muslim dress, dietary laws, and overall conduct.

By the same token, it was not unusual for those who had converted to Islam to retain certain aspects of their previous beliefs; Islam in West Africa underwent a number of reforms in an effort to achieve orthodoxy.[39] However, to the degree that these non-Islamic tendencies were not in conflict with the fundamental tenets of the faith (for example, one God, Muhammad as God's messenger, daily prayer, fasting Ramadan, and so on), the integrity of these practitioners and the veracity of their confession is not open to challenge.

To be sure, the Muslim presence in North America antedates the arrival of the English colonists. Spanish Florida's St. Augustine (and nearby Fort Mose) featured a significant black population.[40] By the middle of the eighteenth century, the third largest African ethnicity in this metropolitan area were the Malinke, a group that certainly contained Muslims.[41] As was true of the Spanish in Florida, the French in Louisiana also imported Muslims, especially from Senegambia, along with non-Muslims from Whydah and Congo-Angola.[42] The Muslim population, although unquantifiable, must have been significant. The runaway notices for Louisiana would support this probability, as they are absolutely replete with references to the Senegalese, including references to males.[43] Finally, Midlo Hall comments that the "slaves of French Louisiana often kept their African names, many of which were Islamic."[44]

The Muslim population in Louisiana was by no means confined, however, to Senegambians. There are a number of references to northern Nigerians in the newspapers. For example, New Orleans' *Moniteur de la Louisiane* called for the return of a runaway from the Hausa nation ("nation Aoussa") in October 1807.[45] The following September, twenty dollars was offered for the return of two individuals of the Hausa nation who had been recently purchased from a slaver.[46] The next month, an auction by Patton and Mossy featured four men and six women "from the Congo, Mandinga, and Hausa nations, in the country eight months, from 11 to 22 years of age."[47] As a final example, "le Nègre HENRY, nation Aoussa" appeared in the runaway notices.[48] The dates of these publications fall within the 1804–12 period of the jihād of Usuman dan Fodio in northern Nigeria, so it is probable that most of these Hausa slaves were war captives, both Muslim and non-Muslim.

While the existence of Islam in Spanish- and French-speaking North America is important and merits further investigation, the preponderance of the evidence concerns English-speaking North America. The anglophone slaveholding society regularly distinguished between the various ethnicities within the African community.[49] Slaves from Senegambia and Sierra Leone, often simply called Mandingo by whites, were generally viewed by slaveholders as preferable to others.[50] Within the categories of Senegambia and Sierra Leone was the bulk of the Muslim imports; both Midlo Hall and Austin maintain that the terms *Mandingo* and *Mandinga* were synonymous with Muslim by the nineteenth century.[51] Although all of these Mande speakers may not have been Muslim, the aforementioned close association suggests that a substantial number must have been. The North American preference for the Mandinka (one component of the Mande world and certainly among those dubbed Mandingo by whites) is reflected in the activity of eighteenth-century North American shippers who, although not responsible for the majority of slave importations into North America, nevertheless confined their activities to those areas of West Africa of greatest interest to planters and for that reason obtained the vast majority of their slaves from Senegambia and Sierra Leone.[52]

Advertisements for runaway slaves contain unique and substantial information on ethnic and cultural traits of individual slaves. With regard to Muslims in early America, these advertisements are important in that they occasionally provide names that are clearly Muslim but rarely identified as such.[53] Names such as Bullaly (Bilali), Mustapha, Sambo, Bocarrey (Bukhari, or possibly Bubacar from Abu Bakr), and Mamado (Mamadu) are regularly observed in the advertisements for runaway slaves. Unless slave owners clearly understood the origin of these names, they would not necessarily associate them with Islam.[54] A good example of this concerns the name Sambo, a possible corruption of Samba (or "second son" in the language of the Fulbe).[55] The 24 May 1775 edition of Savannah's *Georgia Gazette* ran a notice for three missing men, including twenty-two-year-old Sambo, reportedly "of the Moorish country."[56] This association with the Moorish country may be more a reference to Sambo's Muslim identity than to his actually having hailed from North Africa, although small numbers of Moors (from present-day Mauritania) were also imported into North America.[57] Similarly, the 9–12 January 1782 publication of Charleston's *Royal Gazette* sought the return of Sambo, or Sam, described as having a "yellowish complexion . . . and his hair is pretty long, being of the Fulla country."[58] The connections between Sambo, Islam, and the Fulbe become more apparent when the preceding advertisement is juxtaposed with another notice in which a decidedly Muslim name is identified with the same ethnicity: the 17 June 1766 edition of Charleston's *South-Carolina Gazette and Country Journal* features an ad in which Robert Darrington sought the return of one "Moosa, a yellow Fellow . . . is of the Fullah Country."[59] Although the association between the name Sambo and Islam is strong in the preceding examples, it does not follow that the name was the exclusive property of Muslims. Rather, it is more reasonable to conclude that a significant number of African-born males with this name may have been Muslim.

The appearance of incontestably Muslim names in the runaway notices is relatively infrequent. More commonly, slaveholders seeking the return of runaways associated them with particular regions of origin (for example, Gambia or Senegal) or provided an ethnic identity (such as Mandingo or Fula). The *Charleston Courier*, for example, advertised the finding of a "new Negro BOY, of the Fullah nation, says his name is Adam."[60] In the case of either supposed area of origin or ethnic derivation, one cannot conclusively argue that the individual in question is Muslim, but—given both the African background and the tendency among American planters to conflate Muslims, ethnicity, and area of origin—the probability that many of these people were Muslims is high.

Interestingly, examples of Muslim runaways come overwhelmingly from South Carolina and Georgia, especially along the coast, and also from colonial Louisiana.[61] This is probably due to the fact that Charleston (and Savannah to a lesser extent) was a preeminent slave port and was surrounded by major slaveholding areas devoted to rice and indigo cultivation. Senegambians and Sierra Leonians, greatly in demand for their agricultural skills, tended to come from areas in which there was a Muslim presence.[62] Given their preference for slaves from these areas and distaste for Africans from the Bight of Biafra, South Carolinian and Georgian planters paid closer attention to ethnicity. In contrast, Virginians may not have been as discriminating, a topic for subsequent exploration. Their alleged disinterest in ethnicity, as opposed to any actual disproportion, may explain the relative absence of references to Muslims from Senegambia and Sierra Leone.[63]

Further examples of advertisements that clearly refer to Muslims include the notice for "two Gambian Negroes . . . the one his Name is Walley [Wali] the other's Bocarrey."[64] In this notice, a connection is established between Gambia and Muslims. At times a geographic or ethnic affiliation is not given, only the name, as was the case in 1757, when a "negro man named Mamado" escaped from Rachel Fairchild; or again in 1772, when William Wood of Santee advertised for "a Negro fellow named Homady [Amadi, from Ahmad]."[65] Enough time had passed for John Graham of Augustin's Creek and John Strobhar of Purrysburgh to learn the names of their absconded slaves and to seek the return of Mahomet and Mousa respectively, whereas John Inglis of Charleston could only state that three "new" men and one woman had escaped, and that "two of the fellows are of a yellow complection and Moorish breed."[66]

In North Carolina in 1808, one hundred dollars was offered for the apprehension of Arthur Howe, a white man who had taken away a slave named Mustapha, commonly called "Muss," described as "polite and submissive" and a "handy fellow with most tools or about horses."[67] That same year, Charlestonian R. Heriot suspected that "an African wench named Fatima," who was about twenty years old and spoke very little English, may have been "enticed away" and "harboured by some worthless person or persons."[68] However, most Muslim slaves, as was true of slaves in general, were quite capable of stealing away on their own, as reflected in Godin Guerard's report from Georgia in 1792: "A Moor slave man, about 25 years of age, named Mahomet who is badged by that name, but passes by the name Homady in common."[69]

The matter of absconding obviously involves the question of destination. Muslims were no different from other slaves in that, among other places, they sought refuge among Native Americans. In 1781, "Hommady" had been absent from his owner in Savannah for three weeks and was "suspected to be harboured among the Indians."[70] Similarly, someone matching the description of the previously mentioned Mahomet of John Graham's Augustin's Creek had "been seen at a settlement near the Indian Line on Ogechee very lately," three years after his initial flight.[71] While Native American communities may have provided safe havens for slaves on occasion, some Muslims were interested in taking matters a step further by leaving America altogether, as was true of a "new Negro Fellow, called Jeffray, sometimes,

Bram, or Ibrahim. . . . From some hints given by himself and others it is suspected he will endeavor to get on board some vessel."[72]

The preceding discussion concerns obscure individuals. But there are also accounts of Muslims who enjoyed some notoriety. Austin has compiled data on some sixty-five Muslims, of whom only seven who came to North America are discussed in any detail.[73] The question arises: Of all the Muslims who arrived in America before 1865, what was so unique about these seven? An analysis of each case reveals that they attracted attention for a variety of reasons. Umar b. Said, or "Omar ben Said" (ca. 1770–1864), received the greatest amount of interest, apparently because of both his literacy in Arabic and his possible conversion to Christianity.[74] This "Prince Moro," or "Moreau" as he was sometimes called, possessed an Arabic Bible. In fact, he engaged in a campaign of sending such Bibles to West Africa in cooperation with another African Muslim of some renown, Lamine Kaba, or "Lamen Kebe."[75] This, coupled with his repatriation to Liberia in 1835 after nearly thirty years of enslavement, helps explain the latter's fame. An article on the Soninke or Serrakole language was also published based upon an interview with Lamine Kaba.[76]

In contrast to Umar b. Said and Lamine Kaba, Salih Bilali, or "Tom," remained a devout Muslim; the source of his acclaim was his exceptional managerial skills.[77] Born around 1765, he arrived in North America in 1800; by 1816, he was the head driver on a plantation at Cannon's Point, on the Georgia island of St. Simons. Such was his reliability that the owner left Salih Bilali in charge of the entire plantation for months at a time, without any other supervision. Likewise, Bilali (or "Ben Ali"), a contemporary of Salih Bilali, was also a dependable driver and managed a plantation of four or five hundred slaves on the Georgia island of Sapelo.[78] He is noted as well for an extant collection of excerpts from an Islamic (Maliki) legal text known as the *Risāla* of Ibn Abī Zayd.[79] Furthermore, he served as the model for Joel Chandler Harris's caricature "Ben Ali."[80]

Abd al-Rahman, otherwise known as "Prince," was born in 1762 and arrived in New Orleans in 1788.[81] Several remarkable stories surround him, but the one that brought him national fame involves his Mississippi encounter with a white man he had previously befriended in West Africa. Upon the latter's identification of Abd al-Rahman as royalty, a series of events were set into motion that ultimately led to Abd al-Rahman's return to Africa in 1829, where he died within months of arrival. The motif of sudden, unexpected intervention leading to revelation of the slave's noble status is repeated in the life of Ayuba b. Sulayman, or Job Ben Solomon, born around 1702.[82] Arriving in Maryland in 1732, he was a free man and en route to West Africa by 1733, all due to the benevolence of a Royal African Company officer moved by his plea (penned in Arabic) for liberty. Finally, the seventh Muslim of note is Yarrow Mahmud, or "Yarrow Mamout," who in 1819 was living in Georgetown when Charles Willson Peale painted his portrait—apparently because of Mahmud's atypical features.[83]

The extraordinary or unusual circumstances in these seven individuals' lives, not their adherence to Islam, explain their relative prominence in the literature. Indeed, many of the accounts concerning these individuals refer to other enslaved Muslims who, because they did not share in the special circumstance, did not receive recognition. Therefore, the attention these seven are accorded in the literature is misleading in conveying the idea that Muslims were very rare in number. A closer examination of the literature in fact reveals the presence of many more Muslims than previously recognized.

An investigation into the background of these seven Muslims supports the earlier discussion of the regions and conditions out of which most of the Muslim captives emerged. Ayuba b. Sulayman, for example, originated in the upper Senegal valley, from where he traveled to the upper Gambia to (ironically) sell slaves. Unfortunately for him, he fell victim to (other) slave raiders, who ultimately sold him into the transatlantic trade. Also captured and sold with him was Lamine Njai, or "Lahamin Jay"; both would eventually return to West Africa.[84] Similarly, Umar b. Said was born in Futa Toro, along the middle Senegal valley, and was captured and sold in the beginning of the nineteenth century. He himself writes that at the age of thirty-one, "there came to our place a large army, who killed many men, and took me, and brought me to the great sea, and sold me into the hands of the Christians."[85] This particular encounter is only one example of many such conflicts in the middle and upper Senegal valleys and demonstrates the susceptibility of the Muslim population.

Abd al-Rahman represents the Sierra Leone region in that he was born in Futa Jallon and in fact claimed to be the son of Almaami Ibrahima Sori, one of the most important leaders in Guinean history.[86] In the course of a military campaign under his command, he and his army were defeated and captured. What immediately followed is unclear, but at least some of the captives were sold to the Malinke along the Gambia River, including Abd al-Rahman. Eventually, he and fifty of his former soldiers were traded to an English slaver and found themselves transported to the Western Hemisphere. For Abd al-Rahman, then, his path led to the Gambia, whereas other captives from the same company were possibly taken to the Sierra Leone coast. In any event, Abd al-Rahman's personal account underscores the volatility of the region during the eighteenth century and supports the contention that many Muslims from Futa Jallon became captives of war and involuntary participants in the transatlantic trade. Nothing more is said of the other Muslims captured with Abd al-Rahman, except for Samba, or Sambo, who was a part of the former's command in Futa Jallon and wound up on the same Natchez farm with him, thus explaining his mention.

Like Abd al-Rahman, Bilali and Lamine Kaba were also originally from Futa Jallon. Like Ayuba b. Sulayman, Umar b. Said, and Abd al-Rahman, Bilali was also Fulbe.[87] Lamine Kaba, on the other hand, was from the clerically oriented community of the Jakhanke, along the southern reaches of Futa Jallon. His place of capture and point of departure are not clearly indicated and similar information regarding Bilali is altogether missing. Lamine Kaba maintains, however, that it was his search for writing paper along the coast that led to his capture and subsequent enslavement.[88] The need for paper is consistent with the clerical nature of the Jakhanke, and his capture once again illustrates the insecurity that prevailed in the Sierra Leone region.

Origins in the middle and upper Niger valleys are also represented in the list of Muslim notables. The case of Abu Bakr al-Siddiq, who eventually landed in Jamaica and is therefore not a focus of this study, nevertheless demonstrates that the tentacles of the transatlantic trade extended as far inland as the Niger buckle (the stretch of the Niger from Timbuktu in the west to Gao in the east), as he was born around 1790 in Timbuktu and grew up in Jenne, in the floodplain of the upper Niger valley.[89] Salih Bilali was also from the area, specifically Maasina, between the floodplain and the buckle.[90] He was captured around 1790, during the period in which the Bambara were consolidating their control of the upper Niger. After his capture, Salih Bilali was taken south and sold at Anomabu, along the Gold Coast. It has been assumed that captives coming out of the upper Niger were usually traded along the Senegambian coast,[91] but the example of Salih Bilali suggests that those trading in slaves from this area had a variety of options available to them for the disposition of their captives.

Finally, Yarrow Mahmud's origins are unspecified. His appearance, preserved for posterity by Peale, reveals features consistent with those of the Fulbe.[92] That he arrived in North America in the 1730s, as did Ayuba b. Sulayman, suggests a middle or upper Senegal valley origin.

It is difficult to know the extent to which Muslims in early America had opportunities to engage in corporate expressions of faith. At first glance, it would seem highly improbable that the host society would allow Muslims to assemble for the purpose of prayer. But evidence suggests that such assemblies in fact took place. There are recorded instances of Muslims performing *salāt*, or "prayer," as individuals. In some cases such prayer was conducted in a hostile environment. Ayuba b. Sulayman, for example, was chased and otherwise harassed while praying.[93] In other cases, Muslims were allowed to pray in the prescribed manner by their owners. Thus Ayuba, after his initial difficulties, was afforded privacy.[94] There is also evidence that Abd al-Rahman continued to practice Islam, and that after either a flirtation with Christianity or a conscious strategy of dissimulation (to gain support for his repatriation), he immediately reaffirmed his Muslim beliefs upon returning to Africa.[95] Salih Bilali was a devout Muslim who fasted Ramadan; Bilali wore a fez and kaftan, prayed daily (facing the east), and also observed the Muslim feast days.[96] Charles Ball, a slave in Maryland, South Carolina, and Georgia for forty years, also witnessed certain Muslim practices among the slaves, for he wrote: "I knew several who must have been, from what I have since learned, Mohammedans; though at that time, I had never heard of the religion of Mohammed."[97] Ball, like other observers, noticed the behavior but did not know enough to recognize what he saw.

Individual examples of adherence to Islam suggest that many more practiced the religion, perhaps clandestinely, or perhaps in full view of unsuspecting eyes such as Ball's. In any event, the possibility that Muslims congregated for prayer is enhanced by a second factor: the general tendency among slaves to steal away into secluded areas for religious and social purposes.[98] It has generally been assumed that stealing away involved the slaves' pursuit of their peculiar brand of Christianity, or even traditional African religions, but there is absolutely no reason to preclude Muslims from similar activity. Indeed, the probability that such gatherings took place is increased when the question of contact between Muslims is considered. Bilali and Salih Bilali, residing on plantations on neighboring sea islands, were considered the best of friends and were in contact with others who were apparently Fulbe. The sea island Muslim community on Sapelo and St. Simons islands was probably significant, as evidenced by Bilali's response when called upon by his owner to defend the island against the British in 1813: "I will answer for every Negro of the true faith," he announced, proceeding to muster a force of eighty (an event to which this chapter will later return).[99] Religion and religious observances must have constituted an important, if not central, component of Muslims' bond. Abd al-Rahman and Samba, his fellow Pullo (singular of Fulbe) and slave on the same farm, were able to associate closely with each other, and the two communicated with at least one other Mandinka from Natchez.[100] As coreligionists, they surely sought opportunities to pray together.

In addition to the better-known cases of Salih Bilali and Abd al-Rahman, other Muslim slaves may have resided together in significant numbers on the same plantations. For example, thirty-six slaves were taken from Amelia Island, East Florida, in 1813 by white "patriots."[101] Of the thirty-six, the following may have been Muslim: Jack and Samba and their two children Saluma and Pizarro, Adam and Fatima and their one-year-old Fernando, and thirteen-year-old Ottemar or Otteman. The four adults were African-born, and from the names Samba, Saluma, and Fatima it is entirely plausible that these two families were wholly Muslim. Furthermore, fifteen of the thirty-six were African-born, so that even more may have been Muslim. However, the names given to them by their owners, including Hamlet, Neptune, and Plato, make it impossible to know their ethnic or religious affiliation.

An even more intriguing case is the John Stapleton plantation at Frogmore on St. Helena Island, South Carolina.[102] In May 1816, a list of the 135 slaves on the Frogmore estate was drawn up, on which the following individuals appear: Sambo, eighty-five years old and African-born; Dido, a fifty-six-year-old "Moroccan"; Mamoodie and his wife Eleanor, both African-born and age twenty-eight and twenty-nine, respectively; and the family of Nelson, Venus, and child Harriett. Sambo and Dido were probably Muslim. Mamoodie and Eleanor had a child named Fatima in 1814 (who died in infancy), so they were very likely Muslim. The more interesting individuals are Nelson and Venus, who were twenty-nine and twenty-seven, respectively, and both African-born. In a subsequent slave list drawn up in 1818, their child Hammett appears. Hammett (Hamid or Ahmad) is a Muslim name, which would strongly suggest that one or both of the parents were Muslim. Again, the remaining names on the 1816 list are not African, but twenty-eight people are listed as African-born. It is therefore possible that others were Muslim, as were Nelson and/or Venus, but the absence of a corroborating Hammett prevents any such identification. In any event, those who were Muslims would have sought one another's company and ways to corporately express their common faith.

The evidence is sufficient that Muslims struggled to not only bond with one another but also retain their common Islamic educational backgrounds. One Dr. Collins, who wrote a manual on the medical treatment of slaves, stated that many slaves from Senegal "converse in the Arabic language, and some are sufficiently instructed even to write it."[103] LeConte recalled "an old native African named Philip," a Muslim who during the antebellum period demonstrated the outward expressions of the religion "by going through all the prayers and prostrations of his native country."[104] Abd al-Rahman would write the *Fātiḥa* (opening *sūra*, or chapter, of the Qur'ān) for whites who believed they were receiving the Lord's Prayer in an exotic hand.[105] And, of course, Umar b. Said penned his autobiography in Arabic.

Many Muslims struggled not only to preserve their traditions but also to pass them on to their progeny. Thus Bilali bestowed Muslim names upon his twelve sons and seven daughters and apparently taught all but the youngest daughter Pulaar (language of the Fulbe) and possibly Arabic, as they regularly communicated with one another in a "foreign tongue."[106] Samba, the companion of Abd al-Rahman, had at least three sons, and gave them all Muslim names.[107] In 1786, Sambo and Fatima escaped Edward Fenwicke of John's Island; Sambo was "of the Guinea country" and probably Muslim, but Fatima was described as country born, so she either converted to Islam or had at least one Muslim parent.[108] The recurrence of Muslim names among American-born slaves is corroborative evidence of the desire among many to keep their religion and culture alive.[109]

· · · · · · ·

I have already stated that the preponderance of runaway notices featuring Muslims appeared in South Carolinian and Georgian newspapers. Consistent with this pattern is the relatively greater amount of information available on Muslims and their descendants living along the Georgia coast, both on the various sea islands and on the mainland near Savannah. The data provide a rare glimpse into the lives of African-born Muslims, their progeny, and the associated community of believers. What emerges is an incomplete but substantive picture of individuals who pursued their religion with diligence and purpose, and this in an atmosphere charged with the teachings of Christianity and the attraction of African indigenous religions. Further, there is possible evidence of non-Muslim slaves converting to Islam. Finally, one cannot help but notice the pride with which the grandchildren and subsequent progeny speak of these African-born Muslims, suggesting a strong and clear identification with an Islamic heritage, if not an actual embrace of the religion.

As noted earlier, Salih Bilali and Bilali served as drivers on very large plantations located on the Georgia sea islands of St. Simons and Sapelo. It would appear that the number of Muslim slaves in this area was significant. In May 1802, for example, two Muslim men named Alik and Abdalli escaped from Sapelo Island; it is likely that both were African-born, as one spoke "bad English" and the other's command of the language was only slightly better.[110] Toney, Jacob, and eighteen-year-old Musa also escaped from Sapelo Island in March 1807, having belonged to Alexander Johnston.[111] Again, it is conceivable that all three men were Muslim.

John Couper (1759–1850) and his son James Hamilton Couper (1794–1866) owned a number of plantations on St. Simons Island and along the Altamaha River, including the famous Hopeton plantation. In an 1827 document detailing the sale of Hopeton by John Couper to James Hamilton (a close friend) and his son James, 381 slave names are listed.[112] Of these names, Fatima is repeated six times, Mahomet twice, and there is one Maryam: all probably Muslims. However, the principal Muslim on the plantation was Salih Bilali, who is listed as "Tom" in the document. How many more

Muslims there were at Hopeton cannot be discerned from the available data, but it is probable that there were others whose Islamic identities are hidden behind names such as Tom. Indeed, James Hamilton Couper himself wrote that "there are about a dozen negroes on this plantation, who speak and understand the Foulah language."[113]

Ben Sullivan was eighty-eight and living on St. Simons when interviewed by the Works Progress Administration (WPA) in the 1930s.[114] He was the grandson of Salih Bilali, and his father's name was "Belali," a direct indication of the grandfather's desire to pass on his Islamic identity. In addition to his father and grandfather, Ben Sullivan (Bilal ibn Sulayman?) remembered two other Muslims in the community, "Old Israel" and Daphne. Concerning the former, Ben reported: "Ole Israel he pray a lot wid a book he hab wut he hide, an he take a lill mat an he say he prayuhs on it. He pray wen duh sun go up an wen duh sun go down. . . . He alluz tie he head up in a wite clawt an seem he keep a lot uh clawt on hand."[115] The book Sullivan refers to may have been the Qur'ān. Similarly, Daphne prayed regularly, bowing "two aw tree times in duh middle uh duh prayuh," and was usually veiled.

On nearby Sapelo Island was the large plantation of Thomas Spalding (1774–1851), the driver of which was Salih Bilali's coreligionist Bilali (pronounced "Blali" in the Sapelo community), also referred to as "the Old Man."[116] Bilali's large family of twelve sons and seven daughters all "worshipped Mahomet," as one observer stated in 1901 based upon her memories of the late 1850s.[117] Some details of their religious practices are provided by Katie Brown, who at the time of the WPA interviews was "one of the oldest inhabitants" of Sapelo Island.[118] She was also the great-granddaughter of Bilali, or "Belali Mahomet." She enumerated Bilali's seven daughters as "Magret, Bentoo, Chaalut, Medina, Yaruba, Fatima, and Hestuh," most identifiably Muslim names. Margaret was the grandmother of Katie Brown, who went on to say:

> Magret an uh daughter Cotto use tuh say dat Bilali an he wife Phoebe pray on duh bead. Dey wuz bery puhticluh bout duh time dey pray and dey bery regluh bout duh hour. Wen duh sun come up, wen it straight obuh head an wen it set, das duh time dey pray. Dey bow tuh duh sun an hab lill mat tuh kneel on. Duh beads is on a long string. Belali he pull bead an he say, "Belambi, Hakabara, Mahamadu." Phoebe she say, "Ameen, Ameen."[119]

In addition to religious observances, it would seem that Bilali adhered to Islamic prescriptions on marriage, as Brown remarked: "Magret she say Phoebe he wife, but maybe he hab mone one wife. I spects das bery possible."[120]

It would also appear that there was some attempt on the part of Muslims to adhere to Islamic dietary proscriptions. Information is rather meager on this question, but Bailey provides a glimpse with her observation that Bilali's children would not eat "wild" animals or "fresh" meat, and that seafood such as crab was avoided, as were certain kinds of fish.[121]

Taken together, the testimonies of Ben Sullivan, Cornelia Bailey, and Katie Brown provide the essential contours of Muslim life in early Georgia—prayer mats, prayer beads, veiling, head coverings, Qur'āns, dietary laws, and ritualized, daily prayer. The composite picture is consistent with a serious pursuit of Islam.

Bilali's daughters, who may have also been African-born and forced into slavery along with their father, were just as religious.[122] Shad Hall of Sapelo Island, another descendant of Bilali through his grandmother Hestuh, describes the daughters as follows: "Hestuh an all ub um sho pray on duh bead. Dey weah duh string uh beads on duh wais. Sometime duh string on duh neck. Dey pray at sun-up and face duh sun on duh knees an bow tuh it tree times, kneelin' on a lill mat."[123]

A sense of a closely knit community emerges from these WPA interviews. Katie Brown refers to Salih Bilali of St. Simons as "cousin Belali Sullivan." Shad Hall states that his grandmother Hestuh bore a son called "Belali Smith," who in turn was Phoebe Gilbert's grandfather, also a Sapelo resident.[124] Phoebe Gilbert's other set of grandparents were Calina and Hannah, both of whom were Igbo. Sapelo inhabitant Nero Jones was also related to "Uncle Calina and An Hannah" and says that they were "mighty puhticuluh bout prayin. Dey pray on duh bead. Duh ole man he say 'Ameela' and An Hannah she say 'Hakabara.' "[125] The last quote is fascinating, for it strongly suggests that Calina and Hannah were Muslim converts, as the Igbo of southeastern Nigeria were not Muslim.[126] Furthermore, the Igbo population in early America was substantial but hardly ever associated with Islam.

Islam along coastal Georgia was by no means limited to the descendants of Bilali and Salih Bilali. The WPA interviews of Ed Thorpe of Harris Neck, Rosa Grant of Possum Point, and Lawrence Baker of Darien reveal that their ancestors were also Muslim.[127] Like the Bilali families, these early Muslims prayed three times daily in the prescribed fashion, ending their prayers with "Ameen, Ameen, Ameen." In fact, Rosa Grant says of her grandmother Ryna that "Friday wuz duh day she call huh prayuh day." This is not a reference to daily prayer, for Grant had already stated that her grandmother's prayers began "ebry mawnin." Rather, this is a reference to the Muslim observance of Friday prayer, at which time Muslims congregate at noon. Whether Grant and others actually gathered for the prayer is not known, but at least she attempted to keep alive the significance of the day.

There is also the possibility that other Muslims contemporary with Bilali and with names similar to his lived in other areas along the Atlantic coast. Speculation on this point arises from the aforementioned possible Muslim ancestry of Frederick Douglass. His great-great-grandfather was named "Baly," and his grandparents were Betsy and Isaac Bailey of Talbot County along Maryland's Eastern Shore. It was Betsy Bailey's daughter Harriet who gave birth to Frederick Augustus Bailey. McFeely writes:

> In the nineteenth century, on Sapelo Island (where Baileys still reside), there was a Fulfulde-speaking slave from Timbo, Futa Jallon, in the Guinea highlands, who could write Arabic and who was the father of twelve sons. His name was Belali Mahomet. . . . "Belali" slides easily into the English "Bailey," a common African American surname along the Atlantic coast. The records of Talbot County list no white Baileys from which the slave Baileys might have taken their name, and an African origin, on the order of "Belali," is conceivable.[128]

Because Betsy Bailey was born around 1772, she was essentially Bilali's contemporary and therefore unlikely to have been his descendant. However, McFeely's point concerning the structural similarities between Belali and Bailey, coupled with the absence of white Baileys in Talbot County, is an intriguing one, such that the possibility of Muslim antecedents in this particular lineage cannot be ruled out.

The Muslim presence in coastal Georgia (and possibly elsewhere along the Atlantic) was therefore active, healthy, and compelling. Clearly, the history of Africans along the South Carolina–Georgia continuum is more complicated than previously understood; its study can no longer be limited to the Gullah language and associated handicrafts and artifacts, notwithstanding their importance.

Despite the vitality of the Islamic tradition and the strength of their bonds (especially in coastal Georgia), Muslims in early America faced certain distinct challenges to the preservation of their religion. For although they may have gathered in small numbers and clandestine places to pray, they could not openly maintain Qur'anic schools, nor did they have access to Islamic texts. It was inevitable that their collective memory would eventually falter. As an example of not having access to the necessary texts, Bilali, author of the "Ben-Ali Diary," put together passages from Ibn Abī Zayd's *Risāla* in such a haphazard fashion that Nigerian clerics, upon reviewing the document, declared it to be the work of *jinn* (spirits).[129] Likewise, Salih Bilali, although claiming to possess a Qur'ān, could not write Arabic coherently.[130] Allowing for exceptional cases such as Bilali's, the gradual loss of Islamic knowledge, combined with the parochial application of Arabic to religious discourse, constituted a blow to the continuation of Islam in early America.

Additional challenges to Islam include the fact that it was in competition with other African religions, especially prior to the nineteenth century. In the North American setting, most Africans adhered to non-Islamic beliefs. The host society, although at times amused by the religious variations among the slaves, became increasingly concerned with controlling the religion of its captive population as the nineteenth century progressed. The gradual increase in the number of Christian converts among African Americans resulted from both their own desire to embrace an Africanized version of Christianity and a campaign within the post-1830 militant South to use religion as a means of social control. As Africanized Christianity slowly became a force, Islam would have suffered.

The process by which Christianity began to compete with and eventually overtake Islam can be viewed in the Sapelo community. The progeny of African-born Muslims (who tended to restrict their social interactions with non-Muslims) eventually began attending the Tuesday, Thursday, and Sunday night "prayer houses" held by each community on the island, while continuing with their own, Muslim gatherings. With the establishment of the First African Baptist Church in May 1866, however, the open and collective pursuit of Islam became increasingly rare, although it is difficult to say when, exactly, it ended on the island.[131]

In addition to the impact of Christianity, it should be noted that ethnocentricity, combined with other cultural differences, probably restricted efforts at proselytization among non-Muslims. It is therefore probable that the continuity of the Islamic tradition was heavily dependent upon a cultural transfer within existing Muslim families and over generations. This was a formidable task, especially as the importation of non-Muslims into North America greatly exceeded that of Muslims in the late eighteenth and early nineteenth centuries; many Muslims had little choice except to marry non-Muslims. Further, African-born Muslims may have been unable to effectively communicate with their children and grandchildren and would have been frustrated in their attempts to convey the tenets of Islam adequately.[132] Enslavement itself introduced structural impediments to such matters as a formal Muslim education, circumcision, the formation of brotherhoods, the maintenance of moral proscriptions, and the observance of basic dietary rules. The children of African Muslims would have been socialized within the context of the larger, non-Muslim slave culture and deeply influenced by this process. In short, Muslims would have had great difficulty in preserving Islam within their own families, assuming a stable slave family. With Louisiana as a possible exception, such an assumption is most unwarranted.

It is therefore with the children and grandchildren of African-born Muslims that questions concerning the resilience of Islam take on significance. While it cannot be established with certainty that the progeny were Muslim, the Islamic heritage was certainly there, so that individuals bore Muslim names and retained a keen memory of the religious practices of their ancestors. However, whether they themselves practiced Islam is unclear, and a reluctance to be unequivocal on this matter can be observed in the responses of Georgian coastal blacks to the queries posed by the WPA interviewers. Indeed, a careful reading of these interviews reveals considerable anxiety among the informants, understandable given the period's sociopolitical dynamics.[133] If they were practicing Muslims, they were certainly not going to tell it to whites in the rural South of the 1930s.

One account given by the interviewers underscores the ambiguity of religious affinities during this time and supports the contention that the informants did not reveal all. The account concerns one Preacher Little, who was encountered on Sapelo Island and whose physical appearance, demeanor, and dress were initially described as "Mohammedan looking."[134] Although the interviewers were subsequently assured that the minister was a Christian (and they went on to witness the minister preside over a religious service), their first impressions are instructive, especially as this encounter took place after the interviews with the descendants of Salih Bilali and Bilali. Preacher Little could very well have been the embodiment of a certain Islamic-Christian synthesis. Indeed, this possibility is enhanced by the reflections of Charles Jones in 1842, who wrote that African-born Muslims related Yahweh to Allah and Jesus to Muhammad.[135] His observation contains a number of potential meanings, including the possibility that these Africans, while ostensibly practicing Christianity, were in reality reinterpreting Christian dogma in light of Islamic precepts. If this was the case, then such were probably more Muslim than Christian in their worldview, since Islam had already shaped their perspective. It is therefore conceivable that their descendants may have continued this kind of syncretism (or dissimulation).

A further example of this possible syncretism again comes from Sapelo and the descendants of Bilali.[136] Cornelia Bailey's grandmother would tell the former about the life of Harriet Hall Grovner, Bailey's great-grandmother and the granddaughter of Bentoo, Bilali's daughter. Harriet was a practicing Muslim until the First African Baptist Church was organized in 1866, at which time she joined. Although she became very active in the Sunday school, it is possible that, because she frequently retreated into the woods to pray, she continued to practice Islam. It is not clear whether she continued such clandestine activity after 1866, or why she would have found it necessary to do so after that time, unless she was praying something other than

Christian prayers. The fact that Harriet died in 1922 and may have still been practicing Islam at such a late date and as a legacy of an African Islamic tradition is incredibly intriguing.

This inquiry does not purport to make conclusive statements concerning Islam's legacy in America. Rather, it argues that Islam was more important in North America's early development than previously understood, and that it may have influenced African American culture in ways heretofore unimagined. Further, it may be that Islam's most enduring contribution to the African-based community was its role in the negotiation of intrasocial relations, to which the remainder of this chapter now turns.

· · · · · · ·

It would appear that the Muslim community, where it existed, had some impact upon the stratification of African and African American society. Given that it was a slave society, such stratification began with the perceptions of the slaveholders. Vis-à-vis other Africans, Muslims were generally viewed by slaveholders as a "more intelligent, more reasonable, more physically attractive, more dignified people."[137] Phillips has written that planters found the Senegalese to be the most intelligent, as they "had a strong Arabic strain in their ancestry."[138] William Dunbar, a prominent Natchez planter, specifically preferred Muslims from northern Nigeria as opposed to Senegambians, but they were Muslims nonetheless.[139] The belief in the superiority of the "Mohammedans" was apparently a consistently held view throughout the colonial and antebellum periods. As an example, Salih Bilali is described as "a man of superior intelligence and higher cast of feature."[140] To a great extent, this view of the Muslim was informed by the physical appearance of the Fulbe and certain Mande speakers, whose features were believed to be phenotypically closer to Europeans than other Africans.[141] European travelers invariably commented upon Fulbe features: Gray and Dochard described them as "much resembling the European," as did Callié, whereas Jobson stated that the Fulbe were "a Tawny people, and have a resemblance right unto those we call Egyptians."[142]

As a result of their experience and perceived advantage, as well as for reasons to be explored shortly, many Muslims were given more responsibilities and privileges than other slaves. Alford writes that Muslim slaves were used as "drivers, overseers, and confidential servants with a frequency their numbers did not justify."[143] Examples of this general statement include the careers of Bilali and Salih Bilali, who were both placed in positions of high authority and used that authority to jointly quell a slave insurrection. Zephaniah Kingsley, a slaveholder who advocated the "benign" treatment of slaves, recorded that along the Georgia coast during the War of 1812, there were "two instances, to the southward, where gangs of negroes were prevented from deserting to the enemy [England] by drivers, or influential negroes, whose integrity to their masters and influence over the slaves prevented it; and what is still more remarkable, in both instances the influential negroes were Africans; and professors of the Mahomedan religion."[144] This is an apparent reference to Bilali and Salih Bilali. Not only did they crush the revolt but, as previously mentioned, Bilali defended Sapelo Island in 1813 with eighty armed slaves, preventing access to the English. It is likely that the majority of these eighty slaves were Muslim, given the extensive nature of Islam in the area, combined with Bilali's statement that he could depend only upon fellow Muslims, as opposed to the general slave population whom he characterized as "Christian dogs."[145]

As the examples of Bilali and Salih Bilali suggest, there were certain tensions between Muslim and non-Muslim slaves, whether the latter were African-born or not. In the first place, there is evidence that some American-born slaves condescended to newly arrived Africans.[146] To the extent that African Muslims encountered such treatment, they would have experienced pressures to modify or discontinue their Muslim/African practices in order to conform to what was acceptable in the new setting, or they would have found the resolve to remain faithful to their convictions. The evidence shows that, despite pressure from Christianity and African indigenous religions, the majority resisted coercion to abandon their faith.[147] Stories of Muslim piety and determination include that of Salih Bilali, described by his owner as "the most religious man that he had ever known"; another depicted him as a "strict Mahometan" who refused alcohol, holding "in great contempt, the African belief in fetishes and evil spirits."[148] Contrasting examples are few in number and include Abd al-Rahman, whose supposed conversion to Christianity is contradicted by his immediate recommitment to Islam upon repatriation to Africa. And although it is true that Lamine Kaba and Umar b. Said both professed Christianity, serious reservations surround the conversion of the latter.[149]

With this in mind, it is not surprising to read of Bilali's characterization of his fellow (or actually subordinate) slaves as Christian dogs. Neither is it startling to read of Abd al-Rahman's comments to Cyrus Griffin, in which "he states explicitly, and with an air of pride, that not a drop of negro blood runs in his veins."[150] This attitude was confirmed by the children of Bilali, all of whom were Muslims, and who were described as "holding themselves aloof from the others as if they were conscious of their own superiority."[151] Bailey essentially verifies this, stating that not only did Bilali "keep his distance" from others because he "did not like mixing" with them, but that

Muslims and non-Muslims as a whole tended to "keep to themselves," although they generally "got along" and could work together for specific purposes or special occasions.[152] Such behavior is strikingly similar to that of the Muslims of Bahia (Brazil), who also "refused to mix with the other slaves."[153]

The attitude of Muslim superiority, to the degree that it in fact existed, must first be explained within the context of the West African background. The probability that these people themselves had been slaveholders in the Old World influenced their view of slaves. Their African experience was shaped along the lines of highly stratified societies in which the servile population was seen as inferior. The ethnic factor is relevant here as well, in that there are considerable data on the ethnocentricity of the Fulbe of West Africa.[154] Originating long ago in present-day southern Mauritania, many of the Fulbe claim descent from the Arab general 'Uqba b. Nāfi', who in 667 led Muslim armies as far south as Kawar in the Fezzan.[155] This clear fiction reflects the larger truth of their mixed ancestry, resulting, in some instances, in the view of the non-Fulbe as inferior. Park remarked upon this attitude, stating that "the Foulahs of Bondou . . . evidently consider all the Negro natives as their inferiors, and when talking of different nations, always rank themselves among the white people."[156] It is instructive that Wyatt-Brown, in discussing three related yet distinct psychological responses by men to enslavement, cites Ibrahima as a prime example of a Fulbe man who, by virtue of his exclusionary early socialization vis-à-vis other ethnicities, embodies the first category of response, which was characterized by a "ritualized compliance in which self-regard is retained." That is, Ibrahima maintained his culturally inculcated dignity and pride as he reconciled himself to enslavement by remembering his *pulaaku*, the essence of the distinctive Fulbe character and prescriptive code of behavior. Hence, he never descends to the second category of response, which "involves the incorporation of shame," or to the third category, described as "samboism" and "shamelessness."[157] Indeed, to Ibrahima's way of thinking, the internalization of enslavement could only be characteristic of the lesser non-Fulbe.

A second factor in explaining Muslim attitudes of superiority concerns Islam itself. To live as a Muslim in eighteenth- and nineteenth-century West Africa was to live in an increasingly intolerant society. This was the period of jihād, of the establishment of Muslim theocracies, of self-purification and separation from practices and beliefs seen as antithetical to Islam. Abu Bakr al-Siddiq summarized the perspective of the Muslim when he wrote:

> The faith of our families is the faith of Islam. They circumcise the foreskin; say the five prayers; fast every year in the month of Ramadan; give alms as ordained in the law; marry four free women—a fifth is

forbidden to them except she be their slave; they fight for the faith of God; perform the pilgrimage to Mecca, i.e. such as are able to do so; eat the flesh of no beast but what they have slain for themselves; drink no wine, for whatever intoxicates is forbidden to them; they do not keep company with those whose faith is contrary to theirs, such as worshippers of idols.[158]

It is clear, then, that fundamental differences between Islam and other religions could have further militated against a uniform experience of enslavement, along with such considerations as regional differences, urban versus rural conditions, and so on.

But a third factor in Muslim attitudes of superiority is as important as the first two—namely, a number of these Muslim slaves were from prominent backgrounds in West Africa. For example, Abd al-Rahman was a scion of Almaami Ibrahima Sori. Ayuba b. Sulayman's father was a leading cleric in the upper Senegal valley. Several Muslims boasted of extensive educations in West Africa, including Lamine Kaba, Bilali, and Umar b. Said. In fact, it was more common than not that West African Muslims were recipients of an Islamic education and were therefore literate, and the various documents that concern notable Muslims invariably comment on the fact that they could write in Arabic. From the observer's vantage point, this was quite incredible. However, it should be appreciated that literacy within the West African Muslim community was widespread; most Muslim villages and towns maintained *madrasas* (Qur'ānic schools), to which children from ages seven to fourteen went for instruction, boys and girls. At *madrasa*, the Qur'ān was memorized by heart and Arabic grammar was introduced. From *madrasa*, young men (and occasionally young women) of sufficient means moved on to more advanced studies, often requiring travel from one town to another in order to study under the appropriate *shaykh*, or master teacher of a specific curriculum. The most advanced students went on to reputable towns such as Pir and Jenne, where there were concentrations of scholars. Thus the educational process was well established, with a tradition reaching back to at least the fourteenth century.[159] Reducing such an educated elite to the status of slaves—a status shared with those of humble birth—was especially demeaning.

Reflecting the pastoral background of many Africans and referring to considerations of class, it is important to note that some of the Muslim slaves, such as Ayuba b. Sulayman, were completely unaccustomed to agricultural labor, which became evident very quickly.[160] Dr. Collins remarked that the Muslims of Senegambia "are excellent for the care of cattle and horses, and for domestic service, though little qualified for the ruder labours of the field, to which they never ought to be applied."[161] The aristocratic and/or pastoral background of some West Africans, combined with the aforementioned agricultural expertise of others, meant that Muslims were, in the eyes of the host society, better suited for domestic and/or supervisory roles. This determination, it follows, widened the schism between Muslim and non-Muslim, as the former were more likely to receive the less physically demanding jobs.

Finally, it is probable that some Muslims were deeply affected by racist views of whites toward other Africans. That is, they would have been encouraged to distance themselves from the average African and African American, even to the point of denying any kindred relationship to them. Thus there is Abd al-Rahman's claim that he had no "negro" blood. In fact, Abd al-Rahman claimed to be a Moor, and he placed "the negro in a scale of being infinitely below the Moor."[162] The convention of claiming Moorish or Berber ancestry was not unique to Abd al-Rahman, and some maintained a position similar to that of centenarian Silvia King of Marlin, Texas, around 1937: "I know I was borned in Morocco, in Africa, and was married and had three children befo' I was stoled from my husband. I don't know who it was stole me, but dey took me to France, to a place called Bordeaux, but drugs me with some coffee, and when I knows anything 'bout it, I's in de bottom of a boat with a whole lot of other niggers."[163]

Although there is evidence of strained relations between Muslims and non-Muslims, there are also indications of cordiality. For example, Abd al-Rahman himself married a Baptist woman in 1794, had several children by her, returned to Liberia with her in 1829, and expired in her arms a few months later. Charles Ball mentions his acquaintance and friendship with a number of Muslims.[164] These two examples illustrate that, despite Muslim attitudes of superiority, Muslims and non-Muslims necessarily interacted in fundamental ways.

In sum, there are several areas of inquiry related to Islam requiring further investigation. First, the research of Thompson on the relationship between African and African American art and philosophy has revealed that, at least in the area of quiltmaking, African Americans exhibit what are clearly Mande influences.[165] The Mande world contained many Muslims (in addition to non-Muslims such as the Bambara), so that such evidence points to the possible continuity of an Islamically influenced cultural heritage, if not the religion itself. Such a possibility may be supported by intriguing archaeological evidence involving the "recovery of blue, faceted glass beads from slave cabins that were of European manufacture [which] may be related to the Moslem belief that a single blue bead will ward off evil spirits."[166] In any event, it represents a promising avenue of further investigation.

Second, an investigation of the potential influence of Islam upon the practice of Christianity by African Americans in certain areas or communities would be instructive. On Sapelo Island, for example, the congregation always prays to the east, which is the direction in which the church is pointed.[167] Regarding personal prayer, individuals are instructed to pray toward the east because the "devil is in the other corner." The deceased are also buried facing the east.[168] Such details reveal substantial influence indeed, which may even be reflected in the teachings and beliefs of the church. Islam may not have survived as a complete and coherent system of faith, but some of its constituent elements may yet guide and sustain.

Finally, the qualitative testimony is consistent in its view that the Muslim/non-Muslim distinction played a role in social divisions among slaves. Not all lighter-skinned house servants and skilled workers were the result of black-white miscegenation in America; at least some were Fulbe and other Africans with "atypical" features. This point, in turn, leads to the much broader question of the role of ethnicity within the slave community, a topic at the center of the current investigation.

Together with the analysis of the Bambara in Louisiana, the discussion of the Muslim component allows for a more comprehensive picture of the Senegambian contribution to the emergent African–African American community and provides a number of clues into the development of a composite African American identity. To be sure, there were other groups imported to North America's shores from Senegambia via the slave trade, such as the Sereer and other Mande-speaking groups, but the Bambara and Muslim contingents were clearly critical.

The investigation of the Muslim presence in America has introduced more tangible evidence for one of the major foci of this study, namely, that social divisions within the African-based community were to a degree informed by conditions growing out of the African antecedent, and that these divisions necessarily helped to shape the consequent, composite identity. A more rigorous analysis of ethnically driven stratification, however, cannot be conducted until the ethnographic landscape has been completed.

It is important to note that after Senegambia, the second largest source of Muslims for the trade to North America was Sierra Leone, which, however, contained many more non-Muslims. Together with captives from the Gold Coast, these Sierra Leonians were to make a very different kind of contribution and are the subject of the next chapter.

5

· · · · · · · · · · · · · · · ·

SOCIETIES AND STOOLS

SIERRA LEONE AND THE AKAN

Africans from Sierra Leone and the Gold Coast, constituting some 28.9 percent of the total import estimate, transferred unique and significant qualities to emergent African American culture and society. Although found throughout the South, the heterogeneous Sierra Leonians were concentrated in colonies/states different from those of the more homogeneous Akan. The former came to North America from small-scale polities with egalitarian tendencies where gender was concerned, in contrast to the large, centralized Gold Coast states, where women were not as prominent. Sierra Leonians left a legacy on American soil chiefly informed by a distinctive network of associations organized by gender and permeating all aspects of life; those from the Gold Coast communicated a perspective intimately concerned with land and the ancestral realm. Their respective experiences in America were not always the same and provided two additional foundations for subsequent stratification within the African-based community. This chapter therefore begins by establishing the broad context out of which Sierra Leonians came.[1]

A plethora of ethnicities and other collective groupings occupied both the coast and the interior of what is now Sierra Leone and Liberia. Mande speakers included the Mende (or Mandinka), the Susu, the Jallonke (or Yalunka), the Loko, the Koranko, the Vai, and the Kono.[2] Among the non-Mande were groups speaking closely related languages, such as the Temne, the Landuma, the Bulom, the Sherbro (southern Bulom speakers who had separated from their northern kinspeople by the seventeenth century), and the Krim. Others who figured prominently in the slave trade were the Kissi, the Gola, the Baga, and the Limba, the first two of whom were "indistinguishable culturally" from the Mende.[3] And of course there were the Fulbe-Jallonke in the interior.

Many in Sierra Leone did not see themselves as ethnicities during the period of the slave trade. At the same time, however, a number of groups had indeed developed a shared identity. Matthews in 1786, for example, was informed about the various groups and made physical distinctions between them. The "Bullams" and the "Timmanies" differed in that the latter were "remarkable for an open, ingenuous countenance"; the "Mandingoes seem to be a distinct race from any of the others . . . they wear beards like the Jews in Europe"; the "Foolahs . . . are an intermediate race between the Arab and the black"; an so on.[4] Winterbottom in the late eighteenth and Corry in the early nineteenth century also delineated the "Follahs," "Soosoos," "Boolams," "Mandingoes," and others.[5] Again, these are populations' self-ascriptions recorded by foreigners, and although there are inconsistencies, historians have been able to make the necessary corrections, rendering a picture in which ethnicity was clearly operative for many of the principal groups.

A consideration of the coastal peoples and their relationship to both the hinterland and to the succession of European traders along the coast helps develop the context for the purposes of this book. The Portuguese arrived at the peninsula of what they would call "Serra Lyoa" (from "its wild-looking leonine mountains") in the middle of the fifteenth century.[6] There they found the Bulom as far south as the Sherbro estuary; the Temne, who had migrated toward the coast from Futa Jallon sometime in the late fourteenth or early fifteenth century, were living inland at the mouth and to the north of the Scarcies River, beyond whom were the Limba.[7] South of the Scarcies were the Loko, relatively removed from the Jallonke, Susu, and Fulbe of the mountainous interior.

The Portuguese referred to the coastal populations as the "Sapes" (or "Zapes," as they are called in early Cuban documents in which territorial origins are ascribed to enslaved Africans), organized into a series of politically autonomous, small-scale polities.[8] Near the middle of the sixteenth century, the Sapes experienced waves of invasions by groups from the interior, referred to by the Portuguese as the "Manes," southern Mande speakers from either the Ivory or Gold Coast.[9] The resulting Mane Wars were important in initiating a process whereby Sierra Leone became a key supplier of Africans for the Atlantic trade, demonstrating the point that "inter-group hostilities were motivated by and orientated towards the Atlantic slave trade. The melee of peoples on the river Cacheu—Banhuna, Casangas, Djolas,

Papels, and Balantas—was regarded by the slave traders as a paradise."[10] That is, these apparently aboriginal people of the littoral, referred to at times as the "primitives," were circumscribed by Mande speakers and were the early victims of the nascent trade into the Atlantic.

As matters turned out, the Mane, sufficient as a conquering force but too few in number to maintain control over the populations of the littoral, were themselves subsequently overrun by the hinterland Susu and Fulbe and forced to retire to the small polity of "Quoja" at Cape Mount.[11] By the middle of the seventeenth century, the Temne had taken over both the south coast of former Bulom-speaking territory and the Loko domain at Mitombo. It is by the middle of the seventeenth century, then, that the various ethnicities mentioned at the outset of the chapter had more or less settled into their respective places, from which they would all be affected by the intensification of the Atlantic trade.

It is also in the beginning of the seventeenth century that English and Dutch traders began to arrive at Sierra Leone, following the sixteenth-century lead of the Portuguese and Spanish. The French would dominate the region's trade in the first half of the eighteenth century, followed by the English in the second half (who initially sought camwood for the production of red dye, in addition to slaves and ivory).[12] Forts were constructed during the seventeenth century; by 1719 the Royal African Company (RAC), originally established in 1663, was paying the Temne ruler rent fees for the use of Bence Island, its headquarters in Sierra Leone. The English were also operating out of York Island, paying similar fees to the Bulom ruler. During this period a small group of African Portuguese (resulting from the union of European traders and African women living at the factories) functioned as middlemen on Bence Island, some eventually becoming wealthy. In fact, the RAC was momentarily driven out of Bence Island (and Sierra Leone) by the African Portuguese merchant Lopez. The RAC eventually returned and continued to operate out of Bence until the former was terminated as a commercial entity in 1752 and replaced with other British traders. However, Bence Island, later corrupted into "Bance" and finally "Bunce" Island in the nineteenth century, remained a key slave entrepôt.

Trade arrangements negotiated for Bunce and York Islands established the predominant model followed by subsequent European traders—namely, a trade factory was built with the permission of the local ruler, who after consultations with his/her advisors agreed to a landlord-stranger contract.[13] According to the terms of the contract, the stranger (European trader) paid both an annual rent fee and a head tax on all captives exported from the factory. The stranger also provided the landlord with firearms in the event of a crisis. The factory usually included a store, a warehouse, a wharf, living quarters for the merchants, and barracoons for the captives, and was constructed on a riverbank. Caravans bringing slaves to the factory are reported to have negotiated in a "festive" atmosphere taking several days. A trade language, incorporating elements of both local and European tongues, eventually developed.[14]

Sierra Leone has an extremely long coastline; Bunce Island, with all of its activity, was by no means the only source of slaves for this sector of the Atlantic trade. Other examples include the area along the coast and to the south of Cape Mount, where European slavers "often took slaves by force, kidnapping (called 'parrying') unsuspecting Africans who came aboard."[15] In addition and in contrast to the system at Bunce Island, where Europeans traded with the interior through African European intermediaries, Europeans dealt directly with hinterland groups arriving in the Rio Nunez–Rio Pongas area, a site featuring the convergence of several rivers and where, for example, the Fulbe directed their slave caravans. It is therefore evident that the Sierra Leonian contingent to North America was quite diverse in its ethnic and territorial origins.

Notwithstanding the foregoing, it is the trade from the interior, specifically Futa Jallon, that was primarily responsible for supplying the Atlantic trade with Sierra Leonians during the eighteenth century. As discussed in the preceding chapter, the jihād of Futa Jallon was an exceedingly violent affair. The reference to direct European-Fulbe exchange is, in fact, a reference to commerce coming out of this part of Sierra Leone and as a result of this tumultuous period. The overrepresentation of captives from the Futa Jallon conflict, in turn, is indirectly supported by Richardson's estimates of British export figures (see table 2.8). According to those estimates, some 65,570 Africans were taken out of Sierra Leone from 1700 to 1749, compared to some 380,370 from 1750 to 1799, a period that essentially corresponds to the marked expansion of the Futa Jallon jihād. The ratio of the second to first half of the century is nearly 6 to 1, and when it is remembered that the Futa Jallon jihād actually began in the 1720s, Rodney's earlier estimates (Chapter 4) become very plausible.

Given the feasibility of Rodney's proposal, it would appear that a significant number of the captives from Futa Jallon were Susu, Jallonke, and to a lesser extent Fulbe, the latter two having been largely Muslim. Tangible and corroborating evidence for the Muslim categories has already been discussed. What remains is to investigate the non-Muslim littoral and interior populations. Indeed, even from the Futa Jallon interior the presence of such groups was important, as Rodney has written: "The greatest victims of the slave trade may not have been people of the littoral fringe, but rather the Paleo-Negritics, who occupied the interior plateau and parts of the Futa

Djalon."[16] Many captives from the interior described as "Mandingas" were in reality Tenda or "Paleo-Negritics" living under Mande control. This means that although such interior Mande groups as the Susu and Jallonke were enslaved, non-Mande and non-Fulbe groups from the interior were also taken. Together with the littoral peoples sold into the trade, this group was sizable. Having introduced the major groups in the area, along with a brief overview of the development of the trade from Sierra Leone, the focus can shift to those political, social, and cultural structures that served to bridge the differences among such a large and diverse assembly.

The largest political unit in Sierra Leone other than the *almaamate* of Futa Jallon was the small-scale polity, a collection of several villages together with surrounding farm and hunting land.[17] These polities, in turn, sometimes enjoyed loosely held alliances but were in any event politically independent. Such organization, described in one analysis as "semi-centralized," was not on the scale of the larger, centralized states, confederations, and empires from which many in the Senegambia were taken.[18] In fact, it would appear that the extent to which units were centralized in Sierra Leone (especially in the littoral) was a result of such external influences as the Mane and other Mande speakers. In response to both the need to defend against aggression and to either resist or alternatively exploit the Atlantic trade, smaller-scale societies banded together for periods of time.

With the foregoing in mind, the basic and most important unit of political organization in Sierra Leone, whatever the ethnicity in question, was the village. The people of Sierra Leone were first and foremost rural people—farmers, fishers, and hunters. Although most of the people of Senegambia were also rural, there was in Senegambia at least the possibility of an urban experience, with the existence of large, cosmopolitan centers both close to the Atlantic and in the interior, extending to the eastern reaches of the Niger River. With the importance of long-distance trade throughout the area, even those who lived far from urban centers were nevertheless likely to be familiar with the concept of literacy, the exchange of goods manufactured in other parts of the world, and the characteristics of a cosmopolitan life-style. Such was not the case in the littoral and other parts of Sierra Leone; there were no urban areas and only a few small towns. And although trade items circulated in Sierra Leone, hostilities between Mane and Sape and, later, Muslim and non-Muslim militated against the free flow of goods and information and the creation of more tolerant, urbane, transcultural conditions.[19] Sierra Leonians and Senegambians, then, were not simply different territorially but also divergent in their familiarity with town life and large-scale, centralized governments. The alleged provinciality of Sierra Leonians would be an issue in North America, having its origins in West Africa itself.

It was the village, then, that encompassed the lives of most Sierra Leonians. In turn, the village was composed of a number of households.[20] For example, the Mende household, or *mawe* (pl. *mawesia*), was structured around the contours of agricultural life. The largest *mawe* was usually composed of an older man, his wives, some or all of their sons and daughters, the wives and husbands of the latter, and the grandchildren; smaller households consisted of a man, his wives and children, and a few close relatives.[21]

Little describes the *mawe* as unilineal but patriarchal, whereas McCulloch characterizes the society as patrilineal yet retaining important ties along matrilineal lines. The Mande speakers, including the Vai, the Jallonke, the Susu, the Kono, and the Koranko were all patrilineal, as were the Temne and the Sherbro, although the latter may have been matrilineal at an earlier time.[22] The aggregate of several related *mawesia* formed the *kuwui*, or the village or compound, over which was the *kuloko*, who was customarily the eldest, most qualified person.

The position of women in this society will be examined in the course of this chapter, but some details of their circumstances are pertinent at this point. First of all, there is seventeenth-century evidence that Sherbro women exercised political power "on their own," and that Sherbro rulers regularly placed one of their wives in charge of their domains while away.[23] Among the Mende, women were customarily rulers and held less powerful political positions as well.[24] The fact that women wielded political power at various levels in Sierra Leone is a phenomenon closely related to their preeminence in the "secret" societies. This relatively egalitarian tendency was confined to the elite strata of society and was in any event mitigated by the influences of both westernization and Islam.

Concerning agriculture, rice was the staple of the Mende and many others. Because women were its principal producers, it follows that rice cultivation in North America was primarily the contribution of women.[25] Of course, crops other than rice were grown in Sierra Leone, including yams or cassava, sweet potatoes, ground nuts, guinea corn, kola nut, millet, cotton, indigo, and palm fruit, some of which were cultivated exclusively by men. The relationship between cotton, Sierra Leonian women, and the introduction of both into North America is therefore crucial.[26] Complementing agricultural activities were pursuits such as hunting and fishing, the preserves of men. In addition to these industries, Sierra Leone had its share of weavers, potters, and iron workers. Weaving, especially basketmaking and the like, was largely controlled by women and survived the voyage to coastal Carolina and Georgia, where it was and continues as an art form practiced by both men and women, the knowledge of which was often transmitted from mother to daughter down through the years.[27]

Regarding religion, primary, secondary, and anthropological literature all confirm that many if not most of the populations of Sierra Leone posited the existence of a high god and creator.[28] Upon completion of the creation, the creator withdrew and has had little to do with it since. However, he continues to send rain to his wife, the earth. The land, then, becomes a connection with both the distant creator and ancestors, as the latter are buried on family land and continue to live there.[29] As far as the Mende and other Sierra Leonians are concerned, death is the gateway to a realm similar to that of the physical in that agricultural responsibilities are performed by those now living in a "big town."[30] They also believe that reincarnation is a distinct possibility, thus finding further common ground with groups such as the Bambara, Akan, and Igbo.

The Mende ancestral spirits, however, represent only one category of those no longer confined by time and space. A second category consists of the *dyinyinga*, or jinni or nature spirits, who occupy rivers, the bush, and so on. A third group consists of nameless entities who go about creating mischief. But beyond these categories of transhuman existence is the potentially more important genre of spirits known as the *ngafa*, entities associated with the secret societies of Sierra Leone. It is to these societies, then, that attention must be turned in order to more fully understand those who came from Sierra Leone.

From the early seventeenth to the late eighteenth century, and in contrast to their discussion of religion, Dutch and English travelers to Sierra Leone provided some detail on the existence of secret societies, specifically mentioning the Poro male and Bundu female societies.[31] Continuing into the first part of the nineteenth century, an English visitor to Sierra Leone also wrote about the secret societies he found there, explaining that they "seemed to be based upon imperfect principles of justice and retribution," and that the leader of the society "evidently possessed . . . the power of life and death over the members, and even of inflicting summary punishment on others who intruded on the holy precincts of the grove, or who committed offences against the community in general." This visitor concluded by commenting that the "Bundoo" was "perhaps the most singular secret institution in the world."[32] As late as 1984, a Westerner allegedly initiated into one of these societies emphasized the importance of keeping secrets "as an organizing principle."[33] Demonstrating both his commitment to the principle and his respect for the society, the author promptly published a book detailing his experiences.

Westerners label whatever they do not understand about non-Western societies and cultures as secretive and mystical; hence, the most important aspect of a phenomenon is its impenetrability or resistance to explication along conventional lines of analysis.[34] There are many secretive institutions in the West, from agencies of government to clerical communities to health providers. Such organizations are not characterized by their clandestine aspects but by their raison d'être, and it is understood that in order to facilitate or accomplish their objectives, certain kinds of activities and information are best kept out of the public domain.

The secret societies of Sierra Leone were, in fact, the functional equivalents of social, cultural, and governmental agencies, and the secrecy within which they operated was only a means to the realization their purpose. When placed within this context, these societies are not very different from their Western analogues, let alone bizarre. To be sure, secrecy is important and was maintained, but it does not at all follow that these organizations should be reduced to one of their working principles. The use of the term *secret* will therefore be eschewed from this point. Instead, *societies of men and women* or *male and female societies* will be employed, as these terms more aptly approximate the wide-ranging activities and multifaceted aspects of these institutions.

The societies of men and women in Sierra Leone were very complex both in organization and implementation, serving several functions. Politically, they helped resolve diplomatic and commercial differences between otherwise independent domains and villages. At the social level, they helped regulate acceptable standards of behavior and assisted individuals and families in times of crisis. Culturally, they provided formal education regarding what should be known about the world and beyond and supervised the training of males and females for the purpose of producing responsible adults. In other words, the socialization process throughout Sierra Leone, although initially and primarily the responsibility of the household, was formally the responsibility of male and female societies. There were different kinds of societies according to mission, and there were various levels of achievement and status within each society.

Two of the most well known societies were the Sande or Bundu for women and the Poro (or Ragbenle, as it is called among the Temne) for men.[35] The Sande or Bundu was (and continues to be) organized into lodges or local chapters in all of the significant towns and villages. These lodges were autonomous, without a centralized locus of authority, yet their structure and function were so similar that a certain uniformity existed. Indeed, a member of one lodge could transfer membership to another without difficulty.[36] Within the Sande was a series of grades or degrees in a pyramidal structure, from the top of which all decisions flowed to levels beneath. Young women were expected to become initiates prior to or at the onset of puberty, usually around the age of fourteen or fifteen; failure to become a member carried the sanction of sexual proscription.[37] T. J. Alldridge, writing at the turn of the twentieth century, agreed with our nineteenth-century visitor to Sierra Leone that the Bundu or Sande circle of women was far more secretive than its Poro counterpart.[38]

One of the most arresting aspects of the Sande and Poro societies was their ubiquity. Among the Senufo of the northern Ivory Coast, southern Mali, and Burkina Faso, these associations were very strong and vital.[39] Cultivators of dry rice and yams, the matrilineal Senufo were organized into a series of villages or settlements known singularly as the *katiolo*. Each major *katiolo* had its own Poro and Sande societies, the latter known as the Sandogo, a "powerful women's organization that unites the female leadership of the many extended household units and kinship groups of the village."[40] The Sandogo wielded certain social controls, and was particularly concerned with the "sanctity of betrothal and marriage contracts."[41]

Observers referred to the head of the Bundu or Sande among the Temne as the "bunda woman."[42] Winterbottom described her as "an old woman, called boondoo-woman, [who] has the entire superintendence of it, and to her care husbands and fathers consign their wives and daughters."[43] Among the Senufo, the Sando or Sando-Mother was the leader of the Sandogo, and was particularly powerful in that she was the individual responsible for maintaining harmonious relations with the spirit realm, calling upon powers of divination to interpret and mediate between human beings and the spirits of the bush, rivers, ancestors, and deities. As was true of the Bambara, such mediation was unavoidable: "Since the villages must constantly disturb the bush spirits' domain by their farming, hunting, and artisan activities, the diviners' task of regulating appeasement and paying homage to the bush spirits is crucial to the welfare of both household and community."[44] In fact, it can be argued that Senufo women in general, "to a far greater degree than men, assume roles as ritual mediators between humankind and the supernatural world of spirits and deities."[45] Senufo women, as was true of other groups in Sierra Leone, were indispensable to the creation of any new Poro male society and its *sinzanga*, or sacred grove. This was because the founding of the male society required a ritual involving both a man and a woman. Glaze takes matters one step further, arguing that at philosophical and conceptual levels, it was the elder woman who was the real leader of any Poro lodge.[46] Furthermore, the Poro's chief responsibility was to safeguard relations with the deities and ancestors, but the most important of the ancestors were the founding mothers of the matrilineages. Thus not only was the Sandogo clearly controlled by women, but the Poro was also deeply indebted to women both spiritually and psychologically.

The prominence of women in Senufo society is further evidenced by the Senufo belief in a sexually bipartite deity called Kolotyolo when referred to as creator, Katyeleeo when its protective and nurturing qualities are emphasized. And although twins of the same sex were viewed as harbingers of evil or death, male and female twins were received with alacrity, as they represented the "sexual balance" of the Senufo creation account. In fact, it is Glaze's view that the persistence of matriliny among the Senufo, in spite of Islam and Western encroachment, is yet another indication of the "deepseated power" of women.[47] In turn, the Senufo's relatively high regard for the position of women found a certain resonance among other ethnicities throughout Sierra Leone, who were similarly subjected to external influences. In the latter cases gender egalitarianism, to the extent that it existed, only survived into the eighteenth and nineteenth centuries in muted forms. One can glimpse what perhaps once was in the ritual and organization of one of the remaining bastions of female power and autonomy, the Sande society. The question becomes, Given the agricultural contributions and sociocultural autonomy of women in Sierra Leone, did any form of egalitarianism survive the Middle Passage, and if so, what happened to it in the face of influences from other parts of Africa and white America?

The Sande's counterpart, the male Poro, was similarly organized, with grades or degrees of descending status and authority aggregated at the upper strata of the society. The term *poro* is apparently a reference to the laws of the ancestors, and the Poro's oldest society may have been among the Mende, from whom it spread to the Temne, the Sherbro, the Vai, the Loko, and others. Membership in the Poro was mandatory for males, who were usually initiated at puberty by rite of circumcision.[48] As was true of the female Sande, the purpose of the Poro was to prepare each male for full participation in community affairs. Those who were initiated became members of the lower echelon or degree of the Poro, as control of the lodge remained firmly in the hands of the senior members. Sierra Leonians in general pursued higher ranks within the various societies, and in this way anticipate the discussion of the Igbo and their corresponding title-taking proclivities.

Women could join the Poro if they were political rulers, if they were deemed "barren" (membership could generate fertility), or if they had seen a Poro candidate or otherwise learned other Poro secrets.[49] Whether in power, childless, or enlightened, the individual would not be able to advance beyond the lower grades of the society.

Upon entering initiation, candidates were taught to keep a secret, having previously been considered untrustworthy and therefore excluded from deliberations of any substance. Thus Corry recorded of the society: "It is a confederation by a solemn oath, and binds its members to inviolable secrecy not to discover its mysteries, and to yield an implicit obedience to superiors, called by the natives the *Purrah*."[50] Initiates were scarified during the process and underwent a symbolic death to their prior lives and a rebirth to new ones within the society. At the end of the ritual, the initiates, both males and females, were given new names: "A boy has no real name until he goes to the Poro bush, when it is given him at his circumcision."[51] Glaze has described the Poro process among the Senufo as follows:

> In a highly structured sequence of age grades climaxed by advancement ceremonies, the initiate is taught to "walk the path of Poro," which leads to responsibility, wisdom, authority, and power. From the children's primary grade of "discovery" through a long period of training and service that is highlighted by the initiate's ritual death and spiritual regeneration to the final graduation of the "finished man," Poro is preparation for responsible and enlightened leadership.[52]

Passage to higher degrees and the final graduation was marked by "dramatic ceremonies, dances, masquerades, performances, and visual displays."[53] This celebration of death to life through spiritual rebirth would take on new meaning within the North American context; suffice it to say that the concept of spiritual regeneration was by no means foreign to the Sierra Leonians. They not only were acquainted with it but also probably had a more profound understanding of its implications than did their Christian enslavers.

Although these societies helped regulate the various aspects of collective social life, they also had an important political component and function. Matthews, for example, recorded in 1786 that the "most singular law I have yet observed in Africa is what they term the *purrah*, and is peculiar to Sherbro. This wise, political institution is disseminated through the country for the purpose of putting an end to disputes and wars. . . . This law is never used but in the dernier resort; and when it is in force, the crimes of witchcraft and murder are punishable by it."[54] In the event of a dispute between two "tribes or nations," the mediator (usually the ruler of a third state) threatened to "send for the *purrah*" in lieu of a peaceful settlement. If necessary, a contingent of about forty to fifty Poro would visit the offending party at night and "put them to death, or disperse of them in a manner that they are never heard of again."[55] Winterbottom added: "When the *purra* comes into a town, which is always at night, it is accompanied with the most dreadful howlings, screams, and other horrid noises."[56] Whether punishing a capital offense or resolving a political conflict, the Poro operated with utmost authority.

In examining the political and judicial aspects of the Poro among the Mende, Little has written that the society was, "in all likelihood, the means by which a uniform system of government as well as set of customs was possible among a large number of politically separate and scattered communities."[57] In like manner, Wylie concludes that such societies among the Temne "provided for a degree of central power to link the otherwise separate villages and kin groups."[58] This political capacity of the various societies means that in many Sierra Leonian communities there were two sets of authority: the village and small-scale polity rulers, and the leaders of the societies. For the Mende, these authorities were mutually reinforcing in that the Poro, for example, concerned itself with extravillage affairs such as regulating trade between sovereign entities and settling disputes among various polities.[59] The power of the society leaders rested in their very special relationship to the spirit realm. Mende rulers (as opposed to "chiefs," a colonial diminutive) were "purely secular" and unlike Temne rulers, who carried both spiritual and temporal authority.

Although it is important to appreciate the political applications of these societies, one must avoid making assessments based upon the paradigm of centralized government. It would be a mistake to view the intercommunity linkages of the societies as precursors to centralization. Rather, it would be better to view the intricate political arrangements throughout Sierra Leone, via the agency of the various societies, as an achievement of some proportion and in its own right, taking the best of two ostensibly conflicting political theories—local autonomy versus centralization—and creating a hybrid maximizing the former while minimizing the latter. Trade arrangements, defense preparations, and the arbitration of disagreements between polities were all negotiated through the offices of the societies, made possible because of their replication throughout Sierra Leone in the various villages and among numerous ethnicities. For those who valued local independence, such an organizational scheme was ideal.

Given the prevalence and preeminence of male and female societies throughout Sierra Leone, the question becomes: Is there evidence that the structures and/or principles of these organizations continued into the slave quarters of North America? Carter G. Woodson was one of the first to conclude that, although their "traditional" functions could no longer be sustained in North America, these societies nevertheless continued by performing different roles, such as providing for the sick and burying the dead.[60] Washington Creel, in writing about the experience of the Gullah in South Carolina, has also answered the query in the affirmative, arguing that "some adaptive concepts of community (and aspects of spirituality) inherited from secret societies fused with Gullah interpretations of Christianity, becoming part of folk religion in the slave quarters."[61] With regard to the specific matter of societies, she cites the 1833 account of Thomas Turpin, who recorded his observations of a Bull's Island black community that had convened to determine an appropriate punishment for an alleged transgression:

They had three degrees of punishment, and . . . the punishment was in-flicted agreeably to the magnitude of the crime, according to their view of the crime. If the crime was of the first magnitude, the perpetrator had to pick up a quart of benne seed . . . poured on the ground by the priest; and if of the second, a quart of rice; and if of the third a quart of corn . . . they also had high seats and low seats, but incorrect views relative to those who ought to be punished . . . it was also a rule among them never to divulge the secret of stealing; and if it should be divulged . . . that one had to go on the low seat or pick up the benne seed.[62]

Turpin's comment on the Gullahs' "incorrect views" reflects his concern that stealing was not viewed as sinful in this community but tattling on the "thief" was. Washington Creel correctly explains the Gullah view of sin as the violation of "socioreligious authority and loyalty in the slave quarters," consistent with Fanon's discussion of morality from the perspective of the colonized.[63] She then connects the Gullah and Sierra Leone:

The rite the slaves engaged in is reminiscent of high-low seats and a pyramid of degrees in the Poro and Sande in Upper Guinea, and some secret societies in Angola. The Poro inner circle was a social regulating as well as religious body. It stopped quarrels, caught, tried, condemned, and punished social criminals. In Poro-Sande culture, high seats be-longed to a few old religious leaders of high degree. But the way Gullahs employed the use of high-low degrees was unique and reflected their ability to adapt a past tradition to the organization of their slave com-munity. . . . The Gullahs reserved the "low seat" for those who betrayed community interest. . . . Thus picking up the benne seed was reserved for the worst of crimes.[64]

Although maintenance of Sande and Poro formal organization was impossi-ble, informal arrangements would have continued and would have been, due to the clandestine nature of the societies, difficult to detect by outsiders. That such arrangements were indeed in place is suggested by the remarks of former slave John Matthews, who in a WPA interview spoke of his Virginia-born mother transferred to Mississippi, where he himself was raised. He went on: "I believe in spirits. I is seed many one, but it is against my religion to tell about dem; dat is a sacred thing. In fact I have acted de part of de spirit, but dat wus a long time ago. I dont belong to dat sect any more an' cant tell deir secrets."[65] The allusion to acting the part of a spirit as a member of a clandestine organization recalls those procedures performed by male so-cieties and other associations throughout West Africa in general and Sierra Leone in particular. The fact that the practices of this "sect" had been transferred to Mississippi and engaged in by someone who could have only been a child during slavery's last days speaks to the enduring appeal of this form of retention. The foregoing examples demonstrate that the socialization role of the society was far-reaching, instructing those who would become American slaves concerning conflict resolution, courting and marriage, and other matters.

Another possible area in which elements of these societies were retained or merged with non-African influences is freemasonry. Matthews, Winterbottom, and Rankin all likened the activities of the Poro and Bundu to European freemasonry.[66] In 1901, Alldridge similarly characterized the Poro as "a system of Freemasonry amongst the men."[67] Glaze's reference to the "graduation of the 'finished man'" among the Senufo is strikingly similar both in substance and even in wording to the "making of the man" ritual within freemasonry.[68] In fact, it was Americo-Liberians who organized the Masons and the United Brotherhood Fellowship in Liberia as male societies, as there were numerous points of correspondence between the two: Both the Sierra Leonian societies and African American masons were/are extremely secretive about the affairs of the organization; both were engaged in providing a variety of social services to their constituents; both had members who were very loyal to the ideals and the leadership of the associations; both were characterized by degrees, through which one rose after having mastered previous levels of knowledge.

The preceding observations do not mean that European freemasonry was not influential in the African-based community. It does suggest, however, that as was true of the Christian doctrine of regeneration, Sierra Leonians understood the principles of freemasonry long before their introduction to its European version. Indeed, it is plausible that African American freemasonry is an institution derived from West African, and specifically Sierra Leonian, origins, having subsequently assumed a more Western guise.

Finally, the influence of the Sande and Poro upon the African-based community's approach to Christianity is apparent. A more detailed discussion of African conversion to Christianity awaits a subsequent chapter, but it can be stated here that the conversion of slaves took place largely in the latter part of the nineteenth century and only after the religion had been significantly Africanized. As was true of most Africans and African Americans, religion was something to be experienced—it was tangible. As such, conversion often took the paths of "traveling" and "seeking" and going into the "wilderness" to find salvation and enlightenment.[69] The superficial parallels with biblical imagery camouflage the more fundamental association with the Sande-Poro experience, in which initiates undertook a spiritual journey by first retreating to the bush. In fact, there are many conceptual areas in which the religions of Africa and European Christianity converge, including baptism and church organization. As these and other areas will be examined later, it is sufficient here to recall Washington Creel's generalization that "the Gullahs defined life in sacred terms, an inherited African legacy. Their introduction to Christianity reinforced this sense of the sacred."[70]

In addition to drawing attention to the role of societies among the Gullah in coastal Carolina, Washington Creel submits that the terms *Gullah* and *Geechee* may be (at least in part) of Sierra Leonian origin.[71] This is based upon the probability that the term *Gullah*, spelled *Golla* in the eighteenth century and generally believed to refer to the people of Angola, may have also derived from the Gola, an ethnic group in the interior of what is now Liberia. It is her position, therefore, that because both the Gola and Angolans came to Carolina, the term Gullah refers to both. Similarly, the word *Geechee*, used in coastal Georgia to refer to people whose culture is almost indistinguishable from the Gullah in Carolina (and therefore the terms are sometimes used interchangeably), may also be derived from the Kissi (or Gizzi or Kizzi) of Sierra Leone. Then again, the term may have a more immediate source— the Ogechee River.

The scholarship tends to support, if not a direct connection between the Kissi and the Geechee, at least the notion that significant numbers of Kissi were exported from Sierra Leone. Rodney has written that the non-Muslim Mande and the Kissi "seem to have been the main victims" of slave-raiding campaigns.[72] The Kissi were also one of the leading targets of the Futa Jallon jihād, such that "the Sulima Yalunka, for example, sold their defeated Limba or Kisi opponents to Susu middlemen."[73] The association of the Kissi with enslavement was by no means confined to the Jallonke-Fulbe of the interior, for the Mende also looked "down on the Kissi and Kono" because they were recruited so heavily for enslavement by the Mende.[74] Therefore, there is good reason to believe that the Kissi were present in coastal Georgia and Carolina in substantial numbers.

There are in fact references to the Kissi in the runaway slave advertisements. In February 1771, for example, Joseph Heaber of South Carolina sought the return of "Scipio, of the Keshey Country," whose upper teeth had been filed.[75] In February 1773, the administrators of Governor Boone's Ponpon plantation took out an ad for Josey and Morris, "both of the Kishee Country" and missing since July of the previous year.[76] In March 1778 William Maxwell placed a notice for Isaac (missing for two years) and Davy (absent for six months), both around thirty years of age and from the "Kishey country."[77] Andrew Miller of Brewton Hill, Georgia described in July 1784 the runaway Peter as thirty-five years old and "of the Kissee country, has some marks on his face, and his teeth filed."[78] Finally, there is the case of Clarinda, somewhere between thirty and thirty-five years of age, who was picked up as a runaway in South Carolina in 1773 and taken to the "work-house." She is described as a "new negro wench, of the Kisbee country."[79]

The Gola of Liberia are also represented in the slave ads. In one July 1783 notice, a South Carolina owner described Othello and Maria as hailing from the "Gola country."[80] Georgian James Read, who lived along the Great-Ogechee River in 1774, searched for the whereabouts of five "new" people—three men and two women—all of whom were from the "Gola" country and none of whom could speak more than "a little" English.[81] In May 1804 the finding of "a new negro man of the Gullo country, named Cuffey" was reported in Georgia.[82] Similarly, Georgian Martha Wilkins reported the absence of Mary-Ann, a young woman "of the Gulla nation, very small size, and has had one child."[83] A final example comes from South Carolina, where in 1785 Alexander Shinas reported the six-week absence of "a short wench, from the Gulla country."[84]

These advertisements for the Gola are to be distinguished from those that refer very clearly to individuals from West Central Africa, such as Francis Nicholson's December 1770 notice for the return of Dick, described as an "elderly Angola fellow," or the ad placed in August 1784 calling for any information on a sixteen-year-old who was "lately" from Angola.[85] In fact, the notices for runaway Angolans are specific and numerous, whereas references to the Gola are few by comparison.

To be sure, there are a great many references in the runaway notices to people from "Guinea." For example, in September 1767 the following notice was published in Savannah: "Ran away, or stolen, from my plantation, a Guiney Negroe fellow, named July, about 25 years of age . . . can speak very little English, his teeth cut, has his country marks on his arms and shoulders . . . and his face cut."[86] Or take the case of Peter, of "the Guinea Country," who at the age of twenty-seven escaped from John Fisher of South Carolina, speaking "very bad English, but is active and artful; a cabinet-Maker by Trade."[87] The problem with these ascriptions is that "Guinea" is imprecise, and in many instances simply refers to a person born somewhere in Africa.[88] There is therefore no sure method of distinguishing between those from Sierra Leone and those from other places in "Guinea," except in those instances in which there are direct associations with Sierra Leone and the Windward Coast. For the most part, such references can be found in the notices of slave ships arriving at ports of call.[89] An example is the 30 November 1774 edition of the *Georgia Gazette*, which announced the arrival of eighty captives from "Sierraleon, a Rice Country on the Coast of Africa."[90]

Finally, aside from the cultural (and arguably political) contributions of the people of Sierra Leone to those would who become African Americans, some preliminary statements can be made at this juncture about Sierra Leone's role in the development of social relations among people of African descent. As has been stated earlier, North American planters tended to value Sierra Leonians as highly as Senegambians because they were very knowledgeable about rice, indigo, and cotton cultivation. They were therefore valuable as field laborers. There is little evidence, however, that whites acknowledged the cultural achievements of Sierra Leonians or regarded them more highly than other groups of Africans, in contrast to their general view toward Muslims. Consequently, whereas Muslims may have been identified and elevated to other positions, there is nothing in the testimonial record suggesting that slaveholders stereotyped Sierra Leonians as anything other than field laborers.

As a result, there appears to be more of an association of rural, urban-distanced life with such groups as the Gullah and Geechee than is true of other African ethnicities, even though the vast majority of blacks in North America were rural dwellers throughout the period of legal enslavement and even beyond. Indeed, the term *Geechee* carries a pejorative connotation and has come to mean someone who is unsophisticated in the ways of city life, someone considered "country."[91] Some may justify this perception of the Gullah and the Geechee by citing the relative isolation of some of the descendants of the Sierra Leonians along the coasts and among the sea islands of Georgia and Carolina.

It may very well be, however, that an anti–Sierra Leone bias has its origins in Sierra Leone itself. It has been pointed out that the social and political context of Sierra Leone was at some variance with what tended to characterize Senegambia. But within Sierra Leone there is evidence that some groups, particularly the Kissi and the Kono, were seen in a negative light as a result of their repeated victimization during slavery as well as for cultural reasons. The Mende, in fact, looked down upon the Kissi because they were said to "live in 'backward places,' and their customs, such as filing the front teeth, are regarded as particularly degenerate."[92] In view of such sentiments, it is entirely possible that the association of the Sierra Leonians with extreme provinciality began in West Africa and was reinforced by the agricultural regime and relative isolation of North American coastal areas. As such, the Sierra Leonians' opportunity to establish a form of cultural domination in Georgia and Carolina, having arrived in equal numbers with the Senegambians but at a subsequent period to them, was mitigated by the disadvantages of location and perception. Rather than uniformity, then, one can posit the beginnings of both cultural and social divergence, in which the Sierra Leonians, along with others, were not particularly welcomed into the acculturated stream of African American social development. Instead, they added to the culture of the folk, and that largely confined to Georgia and South Carolina, especially along the coast.

Although there were slightly fewer Akan in North America than Africans from the various ethnic groups of Senegambia and Sierra Leone, their presence was potentially more influential in that slaves imported from the Gold Coast, which was territorially smaller and easier to define, tended to be linguistically and culturally closer to one another than those of Sierra Leone, where there were numerous groups covering a vast area. The southern half of the Gold Coast was clearly dominated by the Akan and Ga speakers, the former divided into two subgroups: Twi and Baule speakers. The Baule tended to be concentrated in the western reaches of the Gold Coast, in what is now the eastern Ivory Coast, whereas the Twi inhabited that portion of the region associated with contemporary Ghana. Along the coast itself the Ga speakers constituted a separate source of power.

Myths concerning the ethnogenesis of the Akan underscore both the cultural unity of the group and the important role of women. The ancestresses of the Akan came from either the sky or the earth to the forests of Adanse and Amansie, between the Pra and Ofin Rivers. There they founded the first towns from which all Akan believe they are derived: Adansemanso, Abuakwa Atwumamanso, Asantemanso, Asenmanso, and Abankeseso.[93] The process of clearing the forest was a major undertaking, providing one of the most important clues to Akan thought.

The Akan linguistic subgroups are many: the Asante, the Fante, the Bron, the Akyem, the Akuapem, the Kwahu, the Assen, the Wassa, the Fante, the Nzima, the Ahanta, the Afema, the Sefwi-Bahuri-Aswin, and the Chakosi among them. These subgroups, however, are academic constructs of convenience for purposes of delineation and are "without significance to the people themselves."[94] The Twi branch of the Akan includes the Asante and the Fante, whereas the Baule (or Ayi-Baule) features such groups as the Sefwi and the Ahanta. The sources are in agreement that captives coming out of the Gold Coast were, for the most part, Akan-speaking.[95]

The late seventeenth and early eighteenth centuries witnessed the growth of the slave trade in both the Bight of Benin and the Gold Coast, the latter including the Bandama and Comoe River valleys of the eastern Ivory Coast.[96] Of course, Europeans had been trading along the Gold Coast since the fifteenth century, beginning with the Portuguese and the emergence of Elmina as an entrepôt for auriferous exchange. The Gold Coast was an exporter of gold and a net importer of slaves at that time, but by the early seventeenth century this was no longer the case. Slave exports remained insignificant, however, until the last quarter of the seventeenth century, when the numbers danced around the 2,000 per year mark.

The eighteenth century saw a dramatic increase in Gold Coast captive exports. From 2,500 per year between 1701 and 1710, to 7,300 per year in the 1720s, to a peak of 9,100 in the 1740s, the Gold Coast quickly became an important source of slaves for the West. A depreciation of 25 percent in the 1750s and further decline in the 1770s was followed by an upsurge in either the 1780s or the 1790s.[97] In total, at least 665,000 Africans were exported from the region.[98]

In examining the source of these captives, the twice-told chicken-and-egg quandary resurfaces: although warfare on a relatively large scale generated the captives, the impetus for that warfare is unclear. As was noted in Chapter 4, the rise in the number of slaves coincided with the emergence of Asante as an imperialist power.[99] It remains to be seen, however, whether Asante expansionist policy was adopted in order to take advantage of the Western demand for slaves or if considerable numbers of captives were a by-product of a policy driven by other considerations. From the perspective of the captives, of course, the issue was moot. Factors involved in Asante's rise will be examined shortly, but its push for hegemony involved the whole of the area from the Bandama River and port at Grand Lahu to the Comoe River and port at Grand Bassam, resulting in Baule flight and the displacement of the Senufo and the Guro. Although some slaves were provided via Muslim traders leading south from Kong to Grand Lahu via Boron, most of the captives sold into the Atlantic trade were casualties of war.

As was true of those from Sierra Leone and Senegambia, Africans from the Gold Coast were in great demand in North America, being "highly valued" and "favorites."[100] Wax writes that during the colonial period, captives from the Gold Coast usually received the "highest accolades" and were referred to as Gold Coast or "Koromantin" (or "Coromantee" or "Kromanti") slaves, after the name of the entrepôt at which the British had established a factory.[101] According to Wax, those from Gambia (or Senegambia) received the next highest ranking. In fact, Washington Creel speculates that "Gold Coast Africans were apparently the first black Carolinians," based upon the observation that servile labor for the early Carolina community was provided by Barbados.[102] The characterization of these black Carolinians does not take into account the earlier Spanish settlement there, but it does point to the nature of the relationship between North America and the West Indies in connection with Gold Coast Africans. That is, while South Carolinian planters were willing to pay a premium for Gold Coast captives due to their high regard for them, they were often disadvantaged by planters in the Caribbean, who also valued those from the Gold Coast and who "usually got first choice."[103] Jamaica in particular developed a strong preference for the Gold Coast, such that between 1751 and 1790, some 111,500 out of 138,300

Gold Coast captives went to Jamaica via British slavers, or about 80 percent.[104] It follows that Gold Coast Africans or Akan speakers were the "strongest" numerical representation of Africans in Jamaica.[105]

As a result of the tremendous demand in the West Indies for Akan captives, together with concurrent preferences for those from Senegambia and Sierra Leone, South Carolina may have received fewer captives from the Gold Coast than did Virginia and perhaps Maryland. Higgins, looking primarily at the colonial trade, found that, given their marketability, "surprisingly few" Gold Coast captives entered Charleston.[106] Wax writes that Carolinians were "less committed" to a reliance upon the Gold Coast than were other areas, especially Virginia.[107] A third source goes on to assert (mistakenly) that those from the Gold Coast made up the majority of Virginia's slave population.[108] In light of the relatively substantial Gold Coast contribution, these people had to enter ports and territories somewhere. Although highly speculative, it is not unreasonable to surmise that the African-based populations of Virginia and Maryland contained much higher levels of Akan speakers and their descendants than did South Carolina and Georgia, whereas the latter two featured much larger numbers of captives from Sierra Leone and Senegambia than did the mid-Atlantic colonies/states. The probability of spatially oriented ethnic distribution patterns increases in the case of the Igbo.

The question becomes, Why was the Gold Coast captive so attractive to planters in the New World? This is particularly curious in the case of South Carolina and Georgia, where the cultures of rice, cotton, and indigo go far in explaining the demand for people from Senegambia and Sierra Leone. For the Akan, however, their desirability appears to have been founded upon their reputation as unskilled and vocational laborers. In Jamaica, for example, the Akan were believed to be "stronger" and more industrious than other groups, although prone to revolt.[109] So were they regarded in South Carolina, where they were described as hard workers endowed with physical ability.[110] Littlefield summarizes the English colonial view of the "Coromantees" of the Gold Coast as "especially hardy, ferocious if angered, unmindful of danger, unwilling to forgive a wrong, but loyal if their devotion could be captured."[111] Interestingly, Wax has added that Gold Coast Africans were seen as "docile" and "sensible," as well as the most sturdy.[112] Physical strength and a capacity to work, then, were the principal characteristics by which the Akan were known to whites. Outside of the Caribbean and South Carolina, they were also seen as relatively accommodating to the slave regime. Further background on Akan culture and society is needed, therefore, to determine both the veracity of these stereotypic assessments and the impact, if any, such assessments had on social relations within the African-based community and the African American composite identity.

Any attempt to establish an appropriate context for the discussion of Akan culture and society must first begin with a consideration of those political and economic forces that completely transformed the Gold Coast from the fifteenth to the eighteenth century.[113] It was during this period that commercial ties between this region and the Atlantic began to challenge and eventually eclipse trade relations among the Gold Coast, the West African savannah to the north, and the more distant economies of the Maghrib and the Mediterranean. This reorientation of the axes of trade resulted in fundamental changes in both the sources and configurations of power in the Gold Coast. It is therefore out of a profoundly politically charged matrix that captives bound for North America were extricated.

The Akan gold trade to the savannah and beyond had been important since the opening of the Akan goldfields to Juula merchants under imperial Mali and Songhay, dating back to at least the fifteenth century.[114] In addition, there was an important trade in kola nut to the islamized savannah and elsewhere. The trade stimulated the development of the northern state of Bono, perhaps the earliest of the Akan states, with its capital at Bono-Manso.[115] Thirty to forty miles to the northwest was the town of Bighu (or Bitu), on the northern edge of the forest region. Bighu was a Juula town and important in that it sent gold mined in the Akan fields north to both Kong and Bobo-Dioulasso, also Juula-founded, from whence the gold was carried to the Jenne-Timbuktu corridor and across the Sahara. The Juula networks either traversed or skirted the Mossi kingdoms of Wagadugu, Dagomba, Mamprussi, and Yatenga and were connected to the Muslim kingdom of Gonja (south of Dagomba, north of the Akan).[116]

Following Bono, a number of strong central powers emerged among the Akan, intent upon taking advantage of the lucrative gold trade. However, with the arrival of the Portuguese in the fifteenth century, pressures to control the flow of gold north to the savannah and south to the coast resulted in the combination of increased productivity and competition between polities. The Akan states, dependent upon servile labor to mine the fields (activity abhorrent to the Akan) and perform agricultural duties, imported ever-increasing numbers of slaves from the north and elsewhere.[117] Even so, the rise in the demand for slaves in the New World eventually reversed the direction of captives, so that the eighteenth century saw a substantial outflow of Africans from the Gold Coast, constituting a new, black form of gold.

Bono's longevity is impressive, lasting from the end of the thirteenth century to its apogee between 1712 and 1740, when it experienced defeat at the hands of Asante.[118] Denkyira, the dominant power in the Southwest, also succumbed to the might of Asante in 1701, and the coastal towns of Accra and Adangme fell in 1742.[119] The Fante, on the other hand, created a loose alliance of small states and served as intermediaries between the English on the coast and the Akan in the hinterland, having formed particularly close ties with the former.[120] The coastal Fante in fact acquired considerable wealth from the slave trade and were increasingly influenced by neighboring European settlements, even opening Western schools as early as the eighteenth century.[121] Although the northern Fante fell to Asante in 1765 and the southern Fante in 1807, they would reemerge later in the nineteenth century.[122]

The articulation of the state is therefore a powerful theme in Akan history, and Asante is its quintessential representative. McCaskie writes that Asante society "slowly crystallized in its historic form" in the sixteenth and seventeenth centuries, a time characterized by Wilks as the "era of the great ancestresses" in light of the profound roles women played as advisors and leaders of the matriclans.[123] Established as an empire around 1680 under Asantehene Osei Tutu and pursuing an expansionist policy until the death of Opoku Ware in 1750, Asante was one of the most militarily powerful and structurally articulate polities in all of West and West Central Africa, rivaling the earlier savannah states in complexity if not territorial expanse.[124] The unity of the empire was symbolized in the institution of the Sika Dwa, the Golden Stool, before which all other previously existing stools symbolizing political autonomy were destroyed. At its apex in the nineteenth century, "Greater Asante" consisted of three types of territory: the metropolitan region surrounding the capital of Kumase; the inner provinces; and the outer provinces, beyond which were territories of tributary status. The cultural asantization of the empire radiated from center to periphery; homogeneity was an objective more fully realized in the inner provinces than in those further removed. This is especially interesting given the fact that the subject groups were already Akan in culture and language. After periods of belligerence with the British beginning in 1824, Asante was defeated and brought under British colonial administration in 1896.

Asante's governmental organization included the *asantehene*, the chief executive; the Asantemanhyiamu (Assembly of the Asante Nation), the highest conciliar body of the empire; and the Gyaasewa Fekuo (Exchequer), responsible for the national treasury and tax collection. Gold dust was the standard currency throughout Asante, except for the far northern provinces, where cowries were used instead. Vital to Asante's interests was the maintenance of a "great-roads" system, eight roads over which both commerce and political authority traversed. In fact, an office of "chief inspector of the nuisances and path cleaners" was created in 1764 to oversee the transportation system.

Asante emerged at a time when gold and slaves were exported both north and south, with the trade in slaves to the south taking increasing precedence.

The expansionist policies pursued by Asante were for the most part against neighboring Akan, so that most who wound up in the transatlantic trade were Akan speakers. These people were therefore accustomed to two basic realities: large centralized governments (in contrast to Sierra Leone) within which trading and administrative towns of some size and complexity were distributed and (like Sierra Leone) an atmosphere of insecurity due to Asante imperialism and the labor needs of domestic gold production and New World plantations. It was out of this political context that the Akan came to North America.

Notwithstanding the importance of the gold and kola nut trades, all Akan economies were, at the end of the day, agriculturally based.[125] Yams or cassava, cocoyams, plantains, and such supplied the staples of the diet and were supplemented by fish, game, and livestock wherever the tsetse fly did not prevail. The early struggle to move from forest-based hunting and gathering to subsistence agriculture shaped the collective consciousness of the Asante to the extent that they "were obsessed with order and feared disorder," the latter represented by the forest.[126] The transition explains the development of patriarchy in that men controlled the accumulation of wealth. McCaskie emphasizes that this "principal of accumulation," a consequence of the need to "carve out" cultivable land from the forest, created "in Asante thought and practice a deeply powerful social imperative towards the historical realization of an aggregated cluster of norms and values: fruitfulness, increase, maximization, abundance, plenitude."[127] New World planters may have very well detected this "principal of accumulation" among the Akan, thus explaining their reputation as hard workers.

In addition to agriculture, the Akan were also extremely skilled in crafts; both weaving and woodcarving were important industries. These crafts were usually performed by men only, and although menopausal women could participate in weaving, woodcarving (which involved the creation of stools and drums) was strictly off limits to women. On the other hand, women controlled the making of pottery, a skill handed down from mother to daughter. Akan smiths worked in iron and gold.

Akan society was for the most part matrilineal.[128] The various Akan subgroups (Asante, Fante, Bron, Akyem, and so on) were each composed of clans or lineages. All of the members of a clan, or *abusua*, were believed to be the descendants of a common mother. Although the head of the clan, the *abusua panyin*, was a male, there was always a female head of the clan as well, someone who bore "high moral authority." The responsibilities of the *abusua panyin* included the approval of all marriages and divorces, the arbitration of intraclan disputes, the apportionment of lineage land for farming and other uses, and the maintenance of ancestral stools. The concept of the stool, mentioned in connection with the Sika Dwa, was very important to the Akan, and together with the view of the land will be examined more thoroughly.

The Akan *abusua* was made up of households that, like the Mende *mawe*, were composed of the head male, his wives, their unmarried children; their married sons and their wives and children; and possibly the head male's mother, younger brothers, and unmarried sisters.[129] The head male within a household was often a maternal uncle (*wofa*). In the Akan matriliny, the *wofa* was dominant and could make such decisions as removing his nephew from the father's care if it was determined to be poor, or even pawning a niece or nephew over the protests of the father. The position of the maternal uncle was therefore a powerful one, a fact long remembered by some transported to the New World, where they protested the role of uncles in their sale. "Dey pays de uncles to do it," explained the descendant of one so transported. "Dat's it. In Africky de uncles got charge de chillun. Mammies raise 'em, but de uncles own 'em."[130]

Undergirding the social and political process, and indeed informing it at every juncture, were Akan beliefs. It was Bosman, for example, who wrote that Gold Coast Africans "believe in one true God though in a crude indigested Manner."[131] Called Onyame (or Onyankopon or Odomankama), he created the visible world together with the earth mother Asase Yaa.[132] The high god and goddess were typically "too high and remote to be approached directly" and were viewed by some as unconcerned with daily human existence. Beneath the highest order of deity, therefore, were the *abosom* (sing. *obosom*), or lesser deities, whose numbers reached into the hundreds. Descended from Onyame and deriving their power from him, the *abosom* date "from the very beginnings of Asante society" and were associated with certain natural phenomena, such as bodies of water, trees, rocks, and so on, the most powerful of the *abosom* related to bodies of water.[133] Among the Asante, for example, the four greatest *abosom* were Tano, Bea, Apo, and Bosomtwe, all of whom became important rivers and lakes. In fact, most rivers and streams were not only associated with *abosom*, but were *abosom*, whereas only some trees qualified.[134] Each *obosom*, in turn, had a temple, with priests and priestesses, through whom the *obosom* spoke via possession.

The human level of the ontological scale is divided into the living and the dead. The former are profoundly spiritual and composed of three parts: the *mogya*, the *ntoro*, and the *kra*.[135] The *mogya* (literally, "blood") is the physical aspect of the person (containing spiritual elements) and is derived from the mother. The *ntoro*, or "spirit," forms the individual's personality and is issued from the father. The *kra*, or "soul," comes from God and consists of seven types, depending upon the day of birth. The *ntoro* is sometimes associated with the *kra* and with the *sunsum* or life-force or "activating principle," which is the essence of an individual. It is out of respect for the power of the *ntoro* that children of divorces are left with the father, along with other concessions. Upon death, it is believed that the *mogya* returns to the spiritual world to await reincarnation within the same *abusua*, whereas the *ntoro* joins the ancestral realm and may possibly be reincarnated. This belief in reincarnation recalls that of the Bambara and some of the Sierra Leonians, and certainly anticipates the view of the Igbo.

So then, while part of the person returned to the land of the living, part remained with the ancestors, the *asaman*. The *asaman* inhabit a world similar to that of time and space, where they receive the libations of their descendants. The *asaman* and the *abosom* were critical to the welfare of the living. But an even more important link between the living and the ancestors was the land, which has a power or spirit of its own and was associated with Asase Yaa, the earth mother. For the Akan, the land belonged to the ancestors, from whom "the living have inherited the right to use the land. . . . The land is a link between the ancestors and their living descendants."[136] The land, then, was the source of not only sustenance and values but also corporate identity. It was where one's ancestors were buried and continued to live in another dimension, and to whom one could go in time of need. Displacement was therefore a traumatic, personality-altering experience, especially as it terminated in a sugar cane or tobacco field on the other side of the world.

The ancestors owned not only the land but also the stools, symbols of power throughout what was the Gold Coast.[137] The stools were sacred, then, because they both "symbolize and indeed hold ancestral power."[138] The stools more than represented ancestral power; they constituted the very ancestral presence among a unified community in a specific place and were emblematic of the union of two worlds in a specific location. To put it another way, the "Stool symbolizes the unity of the ancestors and their descendants and the Chief [who] occupies the Stool."[139] As such, the presence of the stool reinforced the Akan perspective that the welfare of the community transcended that of the individual, so that while individual achievement was encouraged, "the notion that something is 'for me' is meaningless unless it is linked with the total idea that it is 'for us.' This is the cardinal principle of Akan communal life."[140] As the concretization of the Akan view of the spiritual realm and the relationship of the living to it, the stool is surely one of the most unique expressions of Akan thought. Given both its symbolism and substance as a sacrum of authority and unity realized in a designated place on earth, the question becomes, How does an individual or group of individuals removed from such a context ever regain it? Given that the stool represents wholeness, how can what it represents ever be reestablished when one or more of the constituent elements is unrecoverable? Indeed, is this not the haunting query of the African tale "Humpty Dumpty"?

The relationship of the Akan to both the land and the ancestors is very reminiscent of the Bambara and groups out of Sierra Leone. Belief in the divisibility of the spiritual nature of human beings, such that part joins the ancestral world and part is reincarnated, also recalls the worldview of the Bambara and some Sierra Leonians. Similarities in social structure and, in the case of the Akan and Senegambians, political organization would have provided even further instances of common ground. Life, it would seem, was understood in similar terms.

The reality of the experience in North America, however, did not necessarily conform to such expectations. First of all, due to disproportionate importations, the rural societies and folk cultures in places such as Carolina and Georgia were not as informed by the Akan as were those of Virginia and Maryland. Their influence was far less apparent in Louisiana, where they did not constitute an important or sizable group.

And although it is useful to point out the commonalities of the various groups examined thus far, it would be inaccurate to leave the impression that the Akan, by virtue of their cultural and social affinities with others, blended seamlessly with these groups. On the contrary, although West and West Central Africans had many points in common, they tended to emphasize and embellish those which were singular. Although the concept of the male and female society was therefore not peculiar to the people of Sierra Leone, Sierra Leonians' development of it was refined to the point of distinction. So it was with the Akan. Virtually all groups venerated the ancestors and understood the connection between the living, the dead, and the land, but the Akan stool carried the conceptualization of the linkages to elevated heights. The Akan brought an acute understanding of the role and significance of land with them to the New World. They were among those who saw the need for a connection between land and political, cultural, and social freedom, a connection both tangible and spiritual. Populations from the next two regions, the Bight of Biafra and West Central Africa, had similar insights.

6

I SEEN FOLKS DISAPPEAH

THE IGBO AND WEST CENTRAL AFRICA

As was true of the Sierra Leonians and the Akan, Africans from the Bight of Biafra and West Central Africa were concentrated in different parts of the South. Certain planters were particularly loath to accept captives from the bight, associated as they were with tendencies inimical to the enterprise of slavery. An examination of folkloric tradition in fact supports planters' concerns, and this, in turn, requires an investigation into the Biafran background. As a result, this chapter offers a more complete picture of how political institutions, religion, and philosophical perspective informed the behavior of the dislocated and argues that significant portions of the West Central African metaphysical view survived the transatlantic passage, deeply influencing African American religion and culture.

It is beyond credulity that the Igbo, a group with such profound impact upon African American society, has received so little recognition in the scholarly literature on North American slavery. In numerable studies on the continuity of African culture in the New World, much is made of the contributions of the Yoruba, the Akan, the Fon and the Ewe, the Bakongo, and so on. Although richly deserved, the attention afforded these groups has tended to minimize the signal contribution of the Igbo, who for reasons better explored elsewhere, have not enjoyed similar prominence and popularity.

The sheer size of the Igbo contingent to North America is stunning. The Bight of Biafra, the Igbo's region of origin, accounted for nearly one-quarter of the total number of Africans imported into North America, placing it in a virtual first-place tie with West Central Africa. The magnitude of this contribution becomes even more pronounced when it is realized that the Bight of Biafra as a region is much smaller than West Central Africa, a construct that runs south from Gabon all the way to the southern tip of Angola. The homogeneity of the Biafran region relative to all the others, with the possible exception of the Gold Coast, adds further distinction to its representation.

Although the Igbo/Biafran contribution to the British trade in slaves was disproportionately high, the demand for them in the New World was by no means consistent. In fact, some of the North American colonies/states preferred not to import Igbo captives. It was Donnan's view that because Virginian planters were simply uninterested in the ethnic origins of the Africans, they imported a large number from the Bight of Biafra, a reflection of the latter's dominant representation in the British slave pool as a whole.[1] In contrast, Donnan stated, South Carolina expressed an abiding preference for Senegambians and Gold Coast captives but were "disdainful" of the Igbo/Biafrans and "short people" in general. With regard to the latter category, Littlefield explains that Africans who were "small, slender, weak, and tended towards a yellowish color, were less desirable. Calabar or Ibo slaves, with whatever justice, seemed to epitomize these qualities."[2] Henry Laurens, a leading South Carolinian planter of the colonial period, wrote that Gambians made the best slaves and should be recruited, but that there "must not be a Callabar among them."[3] Those Igbo/Biafrans who could not be sold in South Carolina, however, were easily transferable to the markets of Virginia.

Wax concurs with Donnan (and Curtin), writing that colonial America sought captives primarily from the Gold Coast and Gambia (and in that order), and that South Carolina "had an intense prejudice against all slaves obtained east of the Gold Coast, especially those from the Bight of Biafra and Calabar."[4] Wax adds, however, that fluctuating market conditions required South Carolinians to purchase undesirables on occasion. Rawley joins the chorus, stating that South Carolina "strongly disliked" those from "the Bight of Biafra and Calabar," whereas Chesapeake buyers "accepted" the Igbo/Biafrans in large numbers.[5] In fact, the divergence between Virginia and South Carolina in their receptivity to the Igbo was such that the former's importation of the Igbo between 1710 and 1760 constituted some 38 percent of its total importation of African captives, a figure that mirrors precisely the overall British export trade from Africa.[6] This estimate is bumped up to 40 percent by Mullin in consideration of the postcolonial trade, and as such qualifies the Bight of Biafra as the region from which the largest group of captives came to Virginia.[7] In contrast, there is the estimate that from 1733 to

1807 South Carolina imported only 2 percent of its African captive population from the Bight of Biafra, a staggering percentage when it is recalled that
South Carolina received some 46 percent of the entire African trade to North
America through 1775.[8] Although Mullin's estimate of 5 percent Igbo/Bia-
fran importation into South Carolina for the whole of the legal trade is
probably more accurate, the South Carolinian rejection of the Igbo remains
both decided and dramatic.[9] On the other hand, the role of the Igbo in North
America, given both the size of Virginia's slave population and its function as
a leading source of slaves for the domestic slave trade, was clearly critical.

There is a fundamental question here. How could two mainland colonies/
states be so diametrically opposed in their attitude toward the largest ethnic
group imported into North America? With regard to Virginia, scholars differ
over what motivated planters to accept so many from the Bight of Biafra.
Mullin essentially agrees with Donnan's characterization of Virginia's indifferent attitude toward the Igbo, arguing the general principle that ethnicity
was only important in relation to levels of resistance; low levels of resistance
translated into indifference toward ethnicity.[10] Littlefield, in contrast, maintains that Virginia actually preferred the Igbo and others from the Niger delta
to those from West Central Africa because the latter traveled a longer distance to the Chesapeake and were therefore physically weaker.[11]

Whatever the reasons for Virginia's receptivity to the Igbo/Biafrans, it
stands in stark contrast to the attitude displayed in South Carolina. The cause
of the latter's discomfort with and disdain for the Igbo/Biafrans is rooted in
the former's perception of the latter's character, and in so typifying the Igbo,
South Carolinians were by no means unique. Both in South Carolina and
Haiti, slaves from the Niger delta, most of whom were Igbo shipped from
the two principal ports of Bonny and Calabar, were considered suicidal.[12] In
Jamaica, Igbo slaves were regarded as manageable but deceitful, while prone
to suicide if mistreated.[13] The unfavorable assessment of the Igbo began
even before they landed in the New World and centered on their behavior
during the Middle Passage, in which, according to Barbot, they were "very
weak and slothful; but cruel and bloody in their temper, always quarreling,
biting and fighting, and sometimes choaking and murdering one another,
without any mercy, as happened to several aboard our ship."[14] Assuming this
is an accurate description, and the behavior so aberrant that it merited
comment, there are several explanations for what took place on this slaver,
some having to do with conditions on the slaver itself, whereas others relate
more to conditions in the Bight of Biafra and its hinterland. An examination
of these conditions will reveal that, whether in the slaver or on North
American soil, the impulse to resist inspired many of the various responses
of the Igbo to enslavement. Of those responses, suicide is the most striking.

Without question, captives from all over West and West Central Africa reacted to enslavement and dislocation by committing suicide. An unthinkable act in Igbo and most other African societies, self-destruction became a plausible solution to many transplanted into the hostile world of white "spirits." It is intriguing, then, to read that the Igbo were perceived as more disposed to suicide than any other group. Mullin writes that the Igbo were viewed everywhere as "suicidally despondent."[15] Phillips records that whereas Igbo women were industrious, the men were "lazy, despondent and prone to suicide."[16] Littlefield summarizes the English depiction of the Igbo as "melancholy and suicidal, sickly, unattractive, and superstitious."[17] The sources are therefore unanimous in ascribing to the Igbo greater self-destructive tendencies; such ascription demands some rational explanation. However, before an explication can be attempted, a more immediate question emerges: Is there any corroborative evidence for this alleged suicidal proclivity?

Interestingly, there does indeed appear to be tentative yet potentially corroborative evidence that more closely associates suicide with the Igbo than any other African group. Specifically, the substantiating information is to be found in folktales of so-called flying Africans. It would be appropriate at this point to initiate a discussion of this body of folklore for the purpose of establishing a more credible link between the Igbo and suicide.

The WPA interviews along the Georgia coast and sea islands uncovered a wealth of information, some of which is used in examining the Muslim presence in America in Chapter 4. Yet another theme (and there are several) emerging from those interviews concerns Africans who could "fly," a theme particularly curious in that it is rarely mentioned in the volumes of WPA interviews of former slaves conducted in other states. In coastal Georgia, in contrast, it was prominent. In the extreme northeastern section of Savannah, in a neighborhood called Old Fort, former slave Jack Wilson had the following to say about the subject: "Some hab magic powuh wut come tuh um frum way back in Africa. Muh mothuh use tuh tell me bout slabes jis bring obuh from Africa wut hab duh supreme magic powuh. Deah wuz a magic pass wud dat dey would pass tuh udduhs. Ef dey belieb in dis magic, dey could scape an fly back tuh Africa."[18] At Tin City, east of Savannah, former bondsman Paul Singleton told a similar tale: "Muh daddy use tuh tell me all duh time bout folks wut could fly back tuh Africa. Dey could take wing an jis fly off."[19] That this was an important topic is evinced by the number of times it is mentioned in the Georgia coastal collection, which is many, and by Singleton's use of the phrase "all duh time." Moses Brown, also of Tin City, testified that his "gran use tuh tell me bout folks flyin back tuh Africa," as did fellow citizen Emma Monroe: "Duh ole folks use tuh tell us chillun duh story bout people dat flied off tuh Africa. I blieb um bout flyin."[20]

The ability to fly was associated exclusively with native-born Africans, who were believed to possess supernatural power capable of such a feat. American-born or country-born blacks are never depicted as having this ability or experience. Some may claim to have witnessed related phenomena, including James Moore of Tin City, who stated, "I seen folks disappeah right fo muh eyes. Jis go right out uh sight. Dey do say dat people brought frum Africa in slabery times could disappeah an fly right back tuh Africa. Frum duh tings I see myself I blieb dat dey could do dis."[21] But others, such as Old Henry Gamble of Frogtown (on the western edge of Savannah), depended on childhood stories: "Wen I wuz a boy I heah lots uh stories bout people flyin. Some folks brung obuh frum Africa could fly off aw disappeah anytime dey wanted tuh."[22] This power was not only the exclusive property of the African-born but also for the express purpose of returning to Africa (as opposed to flying just to be flying), as Dorothy Johnson of Springfield (west of Savannah) made clear: "Duh ole folks use tuh tell bout duh people wut could take wing an fly right back to Africa."[23] These people had no trouble accepting the notion that Africans could fly, for Africa was for them a mystical place and source of great wonder. Thomas Smith of Yamacraw (in Savannah), in discussing the supernatural exploits of Moses and Pharaoh and the fact that they took place in Africa, observed the following: "Well, den, duh descendants ub Africans hab duh same gif tuh do unnatchul ting. Ise heahd duh story uh duh flyin Africans an I sho belieb it happens."[24]

Accounts of flying Africans and the Igbo come together on St. Simons Island, at a place called "Ebo Landing." The account of Ebo Landing is well known throughout the coastal area. According to Wallace Quarterman (b. 1844) of Darien, a group of Igbo workers had just received a beating from an overseer: "Anyways, he whip um good an dey gits tuhgedduh an stick duh hoe in duh fiel an den say 'quack, quack, quack,' an dey riz up in duh sky an tun hesef intuh buzzuds an fly right back tuh Africa."[25] In what may have been an allusion to the same event, Priscilla McCullough, also of Darien and born three years "before freedom" in Sumter, South Carolina, related the following: "Duh slabes wuz out in duh fiel wukin. All ub a sudden dey git tuhgedduh an staht tuh moob roun in a ring. Roun dey go fastuhnfastuh. Den one by one dey riz up an take wing an fly lak a bud."[26] The association with movement within a ring and the ability to fly points to the relationship between African ring ceremonies, the ancestral abode, and relations with the divine.[27] That is, ring ceremonies were very much used to invoke the presence of both ancestors and deities and served as media by which human beings entered into a shared experience with them. It is instructive, therefore, that a ring ceremony would precede the return flight to Africa, as it was very much concerned with entering an altered dimension.

The account of Shad Hall of Sapelo Island, an important source for the early Muslim community in Georgia, is very revealing. After mentioning that Africans knew how to make a hoe work by itself, he turned his attention to the subject of flying:

Doze folks could fly too. Dey tell me deah's a lot ub um wut wuz bring heah an dey ain much good. Duh massuh wuz fixin tuh tie um up tuh whip um. Dey say, "Massah, yuh ain gwine lick me," and wid dat dey runs down tuh duh ribbuh. Duh obuhseeuh he sho tought he ketch um wen dey git tuh duh ribbuh. But fo he could git tuh um, dey riz up in duh eah an fly away. Dey fly right back tuh Africa. I tink dat happen on Butler Ilun.[28]

There are several points to be made concerning this account. First, it is a reference to a signal event, possibly the story of Ebo Landing. Second, the slaves in the account, presumably Igbo, were experiencing suffering unusual even for a slave ("dey ain much good"), owing to the Middle Passage, events leading up to their capture in Africa, or those following their importation to America. Their condition was such that they were unproductive, and rather than accept punishment, they chose to fly back to Africa. Interestingly, they first had to go to the river.

Although it is possible to read into this story the influence of Moses and the parting of the Red Sea, there is something more ominous here. When asked about Ebo Landing, Floyd White of St. Simons stated that he was very familiar with the account, but that he knew the Igbo had not flown back to Africa.[29] That is, Floyd White knew what the contemporaries of these flying Africans also knew, that the Igbo had committed collective suicide by marching into the river and drowning themselves.[30] What the Jamaican planters had reported as their own experience had apparently also taken place in Georgia: When pushed to the wall, the Igbo were more likely than others to take it beyond the limit. Beyond this single, famous incident of group suicide, there is another account of similar phenomena in North Carolina. Although a specific connection to the Igbo is not established in the story, such is a possibility, given the earlier discussion:

About the beginning of this century when the large Collins plantation on Lake Phelps, Washington County, was being cleared a number of negroes just from Africa were put on the work. One of the features of the improvement was the digging of a canal. Many of the Africans succumbed under this work. When they were disabled they would be left by the bank of the canal, and the next morning the returning gang would find them dead. They were kept at night in cabins on the shore of the lake. At night they would begin to sing their native songs, and in a short while would become so wrought up that, utterly oblivious to the danger involved, they would grasp their bundles of personal effects, swing them on their shoulders, and setting their faces towards Africa, would march down into the water singing as they marched till recalled to their senses only by the drowning of some of the party. The owners lost a number of them this way, and finally had to stop the evening singing. This incident was related to my informant by the gentleman who was overseer on this plantation where the incident occurred.[31]

In addition to the foregoing examples, there remain numerous references to individual flights of the African-born, who from time to time cast down their hoes and simply "disappeehed." Some of these stories are probably references to absconding, but the fact that the American-born never similarly vanish suggests that many of these flights were suicides, and that the Igbo were disproportionately represented in these tragedies. In any event, a close link between the Igbo and suicide was clearly established in the minds of many planters, and a self-terminating labor force was clearly out of the question.

To the degree that it existed, how did the African rationalize such behavior? To begin, the belief was very strong within the African-based community that at death one returned to the land of one's birth. Thus flying via suicide was a sure way, perhaps the only way, to get back, at which point one could be reincarnated and live in the land of family and relations, far away from the experience called America. Concerning the African-born, former slave Charles Ball wrote: "They are universally of the opinion, and this opinion is founded in their religion, that after death they shall return to their own country, and rejoin their former companions and friends, in some happy region, in which they will be provided with plenty of food, and beautiful women, from the lovely daughters of their own native land."[32] For the Igbo, then, suicide was perhaps the ultimate form of resistance, as it contained within it the seed for regeneration and renewal. The story of Ebo Landing is an attempt to convey this message, that something more profound than simple suicide had taken place. That the slave community chose to discuss this decision to die in more euphemistic terms is consistent with a metaphysical perspective.

The Igbo may have indeed chosen the option of resistance by way of self-destruction more than did members of other ethnicities. It may also be the case that when they made such a choice, it tended to be dramatic. But of course, suicide was only one form of rebellion. Another was absconding. On this topic, what is striking about accounts of Igbo runaways is the frequency with which women are mentioned. In stark contrast to the Akan and others, there are relatively numerous accounts of runaway Igbo women, so much so that Littlefield comments: "It is remarkable that Ibos as a group and the Bight of Biafra as an area had a greater proportional representation of women among runaways than were produced by the native black populace of South Carolina. In this they differed from all other African entities."[33] Of course, this could be partially explained by the higher proportion of Igbo women imported into North America. However, given that North America imported higher percentages of women in general than did other slaveholding societies, the prominence of Igbo women requires further examination by way of their background and will be undertaken later in the chapter.

With the exception of the first example, which involves a group of runaways, all of the English notices concerning individual absconding Igbo women were found in South Carolina newspapers. Thomas Lamboll of James Island, for example, reported the escape of a group of slaves in August 1765, among whom was "one negro slave Ebo wench, named Amoretta."[34] In August 1773 John Champneys placed an ad for a woman named "Banaba, Of a yellowish Complexion, looks like an Eboe Negroe."[35] The owner further commented that Banaba was a "remarkable fine Seamstress" and expressed concern that she may have been taken away by "evil disposed white Persons." In July 1784, among those held at the workhouse was "a Negroe Wench of the Eboe country, cannot speak English . . . about 20 or 25 years of age, can't tell her master's name or her own name."[36] Then there is the case of nineteen-year-old Tenah of the "Hebo Country," who had escaped from Gerald Fitzgibbon in July 1782.[37]

In August 1779, Jacob W. Harvey placed a notice seeking the whereabouts of a young woman "of the Eboe Country . . . speaks exceeding good English, her country Marks on her Forehead, which will not appear unless closely examined."[38] Edmund Bellinger of Ashley-Ferry reported in August 1768 the disappearance of "Phillis, of the Ebo country, speaks good English, and a little upon the yellowish order; she is supposed to be harboured in or about Charles-Town."[39] In September of the following year, Joshua Beard sought information on twenty-five-year-old Sue of the "Eboe country," who bore a "remarkable scar on her head."[40] Finally, Peter Guerry of St. Stephen's Parish took out an ad in December of the same year for "Becky, of the Ebo country, but looks more like a country born, and speaks tolerable good English."[41]

Although these notices for the most part concern women who ran away as individuals, it is also the case that Igbo women ran away in groups. There are, in fact, sixteen notices in all of the English newspapers consulted in which an Igbo woman ran away with at least one other person. This produces a total of twenty-three notices involving Igbo women, for which the ratio of group-to-individual escapes is about 2 to 1. Many of the group escapes involving Igbo women were actually families on the run. In September 1747, for example, Thomas Chisham of St. Helena Island placed a notice in the *South Carolina Gazette* featuring "Cudjo a sensible Coromantee Negro Fellow, about 45 Years old, stutters, and his wife Dinah, an Ebo wench that speaks very good English."[42] In March 1748 Patrick Brinnon discovered that Prince, a twenty-six-year-old "Angola Negro Man" had escaped with an "Ebo Wench, aged about 19 Years, named Lydia."[43] James Reid of Ponpon, South Carolina, complained that one of his slave families had been missing for twelve months, consisting of "Ben, Guiney born, with his wife, named Linda, Ebo born, and her child. They are supposed to be on Edisto, or some of the small islands near it."[44] Then there was the case of "Andrew of the Angola Country, and his Wife named Affey, a Callabar," who had fled owner John Gaillard in February 1770 and had been missing for over a year.[45] Affey, described as a "tall black Wench" (as opposed to "short" Andrew), had taken "her" infant child with them.

In some instances, women placed their lives in great peril to keep their families intact, as was true of Phebe of the "Eboe Country," described as speaking "tolerably plain, her Teeth filed." In June 1777 Phebe escaped from her owner with her husband Sampson, who was wanted for murder in North Carolina.[46] In other cases, whole extended families sought to leave the state of servility, apparently the situation on Mary Thomas's South Carolina plantation in January 1781, when Old Rose, a "short black Ebo wench" (in anticipation of W. E. B. Du Bois's depiction of Marcus Garvey), decided to take her son Dick, age twenty-two; her daughters Country Sue and Celia, the latter age thirty-six; her granddaughter Elsey (Celia's daughter), age six; and Cato, "an elderly fellow, of yellow complexion, and husband of the above Celia, but perhaps changed," and leave for good. They were accompanied by several others, including the Angolan Kate, "with her country marks about her face," and Town Sue (as opposed to Country Sue).[47]

Unlike examples involving Senegambians, this inquiry did not uncover instances in which women formed exclusive groups and ran away. Rather, when traveling with others, there was at least one male involved, usually someone relatively familiar. It can also be stated that in several of the above examples, specific ethnicities are associated with Igbo women, especially those allegedly from Angola. An analysis of Igbo men reveals similar associations. Such interactions are important and will be discussed later.

The Igbo presence in Louisiana can also be noted. Midlo Hall has determined that those from the Bight of Biafra accounted for 8.6 percent of the slave population between 1720 and 1820, a sizable representation that is reflected in the Louisiana newspapers.[48] For example, "un nègre nouveau, nation Ibo" was advertised as a captured runaway in December 1807; the same person may have been the subject of a January 1808 notice.[49] In October 1806, an unnamed "Négresse" was advertised for sale in New Orleans, of the "nation Ibo, parlant français et anglais."[50] Jupiter and Babb, each in their thirties and of the "Macua" and Igbo nations, respectively, were held in the New Orleans workhouse in January 1809 and were said to both speak "bien français."[51] In contrast, Susanne, an Igbo also held in the work-house, may not have been able to speak French, for she "did not want to say her master's name."[52] Of these four Igbo individuals, three were women.

Regarding the Igbo as a whole, there are a total of ninety-six advertise-ments in both English and French newspapers in which Igbo persons are clearly identified. Seventy involve men only, with thirty-seven running away in groups and thirty-four absconding as individuals, a rough equivalence. When European languages are mentioned, thirteen out of thirty-three men, or 39.4 percent, spoke one or more of these languages "tolerably" or better. This is compared with seven out of ten Igbo women who were able to do the same. These figures are clearly very crude, but they suggest that women, at least among the Igbo, were more prone to abscond after acquiring some proficiency in the dominant language, perhaps viewing it as a tool necessary to the success of the venture.

Slaveholders could be very attentive to details when it came to describing runaway Igbo men. In June 1735, Peter Roberts of Santee, South Carolina, depicted Primus, an "Ebo Negro Man," as having a "very yellow complexion with Scars on each side of his Stomach down his Belly, he is a little Fellow."[53] George Smith Jr. of St. Thomas Parish posted an ad in July 1778 for the return of "Frank, of the Eboe country . . . has his country marks down his wrists, arms and shoulders, his teeth filed sharp."[54] Then there is the case of Dick, who fled B. Casey of Charleston in July 1804. He was believed to be "of the Eboe nation, and had his country marks at the corner of his right and left eyes and another mark just below the pit of his stomach or thereabouts; he can write a tolerable good hand and read. . . . Dick is not a cole black, but rather of the copper colour."[55] There is also the example of Charlestonian David Saylor, who in July 1785 placed the following ad in the *South Carolina Weekly Gazette*: "Run away, and is supposed to be either lurking about town, or between that and the Quarter-House, a negro man of the Callabar coun-try."[56] The man was about twenty-two years old, "yellowish," with filed teeth, having "his face marked with small strokes under each temple, also two scars crossways on the body, one under each breast."

Concerning skilled labor, the runaway slave advertisements provide little evidence to suggest any significant correlation between the Igbo and such positions in North America. Other than the aforementioned Banaba, there is another reference to someone who was possibly Igbo and trained in a vocational capacity. Quamina was characterized in October 1753 as an "Ebo fellow, by trade a cooper, speaks little or no English, very well known in Charles-Town, where he is supposed to be harboured."[57] The absence of skilled Igbo persons in the runaway slave literature reflects at least two factors: one, the Igbo were necessarily in the ranks of skilled workers in Virginia and Maryland, where ethnicity was not emphasized; and two, they were ill-received and numerically few in South Carolina and Georgia, so they were not given such jobs.

What emerges from the foregoing discussion of the Igbo is a group of people who were virtually stigmatized in South Carolina and Georgia, where they responded to their victimization in very emphatic, decisive and irreversible ways, and where such victimization probably explains their prominence in suicide accounts despite their small numbers. In Virginia and Maryland, on the other hand, there is a relative absence of comparable traditions concerning Igbo behavior and response. Without question, the Igbo, along with others, resisted their subjugation. However, non-Igbo methods of resistance did not include, at least not with the same frequency, sensational acts of self-destruction. What is necessary at this point, then, is an examination of the Igbo antecedent, both cultural and historical, which will provide important insights into the Igbo reaction to enslavement and concomitant contribution to the African American identity.

The Bight of Biafra contained a number of ethnic groups, including the Igbo, the Ibibio, the Igala, the Efik, the Ijo, the Ogoni, and so on, representing an area of some cultural and economic diversity. Of these ethnicities, the Igbo, Ibibio, and Ijo form the largest and most distinct groups, which in turn can be further subdivided into smaller cultural communities.[58] However, with one notable exception, the vast majority of scholars working on the slave trade in the region conclude that most of the captives exported from the Bight of Biafra were Igbo. Lovejoy has asserted in one place, for example, that the "overwhelming majority" of slaves from the Bight of Biafra were Igbo, and Ibibio secondarily.[59] He quantified that assertion in another, estimating that for the first half of the nineteenth century, around 75 percent of the captives from Biafra "still came from the Igbo-Ibibio area."[60] Northrup echoes Lovejoy, stating the following:

It was the eighteenth century, however, which saw the greatest growth in trade, as the region became one of the most important sources of slaves. The number of slaves taken from the hinterland of the Bight of Biafra rose to very large numbers after 1730. Indeed, throughout the second half of the eighteenth century this area provided a third of all the slaves taken from Africa in French and English ships and two-fifths of those so taken in the first decade of the nineteenth century. Of these slaves half or more appear to have been Igbo in origin, and the number of Igbo slaves exported in the period 1751–1810 was probably in the neighbourhood of 8,000 to 10,000 a year.[61]

Manning concurs, estimating that captives out of the Bight of Biafra were either Igbo or Ibibio, having been forced to walk relatively short distances from the interior to the coast.[62] Dividing the Bight of Benin into its eastern and western sections, Alagoa and Isichei agree that captives from the eastern Niger delta were predominantly Igbo.[63]

One of the few but notable exceptions to this consensus is Afigbo, who has written that the trade's impact upon Igbo history has been "unduly exaggerated," and that the slave trade was "largely external to Igbo society."[64] Afigbo explains elsewhere that the absence of centralization among the Igbo argues against extensive slave raiding, although he allows for the sale of slaves through market forces, an important vehicle for "a society lacking an organised system of incarceration for prisoners to rid itself of criminals and misfits."[65] Although Afigbo's critique of the means by which slaves were produced is tenable (though his characterization of the victims most uncharitable), he has not produced the kind of argument, based upon a reassessment of the data relating to the trade, that would effectively refute the finding of the majority of scholars concerned. The present study therefore acknowledges Afigbo's dissent but necessarily embraces the consensus.

Historically, Igbo culture and society were characterized by high population densities, political decentralization, and an agrarian economy. The Igbo originated in the Niger-Benue confluence and then migrated long ago to their present homeland, the territory between the Niger and Cross Rivers (although many Igbo live both west of the Niger and east of the Cross).[66] One of the most important sites to develop was the iron-based culture of Nok (floruit 500 B.C.E. to 200 C.E.), whose technology was apparently transferred to the early Igbo community of Igbo-Ukwu.[67] The famous bronzes of Benin and Ife, created no later than the tenth century C.E., are also associated with Igbo-Ukwu.[68]

It is probable that by the beginning of the seventeenth century the major Igbo groups had settled into those areas they currently occupy, but it is by no means incontrovertible that they saw themselves as a distinct ethnicity. Equiano, writing in 1789, certainly seemed to think so, as he very liberally referred to the people of the area as the "Eboe."[69] Passing through a number of villages after his capture (en route to the sea), he produced an argument for Igbo cultural unity by stating that, although "a great many days' journey from my father's house, yet these people [his present captor-hosts] spoke exactly the same language with us."[70] As his trek continued, he marveled that "all the nations and people I had hitherto passed through, resembled our own in their manners, customs, and language."[71] The fact that he was only eleven years old at the time of his kidnapping (1756) suffices to explain his naïveté and enhances his credibility.

Support for Equiano's categorization of the Igbo can be found in two independent sources. The first is the Englishman Baikie's claim that "the name Ibo or Igbo is familiarly employed amongst the natives as London is among us."[72] That the statement antedates colonial rule in Igboland implies that Igbo ethnicity cannot be the brainchild of the district officer (or the metropole). The second source consists of Igbo traditions from their core areas of settlement, traditions which "reinforce the view that many village-groups were aware of the fact that they belonged to the Igbo ethnic group before the advent of Europeans."[73] Examples include Igbo-Ukwu and Amaigbo ("the abode of the Igbo"), communities held in high esteem and seen by many (in the case of Amaigbo) as the ancestral homeland. Thus Cookey's assertion that Igbo communities share "a great many characteristics which have given them, in addition to their language, an identity as a national group" is certainly plausible.[74] At the very least, it is probable that although the Igbo of the eighteenth century were first and foremost loyal to their respective villages and village groups, many were very much aware of their shared qualities. This latent potential of Igbo ethnicity matured very rapidly under the pressures of North American slavery.

The smallest social unit among the Igbo, paralleling the Mende and the Akan, was the extended family, or *umunna*.[75] Most Igbo were patrilineal, but in some cases a double unilineal descent or double descent system was used. Families lived in compounds (singular *obu*, *ezi*, or *obi*), a number of which comprised a village, or *ogbe*.[76]

The free population consisted of the peasantry (*diala*) and the nobility (the *amadi*). The nonfree included semislaves given to creditors to secure loans;[77] full slaves (*ohu* or *oru*), strangers procured for domestic tasks; and the *osu*, individuals "offered to a god as the subject or declared the subject of a god."[78] The *osu* were the absolute dread of Igbo society; there were apparently few slaves or *osu* in the interior of Igboland prior to the eighteenth century and the rise of the slave trade.

It has been demonstrated that Igbo women featured large as runaways in America. Their sense of independence can be traced to Igboland itself, where they distinguished themselves in multiple arenas. In commerce, men usually conducted long-distance trade, but women controlled local exchange.[79] Meek has written that "perhaps the most striking feature of Ibo life is the keenness displayed by the women in petty trade."[80] An Igbo woman had the right to keep any money that she earned "by her own efforts," including her market activity. In addition to trading, women may have also made and sold pottery, keeping the proceeds.[81]

Perhaps in response to the intense raiding of the period, it was Equiano's experience that women regularly defended the village: "even our women are warriors, and march boldly out to fight along with the men." Equiano in fact witnessed a battle between his village and another, in which "there were many women as well as men on both sides; among others my mother was there, and armed with a broad sword."[82] This fierceness of spirit was displayed in the disproportionate number of Igbo female runaways in America and can be seen in the decision to commit suicide.

But it was as mother and wife, responsibilities seen in harmony with her role as keeper of the soil, that the Igbo woman was most celebrated. Matters of fertility, over which the earth mother Ala presided, constituted the special preserve of women. Maidens were expected to be virgins at marriage, and young brides entered "fattening rooms" in order to become more plump and thus appeal more readily to the Igbo sense of beauty and desirability.[83] Once married, a wife expected her husband to provide her with her own residence within the compound, along with clothing and land for farming.[84] Women had the right to abandon their husbands of their own volition and were protected by their relatives from abusive spouses. A woman could hold titles (to be discussed shortly), and although she could not inherit land, she could "be given the usufruct of a piece of land by their father or husband."[85] Whatever property she did own was inherited by her children.

The Igbo institution of "woman marriage" also merits some attention.[86] According to this arrangement, a "female husband" could pay the bride-wealth for a maiden and "dispose of her rights" in the bride by either allowing her husband to cohabitate with her and accept her as a cowife or by allowing the bride to establish her own compound and choosing a lover (*iko*) for her based upon the female husband's own criteria. In either case, the children of these unions belonged to the female husband. The latter were women who either had never had a child, had lost children to death, or had only female children. Beyond alleviating a social stigma, woman marriage had a practical aspect in that, according to Igbo law, a widow without male children could not inherit any movable property from the deceased husband.

There was therefore a relationship between the relative freedom women enjoyed in Igboland and their need to reclaim the same in North America. The Igbo reputation for suicide, on the other hand, may be partially explained by political liberties that paralleled the social. In fact, one of the more distinctive features about Igbo civilization was its village democracies. That is, political power was exercised in Igboland on a part-time basis and only within a limited number of public arenas. There was no single village head, and suprapolitical organization usually did not extend beyond the village group, a collection of several autonomous villages.[87] In contrast to the urbanized Hausa to the north and Yoruba to the west, the Igbo, with some exceptions, did not create large towns and centralized political structures. Rather, they chose to remain rural, decentralized, and highly democratic. The latter characteristic was best demonstrated when a decision had to be made at the village level; village heads were required to convene all of the male adults of the village and engage in an "exhaustive deliberation" of the issue at hand. Igbo democracy would also have implications for the practice of African American Christianity, as will be demonstrated in Chapter 9.

Afigbo has analyzed the political systems of the Igbo along with those of the Ibibio, the Ijo, and the Ogoja, all of which were decentralized and "split into a large number of tiny, politically equivalent and autonomous units."[88] He divides their systems into "the democratic village republic" and the "constitutional village monarchy," the former maintained by the Igbo, Ibibio, and Ogoja, the latter by the riverain Igbo, the coastal Ibibio or Efik, and the Ijo. The state systems of the riverain Igbo were erected and modeled after those of the Edo of Benin and the Igala of Idah, who began to assert their influence along the Niger after the fourteenth century.[89] Here, Igbo states such as Onitsha and Aboh had a king, or *obi*, chosen from a royal lineage.

In addition to the freedoms flowing from democratic institutions, another factor influencing Igbo behavior in North America was their expulsion from the land. In every aspect of Igbo civilization, land was critical. It was not only the basis for the support of physical life but also played a central role in the cosmological and overall philosophical understanding of the Igbo. It is Afigbo's observation that ironworking and agricultural skills led to the Igbo's mastery of their environment: "Largely because of agriculture, land (*ala*) more or less became the center of Igbo existence. It was for them not only the most important economic asset, but also the most vital and the most active spirit force in their lives."[90] Land assumed a "very prominent place in Igbo religion and cosmology. It was worshipped, and it was a hard taskmistress which, on provocation, could cause the harvests to fail and men to die prematurely."[91] Land was ultimately owned by the lineage, not the individual.[92] It was the responsibility of the *okpara*, or lineage head, to oversee the equitable distribution of lineage or communal land, called *ofo* land; for this purpose the *okpara* wielded the *ofo* staff, symbol of ancestral authority.[93] The chief crops included yams (cultivated by men and the most highly prized crop), palm fruit (next to yams in importance), cassava, varieties of cocoyams, maize, beans, plantains, okra, and rice.[94]

To discuss the land is to discuss the goddess of the land, Ala or Ana. The earth mother was functionally the most important deity in most Igbo communities, as she was the most feared and respected, although she was not the high god.[95] The land (*ala*) and the earth mother (Ala) were inextricably associated and represented a standard by which any violation of Igbo law was categorized and subsequently punished.[96] The land "imposed innumerable laws and taboos to guide conduct between man and man and between man and itself. The transgression of any of these rules, known as *omenala* [conduct sanctioned by the land] was promptly punished."[97] Any violation of *omenala*—which included homicide, suicide, kidnapping, adultery, birthing twins or physically impaired infants, poisoning, stealing, and yam stealing (a separate offense unto itself)—was considered an abomination (*nso ani*).[98] Such crimes were not only punished but also required that the land itself be cleansed by way of special rites.[99]

Ala, although occupying a place of great reverence among the Igbo, was but one among a number of Igbo deities. The high god and creator was Chineke or Chukwu, who represented male and female elements (*chi* and *eke*) and recalls the Senufo concept of the high god.[100] *Chi* and *eke* were viewed as two complementary halves of a whole; their unity, Chineke, represented harmony and completion. Chineke also created the *alusi* or *agbara*, or "spiritual forces," including the sun (Anyanwu, who was associated with good fortune) and the sky (Igwe). Whereas Chineke is "always benevolent" (though removed), the *alusi* can bless or destroy, "depending on the circumstances." Other *alusi* were Ifejioka, the yam spirit, and Amadioha, responsible for lightning, sunshine, and rain.[101]

To be removed from the land was to be severed from the ancestors, an additional source of stress for those transplanted to North America. The Igbo ancestors (*ndichie*) were believed to live in the land of spirits (*ala mmuo*), and each village maintained at least one ancestral shrine.[102] The dead maintained contact with the living through the latter's sacrifices and prayers, a relationship dramatized by publicly performed masquerades or masked rituals.[103] Alongside the *ndichie*, however, was the *chi*, a personal guardian spirit or deity assigned to every Igbo person. The *chi* has been described by Isichei as a "personalized providence" that comes from Chineke or Chukwu and returns to him at a person's death. In fact, Chukwu or Chi-ukwu is literally the "great chi," "the ultimate self ordering the course and character of the universe."[104] The *chi*, in turn, was "life conceived as an animate self that guides the course of existence."[105] Henderson explain the "chi in me" as

a spiritual essence of the living self that guides and determines the course of that person's life from birth to death. It is believed that when an individual chooses to "enter the world," he makes a pact with a particular essential being (chi), selecting his length of life and his future activities; the choices so made are marked by the chi on his hand as his *akala-aka* ("marks of the hand"), or "destiny."[106]

The Igbo believed in reincarnation, or what Equiano called the "transmigration of souls."[107] Reincarnation, in turn, involves the *chi* in that, before returning to the land of the living, the deceased works "out a proper role for himself through face-to-face interaction with the creator. Guided by his *chi*— the Igbo form of guardian spirit—the reincarnating soul" chooses for herself or himself from between two options presented by the creator.[108] Only one of these options (such as long life, wealth, and so on) is what the person predicted in the preceding lifetime. A matching choice is best; however, one could make the best of a wrong choice and look forward to making a better one next time.

Uchendu explains that this bargaining session motivates the individual to "make a success of his social position or career. . . . In effect, the Igbo stress on the success goal is ideologically rooted in the reincarnation dogma."[109] That is, the stereotypic success-oriented behavior of the Igbo is a direct consequence of their spiritual beliefs. Uchendu goes on to point out that this "achievement orientation" resulted in both enhanced competition and "a sociopolitical system which is conciliar and democratic," and that the relatively wide latitude of freedom afforded by Igbo culture permitted innovation while allowing for experimentation.[110]

This achievement orientation is therefore an important feature of Igbo culture and very much related to their comportment in North America. It is not a characterization of the Igbo by those outside of the culture, but the self-projection of the Igbo, a means by which they define and thereby distinguish themselves from others. Within the culture, this conceptualization of success is represented by the philosophical construct known as *ikenga*.

Ikenga, or the "cult of the right hand," is often visually represented as a man with ram horns on his head and a machete in his right fist.[111] Meek, in observing *ikenga*'s former association with headhunting, viewed it as "the personification of a man's strength of arm, and consequently of his good fortune."[112] Boston, drawing upon his analysis of Igbo visual art, believes that *ikenga* "symbolises the person as a particular individual, contrasting his own personal achievements with those which can be ascribed to hereditary qualities or to some other external source."[113] This is not to say that Igbo society stressed individualism in the Western sense of the term; on the contrary, there was a very strong sense of community among the Igbo with regard to identity, land, economic activity, and social responsibility.[114] However, within the framework of community there was room for personal achievement, itself a reflection of the fortunes of the lineage. Perhaps even more accurately (and certainly more succinctly), Okpoko has defined *ikenga* as the symbol of a belief system that "emphasizes individual achievement" over "ascribed status."[115] Or as Henderson put it, *ikenga* "represents the essence of a man's will to success."[116]

The spirit of *ikenga*, then, can be seen in the political organization of the Igbo. It can be seen in their agricultural productivity. It can also be seen in the Igbo title system. Meek has written that the "system of title-taking is one of the most characteristic features of Ibo society."[117] There were various kinds of titles conferring different levels of status, and the Igbo, according to Uchendu, "are status seekers."[118] In fact, Uchendu believes that titles are the most important "commodity" the world has to offer to the Igbo. In perhaps overstating the case, Uchendu successfully underscores the importance of titles among the Igbo, the most important of which were found in the *ozo* system. Any individual, man or woman, could take a senior title provided the person had both sufficient wealth and familial right to make the claim.[119] Equiano's father successfully took titles, undergoing facial cicatrization and receiving the distinction of *mgburichi* (literally, "men who bear such marks," Equiano's "embrenche"); many of the country marks in America were actually "marks of grandeur" in Africa.[120]

The prospect of upward mobility, then, was very real within Igbo society. An individual could rise both economically and socially despite most circumstances of birth.[121] When the matter of social mobility is considered together with the political liberties afforded the Igbo in the village democracy, the attraction of such a social contract is evident. To transfer from such a setting to the fields of America, a transition involving the cauterization of relations with the land and the ancestors, was to cause a level of trauma too deep to convey, thus helping to explain why a number of Igbo responded suicidally. But of course this is not the complete picture. The political instability of the period militated against the integrity of Igbo life and culture, so that the Igbo were not simply pulled out of a sociocultural context, but out of a political one as well.

Following the work of Dike, Alagoa divides European activity in the Niger delta into two parts: the fifteenth century to the abolition of the slave trade in 1807; and 1807 to 1885, when palm oil and kernels, used to lubricate European machinery, became the most important export.[122] The Portuguese probably arrived in the delta soon after 1470, creating quite a stir among the coastal populations who, from "a subsistence economy, remote from the mainstreams of trade . . . moved to a position in the forefront of trade."[123] After 1472, for example, the Efik became very active in facilitating the trade between the coast and the hinterland, obtaining slaves and commodities in exchange for firearms and other European manufactures.[124]

The Igbo were exported throughout the life of the slave trade.[125] Overall export numbers were low in the sixteenth century, with a general increase from West Africa as a whole in the seventeenth. By the late 1670s and early 1680s, the coastal towns of Bonny and Elem Kalabari had emerged as major centers of trade, supplying unspecified numbers of captives.[126] Elem Kalabari was the leading entrepôt until the end of the seventeenth century, when Bonny became and remained the chief exporter of human cargo through the nineteenth century.[127] From 1700 to 1807, at the height of the transatlantic trade, the British alone exported some 1,155,590 from the Bight of Biafra (see table 2.8). The French and the Portuguese were also active in the region, although the British were by far the dominant trading partner. The densely populated Biafran hinterland proved to be an extremely rich source of labor for New World plantations.

As Lovejoy has summarized, the vast majority of the captives sold at Bonny, Elem Kalabari, and elsewhere along the Biafran coast came from the interior, not the coast itself.[128] The captives were procured chiefly through small-scale raids and widespread kidnapping; wars and punitive raids are described as having played "only a very small part" of the slave recruitment process.[129] These procurement procedures would have consequences for the affected societies beyond mere population depletion. One was the stimulation of slave markets throughout the region. From such markets as Aboh, Equiano and others were transported in large riverboats through the maze of creeks and lagoons of the Niger delta to the coast and beyond to the waters of the Atlantic.[130]

One of the most important groups to become involved in the slave trade were the Aro, an Igbo subgroup. Hunters and fishers prior to the dawn of the transatlantic exchange, the Aro began to organize themselves, perhaps in the mid-seventeenth century, for purposes of long-distance trading.[131] They established centers throughout eastern Nigeria, and after trading in such luxury items as horses, cattle, beads, and slaves, they soon became exclusively associated with slaves.[132] In exchange, the Aro received textiles, manufactures, firearms, tobacco, alcohol, and ornaments.[133]

The Aro quickly came to control most of the trade routes extending from the Igbo hinterland to the coast.[134] The power and influence of the Aro were generated primarily from their exalted spiritual status among the Igbo, itself a function of the Aro's control of the Oracle of Arochuku.[135] Arochuku was "the seat of the most powerful shrine in the then Ibo land," while the Aro themselves were called *Umuchukwu*, or "children of God."[136] The Oracle of Arochuku played an important role in the acquisition of captives by finding people guilty of crimes or accusing them of witchcraft, thus feeding them into the slave trade via Aro merchants.[137] Should individual villages reject the pronouncements of the oracle, the Aro would employ such mercenaries as the Ada and Aban, Igbo subgroups known for their military prowess, to enforce the promulgations.[138]

As a result of the tremendous demand for slaves in the Bight of Biafra, the level of raiding and kidnapping reached incredible proportions. This, in turn, had a "debilitating, dehumanizing" effect upon Igbo society as a whole, as the "essentially local nature of their loyalties led the little Ibo states to make war on each other, frequently kidnapping each other's members."[139] The Oracle of Arochuku "became an instrument of exploitation among the Igbo" in that the autochthonous system of justice was altered in order to advance slaving interests.[140] Offenders who would have normally paid fines for such crimes as petty theft were now sold as slaves; the innocent were convicted of alleged crimes and likewise sold away. "There was no peace; there was no justice. This meant anarchy, and anarchy produced even more slaves."[141] Indeed, there were over 1 million of them in the eighteenth century alone.

It is out this more complete context, then, that the Igbo came to the shores of North America. Descriptions of sullenness and infighting were, no doubt, reflections of the means by which they arrived at captivity. Igbo culture, with its emphasis on achievement as represented in *ikenga* and its ties to the land via veneration of Ala, was necessarily impacted by the insecurities of the ever-expanding slave trade. It was consequently a very cultured but insecure and vulnerable people who were forced to suffer further humiliation in the ports of the Chesapeake and, to a lesser extent, in the thoroughfares of Charleston, Savannah, and New Orleans.

Faced with the prospect of slavery in a strange land, some Igbo began to think the unthinkable, and to act upon it.[142] In Igboland, suicide was a violation of *omenala* and an abomination; the offender was denied a place in the ancestral burial grounds, "the worst social humiliation for any Igbo."[143] It also increased the possibility of transmigration to an entirely different life form in the next life cycle. It could also involve a period of spiritual limbo, for "unhappy spirits who die bad deaths, and lack correct burial rites, cannot return to the world of the living, or enter that of the dead. They wander homeless and dispossessed, expressing their grief by causing harm among the living."[144]

What, then, could have possibly convinced a number of Igbo to take their own lives, given these risks? How could their basic assumptions about life and death have been so radically altered that they even considered such a course of action? The answer can only lie in their experience as slaves; many must have found it worse than death. Convinced they had entered a horror zone beyond the ability of human endurance, they rethought their existence and reasoned alternatively. They reassessed the meaning of life in light of their novel circumstances. And they concluded that, as they were now living the converse of life, suicide was the means back to that life, back to Africa. They therefore began to fly back to the land of their own people, for suicide in the context of evil would necessitate a meeting with Chineke. At that meeting, each Igbo would renegotiate the next life, and return to the soil of the ancestors, far from the shores of America. For a number of Igbo, then, flying back was a risk worth taking.

. . . .

Rivaling the number of Igbo and others coming out of the Bight of Biafra were the Bantu-speaking populations of West Central Africa, or Congo (formerly Zaire) and Angola. For reasons relating to continuities in culture within West Central Africa and to difficulties in distinguishing between the separate export trades from Congo and Angola, this vast area is treated as a continuum in the literature. Regarding the whole of the transatlantic trade, the contribution of the region was huge, constituting some 40 percent of all Africans transported to the New World between 1500 and 1870, with most going to Brazil.[145]

To be sure, there are several areas that must be traversed in order to reach Congo from southeastern Nigeria. There are two, specifically, that require mention: Cameroon and Gabon, as they are currently known. Living in the former were many different groups, including Bantu speakers (such as the Duala, Bakweri, Isubu, Bassa-Bakoko, Yambassa, Bafia, Ewondo or Pauhin or Fang, Bene, and Bulu); semi-Bantu speakers (including the Bamilike, Banyang, and Tikar); the Aka or Babinga (or so-called pygmies); and northern, Sudanic peoples such as the Fulbe, Matakam, and Podoko.[146] Those slaves who found themselves bound for the Western Hemisphere mostly came from Bantu and semi-Bantu populations organized politically into smaller units. Groups such as the Bamilike and Bamum raided and were raided for slaves, who were collected and brought from the interior by the Bangwa middlemen. The merchant Duala, a patrilineal, decentralized group, bought the captives from the Bangwa and sold them to Europeans who remained on their vessels and did not have direct contact with the interior.[147]

It does not appear that Cameroon played a significant role in the transatlantic trade and in any event did not constitute an important source of slaves for North America.[148] In briefly acknowledging those who did make the fateful voyage, it is instructive to point out that many, such as the Bafut, maintained elaborate rituals featuring a ring ceremony.[149] The climactic moment of the annual ritual cycle was the observation of the year's death and rebirth. At this celebration, the luminaries of the society formed a spiral, around which the "general public dance concentric rings counter-clockwise."[150] This reference anticipates the discussion of ring ceremonies in African American culture. The Cameroonian contingent, though small in number, would have made some contribution.

Sparsely populated and bisected by the equator, Gabon's principal role in the transatlantic trade was supplying navigators with a geographic location from which they could pick up American-bound trade winds, specifically at Cape Lopez, after loading their vessels with captives from the Bight of Biafra. With an interior rain forest populated by the Aka, Gabon did not provide many laborers for New World plantations.[151]

Unlike Cameroon and Gabon, the delegation from West Central Africa was enormous, and of all those who came to North American shores from West Central Africa, some 40 percent were taken to South Carolina (in symmetry with the estimated 40 percent of the Igbo who came through the ports of the Chesapeake).[152] During the 1730s, the figure was more than 50 percent, with "Angolans" arriving in large shipments averaging 260 persons per cargo.[153] Higgins has written that Angolans in particular were the third most preferred group of Africans in South Carolina, after those from Gambia and the Gold Coast, but that tall Angolans were just as desirable.[154] Rawley has also noted South Carolina's "surprising acceptance of those from Angola" but found that Chesapeake buyers positively "disliked" Angolans.[155] Consequently, in contrast to the 40 percent importation of Igbo, the Chesapeake took in less than 17 percent (or less than one-sixth) of its slave imports from West Central Africa.[156]

Although the foregoing references specifically mention Angolans, Thornton contends that West Central Africans in South Carolina prior to 1739 were in fact Congolese, an argument premised upon the distinction between Portuguese trading in Angola (from whence captives went to Brazil) and English activities at Cabinda and points farther north.[157] However, when balanced with subsequent discussion concerning the various phases of the slave trade out of West Central Africa, it is reasonable to conclude that Angolans were among the majority Congolese during this period.

Wood and Washington Creel have put together a reliable periodization for South Carolinian importation of West Central Africans after 1739.[158] By 1740 Congolese-Angolans were numerically superior to other African ethnicities, largely the result of relatively huge Congolese-Angolan importations in the 1730s and little natural increase. This numerical domination is even more impressive given the fact that during the 1730s, "sizeable groups" of Congolese-Angolans fled the Carolina low country for the Spanish presidio at East

Florida, attracted there by the Spanish crown's "proclamation to free all runaways of foreign rivals who arrived and converted nominally to Catholicism."[159] Notwithstanding this seepage, by 1739 some 70 percent of the African-based population of 39,000 in South Carolina (along with 20,000 whites) was derived from West Central Africa; over one-half of all Africans had been in Carolina for less than ten years.

The 1739 Stono Rebellion had a dramatic effect upon the South Carolinian slaveocracy. Fear, anxiety, and insecurity resulted in a prohibitive duty on all slave imports, so that trade for the next ten years was greatly reduced. But with the expansion of rice and indigo cultivation, there was renewed demand for slave labor; between 1740 and 1776 the slave trade to Charleston once again bustled. Due to the perception of the Stono Rebellion as an Angolan insurrection, however, captives from West Central Africa were no longer desirable, whereas Senegambians and Sierra Leonians, knowledgeable in rice agriculture, were heavily recruited. Interestingly, and without benefit of explanation, the period from 1804 to 1808 represents a third and final phase in which Congolese-Angolans again come to constitute the majority of Africans imported into Charleston. This time, the demand was fueled by the spread of upland, short-staple cotton.

The post-Stono image of West Central Africans runs counter to the perception of them preceding the revolt. Littlefield has synopsized the general view of the Congolese-Angolans as "docile, comely, not especially strong, possessed of a peculiar pre-disposition towards the mechanics, but inclined to run away."[160] The reference to docility is echoed by sources in Haiti, of all places, where people from Congo were viewed as "more complacent" than others and therefore disdained by other slaves. Herskovits writes: "Tradition has it that when the blacks rose in revolt, these Congo slaves were killed in large numbers, since it was felt that they could not be trusted."[161] The Haitian material reflects the stereotyping of certain Africans by other Africans, suggesting a complex process between slave and slaveholder whereby public opinion within each was developed via a mutual exchange of information, so that what slaveholders thought of the slaves influenced what slaves thought of themselves. What the Haitian material further suggests, however, is that these influences carried specific information concerning slaves' self-perception, such that it assisted the effort to distinguish the constituent elements of the African-based community. The Congolese-Angolan-led Stono Rebellion, then, probably came to be seen (with the passing of time) as an uncharacteristic expression of Congolese-Angolan frustration, encouraged by homogenic conditions among the slave population (the fault of slaveholders, not slaves). Increased importation of other ethnicities and the expansion of upland, short-staple cotton restored the Congolese-Angolans in South

Carolina and eventually led to their renewed favored status early in the nineteenth century.

Although most from West Central Africa wound up in South Carolina and Georgia, quite a few were imported to Louisiana.[162] Beginning in 1760 and extending through 1799, their numbers were equivalent to both the Senegambians and the Fon-Ewe-Yoruba. Between 1800 and 1820, their imports constitute nearly 40 percent of the entire African trade to Louisiana. As a result, West Central Africans comprised some 35.8 percent of the whole trade to Louisiana from 1720 to 1820.

Notwithstanding their alleged docility, people from West Central Africa were also associated with absconding as much as the Igbo were identified with suicide. In comparison with the 96 ads that feature Igbo runaways, the same English and French newspapers published a total of 256 notices in which individuals from West Central Africa are listed as natives of either Congo or Angola. This 150 percent increase in volume may simply reflect the fact that so many more West Central Africans than Biafrans were in South Carolina and Georgia, where ethnicity was assigned and emphasized, than was the case in Virginia. Even so, such an active record reflects a very clear readiness on the part of West Central Africans to take flight.

It is worth noting that, as was true of the Igbo accounts, men from West Central Africa tended to abscond either as individuals or in groups at roughly the same rate. Of the 256 notices, 216 were published outside of Louisiana, and of those 216, 202 involved men who either ran away with at least one other person (for a total of 93) or by themselves (109 in all). The remaining 14 advertisements featured women who also ran away either in groups, which was less than half of the time, or as individuals. In Louisiana, women accounted for 10 of the 40 instances, or 25 percent, as opposed to their 6 percent share of the non-Louisianan activity.

It is also interesting to point out that every single advertisement in the Louisiana papers described the person(s) involved as having come from the Congo. The term *Angola* simply does not appear. Of course, New Orleans was the site of Congo Square, actually located on the outskirts of the town proper, where slaves would congregate every Sunday afternoon in good weather[163] and perform such dances as the bamboula, the babouille, the counjaille, and the calinda.[164] That Congolese far outnumbered Angolans in Louisiana is supported by Midlo Hall, who found that during the Spanish period some 91.1 percent of those who came from West Central Africa to Louisiana were from Congo, whereas 9.5 percent were from Angola.[165]

Outside Louisiana, examples of Congolese-Angolans seeking to escape include a man named "Soho, [who] speaks very little English, mark'd all over his breast [with] his country mark" and managed to get away from David

Mongin of Charleston in August 1735.[166] In contrast, there was Cordelier, who absconded from Alexander Perronneau of Wando (South Carolina) in November 1751.[167] John Raven of Horse-Savannah reported in July 1761 that his "sensible negro fellow named Dick, Angola born, near 40 years old," had been missing since June of the previous year, and that "he is supposed to be harboured on James Island, where he is well known."[168] Equally "sensible" was Bristol, a "tall Negroe fellow, very black, speaks pretty good English, Angola born," who ran away from George McIntosh's plantation on the Sapelo River in January 1769.[169] Bristol had come "from the West Indies some years ago" and was very familiar with the surrounding communities.

Occasionally the runaway slave ads mention the nonagricultural skills of the individual. For instance, Governor Wright of Georgia placed an ad in a South Carolina paper in 1768 in which Bullock, a forty-year-old Angolan and "a very good sawyer," was featured.[170] In June 1789 John R. Stevenson reported the escape of man "of the Congo country" who was a thirty-year-old cooper.[171] This same Stevenson paid for another advertisement in September 1792 for the return of Ben, "a prime field slave, boatman, and cooper."[172] As Ben was also "of the Congo country," it is possible that he was the same cooper who had absconded in 1789. Likewise, Thomas Miles of Ashepoo, South Carolina, placed a notice in the *South Carolina Gazette* in January 1754 seeking the whereabouts of an eighteen-year-old Angolan named Cudjoe who was trained as a bricklayer.[173] James Donnom of Ponpon, Georgia, stated in July 1764 that he had been searching for two men, Santee and Jemmy, since December 1763. The former had since been recaptured, having confessed that he and Jemmy were "harboured . . . by one Simon Bradley and his friend Samuel Cruse. It is supposed that Bradley has carried off Jemmy, (a short well made Angola fellow, with lifts under his eyes, he understands a little of the cooper business, and formerly belonged to John Gould of Ponpon) and may sell him either in this province or Florida."[174]

James Donnom's dilemma, besides the fact that he had lost a valuable cooper, was the problem of slaves stolen by settlers moving into the interior of Georgia and Carolina. George Tew of Charleston placed an ad in the *South Carolina Gazette* in October 1764 concerning a sixteen- or seventeen-year-old Angolan, stating: "Not having heard anything of the new negro boy I advertised in March last; and having great reason to suspect that he has been carried off by some of the back settlers; I do hereby offer a reward of fifty pounds currency."[175] Mary Thomson of South Carolina also suspected in April 1777 that "Tom, of the Angola country," had been sold "in the back country."[176] Francis Lejeau in July 1762 had similar concerns about two Angolan men named Handy and Fortune, who were previously "seen with a white man in a camp near the upper part of Wassamsaw swamp, and who was suspected to be going to Georgia."[177]

These accounts allude to the precarious nature of running away from a slaveholder in eighteenth-century North America. Not only could the abscondee be caught by the legal owner, but he was also subject to capture by others who would return him to servitude in the hinterland. James Parsens of Ashepoo complained in January 1763 that

it has lately become a pernicious custom for back-settlers when they meet with run away negroes, and for some of the magistrates and others in the back parts of the country when such negroes are brought to them, to publish purposely blind advertisements for a short time of them, and afterwards to keep them at work for themselves, instead of bringing or sending them, according to the law, to the warden or the work-house.[178]

To run away, then, was to venture into even greater uncertainty.

For many West Central Africans, the hazards involved in absconding were far outweighed by the certainty of enslavement and the possibility of recovering some aspects of life as they had known it in Africa. So they ran. In November 1763, six men and one woman, all "Angolans" who had lived in South Carolina for five years, fled their owner.[179] In August 1771, four men and one woman, all "Angolans" who had lived in South Carolina for six months and who could "speak English enough to give an account of themselves," also took flight.[180] There is evidence that these abscondees intended to reestablish their lives independent of their owners. John Vermounet of St. James Parish, South Carolina, was one such owner who in August 1784 found that five of his "new negroes from Congo" were missing, "each having a blanket, kettle, and hoe."[181] The hoe suggests a determination to strike out along a path of independent subsistence.

Abscondees also made preparations for self-defense, as was the case in August 1760, when three newly arrived Angolan men fled John Bulline of Horse-Savannah, carrying "with them an old gun with a small quantity of ammunition."[182] Often the runaways could count on the assistance of others in the African-based community, as was the situation with Angola-born Jack, who in May 1761 removed himself from the property of South Carolinian Henry Smith and was suspected of having been "harboured by negroes in or near the borough."[183] Fear of mutual assistance among the slaves was growing in South Carolina in the 1730s, given the heavy concentration of Congolese-Angolans in the colony. In 1737, two years before Stono and the realization of those fears, Isaac Porcher of Wassamaw searched for his "new

Angola Negro Man, named Clawss," noting that "as there is an abundance of Negroes in this province of that nation, he may chance to be harbour'd among some of them, therefore all masters are desired to give notice to their slaves who shall receive the same reward, if they take up the said run-away."[184] But of course, those who fled desired to get as far away from the source of oppression as possible, and some even sought to return to Africa. In Georgia, for example, three newly arrived slaves "of the Conga country" escaped from John Graham's plantation on Hutchinson Island, taking with them "a canoe and with three paddles, and it is supposed would go towards the sea."[185] Like the Igbo, these also sought to return home, choosing water over air.

Women from West Central Africa were also involved in strategies of escape. In August 1804, Betty and her husband and eight-month-old child ran away. She is described as having come from "the Angola coast, with her country marks plain to be seen in her face and on her body, particularly her back, where there is a numerous quantity of them."[186] In October 1779 Lucy was reported missing from William Clancy of South Carolina, having been depicted as "a short set wench, of the Angola country, about 20 years old, and has her country marks on both cheeks."[187] In June 1736, an ad appeared in the *South Carolina Gazette* seeking to know the whereabouts of an "Angola Negro wench named Flora."[188] Another Flora from Angola, age eighteen, was reported as a runaway from Richard Linter of Charleston in August 1740.[189] Yet another Flora, a "tall Angola Negro wench, about 40 years old," escaped from Mary Elizabeth Timothy in October 1748.[190] "Flora" must have been a popular name for Angolan women, because in February 1779 another Angolan so named, described as having "some of her country marks about her face and breast," abandoned Martha Ellis of South Carolina.[191]

West Central African women could be imported at very young ages, as was the case in December 1738 with a fourteen-year-old who belonged to a Mrs. Skinner of South Carolina.[192] Similarly, South Carolinian Alexander Garden placed an ad in September 1758 for another unnamed girl, age thirteen or fourteen.[193] Perhaps it was this same child who thirty-one years later ran away from Charlestonian Alexander Inglis in September 1789. He called her "Dumba, but very probably will call herself Bella; of the Angola country." He further described her as having been about thirty-five years old, "her country marks on her temples; is sensible and very artful, and may attempt to pass for a free woman. She has of late been very much addicted to liquor, and when under its influence is very noisy and troublesome. Having many acquaintances in Georgia, it is supposed she will endeavour to get there."[194] No doubt, the stress of living life as a woman and an African-born slave took its toll, the bottle yet another means of flight.

West Central Africans brought with them certain political, social, and cultural perspectives. The region encompassed ports from Loango to Luanda and extended to Malebo Pool in the interior. Congo's major feature was the Congo River, which runs some five hundred kilometers from Malebo Pool to the Atlantic, coursing over thirty-two cataracts along the way. The central Congo basin, in turn, contained four ecological zones, characterized by river, swamp, forest, and savannah.[195] Within the basin lived myriad ethnic groups and subgroups, featuring a multitude of languages and dialects with great cultural diversification. However, two elements tended to unify the basin: the abundance of water and the close linguistic association of the various Bantu languages and dialects. Political organization ranged from kingdoms to villages to small-scale units.

Harms has produced a useful reconstruction of Congo's experiences during the slave trade, demonstrating that the history of successive political formations in the region was directly related to, and indeed a function of, the changing and evolving nature and level of its participation in the trade. Keeping this in mind, he has divided Congolese involvement in the trade into three separate phases, the second of which witnessed Angola's eclipse of the Congo basin as the leading source of slaves from the region. This study will therefore employ Harms's overall scheme and will introduce the Angolan background during the discussion of the second phase of the transatlantic trade.

The central Congo basin was first introduced to the vagaries of the Atlantic trade in the late fifteenth century, when the area began supplying captives to the Portuguese for the latter's sugar plantations on São Tome.[196] Soon after 1530, these captives began to arrive in the New World. This first phase was centered upon the kingdom of Kongo, where earlier political consolidation resulted in the establishment of the kingdom late in the fourteenth century. Located on the south bank of the Congo River in what is now western Congo and northern Angola, Kongo was the creation of the Kikongo-speaking people, otherwise referred to as the Bakongo.[197] An absolute monarchy, Kongo was divided into six provinces.[198] From its capital at Mbanza Kongo (later São Salvador), Kongo conducted relations with the Tio kingdom to the northeast, within which was Malebo Pool. Tio was the contact point between Kongo and the upper Congo, and trade descending from Malebo Pool first passed southwest through the capital of Mbanza Kongo and then northwest to the port of Mpinda on the Congo estuary. Although some captives were from Tio and the upper Congo, most were obtained in the savannah to the south of Malebo Pool. Whether from the savannah or Malebo Pool, Kongo engaged in ever-widening campaigns in order to supply the growing demand along the coast. Among the victims were the Mbundu to the south. In the meantime, the ruling family began converting to Christianity in the late fifteenth century, and Catholicism became a royal cult. Resulting disaffection among provincial governors caused the royal family to seek Portuguese intervention in the form of musketeers, who were able to prop up the regime. In this way, Kongo's rulers became inextricably tied to the fortunes of the slave trade.

The second phase of the trade began in the 1560s and was a consequence of two factors: the proliferation of warfare and instability in the Congo basin and the rise of the Mbundu state of Ndongo in what is now northern Angola. In the course of these events, Malebo Pool declined as major source of slaves at the same time that the Portuguese shifted their trading activities from Mpinda to Luanda Bay. There they purchased captives from the Mbundu of Ndongo, who under the political authority of the *ngolas* (or "rulers," from which the term *Angola* is derived) began to reverse their fortunes.[199] The Angolan trade drew most of its captives from the hinterland in what would become Matamba and Kasanje during the second half of the seventeenth century. The Portuguese sought to achieve territorial conquest during the last quarter of the sixteenth century, but they were defeated in a war with Ndongo between 1579 and 1590. During the first half of the seventeenth century, the Mbundu and the Portuguese emerged as the key trading partners, whereas Kongo's role continued to decline.[200] In 1665 the Portuguese, who by now had become a principal force in the political affairs of the region, handed Kongo a crippling military defeat, from which the latter descended into greater political disarray. Six years later, the Portuguese defeated Ndongo as well.

The vacuum created by Ndongo's demise was quickly filled by the interior realm of Kasanje, an Imbangala state, as was Matamba, Holo, and others.[201] The Imbangala were a mixture of Lunda and Ovimbundu peoples who had combined to create roving bands of warriors. More specifically, it was the Ovimbundu *kilombo*, or male initiation and warrior society, that joined forces with the Lunda. Having settled down to establish various states after 1650 such as Kasanje, the Imbangala represented the quickly changing fortunes of polities in the region, most of which were involved in the slave trade in some capacity.

The third phase of Harms's scheme begins after 1750, which saw the focus of the trade move back north to the central Congo basin. In fact, it was during this period that the basin became the leading source of slaves for the transatlantic trade, in response to the boom in demand for slaves in the Americas, peaking around 1780. The state of Loango, also established as an absolute monarchy and inhabited by the Vili, became the center of the trade, exporting from Loango Bay.[202] To be sure, Loango had been trading with the

Portuguese since 1580 (and the Dutch after 1630), but it was the second half of the eighteenth century that saw Loango catapulted onto center stage. The search for slaves went even deeper into the interior and was serviced most successfully by the Bobangi, experts in long-distance trade. In the nineteenth century, Cabinda replaced Loango Bay as the major slave-exporting center of the region, extracting most of its slaves from Boma, a major marketplace for the northern route from Malebo Pool.

The procurement of slaves in West Central Africa was particularly brutal, as it primarily involved escalating warfare over time. In contrast to West Africa, it also witnessed Europeans, principally Portuguese, coming onshore to raid and kidnap in significant numbers. An Englishman, Thomas Clarkson, commented in 1787 about the nature of procurement in Angola, having been there for seven months: "I know of no other way of making slaves there, than by robbery."[203] In the kingdom of Loango as well as others, the slave trade was of great importance, necessitating the creation of a branch of government designed to regulate it.[204] The official in charge of regulating the trade was the *mafuk*, an appointee of the sovereign who, in turn, appointed brokers, or "markedores," middlemen who negotiated between suppliers of the captives and the Europeans. The following concerns the *mafuk*: " 'The first thing you must do when you come to the Coast of Cape Binda or Malimba,' advised a 1714 Memorandum of the Way of Trade on the Coast of Angola, 'is to go on shore and agree with the Maffoca and Gentlemen for your customs which you must endeavour to get as cheap as you can, for there is no set price. . . . But note that before you pay your customes you must be sure to agree for the Price of your Slaves.' "[205] As most captives were obtained in the hinterland, they arrived at the coast via caravans. Those who did not offer resistance were allowed to travel unfettered, whereas resistors had their hands tied behind them and a forked piece of wood, called a *bois mayombé* by the French, placed over their heads.[206] Overall, there is every evidence to suggest an efficient system of slaving.

The trade from West Central Africa was characterized by shifting foci of activity both along the coast and in the interior and was the primary factor in the rise and fall of many states. The resulting picture, mirroring similar conditions in southeastern Nigeria, is one of incredible political instability and social chaos, radiating in every direction in steadily expanding circles. The Portuguese were operating along the southeastern stretch of Africa at the same time, so that the populations of Angola and what is now Mozambique were in effect caught in a vise, with the Luba, Lunda, and the Lozi states, as well as the Swahili city-states along the southeastern coast, affected. West Central Africa is the primary focus of this discussion, however, and it is left to determine those qualities of society and culture that were able to survive the political upheaval there, only to face a challenge of a different kind in North America.

It has been stated that West Central Africa was home to numerous groups. A few have been mentioned; to give an idea of just how extensive the list could be, the ethnicities include the Bushoong, Ngunde, Pyaang, Bulaang, Bieeng, Ilebo, Idiing, Kaam, Ngongo, Kayuweeng, Kel, Shoowa, Bokila, Ngoombe, Maluk, Kete, Coofa, Cwa, Mbeengi, Leele, and the southern Mongo.[207] The Bakongo or Kikongo speakers, founders of the kingdom of Kongo, include subgroups such as the Sundi, Bwende, Kamba, and Dondo, who can be further divided into the Mpangu, Ladi, Bembu, Kunyi, Yombe, Lumbu, Bussi, Puno, and Tsangui. The list could go on, the point being that with regard to diversity, West Central Africa is a region par excellence.

In view of the foregoing, to speak in generalities is to invite inaccuracy and oversimplification. To be sure, there are commonalities in the region, such as the series of closely related, though not mutually intelligible Bantu languages.[208] But as Harms has written, the area is truly paradoxical, containing both convergent and divergent elements. This is especially true of ethnicity. Within states such as Kongo, Ndongo, Kasanje, and Loango, ethnicity was the basis of the polity and was strengthened by intense regional hostilities. At the same time, there were numerous communities beyond the recognized authority of the state, where loyalties did not transcend the smallest village unit. Once removed from the West Central African context and relocated to America, however, the commonality of the Bantu languages and cultures, their treatment as a single people by their captors, and the need to effect strategies of resistance necessarily encouraged the Congolese-Angolans to see themselves anew and forge ties of community.

As was true of the other regions discussed so far in this study, agriculture provided the material foundation for societies in West Central Africa. Various economies were based upon hoe cultivation of such crops as manioc, yams, taro, groundnuts, maize, and palm and fruit trees.[209] Agricultural work, with the exception of clearing the land through means such as slash-and-burn, was usually performed by women. In this way, West Central Africans were consistent with other regions discussed thus far (with some exceptions). Men in West Central Africa tended to be exclusively responsible for fruit and palm trees, so that there was a clear division of agricultural labor with respect to gender. Hunting was also a male preserve, although Lega women, for example, could fish and gather as did the men.[210]

The consideration of agriculture is related to matters of land ownership and social organization, as both were determined by the nature of the agriculturally based economy. Land tended to be owned by clans or extended families, or lineage-villages.[211] Among the Kikongo speakers these were matrilineal descent groups, or *kanda*.[212] In contrast, the Lega and Bembe were both patrilineal.[213] All of these groups, however, featured descent systems that compensated for their unilineality, so that if matrilineal, there remained important aspects of identity and status accorded through the male line, and vice versa.[214]

In seventeenth-century Kongo, two-thirds to three-fourths of the population lived in rural villages, the *mabata* (sing. *lubata*); the residents of the towns, or *mbanza*, controlled agricultural surpluses and therefore wielded political power over the *mabata*.[215] Although the apparatus of the state functioned well at times, the reports of da Caltanisetta and da Lucca suggest that the nobility, the *mani*, enjoyed independent sources of power.[216]

With respect to religion in the lower Congo, it is Jacobson-Widding's contention that "the same main features are found east and south of the Lower Congo, among all the ethnic groups belonging to the matrilineal belt of western Central Africa."[217] As such, there was belief in Nzambi or Nzambi a Mpungu, the creator of the earth and of the first human couple (who subsequently withdrew from that creation). The Lega of eastern Congo, on the other hand and by way of example, believed in a trinity: Kikunga, Kalaga, and Kaginga.[218] In this way, the Lega differ from both the societies of the lower Congo as well as those in the eastern portion, who tend to posit large pantheons of deities.

It was also the case, however, that Christianity was present in West Central Africa since the dawn of the slave trade. Thornton asserts that "Kongo had been a Christian kingdom since the late fifteenth century. . . . By the eighteenth century, Christianity was the source of Kongo identity, and virtually all the population participated in and knew its rites and tenets."[219] He adds that the eighteenth-century "Kongolese were proud of their Christian and Catholic heritage," having established "a fairly extensive system of schools and churches in addition to a high degree of literacy (at least for the upper classes) in Portuguese."[220]

The comments of contemporary observers, clerics no less, are at some variance with Thornton's overall characterization. For example, da Caltanisetta's writings are filled with references to burning the paraphernalia, symbols, and sanctuaries of the "féticheurs" or *nganga*, local leaders of traditional religion. The impression is one of an uphill, state-sanctioned campaign against the *nganga* and indigenous beliefs. The following anecdote captures da Caltanisetta's sentiments:

> At one point some men and women told my interpreter that my mission was evil because I showed myself to be an enemy of the "féticheurs"

and burned their idols; they added that they were unable to forsake the practices of their country; as Christians, they initially went to God for the healing of [a particular illness]; not having obtained it, they turned to the "féticheurs" in order to get the healing from the devil, honored in these idols. This response demonstrates the profound disposition of all the inhabitants of this unfortunate kingdom of Kongo.[221]

Similarly, da Lucca, in passing through Kongo in the early eighteenth century, observed of a particular area that "the ignorance of the people of this region was unbelievable. Many did not know how to make the sign of the cross. There were even those for whom [the idea of] the immortality of the soul was strange and who imagined that the soul died with the body."[222]

Thornton's response to the foregoing is that such clerics may have questioned the orthodoxy of the Kongolese but never their sincerity, and that "whatever modern scholars or some eighteenth-century priests thought, the Kongolese regarded themselves as Christians."[223] He acknowledges that "the actual practice of Christianity was highly mixed with African religions," but that this form of "African Christianity" was nonetheless accepted by clergy with strained resources in Africa and the Americas. Probably the most arresting example in support of this thesis is the life of Dona Beatrice Kimpa Vita, leader of the early-eighteenth-century Antonian movement, a movement so inclusive of both Christian and indigenous elements that its broad appeal explains its success in ending Kongo's civil wars.[224] Thornton's work has implications for the development of Christianity in North America and will be discussed in that context. What can be said here is that whether appropriately designated Christian or not, autochthonous religion remained strong and important in Kongo throughout the period of the trade.

Seventeenth- and eighteenth-century Kongo indigenous religion had a number of relevant features. Hilton has developed three categories of "other worldly power": the "named dead," for whom rituals were performed by the *nganga atombala* ("priest of the resurrected," one type of "féticheur") to remove the influence of the deceased from the living; the "*mbumba* dimension," apparently a fertility cult associated with water and earth spirits; and the *nkadi mpemba*, a white-colored realm associated with death and the grave.[225] Amulets or charms derived from *mbumba* rites were called *nkisi* or *minkisi*; according to da Caltanisetta, there were many types of *nkisi*, about which more will be written later.[226] Powerful *mbumba*-based associations, the *impasi* (sing. *kimpasi*) led by "priests" known as *kitomi*, were a source of great concern to missionaries.[227] Dona Beatrice is perhaps the best known example of a *kitomi* whose Antonian movement was *mbumba*-based.[228]

Hilton's category of the "named dead," or what Jacobson-Widding calls the recently dead, is directly related to the third category of the *nkadi mpemba* or *mpemba*.[229] In this instance the historical and anthropological literature converge in that the recently dead were divided into the evil *bankugu* and the good *banzambi bampungu*. The former either dwelled in the forest or were forced to wander about homeless. The *banzambi bampungu*, however, lived in the land of the good spirits, *mpemba*, after having spent from six to ten months in the grave. Now, the thing about *mpemba* is that it was located beneath the ground, "on the other side of the water," where white clay is found (that is, at the bottom of rivers and lakes). During the six-to-ten-month period in the grave, the deceased are believed to change color, turning white before entering *mpemba*.

Explained in another way, the world was conceived as resembling "two mountains opposed at their bases and separated by water."[230] The barrier between these two sections of the world was called the *kalunga*, a reference to an ocean or large body of water. The dead had to pass through the *kalunga* to reach the other mountain, the dwelling of the recently dead, *mpemba*. It does not take a great leap of the imagination to identify the Atlantic Ocean with the *kalunga* and Europeans with "the returned spirits of the dead who lived at the bottom of the ocean."[231] This, of course, would explain their color. However, it could not explain their activities, by which it became abundantly clear they were no ancestors of West Central Africans. Upon realizing this, a new twist was added to the account that did not violate the Congolese or Angolan view of the afterlife but was in fact consistent with it. To account for the slaving interests of these "spirits," the notion developed that beyond the Atlantic were "blood red-skinned followers of the great Lord of the Dead, Mwene Puto. . . . These people of Mwene Puto, it was well known, were cannibals who took their nourishment from the flesh of the blacks they so avidly sought."[232] Mwene Puto was Portugal (and by extension, Europe). Death, the slave trade, and white people were therefore all inextricably linked, and to embrace one was to unavoidably come into contact with the other two.

Once across the Atlantic, those West Central Africans who survived the ordeal of capture, transport, and seasoning in the New World were forced to adjust their thinking, as were the Igbo. They were not physically dead, although they had certainly undergone a different kind of death. The New World was not the type of *mpemba* they had anticipated. Rather, they had to come to terms with servility and racism simultaneously and in their most devastating forms. Which of their previous values, principles, and world-views could be appropriated and modified to help them make sense out of this bizarre situation?

Fortunately, a substantial amount of work has been done on the continuity and transformation of West Central African culture and society in the Americas, particularly by Thompson and Stuckey, and this inquiry is in the enviable position of attempting to build upon their foundation. Thompson, in his study of the relationship between art and philosophy throughout parts of the African diaspora, has determined that Congolese and Angolan influences are to be found in "herbalism, mental healing and funeral traditions among black people of the Old Deep American South."[233] In fact, he makes the emphatic point that "nowhere is Kongo-Angolan influence on the New World more pronounced, more profound, than in black traditional cemeteries throughout the South of the United States."[234] The matter of funeral traditions has been addressed elsewhere and in sufficient detail, so that only specific aspects of it will be reviewed later in this study. More also remains to be said regarding herbalism; suffice it to state here that the West Central African practice of *minkisi*, or "sacred medicines," is the basis for what has been called hoodoo in the American South.

To be sure, there are a number of other West Central African survivals in North America. To cite two linguistic examples, the word *toby*, which refers to a charm or amulet, is probably derived from the Kongo *tobe*, or good luck charm originally consisting of graveyard dust and palm wine. Also, the term used by conjure folk (men and women) for graveyard dust, *goofer*, may be a corruption of the Kikongo verb *kufwa*, which means "to die," as graveyard dust was intimately associated with the spirit of the deceased party.[235]

The *tendwa nza Kongo*, the Kongo cosmogram depicting a cross within an ellipsis, is also of great interest. Of the *tendwa nza Kongo* in lower Congo MacGaffey has commented: "Contrary to what many students have said, the sign of the cross was not introduced into this country [lower Congo] and into the minds of its people by foreigners. The cross was known to the Bakongo before the arrival of Europeans and corresponds to the understanding in their minds of their relationship to their world."[236] The *tendwa nza Kongo* also refers to the West Central African notion of death and is therefore closely related to the experiences of the slave trade. Given the belief that the worlds of the living and the dead are likened to mirror mountains separated by water, the rising and setting of the sun was seen as the exchange of night and day between these worlds.[237] Nzambi a Mpungu is at the top of the cosmogram, the dead are at the bottom, and the *kalunga*, or "water," is represented by the horizontal *yowa* line. There are four disks for each point on the cross, representing the "four moments of the sun." The top disk symbolizes the sun, the masculine element, the north, and the apex of a person's earthly life; the bottom disk stands for midnight, the female element, the south, and the height of a person's "otherworldly strength." The other two disks represent dawn and sunset, so that whatever takes place in one world is mirrored in the other. Movement from dawn to dusk is counterclockwise.

To actually trace out the cosmogram in the ground while singing Kikongo words was believed to bring about the "descent of God's power upon that very point."[238] It became a "sacred 'point' on which a person stands to make an oath, on the ground of the dead and under all-seeing God." There was a very strong connection, then, between West Central African cosmogony and ritual involving circular movement. The latter was a visual expression of the former and was deemed necessary in order to access the divine. It is Stuckey's view that this visual, physical circumlocution, this expression of the West Central African perspective of the relationship between the living, the dead, and the divine was incorporated into the ring shout, a ceremony in the American South in which participants move counterclockwise in a circle during religious worship.[239] In fact, it is his argument that the ring shout, primarily a West Central African contribution, was the foremost means by which a sense of community was forged among the African-based population. There is a great deal to be said about this provocative thesis. At this point, however, it is enough to suggest that West Central Africa played a crucial role in shaping African American culture and society.

· · · · · · ·

North American discriminatory tendencies resulted in distinct patterns of ethnic distribution throughout the colonies/states. The recovery of such patterns assists immeasurably in any analysis of subsequent sociocultural development, operating under the premise that black life and culture in a given area evolved out of and in creative tension with norms associated with specific ethnic groups imported via the slave trade. To be sure, people of African descent moved from locale to locale throughout North America and over time, so that their insularity was steadily mitigated the longer their sojourn in America. However, it is necessary to identify the respective cultural milieux out of which they came in order to understand how they contributed to successive settings.

It has been established that the Bight of Biafra, West Central Africa, and the Gold Coast were early and consistent sources for North American markets. Senegambia was also an initial contributor but was replaced by Sierra Leone from 1750 to the end of the legal trade, while the Bight of Benin was prominent only in Louisiana. The first four regions, then, supplied the ethnicities which would form a foundational African society in North America. The Igbo and the Akan, along with the Senegambians, Angolans, and

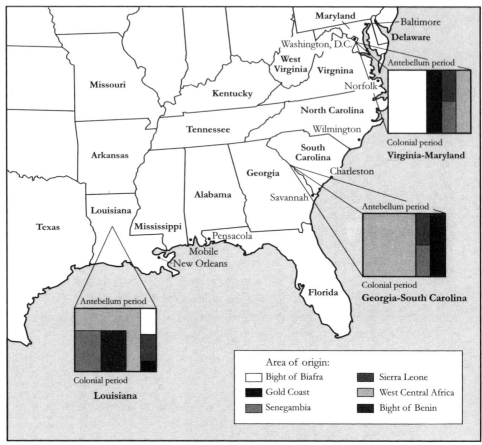

MAP 6.1 Africans in the American South by Area of Origin

Congolese, featured large as the progenitors of an eventual African American population. However, their spatial deployment supports the argument for African ethnic enclaves in North America.

Virginia and Maryland were the preserve of the Igbo. There were also relatively substantial numbers of Akan speakers in Virginia and Maryland, as those from the Gold Coast were universally acclaimed and sought. Senegambia was represented as well, although the combination of a large Igbo presence and the heavy demand for Senegambians in South Carolina and Georgia supports Rawley's estimate that less than 17 percent of Virginia's slave imports came from Senegambia.[240] Finally, the West Central African and Sierra Leonian populations would have been less than the others.

South Carolina and Georgia, on the other hand, were almost diametrically opposed to Virginia and Maryland with regard to the ethnic composition of its African population. In these two contiguous areas, it was the West Central

Africans who contributed to the slave lists in the same proportions as did the Biafrans in Virginia and Maryland. However, the Senegambians were also highly valued there, so that they possibly comprised the second largest ethnic matrix in this instance, followed by the ubiquitous Akan speakers. Into this mix would be added the Sierra Leonians from the second half of the eighteenth century on. How the Congolese-Angolan-Senegambian-Akan base was altered by this subsequent but substantial addition is a fascinating question, about which more will be stated.

Louisiana, then, remains. The Senegambian presence, together with that of the Fon-Ewe-Yoruba, were foundational. By the Spanish period, the Fon-Ewe-Yoruba contingent rivaled that of Senegambia, which in turn was nearly equaled by the Congolese and other West Central Africans. The Igbo were also well represented by the late eighteenth century and went on to comprise some 8.6 percent of the African population for the whole of the trade, whereas the Akan (1.1 percent) and the Sierra Leonians (5.3 percent) were in the minority. However, the relative percentage of West Central Africans imported between 1780 and 1820 was immense, resulting in Congolese-Angolan numerical dominance.[241]

These, then, constitute the ethnic bases upon which the subsequent African American composite would be constructed. When first-generation American blacks from Virginia and South Carolina met, they carried with them varying cultural perspectives and experiences that could not be explained by differences between tobacco and rice cultivation. Their differences, and their points of correspondence, extended to the other side of the Atlantic.

This analysis can be taken one step further by considering the confluence of cultures within the various colonies/states. Virginia and Maryland, for example, developed a servile population largely out of Igbo (in the majority) and Akan antecedents. When individuals from these two groups met, they would have realized their similarities in short order. Both groups were largely rural, their diets equally dependent upon root crops. Both had established a high regard for women, reflected by such evidence as the veneration and popularity of the earth mothers Asase Yaa and Ala, the perfection of gender balance represented in the name of the high god Chineke, the matriliny of the Akan and some of the Igbo, and the freedom with which Igbo women engaged in commercial and civic enterprise. The reverence for earth mothers, in turn, created a strong sense of union (physical and mystical) with the land and the ancestors, symbolized and concretized by the Akan stool and the Igbo ancestral staff. Given the separation from African soil, the association of the Igbo with suicide as a means of returning to that soil would have been readily understood, if not always emulated, by the Akan.

Although land was central to both the Igbo and the Akan, they would have possessed somewhat different experiences regarding social and political order. The former were decentralized for the most part, as opposed to the Akan, many of whom were familiar with sprawling, well-articulated, large-scale systems of government. It can be argued that because neither group had opportunities to reconstruct polities, their experiences in this area are immaterial. It must be kept in mind, however, that slaves had to develop mechanisms by which they could address problems arising in the quarters, or were otherwise unique to their lives and separate from their relations with the slaveholder. In order to adjudicate cases and resolve disputes, they would have necessarily drawn from the wealth of their experiences in Africa. Further research into these matters is required before one can know whether the more egalitarian system of the Igbo prevailed over the pyramidal structures of the Akan. The sheer numbers of the Igbo would seem to argue for the former. It also remains to be seen whether the Igbo concept of *ikenga* could have survived in the New World, and if it could have possibly provided the basis for a work ethic among Igbo slaves. It must be pointed out, however, that material conditions were so altered that it may have been impossible to reconcile the principles of *ikenga* with the consequences of a perpetual "social death," by itself an explication for the spectacular incidence of flying Africans.

In the case of South Carolina and Georgia, it is clear that West Central Africans were the dominant group. Their perspective of the corresponding, mirror images of the realms of the living and the dead would greatly influence the African-based community, as would their complex system of *minkisi*. These beliefs were expressed most clearly in the area of religion, in which the West Central African use of ring ceremonies was the main source for the development of the ring shout and the *minkisi* the basis of hoodoo.

Although all the various ethnicities were first and foremost agriculturalists, Senegambians possessed greater potential to have emerged out of a cosmopolitan environment. Given the interconnectedness of the Senegambian region, they would have been accustomed to interacting with people of differing backgrounds. Concomitantly, some of them, particularly the Muslims (along with the Muslims of Sierra Leone), would have experienced sharp differences with the Congolese-Angolan majority, and such clashes would have contributed to social differentiation within the slave community. Ensuing segmentation would have found ideological support in the nearly ubiquitous Senegambian tripartite division of society. The potential for stratification has already been introduced in the discussion of the Muslim community, and will again be explored at greater length. But clearly, the Congolese-

Senegambian exchange held the greatest possibility for conflict as opposed to convergence.

On the other hand, non-Muslims from Sierra Leone may have found greater affinity with the Congolese-Angolans due to the fact that they had less opportunities than did the Senegambians for urban-based experiences. The more egalitarian nature of Sierra Leonian society with regard to gender, a result of both the prevalence of female societies and the centrality of women as cultivators and political officeholders, would not necessarily have been rejected by the Congolese-Angolans, as societies and women office-holders were found throughout West and West Central Africa. As a result, it is very likely that those from West Central Africa and Sierra Leone were able to build upon their similarities. Indeed, scholarly uncertainty over whether the term *Gullah* derives from Angola or Gola or both may in fact reflect the affinities that quickly developed between the two groups.

Concerning Louisiana, it has been established that the Senegambian Bambara were an important population whose warrior-cultivator tradition and perception of the spirit world were both carried over into Louisiana, finding expression in a number of violent "conspiracies" and the manufacturing of numerous amulets and other assorted agents of spirit-world manipulation. The Congolese practice of *minkisi* mirrored the Bambara worldview and use of charms, as did Fon-Ewe-Yoruba voodoo. The Igbo certainly understood such concepts. However, the Senegambian Muslims, a minority among whom were Wolof women, would have necessarily suffered irretrievable loss under this preponderance of non-Muslim culture and activity. The substantial numbers of Fon-Ewe-Yoruba, their early presence and steady replenishment over the years, their notoriety in New Orleans, and their resonance with both Bambara and Congolese perspectives help explain their apparent and eventual cultural preeminence.

7

TALKING HALF AFRICAN

MIDDLE PASSAGE, SEASONING, AND LANGUAGE

With the African antecedent in view, it becomes possible to more fully comprehend the change, the transition, from a socially stratified, ethnically based identity directly tied to a specific land to an identity predicated on the concept of race. This chapter argues that there were specific mechanisms in each phase of the African's experience—the initial capture and barracoon, transatlantic trek, and seasoning—through which he was increasingly nudged toward reassessment of his identity.

The question of the nature of enslavement and its attendant impact upon the slave is a complex one, to which Patterson has made one of the more signal contributions to date.[1] Clearly, the very process of enslavement directly informed the restructuring of the slave's identity. The slaveocracy attempted to define the African's condition for its own purposes, manipulating cultural symbols with such efficacy that in some cases the slave ultimately adopted and embraced the perspective of the slaveholder as her or his own. On the other hand, many slaves understood the objective of the enslaver and often opted to resist. In addition to insurrection and other forms of rebellion, continuity of culture was a principal weapon, forged and reforged with varying degrees of success. Within the context of a political struggle, which is exactly what slavery was, it ceased to matter whether specific cultural forms could be maintained over increasing spans of time and space. What mattered instead was achieving a self-view in opposition to the one prescribed by power and authority. To this end, the African antecedent formed the wellspring of cultural resistance.

The transformation of the African into the African American actually began on African soil. Africans chosen for the fateful transatlantic voyage all experienced the barracoon phase of the exchange; that is, the stage at which those who had been captured by various means were transferred to points along the coast to await embarkation.[2] Depending upon the specific location, captives from more than one ethnicity may have found themselves hold up in the same barracoon, thus initiating the message that the one thing they all shared was their blackness, a message that became even clearer upon considering the contrast with their European captors.

At the point of initial capture, anything was possible. The captives may have escaped, or they may have been channeled north into the transsaharan trade. An even greater likelihood, depending upon the precise period in question, was their retention by the host society for use in either domestic or productive capacities.[3] In the case of the latter scenario, captives remained subject to eventual export via the Atlantic. However, once they entered the barracoons, expulsion from the continent was the likeliest of fates.

Manning's research supports the earlier contention that for Senegambia, distances varied significantly and over time; the journey in the seventeenth century averaged one hundred kilometers, increasing to three to six hundred kilometers in the eighteenth with the recruitment of the Bambara from the upper Niger. The Bight of Biafra and the Gold Coast also averaged just over one hundred kilometers, with distance in the Gold Coast increasing to as many as three hundred in the eighteenth century. Sierra Leone and the Bight of Benin averaged less than two hundred kilometers, but in West Central Africa there was an increase from three hundred kilometers in the seventeenth century to six or seven hundred in the nineteenth, "a four-month journey for a slave coffle."[4] Loss of human life from initial capture to the barracoon averaged 10 to 15 percent, reaching as high as 40 percent in the specific case of Angola.[5]

The period of awaiting export from the barracoons could last for months, depending upon at least two conditions: the availability of slavers capable of taking on additional slaves and the health of the captive. With regard to the latter, captives invariably needed to convalesce following their initial capture and march to the sea. Concerning the former, the rate of available vessels was directly related to the particular coastal point in question. Sizable port towns with established and regular traffic attracted larger numbers of slavers with greater frequency.

The barracoons themselves differed in type and size. Some were simply exposed pens set up along the coast and possibly adjacent to the factories of

European traders. Others ranged from weather-protected dwellings to fortified castles. Still others were in fact compounds of nearby communities used to house captives until the previously mentioned conditions were satisfied. Such was the case toward the end of the eighteenth century, when Mungo Park, commenting on the arrival of slave caravans at the Gambian coast, observed that "if no immediate opportunity offers them to advantage, they are distributed among the neighbouring villages until a slave ship arrives, or until they can be sold to black traders who sometimes purchase on speculation."[6] Park goes on to comment on their circumstances, stating that "the poor wretches are kept constantly fettered, two and two of them being chained together, and employed in the labours of the field; and I am sorry to add, are very scantily fed, as well as harshly treated."[7]

The symmetry between the Gambian and Angolan experiences is striking. The latter involved caravan operators, or *sertanejos*, who led coffles averaging one hundred captives from the hinterland to the lower Kwanza or Luanda. From capture to barracoon, these people were fed the "cheapest rations available, often spoiled, and each slave carried his or her own provisions, mainly maize, beans, and manioc flour."[8] Bound and harshly treated, captives were taken to Luanda, where conditions remained deplorable. Conrad, in discussing the possible importation of more than 5 million Africans into Brazil alone, has provided a detailed account of the barracoon experience at Luanda:

> At the port of embarkation, suffering continued. . . . As proof of payment, a royal coat of arms was burned into each slave's right breast with a silver instrument, after which frequently a mark of ownership was placed on his left breast or arm. Even baptism, a ceremony which in the early nineteenth century was performed for a fee of 300 reis per slave, and so was sometimes neglected, was often a painful experience. According to one witness, slaves were usually baptized at the port of embarkation, and then a hot iron was used to put a small cross on each one's chest. Thus converted and marked with the most sacred symbol of Christian Europe, slaves were lodged in warehouses and in open-air compounds enclosed by high earthen walls or palisades. Exposed to the weather, poorly fed and clothed, sometimes still chained together or placed in stocks, they waited to be put aboard a ship. It could take weeks or months for a vessel to arrive. Meanwhile, another witness wrote, the slaves lived in close confinement, eating, sleeping, and seeing to other bodily needs—and infecting the houses and the city with "putrid miasmas." Oliveira Mendes claimed that ten or twelve thousand arrived each year at Luanda, but only six or seven thousand survived for shipment to Brazil. The number of the dead, he wrote, was "unspeakable."[9]

While Conrad is specifically addressing the trade to Brazil, it should be recalled that a quarter of those imported into what would become the United States were from West Central Africa. Many therefore endured similar experiences.

People not only were detained in facilities on land but also found themselves waiting for the final excursion in slavers offshore. This was because a slaver did not always take on its full complement of captives at one port of call. In fact, it was often necessary to sail from barracoon to barracoon until the quota was reached. In this way, the period of confinement for Africans was further prolonged by the process of collecting additional captives, during which time those already boarded remained in the bowels of the slaver for another several weeks or months. To therefore speak of a Middle Passage transition of only two or three months' duration is an oversimplification of a potentially much longer, more complex, more arduous experience.

A prime example of the foregoing was the voyage of the *James*, commissioned by the Royal African Company to engage in the slave trade. The *James* departed from England on 5 April 1675 and did not arrive in Barbados until 21 May 1676.[10] Having reached Assini (Gold Coast) on 30 August, the *James* proceeded to exchange goods for both gold and slaves at several points along the coast until 11 January 1676, when the vessel arrived at the English factory near Wyemba. There the slaver boarded slaves each day for about a week, most of whom were described as "very thin ordinary slaves," suggestive of the preceding experience inshore. The *James* made yet another stop at Anomabu and did not set sail for Barbados until 8 March 1676.

Similarly, the Dutch slaver *St. Jan* began to take on captives at Ardra, on the Slave Coast (Bight of Benin) on 4 March 1659.[11] The ship continued east, picking up additional slaves and supplies in the Bight of Biafra. By the time the *St. Jan* left the Biafran area for the Cameroon River on 22 May, it had acquired 219 Africans. From that time to 17 August, the vessel searched the coast as far south as Cape Lopez (just south of the equator), not for additional slaves but for provisions to feed the slaves.

The search for food was a major preoccupation of slave vessels, contributing tremendously to the time spent along the coast. The captain of the *James* complained of his "great trouble" trying to find provisions for his captives.[12] The captain of the *Arthur*, operating in the Biafran Bight in February 1678, had similar concerns: "This day we sentt our Boat att Donus to see whatt might be done there, wee findinge negroes to be Brought on Board of us fast enough but wee nott free to deale in many fearing lest wee should take in negroes and have noe provisions for them."[13] It was Barbot's calculation at the beginning of the eighteenth century that a "ship that takes in five hundred slaves, must provide above a hundred thousand yams; which is very difficult, because it is hard to stow them, by reason they take up so much room."[14] Provisions competed with human beings for space in the slaver, a contest the latter could not win.

Two new realities gradually began to dawn on those Africans awaiting export to the New World. The first was that they had been severed from their people and their land; the longer the period of separation, the less the likelihood of reunion. The second was they were now in close proximity with Africans of differing ethnicities. Without doubt, many were already familiar with other groups, especially in the closely connected Senegambian region. However, they were now interacting in a new capacity—not as traders, travelers, or possibly even coreligionists, but as captives. This new condition, unlike previous interactions, suggested the need to adjust their self-perception. The suggestion would only grow more persistent with the Atlantic trek.

. . . .

The Middle Passage was one of the New World's most crucial and formative phases. The intensity of the suffering provided the survivors an opportunity to bond with others of differing backgrounds. Rites of passage were well understood in Africa, and the Middle Passage certainly qualified as one of the most challenging. As a consequence, those who bonded were taking the first faltering steps in the direction of redefinition.

The transition from the barracoon to the passage differed from locale to locale. Depending upon the type of barracoon and the nature of trade relations between European merchants and the area and regional powers, slavers would either wait offshore for a succession of canoes bearing captives, as was the case at Bonny in the Bight of Biafra and points along the Gold Coast; or the technique of "boating" would be employed, whereby European sailors took vessels upriver to obtain captives from villages along the banks, as was practiced along parts of the Windward Coast.[15] The latter method could be very time consuming; sometimes only eight to twelve captives had been gathered after a three-week expedition.

Male slaves, upon entering European vessels, were chained together at the wrists and ankles in groups of two in order to prevent mutiny and escape.[16] Women and girls were physically separated from the males and usually unfettered. This arrangement had become standard procedure by the last quarter of the eighteenth century, as Europeans came to appreciate the capacity of the African to rebel. In fact, the lesson was learned as early as 1651, when the Guinea Company commissioned Bartholomew Haward to sail for the Gambia in search of slaves, instructing him that "there is put aboard your Pinck *Supply* 30 paire of shackles and boults for such of your negers as are rebellious and we pray you be veary carefull to keepe them under and let them have their food in due season that they ryse not against you, as they have done in other ships."[17] In some cases the shackles were removed once the ship actually set sail for the Western Hemisphere; a number of captains removed the chains only during the day, whereas others never removed them.[18]

In order to avoid paying additional fees to African authorities for continuing to house captives once they had been purchased, European traders took the captives on board as quickly as possible.[19] Branded on the chest with the company's coat of arms or name, it was Bosman's experience in 1699 that these Africans were stripped of all clothing, "so that they came aboard stark-naked as well women as men; in which condition they are obliged to continue, if the master of the Ship is not so charitable (which he commonly is) as to bestow something on them to cover their nakedness."[20] The comments of Mayer in 1826 regarding this denuding, some 127 years after those of Bosman, are instructive. Two days before loading captives onto a slaver, the heads of both males and females were shaved. Mayer then records:

> On the appointed day, the *barracoon* or slave-pen is made joyous by the abundant "feed" which signalizes the negro's last hours in his native country. The feast over, they are taken alongside the vessel in canoes; and as they touch the deck, they are entirely stripped, so that women as well as men go out of Africa as they came into it—*naked*. This precaution, it will be understood, is indispensable; for perfect nudity, during the whole voyage, is the only means of securing cleanliness and health.[21]

Notwithstanding Mayers's reference to hygienic concerns, the psychological implications of denuding are both clear and clearly intended—profound humiliation and disintegration of identity.

Their dignity assaulted, the captives were immediately herded into the hold of the ship.[22] The segregation of the sexes was maintained throughout the voyage except when permitted on deck, where they were allowed to converse. It was often the case that captives were kept below until the African shoreline was no longer in sight. This was due to the fact the African, if allowed to maintain visual contact with Africa, very often sought to return. The *Hannibal*'s Captain Phillips remarked: "The negroes are so wilful and loth to leave their own country, that they have often leap'd out of the canoes, boat and ship, into the sea, and kept under water till they were drowned to avoid being taken up and saved by our own boats, which pursued them; they having a more dreadful apprehension of Barbadoes than we have of hell."[23] Phillips did not realize how insightful his remarks were, for Barbados, from the perspective of the African, was indeed hell, literally and figuratively.

One of the African's greatest fears was that whites were cannibals, and that he or she was going to be eaten.[24] Barbot records that it "has been observ'd before, that some slaves fancy they are carry'd to be eaten, which make them desperate; and others are so on account of their captivity: so that if care be not taken, they will mutiny and destroy the ship's crew in hopes to get away."[25] In addition to the fear of cannibalism, there was also the strong suspicion that whites were not human. Equiano articulated both concerns:

> The first object which saluted my eyes when I arrived on the coast was the sea, and a slaveship, which was then riding at anchor, and waiting for its cargo. These filled me with astonishment, which was soon converted into terror, which I am yet at a loss to describe, nor the then feelings of my mind. When I was carried on board I was immediately handled, and tossed up, to see if I were sound, by some of the crew; and I was now persuaded that I had got into a world of bad spirits, and that they were going to kill me. . . . When I recovered a little, I found some black people about me. . . . I asked them if we were not to be eaten by these white men with horrible looks, red faces, and long hair.[26]

These apprehensions were particularly well developed in West Central Africa, where indigenous cosmology and white-skinned foreigners converged with fantasy and fact, fused at the ankles and wrists in the surrealism of the transatlantic slave trade. The European advent represented death, the Europeans themselves spirits. Face to face with messengers from the ultimate netherland, a quintessential encounter with the other, the African did everything in her power to escape prior to setting sail. Such was the fear of what lie ahead in the white world, such was the grief over severance from family and land, that starvation and leaping overboard were options exercised by many during the course of the Middle Passage. Death was not a fate to be feared and was, at any rate, preferable to life under the control of beings from beyond the *kalunga*. But of course, most did not go over the side, nor starve themselves to death.

Notwithstanding the nefarious nature of the enterprise, the slave trade was, after all, a business venture. Given that the African was central its success, measures were taken to ensure his fit arrival in the New World. To this end, Africans were often fed twice a day aboard the slavers.[27] In some instances they were divided into groups of ten around a grub-containing flat tub and given wooden spoons. Because they were allowed on deck, mealtime also represented an opportunity to mutiny; hands not actually feeding the captives stood guard with guns trained.[28]

In the eighteenth and nineteenth centuries, it was the custom of the English to give captives a steady diet of horse beans to "fatten them up." Rice was also frequently provided, but meat was very rare. Yams, limes, lemons, and palm oil supplemented the diet at times; water was the principal drink. Earlier in the seventeenth century, and based upon the voyage of the *James*, fish caught along the way were also made available to the captives on occasion.[29] During the same century, the *Hannibal*'s Phillips recorded that the chief meal was ground Indian corn mixed with water and boiled into a porridge.[30] Whereas horse beans were served throughout the trade, the use of Indian corn declined.[31] Summarizing the problems with diet and health, a survivor of the *Clotilde* stated: "We get almost nothing to eat. We get seek. Two of us die. They geeve us leetle water—one swallow twice each day. They give it in a leetle can. When we swallow they snatch it way and geeve it to the next man."[32]

The relationship between the captive's diet and his health was obviously important. To promote the latter and monitor the former, it was not unusual for slavers, with the exception of the North Americans, to include among its staff at least one surgeon.[33] These were frequently medical practitioners who had fallen upon hard times in Europe and whose abilities were very much in question. Although slavers carried medical manuals as early as 1729, it was not until 1788 that English law required each slaver to employ at least one certified surgeon, whose responsibilities included recording the number of captives taken aboard and keeping track of their deaths, along with those of the crew. It was the surgeon's task to examine captives held in the barracoons to determine their fitness, for men could not be "ruptured" and women could not have "fallen breasts." Once the ship entered the passage, the surgeon was to monitor the health of the captives on a daily basis, segregating those who were seriously ill and treating them with various medicines, especially wine and sago, a starchlike substance.[34] It also fell to the surgeon to prepare the captives for market once the Americas had been reached. At this point, diseases had either been successfully treated or expertly concealed.

Given the limited resources and dubious skills of these surgeons, the seriously ill were in the gravest peril. Diseases assailing the captives included dysentery (usually called the "flux" or the "bloody flux," perhaps indicating degrees of severity), measles, scurvy, and "fever."[35] Ophthalmia, a condition leading to blindness (and therefore possibly related to river blindness), "afflicted Africans in great numbers." Yaws, evidenced by dark swellings, was both widespread and potentially fatal. Intestinal worms also contributed to poor health. But aside from the bloody flux, which was essentially contracted from food and water contamination, smallpox was of particular concern. It was due to the pox that whole ships, having reached North American ports, were quarantined until the disease had run its course and was no longer contagious.

In addition to malnutrition and unsanitary conditions, there is also the question of spacing and its relationship to sickness and mortality. Scholars disagree over the frequency and significance of "tight packing" aboard slavers. Rawley, for example, has taken considerable time to investigate the alleged phenomenon, and his characterization of it bears repeating:

> Few stereotypes about the Atlantic slave trade are more familiar than popular impressions of the Middle Passage—the crossing from Africa to America. Huge ships—crammed to the gunwales with Africans, packed together like spoons, chained to one another, daily exposed to white brutality, meager provisions, and hygienical neglect—in long, slow voyages suffered abnormally high mortality rates for their hapless passengers.
>
> A diagram of the Liverpool slave vessel, the *Brookes*, has for nearly two centuries nourished this stereotype. A nauseous sketch depicted a large ship of three hundred and twenty tons, whose narrow and shallow decks were packed with slaves "like books on a shelf." The diagram was printed in 1788 when Parliament was deliberating upon a law which in effect would have restricted the *Brookes* to a cargo of no more than 454 slaves. It was calculated that if every man slave was allowed six feet by one foot, four inches, platform space, every woman five feet ten by one foot four, every boy five feet by one foot two, and every girl four feet six by one foot, the *Brookes* could hold 451 slaves. A witness who had been on the *Brookes's* voyage of 1783 testified that "they brought upwards of 600 slaves, and lost about seventy in the voyage."[36]

Rawley points out that the sketch of the *Brookes* and the accompanying calculations were prepared by London abolitionists, who then distributed their propaganda throughout Britain, France, and the United States and achieved their objective of creating an "impression of horror." The author concludes with the observation that 320-ton ships such as the *Brookes* were not the norm in the 1780s, and that most slavers were not specifically designed to carry human captives.

Evidence presented heretofore, some of which is derived from Rawley's own findings, clearly demonstrates that insofar as brutality, unsanitary conditions, and malnutrition are concerned, we are not dealing in stereotypes but in a preponderance of factual information. With regard to the matter of the *Brookes*, that its records were used by abolitionists is neither surprising nor in any way improper. Further, the size of the *Brookes*, or any other ship for that matter, has nothing to do with the question of tight packing; the latter could (and did) occur on vessels both large and small.

Klein takes a different approach. Rather than deny the frequency of tight packing, he rejects any causal relationship between it and mortality, focusing instead on the duration of the voyage and arguing that the mortality rate of death remained constant whatever the duration.[37] Hence, we are back to the fact that not only were Africans packed into these vessels in a way to maximize profit, but that they were in all probability adversely affected by that arrangement in addition to other factors. It is not necessary to demonstrate a direct relationship between tight packing and death. Common sense dictates that such a practice would induce considerable suffering.[38]

Although it has been estimated that the Middle Passage suffered a mortality rate of approximately 15 to 20 percent, it is difficult to feel comfortable with these figures.[39] First of all, the rates varied according to port and period. It would appear, for example, that the mortality rate declined during the eighteenth century, primarily the result of the accumulation of slaving experience.[40] But there is also a problem with the reliability of the slaver's logs. Underreporting the number taken aboard and overreporting the number of deaths en route was widespread and encouraged by the fact that a captain in the employ of a particular company could make more money by selling Africans on his own and reporting them as fatalities. Hence, the records of the RAC reveal the suspicion that the *Sarah Bonaventure* in 1685 made an unauthorized stop at Barbados on its way to Jamaica and sold "some of his choicest Neg'rs but of that wee have yet noe certaine proof."[41] The vessel reported that only 250 of the original 530 captives reached Jamaica. However, it was discovered that the captain concealed 49 captives in the hold. Similarly, in 1679 the RAC received word from agents in Barbados that the *Marigold* had understated the number of its captives in order to sell some on their own; instead of 118 survivors as claimed by the captain, the total number was discovered to be 180 (out of 293 originally).[42]

Tight packing, disease, and malnutrition all contributed to the mortality of the captives. The Dutchman Bosman, while claiming that Dutch vessels were clean and well ordered, charged that the English, French, and Portuguese ships were "always foul and stinking."[43] "The stench of a slave ship could be scented for miles," according to another account, citing an eyewitness who described the slave deck as "so covered with blood and mucous that it resembled a slaughter-house."[44] Altogether, these factors exacted both a physical and a psychological toll obvious even to traders. The surgeon Isaac Wilson was convinced that two-thirds of the 155 (out of a total of 602) who perished aboard the *Elizabeth* died from "melancholy." He observed that once the captives were taken on board, "a gloomy pensiveness seemed to overcast their countenances and continued in a great many."[45] "Characteristic of many slavers," according to another account, "was a 'howling melancholy noise' with the women occasionally in hysterics."[46] Such medicinal agents as malagetta and Indian pepper, administered to combat the bloody flux, were of no use in the battle against deep depression. In an effort to do something, captives were brought on deck and forcibly made to dance. Thus, Captain Phillips of the *Hannibal* wrote that the Africans were taken from the hole in the evenings to "air themselves, and make them jump and dance for an hour or two to our bag-pipes, harp, and fiddle."[47] Falconbridge wrote that captives were sometimes "obliged" to dance on deck, weather permitting; if reluctant, they were flogged. They were also forced to sing, "but when they do so, their songs are generally, as may be expected, melancholy lamentations of their exile from their native country."[48]

As a consequence of the combined trials and tribulations of the Middle Passage, Africans died by the scores. In addition to those who succumbed to disease and hunger, there were many who voluntarily gave up the ghost.[49] They found various methods of self-destruction, including refusal to eat. The last option was so frequent that, according to one witness, "compulsory feeding was used on every slave ship with which he was familiar."[50] Those who refused were given a "cat," or flogging, to break their resistance.[51] Those who could went over the side; those who could not often went insane.[52] Mutinies and shipwrecks added to the number of the dead.[53]

The Middle Passage was a transition like no other. No other. It would have been difficult indeed to convince those from West Central Africa that they had not in fact passed through the *kalunga* to *mpemba*. For all practical purposes that is exactly what happened. The means by which they were transported was of such violence, the anguish they suffered of such depth, that their memory was veritably seared into the consciousness of both the African and her American-born progeny. One experiences this generational transfer in the words of Uncle Ephraim, whose grandfather was African-born:

> Waves beatin' 'gainst de boat, 'cause it's stormy. No big steamships lak dey got terday. Jes' little sailboats. Grandfadder say dey got rows o' cells lak a jailhouse. Dey puts de men on one side de boat, an' de women on de udd'ah. Tuk a month ter come 'cross. Nobody couldn' eat nothin' fo' longes' time. . . . Some of 'em hit dey haids 'gainst de iron ba'hs an' died. Dat night—"Ker-plunk!"—into de ocean . . .
>
> By 'n by de wind calm down. Folks got well an' started eatin'. If niggah kin eat, he's happy! So dey lets all but de mean ones come up on deck. Keeps dozen or so chain togedd'ah. Feed 'em good, an' dey sits on de deck watchin' de sun go down an' de moon come up. Den dey sings. One sings. One sings, an' de res' hum, lak. What dey sing? Nobody don' know. It's not ou'ah words. Dey sing language what dey learn in Africa when dey was free![54]

The passage was indeed stormy. But when the wind calmed down, the survivors began their collective reflection by way of call-and-response. The grandson could know something of the passage, something of what was left behind in Africa. He would even learn to call and respond. But the passage was transformative as well, so that Ephraim could not know what he wanted to know about his grandfather and about Africa, for not only had the words changed, but so had the material conditions.

In this way, millions of Africans embarked upon one of the most difficult experiences in recent human history. In the end, they would be forced to reinvent themselves. The barracoon and Middle Passage constituted the hazy beginning of the process. In the midst of turmoil and confusion, in the center of the storm, certain facts gradually began to come into focus. The first was the most obvious: all who were in chains were black, and nearly all who were not were white. This would suggest to the former that skin color was in some way central to the call to suffer. Africans of varying ethnicities, who had never considered their blackness a source of reflection let alone a principle of unity, became cognizant of this feature perhaps for the first time in their lives. But it was still quite early in the game; such impressions were at best superficial and incapable of challenging, let alone supplanting, the much deeper, more fundamental self-concept of the individual as Mandinka, Igbo, Wolof, and so on. To be a captive Pullo, having been a free Pullo, was to remain a Pullo in the belly of the whale.

A second factor also encouraged a sense of community among those remaining at journey's end: their very survival. They had survived the death angel's passover only to enter a whitemanmade Hades on Earth. They had witnessed starvation and suicide. They had endured the dizzying days and the sickening nights and somehow remained. They were those who fought and scratched and clawed their way through, yet comforting one another in their collective despair. They had shared what little they had with those who were on the verge. They had made the necessary sacrifices and had extended themselves in so many charitable acts, large and small, none of which has been preserved for posterity. But that they occurred is beyond doubt, for how else could they have emerged from the belly of the great fish?

Goveia, in citing Bryan Edwards, writes that slaves were "strongly attached to people of their own country, and 'above all, to such as their companions as came in the same ship with them from Africa.' "[55] Patterson, in turn, explains that captives who formed close friendships during the ordeal were called "shipmates," and that "their love and affection for each other was proverbial."[56] Curtin, in his study of Jamaican slavery, also discussed "the strange bond between 'shipmates,' who had made the middle passage together. In Jamaica this was considered almost as strong as blood relationship, and it passed from one generation to another—a young man felt that the 'shipmate' of his father was his own relative as well."[57] In those slavers that carried an ethnically homogeneous human cargo, such bonds of affection would have been natural. Their heterogeneous counterparts would have had linguistic and cultural differences to surmount, so that the bonds may not have been so immediate or have become as intimate. Even so, to endure would have required some degree of cooperation, some level of mutual response. That they survived is testimony enough.

But a third factor had more potential than anything else to bring the African to the aperture of reevaluation. The recognition that all who were in chains were of dark hue was significant and had some impact, but it probably did not result in moving Africans away from their previous self-perception to any appreciable degree. The more important bonding was on the basis of a shared experience in suffering, which led to the concept of a special tie between shipmates. That this association was crucial is evidenced by the fact that it would not only be remembered by the progeny of the shipmates but also serve as a foundation for future and enduring fictive relationships. The contributions of these first two factors to the onset of the reidentification process are therefore clear. However, it is possible that a third factor, the sexual exploitation of African women, held even greater significance for the process.

The rape of African women by European men began its long and sordid history aboard the slaver itself, before the former were ever sold to New World masters (who would promptly go out and do the same). Indeed, it was the practice among many vessels to give their crews such sexual access as a matter of policy.[58] It mattered not that the violation was with great or little frequency, or that the number of women so violated was large or small. A small number of women violated infrequently would have been sufficient to convey at least two messages to all aboard the vessel. First, African women (or young girls in many instances) were completely vulnerable. Second, African men were at a tremendous disadvantage were they to attempt intervention.

Davis's reflections on the political content of rape during slavery continues to instruct.[59] Her depiction of rape as a tool of deterrence against revolt and other forms of resistance on farms and plantations is just as applicable to the slave ship itself, where a calculus of domination and violence was also essential to the success of the mission. What is crucial to the present investigation is her argument that enslaved men were also targeted by the rape of women and that they unavoidably suffered from their inability to protect. Their suffering, in turn, resulted from the fact that these women and children were their wives, daughters, sisters, and friends. They constituted a community, separate and distinct from that of slaveholders and other whites.

The point is this: To the extent that African men and women suffered aboard the slaver what they and their progeny would suffer on the plantation, there developed a reorientation of identity, a rethinking of who and what constituted the community. For in order to suffer at all, an identification with those so violated had to take place. In order for there to be any anguish, there would have necessarily been some reflection on the loss of power, on the inability to defend. In turn, the sensation of powerlessness and the outrage over the incapacity to shield was predicated on the need for power and the obligation to defend. The desire to intervene strongly suggests the beginning of a movement away from a previously defined, ethnically based identity to one in which the new community consisted of those jointly experiencing the ignominy. Those who reacted to the rape of African women moved into the continuum, whether or not they were conscious of it.

Having begun the process of reidentification by virtue of that which they withstood, Africans from all over West and West Central Africa poured into the fields and towns of the New World. They emerged from the holds of the slavers in various states of physical and mental health. They now had the potential to forge a new self-consciousness, informed by their common color, related cultures, and shared pain. To be sure, the direction of a reconceptualized community would be influenced by additional factors such as labor status, periodization, location, and so forth, so that the composite personality or set of personalities would vary. But with each new period, with each new task, in each and every locale, the African and her progeny made choices with regard to the preferred response to such stimuli. That is, the African had to make decisions concerning the meaning of her environment and what constituted a proper response. Some order and sense had to be fashioned out of New World disorder. To achieve this, the African antecedent was drawn upon, and in the process the African-based community began to see itself in heretofore unimagined ways.

· · · · · · ·

The African was brought onto the shores of North America in Charleston, in Savannah, in Mobile, in New Orleans, and in the various ports of the Chesapeake in the same way she had been removed from her native land—stripped of both mantle and honor. Nicholas Cresswell witnessed such a landing at Bridgetown, Barbados, in September 1774: "One of the most shocking sights I ever saw. About 400 Men, Women, and Children, brought from their native Country, deprived of their liberty. . . . They were all naked, except a small piece of blue cloth about a foot broad to cover their nakedness, and appear much dejected."[60]

The arrival of the African was more seasonal than not. According to Galenson, it was the pattern in the West Indies to receive relatively large numbers of vessels from late winter to early summer, with peaks in May and June; conversely, August to early winter witnessed the arrival of far fewer ships.[61] The timing was informed by weather patterns in both West Africa and the Caribbean. With regard to the former, slave traders sought to avoid the rainy season, when efforts were hampered by high levels of disease and mortality. Concerning the Caribbean, vessels preferred not to run the risk of sailing into island ports in the middle of hurricane season (August to October).

Of course, North American ports were not necessarily concerned with hurricane season, although the same vessels tended to make stops in North America and the West Indies, delivering partial cargoes in both places. For North America specifically, the season for the importation of Africans ran from late spring to late summer.[62] In addition to the consideration of West African rains, it was also believed that cold weather could be fatal to the new arrivals. Therefore, September marked the end of the season for purchasing Africans.[63]

Once the captives were transferred from the slavers to various buyers in North America, they were plunged into a period of seasoning. They had to adjust to different weather patterns, different food, different clothes, a different land. Much more profoundly, they had to come to terms with the idea of being a slave in North America. Gradually, the transplanted African would come to realize that the general dishonoring she was experiencing was much more directed toward and a consequence of her Africanness as opposed to her new status as a slave.

The various terms employed in the sources to refer to the African-born tend to be used interchangeably, but they were apparently intended in the original instance to locate the African within the phase of her acclimation. Thus newly arrived Africans were classified in the North American lexicon as "outlandish" in that they were "strangers to the English language" and had yet to learn their new roles.[64] Once the period of seasoning had been completed, these slaves were often thereafter known as "new Negroes." It is important to note, however, that the terms *new* and *outlandish* were not always applied uniformly. Mullin, for example, asserts that the latter was not used outside of the Chesapeake, so that these terms are not necessarily reliable indexes by which Africans could be located within the acculturative process.[65] However, the distinction between African-born (at whatever phase in their "development") and American-born blacks was consistently made by whites; the former were politely called "salt-water Negroes" and the latter "country-born Negroes" (although "nigger" was the only noun slaves ever heard following the modifier). Consideration of these appellations is not mere pedantry, for such labeling was of profound significance not only at the individual level but also at the corporate level.

The nakedness of the African arrival was covered, and his new death-in-life symbolically redefined, when upon disembarkation he was issued his "Osnabrugs," a type of clothing widely worn by slaves and made from coarse flax and tow, having been originally produced in Osnabrück, Germany.[66] At this point he began a process of seasoning that could last from one to three years.[67] As has been established earlier, the vast majority of Africans were imported directly into North America and not via the Caribbean, and therefore experienced their initiation into servility in Virginia, Carolina, Louisiana, and so on. Many, having survived the barracoon and the passage, died during this period.

There was no single method of seasoning Africans, so that the specific content of the process varied according to region, time, and idiosyncratic tendencies. Broad patterns, however, are somewhat discernible. Mullin, for example, insists that outlandish Africans in Virginia were not seasoned or broken in at all; rather, they were immediately placed in the fields to gather the year's final harvest.[68] Early in the colonial period and along the South Carolinian coast, on the other hand, a gang of newly arrived Africans would be assigned to drivers, reliable slaves who broke them in by way of alternate instruction and minor punishment, including the withholding of food.[69] It was the task of these drivers to teach the new arrivals the skills they would need to perform the work. In order to do so, the drivers had to communicate with the outlandish in "broken" English. The relationship between language and identity is direct and didactic, meriting closer scrutiny.

By the end of the year, the South Carolinian driver would have discharged his responsibilities. The "new Negro" would now be supervised by either the owner or the overseer, having joined others "who had long since learned to obey orders, to arise when the conch blew at 'day clean,' to handle a hoe in listing and banking, to stand still when a white man spoke."[70] Thus a political education was embedded in the vocational training. White men, who in Africa were viewed as equals to their African trading partners, had emerged as the sole power brokers during the passage, and now represented ultimate authority on the plantation and farm. The objective of the African's forced migration from outlandishness to newness was to fully appreciate this aspect of the white man, of whiteness. White was associated with power and control; black, blackness, black was the equivalent of subordination. The moral attributes of good and evil would soon be added to the African's repertoire of color association. The new language itself was fashioned to contain words and meanings reinforcing such associations. But whatever the dimension of the education received by the African, in whatever phase, there was one consistent, insistent, and unifying theme to them all: difference was inherent. What she had become, a slave, was not a function of circumstance; rather, it was who she was all along, what she was providentially meant to be. Destiny, she was taught, was derivative of birth.

In contrast to the procedures described for Virginia and the South Carolinian coast, Africans imported into Louisiana received a somewhat different welcome. "Negroes bought from the importers and carried home by the purchasers are ordinarily treated differently from the old ones. They are only gradually accustomed to work. They are made to bathe often, to take walks from time to time, and especially to dance," a regimen readily remembered from the slave ship.[71] Newcomers to Louisiana were divided into small groups and placed under the tutelage of older slaves. This more gradual approach was informed by prior experience that saw slaves, pushed too far too fast, either abscond, die from disease and distress, or commit suicide.[72] The African was all too familiar with "melancholy" from the days of the passage. Slaveholders had to therefore exercise restraint lest they minimize the return on their investment.

Whatever the specifics of the seasoning process, the newly arrived African had been brought to the shores of North America for a single purpose: to work. She would have to learn what was expected of her and either employ skills she already possessed or incorporate new information in the performance of her tasks. He would need to understand appropriate and inappropriate behavior in the presence of the slaveholder and what his conduct should be toward whites in general, particularly white women. Back in the slave quarters, it would be necessary to interact with fellow slaves in meaningful ways. There would have to be some general understanding of the rules or the expectations governing social engagement within the African-based community. Somehow, the politesse of the slave quarters had to be established, and the most effective means of communicating social and political organization was language. Language is indispensable to social order.

The question of language is absolutely critical to understanding the transformation of the African into the African American.[73] It has served as a primary facilitator of that transformation, carrying within it the very essence of race and class conflict. As the articulation and explication of consciousness, it conveys messages of domestication and resistance. It reflects social distance and assists in maintaining it, succeeding in creating requisite proximity and locking the participants into place. It is both the bridge and the void over which it extends. Its words, its multiple constructions, its various rhythms speak of power, privilege, and deprivation. Language is a world of polarities, polarizing in its use, a tool of incredible destruction. A weapon of war, it constitutes a war unto itself. It is a primary theater of conflict, a principal site of contention.

To listen to America's internal dialogue is to comprehend the ability of language to transcend parochial aims. In arguing that conventional education domesticates, Freire focuses on questions of content and methodology.[74] To be sure, the instruction Africans received and the means employed to reinforce it were certainly intended to domesticate, to produce a new Negro. But in the North American (and arguably even the Brazilian) context, the medium of instruction itself collaborated with the curriculum. In fact, as a tool of adjustment, it was just as important as content. Language was co-conspirator in the process of enslavement, a veritable "colonization of the mind."[75] Language became synonymous with the condition of servility, and as such was reinvented, having vaulted over symbolism to achieve substance itself.

With this understood, it is no longer sufficient to view the question of Africans speaking European languages as a function of cognitive skills, physical age, approximation to whites, relationship to specific tasks, and so forth. Admittedly, these are issues to consider, but none go to the heart of the matter. The real question is not, How difficult was it for Africans to learn English words? Rather, the truly important queries are, What did it mean to the African to hear and at some point repeat words associated with his captors? What did it signify to the African to be expected to learn and embrace concepts which further concretized his condition of social death? What was it like to have the world renamed, redefined, and reimagined for him? Sober reflection leads to the conclusion that the African understood the political nature of his predicament. And in that setting, he also understood that this new language was profoundly political. It stands to reason that he would respond in kind.

The enslaved had several matters to consider. To be sure, new words were necessary. But the degree to which the African chose to ever utter these words was very much an individual choice. The fact that she may have spoken "broken" or "bad" English does not at all mean that she did not understand the language. Although it is obvious that some would have picked up the rudiments with ease and would have spoken the tongue with facility, others may have simply refused to speak it, or to speak it very much, out of a conscious decision to resist their oppression. As Caliban used Prospero's words to curse him (and Miranda), the African may have cursed the words themselves.

But in addition to interfacing with the world of white folk, and of far greater significance, was the need for the African-based community to self-dialogue. And it is in this arena, and for the purpose of promoting such fellowship, that the community was forced to invent a lingua franca of its own. There exists sufficient evidence to demonstrate that many, if not most, Africans continued to speak their native language in North America. Those of shared ethnicity or from a region in which more than one language was familiar would have continued in this vein. But the need to communicate with Africans of dissimilar background, combined with the challenge of passing on something of themselves to their American-born progeny, meant that some other means of communication had to be found. In anglophone North America, English was the obvious solution.

But it could not be white folk's English. The African could not simply parrot what he heard from the very fount of oppression. No, the words had to be altered. The syntax had to conform to that which was more reminiscent of home. The meter required attenuation so that when spoken, the language would be as deracinated as possible. So the African put his indelible, undeniable imprint on the language, re-creating it in his own image to the degree that was possible. As Herskovits observed some time ago, "Whether Negro speech employs English or French or Spanish or Portuguese vocabulary, the identical constructions found all over the New World can only be regarded as a reflection of the underlying similarities in grammar and idiom, which, in turn, are common to the West African Sudanese tongues."[76] In this way, the African American community linked arms with diasporic communities throughout the hemisphere, so that everywhere European languages were heard spoken through African modulations and tonalities.

It is important to place the discussion of the political implications of language here, at the outset of the consideration of acculturative forces. It is crucial to see that such forces do not proceed in a vacuum, totally oblivious to their surroundings and unaffected by them. It is inescapable that the interplay between culture and sociopolity is extensive and mutually conditioning, whether the society is free or enslaved, and especially in the case of the latter. One cannot undertake a serious study of acculturation in a society so extremely polarized without taking into consideration these dichotomies. Without such inclusion, the investigation may provide provocative models and theories, but remain far from the essence.

When I speak a word, I am extending myself to the listener. I am drawing from that which I understand about myself and my relationship to my reality and sharing it with another person. My isolation, my separateness, my aloneness is transcended by means of language; I have the power to break out of my insularity when I utter a word meant to be heard. In this way, I affirm and reaffirm my essential humanity and identify myself with my community. I engage that community, link with it, merge with it in the very process of speaking through space into the receptive capacity of the community. That I can speak a word and have it understood, and can in turn understand the words of others in my community, constitutes a celebration of my belonging to others of like mind. The bond between us is very much formed and strengthened by our words. Our words represent us, for they are our words. Our words declare our vision of the world and our relationship to it. We are our words.

To be forced to employ the words of another is beyond oppression as such. It represents more than a socioeconomic inversion. It goes beyond the physical. It is a violation of my psychic space, an intrusion into the deepest recesses of my being. To completely acquiesce is nearly impossible, for it would mean the total collapse of the personality. I may therefore learn a few words, and may even speak them, but I will speak them in my own way, in my own cadence, and with my own meanings. And I will share this attitude with my children and my children's children. I will subvert this language.

It is the political context, then, that best prepares the inquiry into intercultural exchange. The African began the process once he stepped onto American shores and entered the period of seasoning; the process has yet to end. As an outlandish fellow, he would have been introduced to a few English words as a necessary prerequisite to performing various tasks. Blassingame writes that the African acquired this limited vocabulary "in a relatively casual and haphazard fashion."[77] This led to a kind of pidgin English, allowing for communication between slaveholder (or overseer) and slave. But back in the quarter, the African would have continued to speak in his native tongue whenever possible. This is because there is no hard evidence to support the popular notion that newly arrived Africans of the same ethnicity or area of origin were separated. Rather, there is every reason to believe that they were kept together.

Huggins, as late as 1977, wrote that slave traders and slaveholders "preferred to mix the Africans, avoiding concentrating any one people together."[78] But Herskovits, as early as 1941, assailed as a fallacy the belief that Africans "as a matter of policy, were distributed in the New World so as to lose tribal identity, [so that] no least common denominator of understanding or behavior could have possibly been worked out among them," and that such a misperception contributed to the Western mythological construction of the African experience.[79] In the absence of information that would support intraethnic divisions as a general phenomenon, one can only posit the likelihood that captives from the same area were purchased and housed together. If slavers were successful in filling their quotas from one region, that success would have been reflected on the plantation or farm of the eventual purchaser. Activity in more than one region would have also been evinced on plantation rolls. When the specific preferences of many planters are coupled with the demographic data suggesting high densities of certain ethnic groups per colony and state, it becomes even more unlikely that intraethnic divisions took place on a significant scale, or that planters were even in a position to carry out such a scheme. This was especially true of French colonial Louisiana, where due to Haiti's domination of imported African labor, planters kept families of the same ethnicity together to promote a stable and self-sustaining servile population.[80]

The outlandish, therefore, had in all probability sufficient occasion to commune in their own languages in the quarters while they learned to differentiate the harsh sounds of English speech. Blassingame has found that on the larger plantations, where contact with whites was at a minimum, Africans were "remarkably successful in retaining elements of their native language."[81] But the ability to retain one's native tongue did not rest on the degree of contact with whites; after all, Bilali and his family on a large estate in Georgia and Abd al-Rahman and Samba on a very small Mississippi farm all spoke their native language. Martha Page, who was eighty-four years old and lived in the Yamacraw section of Savannah during the time of the WPA interviews, remembered that her African grandfather used to talk with two others on the plantation in a foreign language.[82] Anna Miller of Frogtown and Currytown, on the western limits of Savannah, also testified in the 1930s that several of the older workers on the Butler Island plantation spoke a "funny language."[83] Tony William Delegal, more than one hundred years old at the time, could even sing an African song, which was recorded by the interviewer as follows:

Wa kum kum munin
Kum baba yano
Lai lai tambe
Ashi boong a nomo
Shi wali go
Ashi quank
Kum baba yano
Lai lai tambe
Ashi lai lai lai
Shi wali go
Dhun.[84]

The fact that Delegal (a form of Senegal?) could remember these words is itself testimony that African languages were kept alive by the African-born and passed on to descendants in certain instances.

The native African, with rare exception, did not forget her own language, whether or not she ever learned or demonstrated that she had learned the

English dialect. The most profound testimony to this fact can be observed in accounts concerning the survivors of the aforementioned *Wanderer* and *Clotilde*, two slavers that illegally entered North American waters in 1858 and 1859, respectively.[85] The *Wanderer* first landed at Jekyll Island, Georgia, from which point some of the captives were sent to Florida, then taken up the Saint Johns River and sold. In addition, about 170 Africans were brought up the Savannah River to about two miles north of Augusta, on the Carolina side of the river. From there they either remained in the area or were sold as far away as Mississippi. A number were still alive in 1908, including Mabiala, who had been given the name Uster Williams. Living near Augusta, Mabiala had managed to retain "his memory of African words and customs in a remarkable degree." Two others, Cilucangy (Ward Lee) and Tahro (Romeo) of Edgefield County, South Carolina, "seem to speak fluently their native language, and remember much of the life in Africa."[86] This, after fifty years in America, most following the Civil War.

Similarly, the *Clotilde* entered Mobile, Alabama, with a cargo of 116 Africans purportedly recruited at Whydah. Some were dispersed to the plantation of John Dabney below Mount Vernon, Alabama. A smaller group was subsequently taken to Magazine Point, Alabama. At the time of Roche's writing in 1914, eight of this last group were still alive, having all come from the same village of "Tarkar." They were said to all "bear upon their faces the Tarkar tribal marks—two lines between the eyes and three on the cheek." The interviewer went on: "Among themselves they speak the Tarkar language. Their English is very broken and is not always intelligible even to those who have lived among them for many years." That is, there were Africans in the United States who still spoke their native tongue but had yet to demonstrate mastery of the English language after fifty-five years of life in America. In 1914, no less. And because these examples come from so late in the period of slavery and beyond, it would appear that the matter of Africans learning English was not necessarily a function of the specific period in question.

The ability of Africans to communicate in their own language with others of like background was a factor influencing the manner in and degree to which they acquired English and must be considered in tandem with the political implications of declining to speak English. Convenience may have joined the impetus of cultural resistance. These two factors should at least be recognized as consequential, and in all probability outweighed questions of individual capacity. It would appear, in fact, that some African-born slaves absolutely refused to engage the language. For example, in 1724 the minister of Christ Church Parish in Virginia explained the insignificant number of conversions by appealing to the barrier of language: "A great many Black bond men and women infidels that understand not our Language nor me their's: not any free."[87] Just before the end of the colonial period, one Smyth visited Virginia and was of the opinion that at least two-thirds of the population were black. He went on to say, and in so stating supported both the idea of cultural resistance and clustering in Virginia, that one "cannot understand all of them, as great numbers, being Africans, are incapable of acquiring our language, and at best but very imperfectly, if at all; many of them speak a mixed dialect between the Guinea and English."[88] It is instructive that the phenomenon continued right up to the Civil War, for Olmsted, in the course of his southern journeys in the 1850s, writes that he encountered an old African woman who had been enslaved as a young girl but "spoke almost unintelligibly."[89] Another observer notes that by the time of the Civil War, there were still slaves who could not "make themselves understood in English."[90]

The descendants of the African-born bear witness to the accounts of observers external to the community. Eighty-one-year-old Charley Barber of Winnsboro, South Carolina, in discussing his African-born parents Jacob and Jemima in the 1930s, stated that they "never did talk lak de other slaves, could just say a few words, use deir hands, and make signs."[91] Mary Gladdy, who was born around 1853 near Columbus, Georgia, described her grandfather as "a very black, little, full-blooded African Negro who could speak only broken English. . . . I don't believe he was over five feet high, and we could hardly understand his talk."[92] Richard Jones of Union, South Carolina, who was either 93 or 125 years old in 1937, offered the following: "Uncle Tom come 'long wid Granny Judith [from Africa]. . . . When dey talk, nobody didn't know what dey was talking about. My granny never could speak good like I can. She talk half African, and all African when she git bothered."[93] Mary Smith, also of Union and 84 years of age in 1937, simply said that her African grandfather "talked real funny."[94]

The foregoing evidence makes it clear that many African-born slaves never demonstrated significant facility with the English tongue, and continued to speak their own language. But the same examples also contain information on the evolution of an Africanized English among other Africans. Johnson recalls the words of Cass Stewart, who in 1934 was about eighty-five years old: "I was wid de Africans. Dey couldn't understand what dey was saying deyselves."[95] That is, people of like background could get along just fine, but those of different ethnicities had to somehow bridge the gap. Not all were as versatile as Betty, who in October 1785 had run away from Samuel Beecroft of Georgia and could speak "tolerable English, and understands two or three different African languages."[96] Nor were all as conversant as Moses, an American-born slave who at age fifty could speak "several African languages."[97] They therefore lighted upon the scheme of developing an Africanized form of English sufficient to both facilitate their internal dialogue and to interface with whites. Thus Smyth's earlier reference to a "mixed dialect between the Guinea and the English" is precisely what Blassingame means when he writes that in the course of the eighteenth century "a patois containing English and African words developed in the quarters."[98] The patois, however, consisted of more than just African words; it also used African syntax and meter. What is more, it was this Africanized version of English that reissued from within the slave community and made a lasting impact upon the speech of the South, such that Herskovits observed:

> Certain aspects of American speech, particularly the pronunciation of English by Southerners, whether Negro or white, must also be referred to Africa. . . . What happened, then, when the Negroes came to the New World? They learned new words—in English, Spanish, Portuguese or French—but they spoke these words with a West African pronunciation, and poured their new vocabulary into the mold of West African grammatical and idiomatic forms. And, having done this, many of them were entrusted with raising the children of their masters.[99]

The Africanization of the English language influenced even whites to unwittingly participate in its alteration. But in adjusting to the African influence, whites retained all the prerogatives of power, and at the end of the day, African Americans continued to tinker with the language in order to maintain distance, distinctiveness, and some sense of ownership.

The imposition of English was therefore not a complete victory for the slaveholders; the process was, in the end, transformative for all parties involved. Africans were taught one brand of English but gave back another. In so doing, they manifested a continued desire to resist the slaveocracy and to name the world, even if it did not belong to them. It is therefore the combination of political defiance and both intra- and interacculturative forces that together informed the process of learning and Africanizing the English language. The experience would slowly but surely alter the African self-perception as well.

A detailed analysis of the relationship between the African-born slave population and the English and French languages, based upon runaway slave ads, is instructive. Factors such as time period, age, region, and ethnicity have been correlated to determine any discernible patterns. However, it should be remembered that the languages under consideration were almost invariably Africanized. We are not here dealing with the King's English.

An examination of newspapers consulted for the purposes of this study has produced the categories and tallies found in table 7.1. The designations "none," "little," and "very little" employed in the table are all imprecise and conceivably interchangeable. Similarly, terms such as "bad," "very bad," and "broken" are not always used consistently, so that these words may have conveyed slightly different meanings to different people. It is likely that such characterizations as "very little" and "very bad" were in fact functional equivalents, so that the first two columns should be viewed as a continuum of those who, for all practical purposes, could not speak English or French effectively. On the other hand, Africans who spoke the language "tolerably well" or "good" were clearly those who could make themselves understood to whites.

The above categories reveal that more than 71 percent of all those Africans mentioned in the consulted newspapers did not speak English/French effectively. Nearly 70 percent were twenty-nine years of age or younger, whereas nearly 50 percent of those who spoke "good" English/French were thirty years old or older. This suggests that the latter group's greater facility was a consequence of longer exposure, a generalization consistent with the evidence that almost 50 percent of those who had spent more than three years in North America spoke the language "tolerably well." In contrast, only 25 percent of those who has been in the country between one and three years could speak "good" English/French.

It is interesting to note that some 68 percent of the ads featuring individuals who could not speak English/French effectively were published between 1800 and 1830, down only slightly from the nearly 72 percent featuring similar persons prior to 1800. This suggests that although those who were longer exposed to English/French became progressively better at speaking it, the phenomenon of nearly three-fourths of all Africans either unable or unwilling to speak the language continued well into the nineteenth century. Interestingly, whereas 72 percent of the men did not speak effectively in a European tongue and 28 percent did, the figures for women were somewhat different in that 39 percent spoke English and French well enough and 61 percent did not. The database is simply too small, however, to further extrapolate on the basis of gender.

Concerning the various colonies/states and regions of origin, the statistical base is too narrow to draw any conclusions upon which a composite picture of the African-born community can be predicated. There is nothing to suggest, however, that certain ethnic groups demonstrated any significantly greater facility in a European language than others, with the number of Africans speaking "no" or "bad" English/French ranging from 56 percent (Bight of Biafra) to 69 percent (Sierra Leone) to 76 percent (Africa). In fact, the percentages for Senegambia, the Gold Coast, Sierra Leone, and West

TABLE 7.1 Quality of English or French Spoken by Africans

	None, Little/ Very Little	Bad/ Very Bad, Broken	Good/ Very Good
Total	435	269	285
QUALITY SPOKEN BY AGE OF AFRICANS			
Age 12 or under	9	0	2
Ages 13–29	113	64	79
Age 30 and over	32	49	83
QUALITY SPOKEN BY GENDER			
Male	379	240	239
Female	49	27	48
QUALITY SPOKEN BY COLONY/STATE			
Virginia	39	36	24
Maryland	14	10	15
South Carolina	194	81	122
North Carolina	4	7	5
Georgia	165	122	94
Louisiana	12	7	20
Tennessee	0	1	11
Mississippi	4	5	3
QUALITY SPOKEN BY REGION OF ORIGIN			
Senegambia	35	14	24
Gold Coast	24	4	14
Sierra Leone[a]	68	66	61
Bight of Biafra	17	13	24
West Central	54	29	51
"Africa"	235	142	109
QUALITY BY PERIOD OF TIME			
To 1750	29	14	26
1750–1800	336	202	205
1800–1830	59	53	53
QUALITY BY NUMBER OF YEARS IN NORTH AMERICA			
1 year or less	25	9	0
1–3 years	22	6	7
More than 3 years	0	18	16

a. I have placed those who were said to have come from "Guinea" into this category. The "Guinea" designation could have been a reference to Africa in general or to some other location, but in most instances this is not clear. I have also placed those from "Gola" (not more than ten individuals) into this category, although it is possible that Angola would be more appropriate. As a result, the numbers in this category are in all probability greatly inflated.

Central Africa are practically identical (67 percent, 67 percent, 69 percent, and 62 percent, respectively). With regard to states/colonies/territories and concerning the same category of Africans, there is a much wider range, beginning with Louisiana's 49 percent and ending with Mississippi and Georgia's 75 percent. Again, however, the database is uneven and inexhaustive.

The foregoing discussion raises interesting implications. At any one time prior to 1830, it is possible that from two-thirds to three-fourths of all African-born slaves either could not or did not speak recognizable English or French. This means that they were either speaking their native languages to one another or a version of English/French so Africanized as to be unintelligible to whites, or both. Implicit in such high percentages is the political posture of cultural resistance discussed previously.

The restructuring of the African identity, principally involving a move away from ethnicity toward race, would have been greatly facilitated by the creation of a lingua franca emblematic of the African's altered condition in the New World. Cooperation between individuals of different ethnicities would have met with varying degrees of success or failure depending upon their ability to effectively communicate. One of the most important corporate ventures that Africans could have undertaken was to abscond. That Africans regularly crossed ethnic boundaries and literally took steps in the direction of redefining themselves is amply documented in the runaway slave advertisements, examples of which are provided in the previous chapter, especially as they relate to the Igbo.

Consistent with interethnic, familial cooperation but with a different twist was the case of Charles and Peggy and Breetchie and Venus, who in February 1790 took off from Mrs. Elbert's plantation on Argyle Island. Both couples are described as husband and wife, but the first couple is depicted as Angolan, whereas both members of the second were Igbo.[100] That these two families had decided to embark together upon a most dangerous venture implies that sufficient mutual respect and good will had been established between the couples. The fact that Breetchie spoke "good" English and Charles did not underscores a strategy whereby Africanized English was developed to promote communication within the African-based community; once achieved, the language could be used to facilitate escape.

The example of the above couples is a wonderful illustration of the process by which Africans began to reexamine ethnicity. Charles and Peggy probably went to their graves viewing themselves as Angolan; however, implicit in their mutual exploit with the Igbo couple was the perception of common ground with the latter. Without question, the sameness of their condition had already been reinforced by way of common experiences, for example, the Middle Passage, seasoning, the rationing of uniform clothing, the similarities of agricultural tasks, and the reality of the external, white world. It was the acquisition of English, though, that allowed the two couples to plan their departure.

In some instances an African language served as the chief means of communication. In many such cases, it was not unusual to learn that the majority of the abscondees were from the same area, thus minimizing communication difficulties. This can be observed in the 1769 publication of the *Georgia Gazette*, in which was discussed the escape of three men and three women from the Georgia plantation of Lachlan M'Gillivray, none of whom could "speak English, nor tell their master's name."[101] All were of the "Guinea country," except for one of the men. It would appear, therefore, that the six were pairs, and that the one interethnic pairing had received the approbation of the others. The lone "non-Guinean" must have found other means of communicating with the larger group, of identifying with their dissatisfaction and resolve to change their circumstances. The tendency for non-English speaking abscondees to form nearly homogenic groups was clearly a response to the need for participants to coordinate their efforts as best as possible. The pattern can be observed in nonfamilial groupings as well, as is evidenced in the November 1761 notice of Thomas Middleton of South Carolina, who awakened one morning to find that eight men had fled the manor. Seven were "Coromantee negro men," and the other was a "Calabar." Middleton went on to state that they all "have been in the province about 15 months, and speak little English."[102]

On the other hand, many who were not ethnically similar ran away together. South Carolinian William Martin reported in 1738 that nineteen-year-old Levi, "an Angolan," had escaped with an Igbo named Kent.[103] Levi could be identified by the "silver Bobb in his right Ear" (not the only reference to male Africans and African Americans wearing earrings). A 1774 case featured "Homidy a Guinea negro . . . ears bored" and "Polydore, or whose country name is Savey, a Congo negro, 25 years old . . . the fore teeth of his upper jaw filed."[104] Yet another example of interethnic cooperation (sans the earrings) was originally filed in April 1743, when Edward Fisher reported the absence of "Cyrus and Caesar, the former is an Ebo, and the other an Angola Fellow," both of whom spoke "pretty good English."[105] Peter and Flanders, an Angolan and a Gambian respectively who both spoke English well, had no intention of being recaptured in April 1769, having taken with them two guns and a cutlass.[106]

Africans of varying ethnic backgrounds absconded in both large and small groups as well as traveled alone. The group could be as small as two or three, such as was the case in 1806, when a Congolese, a Bambara, and a third man fled a Louisiana plantation.[107] Higher numbers were also not unusual, as is evident from both previous examples and from such ads as the one placed in the *Columbian Museum and Savannah Advertiser* calling for the return of six "new" men from the Angola and "Coromantee countries."[108] Or the count could be extraordinarily high, constituting a virtual jailbreak, as was the previously mentioned 1813 case in Florida, when thirty-six slaves, among whom were fifteen Africans, escaped from Amelia Island following the War of 1812.[109]

Of course, an important question to ask is, Where did these people think they were going? If they had limited knowledge of English, or were unfamiliar with the concept of "the North" (especially during the colonial period, when the North had yet to emerge as a place of refuge), what place did they perceive as constituting asylum? For some, a brief respite in the woods, just long enough to clear their heads, was the objective. Others returned to the plantations of previous owners, where they could rejoin those with whom they shared amicable or familial bonds. But others were clearly after a more permanent solution, a more enduring alternative to life as a slave. Thus many absconded into the woods never to return, electing to live out their lives as Maroons. Mention has already been made of the Maroon formations in Louisiana and their impact upon the development of that area. It is also known that a number of blacks absconded from Carolina and Georgia into Florida, where they created either independent Maroon societies or became part of existing Seminole communities.[110]

By the last quarter of the eighteenth century, people of African and Native American descent had established a number of settlements along the Suwannee and Apalachiola Rivers, in addition to those of longer standing in eastern and central Florida. Tensions between Georgia and the Seminoles over the status of absconded slaves led to even greater affinities between the latter and their African refugees. In 1812, Seminoles and Africans were successful in defeating an army raised in Georgia, and by 1814 the former alliance had gone on to create, with British assistance, a fortified position thirty miles above the mouth of the Apalachiola River, "generally called the Negro Fort" but officially named Fort Blount.[111] The fort provided security for a number of African Seminole farming settlements. Such was the threat of the African Seminoles that Andrew Jackson personally led an assault on Fort Blount in July 1816. When Florida was claimed by the United States in 1821, Africans and Native Americans responded by retreating more deeply into the "fastnesses of the Florida swamps and forests." The so-called Seminole Wars ensued, lasting until 1842.

But Florida and Louisiana were not the only areas in which Africans sought to restructure their lives. Similar attempts were made in the more remote places of Georgia and South Carolina. Evidence for the former can be found in the October 1786 publication of the *Georgia State Gazette or Independent Register*. A careful reading of the following article reveals that there was clear intent to fashion an autonomous, self-sufficient community on the part of the African-based community, and that such intent was met with murderous resolve:

> SAVANNAH. October 19. A number of runaway Negroes (supposed upwards of 100) having sheltered themselves on Belleisle Island, about 17 or 18 miles up Savannah river, and for some time past committed robberies on the neighbouring planters, it was found necessary to attempt to dislodge them. On Wednesday the 11th inst. a small party of militia landed and attacked them, and killed three or four, but were at last obliged to retreat for want of ammunitions, having four of their number wounded. Same evening, about sunset, 15 of the Savannah light infantry and three or four others drove in one of their outguards, but the Negroes came down in such numbers that it was judged advisable to retire to their boats, from which the Negroes attempted to cut them off, but were prevented by Lieutenant Else of the artillery, who commanded a boat with 11 of the company, and had a field piece on board, which he discharged three times with grape shot, and it is thought either killed or wounded some of them, as a good deal of blood was afterwards seen about the place to which the shot was directed. On Friday morning General Jackson with a party proceeded to their camp, which they had quitted precipitately on his approach. He remained till Saturday afternoon, when he left the island, having destroyed as much rough rice as would have made 25 barrels or more if beat out, and brought off about 60 bushels of corn, and 14 or 15 boats and canoes from the landing. He also burnt a number of their houses and huts, and destroyed about four acres of green rice. The loss of their provisions, it is expected, will occasion them to disperse about the country, and it is hoped, will be the means of most of them being soon taken up.[112]

These abscondees had planted and harvested a considerable amount of food; they had set up security systems, and they were determined to defend themselves.

The following year, South Carolina was encountering similar problems with absconded slaves. As was true for Georgia, a lengthy reproduction of the account is helpful as it constitutes in itself an important document, casting new insights into the ubiquity of the Maroon as a form of resistance:

> SAVANNAH, April 26. The Legislature of South-Carolina, taking into consideration the daring state of the runaway slaves, ordered, at their

last session, a company of minutemen, and a draft of the Granville county militia, for the purpose of keeping the field till they are totally broken up.

SAVANNAH, May 10. In consequence of the orders of the Executives of the two states a co-operation against the banditti of runaway slaves commenced the 1st instant, and a junction of troops . . . took place at the old camp in the fork of Abercorn, and Collins's Creeks. . . . [The mission discovered] a negro camp at Patton's Swamp [which was successfully defeated]. A correspondent observes that the late decisive effort made by Col. Gunn to break up the camp, and destroy the confidence and strength of the runaways, cannot fail of producing the best effects, as they had got seated and strongly fortified in the midst of an almost impenetrable swamp, and opening a general asylum, which no doubt would have been embraced by many on the approach of hot weather. Indeed running away had already become more prevalent than usual.[113]

The Maroon experiences of Carolina and Georgia, combined with those of Florida and Louisiana, suggest that within the African-based community there resided a strong aspiration to return to life as it had been lived prior to the initial capture. To the extent that these communities consisted of multiple ethnicities and Native Americans, they would have been challenged to reconsider and reshape their corporate identity in response to yet again altered circumstances. But the removal to the Maroon was an attempt to re-create Africa in the swamps and inner recesses of America, and as such would have entailed to some degree a reaffirmation of ethnicity as previously understood.

Other Africans who took flight were even more ambitious than the Maroons. Twenty-two-year-old Tom, for example, had been in Maryland for two and a half years when in 1761 he took his leave from the plantation of Robert Peter at Rock Creek. Peter also reported that a canoe was missing and surmised that Tom had probably used it to escape, given that the African had made an earlier escape to "get to sea in an open boat."[114] Charleston's *South-Carolina Gazette and Country Journal* published a similar notice in November 1769, in which five Angolan men stole away from the Brother-hood plantation on the Great Pee Dee River. Bearing their country marks, they were said to have headed east, "thinking to return to their own country that way."[115] Interestingly, the five men had been missing since August of the previous year.

A final example of Africans seeking to return to "their own country" comes from the *South-Carolina and American General Gazette*, which in January 1775 solicited information on the whereabouts of four African men and a woman who was probably American-born. This likelihood is enhanced by the details: "These people went away with the wench in a small paddling canoe, and put her ashore somewhere near White Bluff, where she was taken up by one Mr. Johnston, and on examining her since she says the other negroes told her they intended to go to look for their own country, and that the boat was not big enough to carry her with them."[116] What is interesting is not that the Africans sacrificed the woman in their attempt to return to Africa, but that the woman had also elected to embark on the same journey. Perhaps one or both of her parents were African-born; whatever her background, she had made a concrete identification with the land of her forebears.

Attempts to return to Africa, along with the creation of numerous Maroon communities throughout the South, underscore the fact that although Africans may have left Africa, Africa never left them. Freedom, whatever it would eventually come to mean within the North American context, meant to these people nothing less than reversing the direction and consequences of the Middle Passage. Of course, most would not achieve such an end; they could not avoid the reality of North America and were forced to reexamine their individual and collective identity in the light of radically changed material conditions. This chapter has looked into the question of interethnic relations and has argued that the commonality of experiences extending from the barracoon through the period of seasoning began a process whereby Africans moved along a continuum from ethnicity to race. It should be understood, however, that such movement was modest at best. These experiences, traumatic and invasive as they were, were not sufficient to overturn the construct of personhood so carefully and thoroughly erected on Africa soil. Yet a beginning had been made.

To some extent this chapter (and certainly those that follow) has maintained the book's focus on the development of an African-based society in America from its inception to 1830 (with some unavoidable commentary on subsequent years) while differing from the preceding chapters in at least one of two ways: one, the sources for the period are for the most part recorded after 1830; and/or two, interpretations of phenomena associated with the period are largely formulated after 1830. The next chapter is illustrative in that its investigation of the complex question of African–African American relations, out of which will eventually emerge the latter's conception of identity, are very much informed by the WPA interviews of the 1930s.

8

. . . .

TAD'S QUERY

ETHNICITY AND CLASS IN AFRICAN AMERICA

It would take some time for Africans to assimilate the battery of novel and strange information with which they were assaulted upon their arrival in North America. They would have to make adjustments to a world of white domination in which they were forced to assume a different socioeconomic station in life. Whites clearly perceived them in certain ways, primarily as primates predestined to draw and hew. But it is the self-perception, the self-view of the African-born with which this book is concerned. Africans would indeed begin to revise their self-definition, but this would prove to be a time-consuming process informed by a number of factors, including the African precursor, the material conditions of servitude, the interpretation and rein-terpretation of religion, regional and local permutations in the organization of slave society, cultural and social interaction with others of African descent, and resistance to hostility. The African himself had a great deal to say about how all of these elements would combine to fashion a coherency capable of supporting the struggle to survive.

Throughout their sojourn in America, Africans were quite unimpressed with the culture and achievements of the slaveholder. As Ball reported in the nineteenth century, the

> native Africans are revengeful, and unforgiving in their tempers, easily
> provoked, and cruel in their designs. They generally place little, or even

no value, upon the fine houses, and superb furniture of their masters; and discover no beauty in the fair complexions, and delicate forms of their mistresses. They feel indignant at the servitude that is imposed upon them, and only want power to inflict the most cruel retribution upon their oppressors; but they desire only the means of subsistence, and temporary gratification in this country, during their abode here.[1]

That is, many Africans responded to their new environment by rejecting the acculturative process. Although there were surely those who acquiesced to their enslavement to the point of obsequity, it is important to note that the overwhelming characterization of the African-born was consistently one of defiance. One of the most vivid examples of African antagonism to slave-holders comes from the pages of the *Gazette of the State of Georgia*, which in 1789 featured the following story entitled "African Humanity":

A MOORISH slave, having been severely beaten by his master, resolved on taking vengeance, which he executed in the following way: During the gentleman's absence he secured the gates (the house being in the country) in the strongest manner; and having fast bound his mistress and her three children conveyed them to the roof of the house, where he sat with the greatest composure. The gentleman returning, and ringing for admittance, was surprised at seeing the slave in that situation, and threatened him with the severest punishment, if he did not open the gate immediately. The slave tauntingly replied, "He would soon make him alter his language." Then taking up two of the children, and bidding them go open the gate, he flung them over the battlements. The father, in the greatest consternation, promised him not only pardon for the two murders, but even freedom and money, if he would spare his wife and third child. "I will never believe you," exclaimed the slave, "unless you convince me you are in earnest by cutting off your nose." This injunction being complied with, the villain immediately flung down the child and mother, and on hearing the piercing outcries of his master, advised him to go hang himself, as his only resource. To complete his savage triumph, he threw himself after them, and expired without a groan.[2]

To be sure, the preceding account is melodramatic to the point of incredulity, but whether invented, embellished, or factual, the story is clearly instructive in that it warns slaveholders of the dangers of both excessive punishment and excessive trust. That the slave would be left alone with the owner's family suggests the latter. That he was a "Moor" underscores this likelihood, given the earlier discussion of Muslims. The moral of the story is inescapable: even a privileged Muslim cannot be fully trusted, so have a care for the non-privileged African-born, as they are particularly dangerous.

The perception of the African-born as potentially threatening has a basis in fact; slaveholders were more than justified in their apprehension. In addition to the dehumanizing experience of the plantation system itself, Africans resented their removal from ancestral ground. Those transported to North America were initially single-minded in their desire to return to their native land. Whether they returned in this life or the next, they knew that America could never be their home; Africa remained their mental and emotional center.

"The case is different with the American negro, who knows nothing of Africa, her religion, or customs, and who has borrowed all his ideas of present and future happiness, from the opinions and intercourse of white people, and of Christians."[3] This statement, published in 1837, is a vast oversimplification of the alleged dichotomy between African- and American-born blacks, having as its purpose the promotion of abolitionism through emphasizing cultural distance between the two groups, thereby lending credence to the notion that blacks were capable of "progress." Even so, the quote is useful in that it reflects a class rift that would eventually develop between assimilated and non-assimilated blacks. With the advance of time and the decline of the African-born population vis-à-vis its burgeoning American-born counterpart, a significant proportion of the latter would begin to seek some form of rapprochement with American society and would promote the cause of inclusion. On the other hand, a substantial number of American-born blacks would continue to identify, or be identified with, those social and cultural norms firmly associated with Africa. It was not simply a matter of different culinary tastes or sumptuary preferences. It was more than a question of linguistic divergence or theological and philosophical departures. The sum total of these developments meant that these two basic components of black society, the one African-centered and the other American-centered, were traveling in opposite directions, headed for qualities of distinction. By the middle of the nineteenth century, perceived differences had crystallized: the two camps viewed themselves as related but separate and discrete. The Negro had fully evolved.

Although the African-born desperately yearned to return to Africa, it is obvious that many would die in such a state. At some point between disembarkation and the grave, between sowing and harvesting, picking and laying by, somewhere between sundown and sunrise, relations were consummated and children conceived. The African's dilemma intensified as soon as the child took its first breath, for here was an undeniable extension of the chain of life, stretching back to Africa itself. Here was a manifestation of Africa born on American soil: What were the implications of such a development? What indeed would be the precise nature of the relationship between the African parent and the American child? The African-born belonged to the soil of Africa, their native land. They would surely return to that land at their death. But what of their offspring? Could the same be said of their children? Where would their spirits travel upon death? To what land did they belong? Although the answers to such questions were not at all obvious, it is clear that it is with the replication of Africa on American soil that Africans began to experience conflicting sentiments. Although their ties to Africa were by no means mitigated, they were now in the tenuous position of parenting children who had clear connections to a sorrowland. The African parents would have experienced some ambivalence, but it is their descendants who would necessarily go through a more complete and painful examination of their identity.

At first glance, the sources appear to conflict when reporting on relations between the African-born and their American-born descendants. Charles Lyell, traveling through coastal Georgia during the second quarter of the nineteenth century, remarked that one-fourth of the lower country was African-born, "and that it is a good sign of the progress made in civilization by the native-born colored race, that they speak of these 'Africanians' with much of the contempt with which Europeans talk of negroes."[4] Puckett, writing in the early twentieth century, employs virtually the same language in maintaining that slaves "looked upon the new African arrivals with much the same contempt with which the whites regarded Negroes in general—a fact which would tend to make the Negro arrivals take on the outward signs of white culture as soon as possible."[5] Puckett provides no evidence to support the contention of African cultural suicide, and my findings suggest that there is very little such evidence to be had.

But the issue of the reception of Africans by the existing slave population is another matter. Indeed, Stampp concurs with Puckett in stating that the latter were "contemptuous" of newly imported Africans.[6] Patterson, in discussing Jamaican slavery, argued that new African arrivals were "quite often ill-treated by the older slaves who were elected to supervise them," and that Creoles or Jamaican-born blacks referred "contemptuously" (the characterization of scholarly choice) to the newly arrived as salt-water Negroes and "Guineybirds."[7] Johnson, in his 1934 study of slavery in Macon County, Alabama, similarly found that older slaves looked upon "salt water niggers" with both fear and "contempt."[8] Based upon these kinds of statements, Frazier did not hesitate to assert that new arrivals faced "the disdain, if not the hostility, of Negroes who had become accommodated to the slave regime and had acquired a new conception of themselves."[9] He goes on to support this perspective by citing the 9 March 1859 edition of the *Atlanta Daily Intelligencer*, in which appeared a passage discussing the plantation experiences of four African-born slaves: "Our common darkies treat them with sovereign contempt walking around them with a decided aristocratic air. But the Africans are docile and very industrious and are represented as being delighted with new homes and improved conditions. The stories that they are brutes and savages is all stuff and nonsense. . . . As to their corrupting our common negroes, we venture the assertion would come nearer the truth if stated the other way."[10] All of these statements are consistent in describing relations between Africans and African Americans as antagonistic. Further analysis of the data, however, reveals a more complicated picture.

In evaluating the foregoing assessments of African- and American-born relations, it is important to recall what Herskovits wrote on the subject: "It is customarily assumed that during the 'seasoning' process, whereby newly arrived Africans were taught the manner of life on the plantations, the scorn of the teachers for savage ways prevented any interchange that could have reinforced Africanisms present in the behavior of those in charge of the newcomers. Yet the relationship between Africans and their teachers, except as concerns plantation routine, has never been systematically studied."[11] The basic lament, although published in 1941, remains as poignant now as it was then. It is hoped that this book will contribute something to the resolution of these issues.

First of all, it is probably not coincidental that evidence presented by scholars such as Frazier bolsters their arguments regarding the transmission of African culture into North America. To such an end, the evidence is presented uncritically. For example, the *Atlanta Daily Intelligencer* article seems to have as an objective the assuaging of anxieties over introducing newly arriving Africans into the slave population as late as 1859. To be sure, the depiction of happy-go-lucky newcomers is at complete variance with the preponderance of information provided heretofore that consistently describes the arrivals as angry, somber, despondent, and rebellious. Second, the frequency with which the word "contempt" is employed by such scholars suggests that they were not as original as they would have us believe. Third, it is possible that this contempt, to the extent that it existed, was more of a reality for those entrusted with teaching the arrivals than for those who were not. Presumably, those who taught had themselves been taught; that they looked upon the African with disdain is not at all surprising.

But the most glaring problem with these assessments is their lack any sense of periodization, and this is crucial. For African–African American relations in the second quarter of the nineteenth century were not the same as those that characterized the dawn of the eighteenth century, and so on. As the ratio of African- to American-born changed over the decades, so did the nature of the exchange between these two components of the slave community. In this context, it is instructive to point out that most, if not all, of the firsthand observations regarding African–African American relations were made after the first quarter of the nineteenth century; subsequent, secondary studies are largely premised upon such observations.

In contrast to reports of African–African American estrangement are accounts that cast a very different light on the subject, such that Blassingame has written that the most esteemed members of the slave community were the African-born and elderly.[12] Support for this view can be found in Cobb's *Mississippi Scenes*, in which he discusses "Capity, Saminy, Quominy, and Quor," native Africans who were the last purchased by William H. Crawford and who, along with a fifth native African who had been in the United States for a longer period of time, enjoyed "marked respect by all the other negroes for miles and miles around."[13] As a boy, Cobb would

> hunt up these old Africans, and gather their stories of their native clime. . . . I have sat for whole hours of a summer day under the shade of a spreading oak, or by the cheerful fire of their rude and homely ingle-sides when in winter, and listened with intense delight to the history of the fierce wars which had raged between hostile princes in their native country, or to some dangerous and interesting personal adventure with wild animals of the desert or forest. . . . Sometimes, on these occasions, the old Africans would become so completely absorbed in their own narratives, or so carried away by early grateful recollections, that they would involuntarily slide into the dialect, or rather *lingo* of their native country, and . . . continue to jabber away for hours at a time.[14]

Clearly, these Africans were not at all interested in taking on the "outward signs of white culture as soon as possible." Rather, it was their African ways and disposition, their cultural posture, that was the source of attraction.

The high regard by the country-born for the native African can be observed in Rias Body, born around 1846, who told his WPA interviewer in 1936 that "among the very old slaves whom he knew as a boy were quite a few whom the Negroes looked up to, respected, and feared as witches, wizzards, and magic-workers. These either brought their 'learnin" with them from Africa or absorbed it from their immediate African forebears."[15] Le-Conte, born in 1823, echoes the testimony of Body when he writes of several old Africans who lived on the same plantation as he during his childhood, carrying with them memories of their homeland. These were cared for in their old age; especially Sessy, who was "extravagantly fond of alligator meat, and always begged us boys to bring him the tails of any alligator we might kill." LeConte's experience is consistent with Cobb's when he writes of "an old native African named Philip," a Muslim who lived on a neighboring plantation. The old African, "who was a very intelligent man . . . used to tell us all about the customs and religion of the country from which he came."[16] The picture from such depictions is one in which the African-born are accorded special recognition and are viewed as an integral part of the African-based community.

High regard for native Africans by the country-born can also be seen in the story of "Little Luce," as told by seventy-four-year-old Lucy Galloway in 1936. The entire community was very much taken with the African woman: "We wuz all crazy about 'Little Luce.' Dat wuz what we called her, cause she wuz little, but my! she wuz strong and could whup anybody dat fooled wid her." The country-born also learned something about the African side of the slave trade through Luce's experiences, for she "remembered her mother who wuz also a slave in Africy. Their master over dere wuz a black man and he wuz mean to dem; would beat 'em when dey didn't do to suit him." As a consequence of Luce "fighting the black man over dere," she came to America minus one front tooth, but with a fierce spirit of resistance very much intact. "She said dat wuz de reason dey sold her because she was so bad about fightin' and bitin'—she wuz strong and could fight jes' like a cat." Luce was a "good-lookin' gal—jest as black and slick as a—gutta-pucha button. She had bright, black eyes, and purty white teeth." She enjoyed not only the admiration and respect of her fellow slaves but also the esteem of her owners by virtue of her industriousness: "Her Old Mistress would never hear to selling Lucy [she had married and taken the name Lucy Hutson]. She said she wuz too smart and 'responsible' fer her to part wid her!"[17]

The slave community's veneration of individuals such as Sessy and Philip, coupled with its respect, even awe of personalities similar to Luce suggests a foundation for African–African American relations other than that of contempt. The question regarding which characterization more closely approximates the historical reality is still, however, very much on the table. Resolution of the problem lies in a full appreciation of two factors: periodization and familial ties. With regard to the former, it is critical to keep before us the shifting ratios of African-born to American-born blacks over time. With that understood, it stands to reason that significant levels of native Africans within the African-based community would certainly tend to prevent the cultivation of an anti-African bias within that community. The presence of substantial numbers of native Africans suggests a society more African in culture and perspective than not, and consciously so.

Based upon the information contained in table 2.4, virtually every black person in North America was African-born through 1640. From 1680 to

1720, the native African population averaged slightly more than 50 percent, meaning that the remaining black population was largely first-generation and, to a lesser extent, second-generation African American. These first-generation American-born were raised by native Africans, so that they were socialized within the slave community according to the only set of principles and ideals known to their parents—African ones. For all practical purposes, then, these progeny were much more African in outlook and culture than American, whatever that concept might have meant for a black person living in 1720. The African parent would have constituted the leadership in the community, as is clear in this 1785 account by Bryan Edwards concerning the Caribbean:

> On my return to the West Indies, I was surprised to find the old-established Negroes, when young people newly arrived from Africa, were sent among them, request, as a particular instance of favour and indulgence to themselves, the revival and continuance of the ancient system [of receiving newcomers]; assuring me they had the means of supporting the strangers without difficulty. Many who thus applied, proposed each of them to adopt one of their young country-folks in the room of children they had lost by death, or had been deprived of in Africa; others, because they wished, like the patriarchs of old, to see their sons take to themselves wives from their own nation and kindred; and all of them, I presume, because, among other considerations, they expected to revive and retrace in the conversation of their new visitors, the remembrance and ideas of past pleasures and scenes of their youth. The strangers too were best pleased with this arrangement, and ever afterwards considered themselves as the adopted children of those by whom they were thus protected, calling them parents, and venerating them as such.[18]

Although the preceding account does not emanate from North America, the ratio of Africans to African Americans in North America was so overwhelming, and the preferences for certain ethnicities in the various colonies so pronounced, that it is reasonable to conclude that relations among Africans in the colonial American mainland were not inconsistent with the West Indian experience. As has been demonstrated, ethnic affiliations were very important in North America, and given the relative absence of an American-born component during this time, the movement toward an African American identity would have largely consisted of interethnic negotiations.

Smith states the importance of knowing the "specific provenance" of initial African arrivals, for they "tended to structure the situation. Other Africans, arriving later, adjusted their slightly different behaviour to the already existing situation."[19] That is, the African-born community provided the basis for all subsequent social and cultural development in African-derived society. Although Smith does not sufficiently allow for the possibility that subsequent African arrivals could come in such numbers and with such rapidity that they overwhelmed the earlier population, his point retains great validity.

For our purposes it is necessary to extend Smith's comments to include not only later African arrivals but also the emergence of an American-born, or Creole, population. That is, the culture and society of the latter would also be largely shaped by the African antecedent. Such a conclusion is inescapable, for no matter how intrusive slaveholders may have been in the lives of the slaves, there would have been too many instances in which the slaves experienced autonomy. Slaveholders could not have dictated how a mother nurtured her child, or how that child learned to conduct herself in the presence of her elders, or the substance of communications between father and child, or even the form and manner of expression. But it is precisely these sorts of things, familial and communal interaction, that shape and mold culture and individual behavior. The slaveholding superstructure could not possibly inform the socialization process in every way that was meaningful and prescriptive; indeed, the evidence, from the southern drawl and vocabulary to cuisine to architecture to agriculture to music to everything in between, suggests that it was from within the slave community that formative powers of enculturation were generated.

In 1720, then, the slave community was for all practical purposes African. The American-born constituent was present, and continued to grow from 1740 to 1760, during which time the American-born came to account for 60 percent of the black population. However, many of these were first-generation Americans, so that they would have fallen under the enculturative provenance of African parentage. The combination of these first-generation blacks and a native African population resulted in their domination of second- and third-generation African Americans, a phenomenon similar to that which obtained in Jamaica, depending upon the period in question.[20] The second and third generations would have known African grandparents in addition to other native Africans who were a significant part of the community.

The period of 1780 to 1810 saw a further decline in the percentage of native Africans in the African-based community, averaging around 20 percent. During this period, second- and third-generation African Americans outnumbered both the African-born and their first-generation offspring. By 1830, the number of African-born slaves dropped into the single digits—a clear majority were two or more generations removed from African soil. To be so removed possibly meant that a large number of individuals had no recollection of their African grandparents and therefore no conscious, personal link to the African antecedent. The forces of acculturation with respect to the external white world would have accelerated by this time as well, so that within such a context, there was increased potential for social divisions between African- and American-born blacks. And although these divisions were more apparent than actual, perception can be everything. It is under such circumstances that contempt by the American-born for the African could have developed. As such, it was a relatively late development, and by 1830 evinced not only cultural differences but class distinctions as well. To the extent that divisions between Africans and African Americans were grounded in class, it is probable that such divisions were more a preoccupation for the few who had achieved a higher status, as opposed to the masses of blacks whose concrete, leveling experience in agricultural slavery converged with elements of cultural continuity to reinforce the bonds between the African and her American-born counterpart.

But even with greater interaction between the black and white communities after 1830, there is plenty of evidence that the African parents and grandparents of slaves who lived during and after this time were respected, and often remembered with great affection, even though they may not have been well understood. For example, there is the 1918 oral and written account of Eliza J. Kendrick (Lewis) Walker, completed in 1924 for posterity by her daughter Anne. Eliza was born around 1836 in Columbia County, Georgia, and had been raised by Mammy Lucy along with seven other children. The manuscript, entitled "Other Days," reveals that both Mammy Lucy and Uncle Pad were loved and revered: "Mammy was a mixture of Spanish-Africa, very bright in complexion, handsome and alert, and noted for her good judgment and sound sense. Her husband was pure African, Patrick by name, and 'Uncle Pad' in the affectionate regard of we children."[21] Notwithstanding Mammy Lucy's apparent Spanish background, she was very African in outlook and probably practiced some form of African medicine, as is suggested by the remark that "Mammy reigned supreme among the other servants in the household. . . . The other servants looked up to her as if she possessed supernatural powers, and she enjoyed her sway over them."[22] No doubt, her powers grew not only out of her personal abilities but also out of her marriage to a "pure African," who was cherished more than feared throughout the community.

Further corroboration of intimate and vital links between the African- and the American-born slave can be found in newspaper advertisements for runaways. As has been observed earlier, a conspiracy of two or more individuals to escape slavery has at its foundation more than a modicum of trust. So it was in December 1782 when twenty-two-year-old Will, an outlandish fellow with rings in his ears, proceeded to run away with twenty-five-year-old Cato, described as country-born.[23] In September 1811, Virginia-born Ben managed to steal away with Aplin, an eighteen-year-old African described as "very handsomely marked on his chest."[24] In August 1764, three men, two of whom were country-born, escaped from Monmouth plantation in Georgia in the company of an accomplice described in such detail as to suggest a greater interest in him as opposed to the others: "A lusty well made new negroe, speaks little English, is a little bow-legged, and has one of his teeth broke out."[25] In May 1817, Samuel W. Butler of New Orleans placed an ad reporting that Sandy, a thirty-eight-year-old African recently brought from Kentucky, was missing along with Toney and Isaac.[26] James Denmark, who lived near the Pearl River in Mississippi, offered a fifty-dollar reward for the return of twenty-seven-year-old Adam, a native of Savannah who was thought to be headed back in that direction, and July, a thirty-year-old African.[27]

Africans and African Americans did not necessarily limit the circle of conspiracy to two or three. In September 1819, for example, five men absconded from the plantation of Benjamin Jewell at Pointe Coupee, including Alfred; York, a light-complected African; Peter, a dark-complected African; Liverpool (these names); and Joe.[28] Patrick Mackay's Hermitage plantation suffered an even greater loss earlier in 1765, when nine men, including one Bomba John, took their leave.[29] Three years later, Robert Bradley of Pensacola likewise found that three newly arrived Africans, Neptune, Bacchus, and Apollo, were led away by a "seasoned fellow, called Limerick" who spoke "good English, and is very much marked on the back, etc. by severe whipping."[30] It was believed that the men had found "their way through the Creek country."

Of course, in addition to exclusively male conspiracies, it was often the case that families featuring African and African American spouses and partners ran away together. In 1819, Fortune and Dinah belonged in this category, as "Dinah has an infant at her breast. Fortune is by birth an African."[31] Twenty-one-year-old Jim, who could be easily mistaken for country-born as he had "none of the African marks" and spoke "very plain," left John Norris's Alabama plantation in 1825 along with his eighteen-year-old American-born wife Nelly.[32] John Morel of Ossabaw Island reported the absence of nine people in October 1781, including the Angolan Hercules, his wife Betty, and their two children.[33] The following year, Will and Kate fled the property of Leighton Wood Jr.[34] Will had "been in the country for many years, but his speech may easily discover him not to be a native." Kate, on the other hand, "has many scars about her neck and breast, her back will prove her to be an old offender." The fact that Kate had all the scars suggests that she was much more openly defiant.

It was often the case that African women agreed to either lead or join their American-born husbands in a bid for freedom. Some examples of this include the story of Juno and Jack, age twenty-eight and twenty-three, respectively.[35] Juno was "of the Guinea country" and a good seamstress, whereas Jack was country-born. They had joined a fifty-year-old man and his thirty-five-year-old wife, both "Guinean," in escaping from Edward Fenwick in 1788. In September 1766, twenty-year-old Jack and nineteen-year-old Mindo fled together from William Guess of South Carolina, the latter having been a "new Negro woman" with filed teeth and "plenty of her Country Marks on her breast."[36] There is the case of Peter and Jude, detained in South Carolina, having been found traveling "almost entirely naked of cloathing." Peter was a fifty-year-old native Carolinian, whereas Jude appeared "to be old, out-landish, and has her country marks on her face."[37] Some of the runaway notices feature African- and American-born women exclusively, as in the obscure 1732 instance of two women, one of whom hardly spoke English.[38] Then there is the 1825 case of Venus, a forty-year-old African woman who had run away from S. J. Morgan along with Betsy, "a good looking intelligent Negro, aged about 22."[39] They were carrying a three-year-old child with them.

As is obvious from some of the examples cited, it was not always necessary for individuals to be related in order for them to plan their collective escape. In many instances friendships and subsequent plans developed as a result of individuals working together. Close working conditions were not at all confined to the fields, however, and there are instances of skilled slaves who took advantage of their proximity to flee together. In 1835, for example, forty-year-old George and twenty-eight-year-old John fled their owner in Florida. John was African born, and they were both "jobbing carpenters."[40] There is also the 1782 ad featuring two other runaways named "Galba, a cooper by trade, about 30 years of age, and the other a country born sensible young fellow, about 20, a carpenter by trade."[41]

There are many such references to Africans and African Americans who absconded together. These constitute further evidence of cooperative relations between these two components of the slave community. In addition to runaway slave advertisements, however, the WPA materials also address the question of African–African American relations. These interviews are peppered with allusions to African parents and grandparents who were instrumental in the lives of the former slaves. Even though the informants grew up during the latter stages of slavery, when the percentage of the African-born among the black population had declined (4 percent by 1840 and 1 percent by 1860), they remain careful to honor their African forebears. In many instances there is only the mention that a parent or grandparent was African, as was the case with eighty-one-year-old Fred James of Newberry, South Carolina, or centenarian James Cape of Texas.[42] Seventy-seven-year-old Irene Robertson of Mississippi (born in South Carolina) in like manner stated that her mother "was a guinea woman," and that her grandfather was a "pure African, black as an ace of spades."[43] Margaret Goss, who was purported to be 113 years old in 1937, also recalled her mother as "very black, small, and quick in her movements," who spoke "with a strong African dialect. People speak of her as a Guinea negro."[44]

Susan Snow, born in Alabama in 1850, remembered that her "ma was a black African, an' she sho' was wild an' mean. She was so mean to me, I couldn't believe she was my mammy."[45] A great deal can be read into this statement, including the relationship between the mother's callousness and the brutality of slavery. But Snow was not the only person who respected and feared this woman; the larger slave community apparently did as well, for "dey used to say my ma was a cunjer an' dey was all scared of 'er. But my ma was scared o' cunjers, too!" Snow also observed that her mother, consistent with evidence presented earlier in this chapter, did not much care for the Western life-style: "Every nigger had a house of his own, but my ma never would have a board floor. Only dirt, cause she was an African." Snow's mother was fiercely independent yet filled with a sense of rootlessness, such that she "was de first to leave de plantation after de surrender. All de other niggers had a contrack to stay, but she didn't, an' she went to Newton County an' hired out. She never wanted to stay in one place, nohow." The WPA interviews also contain sketchy references to either the forebear's experiences in Africa or the Middle Passage. Henry Brown's grandmother and grandfather, for example, were married in Africa.[46] The interviewer of Georgian Phil Towns, born around 1824, reported that "his grandfather and grandmother were brought here from Africa and their description of the cruel treatment they received is his most vivid recollection."[47] Finally, there is the testimony of eighty-five-year-old South Carolinian Phillip Evans of Winnsboro, who encapsulates the problem of malnutrition and disease during the Middle Passage in the simple statement that his African grandfather was "powerful sick at de stomach de time he was on de ship."[48]

There is sufficient evidence, then, to advance the proposition that relations between Africans and African Americans were characterized by warmth and harmony more so than strife and hostility, and that significant difficulties developed well after the first quarter of the nineteenth century, by which time class issues within the African-based community had taken on greater significance. Stratification among those of African descent constitutes a subsequent focus. What remains at this juncture is to examine two key concepts that lend insight into the dynamics of African–African American relations, followed by an analysis of runaway slave advertisements that pertain to those concepts.

The first key concept concerns the procurement of Africans for the slave trade. To this end, a significant proportion of the WPA's interviews of former slaves focuses specifically on the matter of the African's initial capture. These stories tend to be very consistent, clearly indicating that numerous accounts of the initial capture had circulated throughout the slave communities of the South—and to a degree that comparisons were made and consensus reached on a version that, for reasons to be explored shortly, was more appropriate for the slave population. The uniformity of these capture accounts is quite remarkable, soliciting an examination that should reveal something more of the collective consciousness of the African-based community. These stories are presented here, rather than in an earlier chapter largely devoted to the Middle Passage, because they are much more a reflection of subsequent African–African American relations than a precise account of the slave trade.

The WPA interviews are the testimony of former slaves who for the most part were some generations removed from Africa. Nevertheless, a number of informants were the grandchildren or great-grandchildren of Africans, and they were asked by their interviewers about their progenitors' experiences in Africa. Their responses concerning the initial capture of their forebears make it clear that they were not simply passing on what they had heard as individuals; rather, the consistency of the replies points to the probability that the matter of the African's initial capture had been a subject of negotiation between the Africans and their descendants. That is, the story of capture represented an intergenerational crafting by those who were actually captured and by those who were born on American soil. The story was not told as it actually happened but recast to convey what the African-based community perceived as the essential truth of the experience. This is critical, for the presentation of facts alone, to the African way of thinking, cannot communicate the full meaning of an event. What physically happened and the deeper meaning of what happened are very different things. And for the sake of the African-based community, for whom these accounts were expressly designed, it was crucial that they grasp the deeper implications.

At the core of the initial capture accounts is the notion of deception: Africans were tricked by Europeans, resulting in their capture and deportation. This is the most important aspect of the trade to understand and the most consequential lesson to learn about dealing with white folk. As such, the initial capture accounts fall within the genre of the West African trickster story. Trickster folklore usually includes the following elements: an offer of false friendship by the trickster, a contractual agreement with the trickster, violation of that contract by the trickster, further trickery, deception involving acceptance of the trickery by the deceived, and the trickster's escape or reward.[49] Several of these elements can be detected in the initial capture stories, from which the white trader emerges as the ultimate trickster.

Charlie Grant of Marion, South Carolina, eighty-five at the time of his interview in 1937, gave the following account: "Dey fooled dem to come or I calls it foolin' dem. De peoples go to Africa en when dey go to dock, dey blow whistles en de peoples come from all over de country to see what it was. Dey fool dem on de vessel en give dem something to eat. Shut dem up en don' let dem get out."[50] The element of deception is prominent in Grant's story, as Africans were drawn to the European ships by the sound of whistles. They were invited to come aboard, and were fed, all suggestive that the European desired friendship. But before they knew it, they were detained and taken away. They had been deceived by the European's feigned display of goodwill.

Alabama-born Josephine Howard, whose age was unknown when she was interviewed in Texas, reported that both her mother and grandmother were from "Africy."[51] They may have lived in proximity to the coast, for Howard said that "dey lives clost to some water, somewheres over in Africy, and de man come in a little boat to de sho' and tell dem he got presents on de big boat." As opposed to whistles, the elements of attraction in this instance are "presents." Howard seems to suggest that this particular deception was gender-specific, for she says that "most de men am out huntin' and my mammy and her mammy gits took out to dat big boat and dey locks dem in a black hole what mammy say so black you can't see nothin'." The phrase "gits took out" is instructive because, although it leaves much to the imagination regarding how these people were transported to the slaver, Africans are clearly portrayed as unwary if not reluctant participants. Having arrived at the coast, the true intentions of the European are revealed, and Howard does not hesitate to pronounce her moral judgment: "Dat de sinfulles' stealin' dey is." Remaining in the black hole, both mother and grandmother are taken to Mobile, where they are "put on de block." Mother, who is twelve years old at the time, is sold along with grandmother to "Marse Tim, but grandma dies in a month and dey puts her in de slave graveyard."

Although the preceding stories are consistent with those that follow concerning matters of guile, they differ in that the overwhelming majority of the following accounts include as the source of attraction some form of cloth, usually red in color. To be sure, textiles were the principal imports exchanged for captives in West Africa and were used for both currency and clothing.[52] But the way in which textiles are featured in the stories makes it clear, from the perspective of those who were victimized, that the trade between Europeans and Africans was never an equal exchange, and that it was not typified by good faith negotiations.

A primary example of the "red cloth" version of the initial capture was offered by aforementioned South Carolinian Richard Jones in 1937.[53] Jones, also known as "Dick Look-up" for his habit of constantly peering into the sky, stated that his grandmother Granny Judith was from Africa. It was her report that "some strangers wid pale faces come one day and drapped a small piece of red flannel down on de ground. All de black folks grabbed fer it." This is a reference to the European initiation of the trade. European cloth found a ready market in Africa, conveyed by the remark that Africans "grabbed fer it." Jones continued: "Den a larger piece was drapped a little further on, and on until de river was reached." That is, the volume of trade between Africans and Europeans grew steadily and finally reached a point at which Africans became accustomed to the trade and dependent upon European textiles. They had reached a point of no return in their commercial dealings with Europe; they had reached "de river" and were now inextricably involved. "Finally," Jones concludes, "when de ship was reached, dey drapped large pieces on de plank and up into de ship 'till dey got as many blacks on board as dey wanted." Africans, blinded by the allure of European commodities, suddenly found themselves enslaved. The delusion was widespread, for Europeans "got as many . . . as dey wanted."

Eighty-seven-year-old John Brown of West Tulsa, Oklahoma, tells a similar story.[54] Born on an Alabama plantation of three hundred slaves, it was his testimony that the oldest of the slaves were from Africa, one of whom was his own grandmother. "Mammy told it to me," he said regarding the tales he heard from grandmother concerning her home. Included in this repertoire was the account of her capture: "One day a big ship stopped off the shore and the natives hid in the bush along the beach. Grandmother was there." The story begins by giving the listener a sense of distance between the European and the African, as the latter had little or no experience with such foreigners, at least in this instance. "The ship men sent a little boat to the shore and scattered bright things and trinkets on the beach. The natives were curious." The cultivation of the market had begun. "Grandmother said everybody made a rush for them things soon as the boat left," but there was a problem, for "the trinkets were fewer than the peoples." The scarcity value of the European manufactures only increased the demand for them. "Next day the white folks scatter some more. There was another scramble. The natives was feeling less scared, and the next day some of them walked up the gang plank to get things off the plank and off the deck." Once again, as with the preceding stories, commodity attraction led to the fatal mistake of boarding the slaver. What is unique to Brown's story is his emphasis on the lessening fears of the Africans and their concomitant growing trust in the goodwill of the white traders. Implicit in this depiction is that the latter were duplicitous. The Africans, their anxieties lessened, discovered that the "deck was covered with things like they'd found on the beach." Once on board the vessel, however, the Europeans ended the masquerade, and the Africans were trapped: "Two-three hundred natives on the ship when they feel it move. They rush to the side but the plank was gone. Just dropped in the water when the ship moved away." The ruse was uncovered too late. The next thing she knew, Brown's grandmother was in Charleston.

The speed with which the deception was played out is a constant in the various accounts. The Africans simply had no time to react. They had reservations about the strangers, but they had allowed their collective guard to lower just enough to become ensnared. Della Fountain, who was born and raised in Louisiana, told her story in 1938 at the age of sixty-nine.[55] Her grandmother was African, and according to her, "traders come dere in a big boat and dey had all sorts of purty gew-gaws—red handkerchiefs, dress goods, beads, bells, and trinkets in bright colors. Dey would pull up at de shore and entice de colored folks onto de boat to see purty things." The ploy was as swift as the "gew-gaws" enticing, and "befo' de darkies realized it dey would be out from shore."

Although minor details change from story to story, all of these accounts agree on at least one thing: the African was deceived by European professed sincerity and thereby duped into slavery. This same message is to be found in much terser references to the initial capture. Eighty-five-year-old Martha King, for example, stated that her African grandmother had been tricked onto a slaver by the lure of a red handkerchief.[56] Georgian Shang Harris, age ninety-seven in 1936, maintained that her African grandfather, along with other Africans, were also "tricked" onto slavers by way of "red flags."[57] Eighty-four-year-old Hannah Crasson's great-grandmother was called "granny Flora. Dey stole her frum Africa wid a red pocket handkerchief."[58] Annie Groves Scott of Oklahoma concurred. Born in 1845 in South Carolina, she reiterated that Africans were "fooled" and "tricked" onto the slave boats.[59]

The African–African American version of the initial capture was therefore well known throughout the black community. It had probably become standardized, with the essential elements of European manufactures and cunning, sometime during the second half of the nineteenth century. The regularization of the account, featured in the stories given to WPA interviewers, is probably better represented by the story of "Gullah Joe," first published in 1928 and therefore a bit older than the WPA materials.[60] The story emanates from the Congaree valley of South Carolina, near Columbia. Gullah Joe was born in Africa, where he and a number of others were enticed onto a slaver with "all kind er bead an' calico an' red flannel, an' all kind er fancy thing." Having been baited to board the vessel, the deception was eventually completed: "An' one day dey hab de boat crowd wid mens an' womens an' chillun, an' when dey find dey self, de boat was 'way out to sea." Gullah Joe is successful in depicting a process that is not only beguiling but sufficiently swift and relatively absent of conflict; by the time he and the others could "find dey self," there was not much they could do about it. "An' some er dem niggers jump off an' dey was drowned. But dem white folks overpowered dem what was on de boat, an' th'owed 'em down in de bottom er de ship. An' dey put chain on 'em an' make 'em lay down moest of de time." Resistance, though offered, was often successfully repressed.

There is more to Gullah Joe's story. What follows does not appear in the WPA interviews, as it is not something that slaves and their descendants would want to volunteer to white interrogators. But as it is a part of the initial capture account, it is very likely that the black community was just as acquainted with it as it was with what has preceded. As such, the entire account represents what the slave community understood about the Middle Passage—it is the standard version of the experience. The community was concerned with preserving knowledge not only of the initial capture but also of what transpired thereafter. As the captains of the slavers and other white passengers recorded their observations of the passage, so did the Africans. What they told their progeny is very likely consistent with the words of Gullah Joe:

> Dey been pack in dere wuss dan hog in a car when dey shippin' 'em. An' every day dem white folks would come in dere an' ef a nigger jest twist his self or move, dey'd cut he hide off wid a rawhide whip. An' niggers died in de bottom er dat ship wuss dan hogs wid cholera. Dem white folks ain' hab no mercy. Look like dey ain' know wha' mercy mean. Dey drag dem dead niggers out an' throw 'em overboard. An' dat ain' all. Dey th'owed a heap er live ones wha' dey thought ain' guh live into de sea.
>
> An' it look like we been two or three month in de bottom er dat ship. An' dey brung us to dis country an' dey sell us, an' a slave trader brung me here an' sold me to ole Marster.

Interestingly, there is plenty in the accounts of white observers to verify Gullah Joe's version.

Given the distressing nature of the passage, failure to find many doleful references to it in the WPA interviews is at first surprising. In fact, one finds just the opposite, or what would appears to be the opposite. In an amazing and instructive example of dissimulation, the same Richard Jones of South Carolina continued his account of what happened to his African grandmother: "On de ship dey had many strange things to eat, and dey liked dat. Dey was give enough red flannel to wrap around demselves. She liked it on de boat. . . . No, I ain't never had no desire to go to Africa, kaise I gwine to stay whar I is."[61] Although Jones appears to be in a state of obsequity, groveling before his "marsters" with claims that, in contravention to both the evidence and common sense, his grandmother and others enjoyed the Middle Passage, the key to understanding his statement is his reference to "red flannel." It was red flannel, in fact, that Jones had identified as the very instrument of deception by which his grandmother had been captured. That is, red flannel in this context is intimately and expressly associated with deceit and guile. In saying that the Africans on board the slaver wrapped themselves in red flannel, Jones was saying that they had been wrapped in the deceit of the European. They were surrounded and totally engulfed by it. The white interviewer would have heard the words "and dey liked dat" and reached one conclusion. But blacks would have deciphered the code and come away with an entirely different understanding:

Got one mind for white folks to see,
'Nother for what I know is me,
He don't know, he don't know my mind.[62]

The color red also seems to have some special significance in the various stories. Paul Smith, who was seventy-four years old when interviewed in Georgia, had a straightforward explanation for its relationship to the enslavement process: "Whilst us was all a-wukin' away at house and yard jobs, de old folkses would tell us 'bout times 'fore us was borned."[63] The chain of cultural transmission, therefore, was already established by the time of Smith's birth (which must have been in the 1860s); that is, tales explaining the initial capture had already been subjected to standardizing processes. "Old folkses said dey had done been fetched to dis country on boats." Smith, in making such a statement, would seem to suggest that the "old folkses" were all Africans by birth. By the 1860s, however, the ranks of the aged were necessarily and overwhelmingly filled with American-born blacks. The statement is therefore even more revealing, with the strong implication that the elderly identified very closely with Africa. "Dem boats was painted red, real bright red, and dey went plumb to Africa to git de niggers. When dey got dere, dey got off and left de bright red boats empty for a while. Niggers laks red, and dey would git on dem boats to see what dem red things was." According to Smith, then, it was the color red, not the commodities of themselves, that attracted the attention of Africans.

Phoebe Gilbert of Sapelo Island told a different story, but in so doing supported Smith's preoccupation with the color red.[64] She relates that her grandfather, Belali Smith, was captured as a child while playing on the beach: "He say he playin on beach in Africa, an big boat neah duh beach. He say, duh mens on boat take down flag, an put up big piece uh red flannel, an all chillun dey git close tuh watuh edge tuh see flannel an see wut doin." In Gilbert's version, the youth and inexperience of the targeted African population are salient, for eventually "duh mens comes off boat an ketch um, an wen duh ole folks come in frum duh fiels dey ain no chillun in village." The vulnerability of the young African population is emphasized here, and it comes up in other accounts and contexts as well. The message is clear: those who were captured were not only naïve but also unprotected by those elements of society who held such a responsibility.

At first glance, the notion that people were drawn to their destruction by a color seems preposterous and unworthy of scholarly consideration, and that may very well be. However, a modicum of speculation is not out of line. For although imported textiles were popular in West Africa, and many were red in color, there is surely something more involved than the apparent.[65] In her analysis of Congolese ritual symbolism, Jacobson-Widding focuses specifically on the question of the relationship between colors, symbolism, and conceptualization. She found that the color red could be associated with beauty, sexual maturity, and heroism; and alternatively, with physical weakness and death.[66] The frequency with which the color red is mentioned in connection with slaving may perhaps represent the process by which people were tricked into enslavement. Such a possibility finds support in the statement of Patsy Moses, who was born around 1863 in Texas. With regard to charms she made the following observation: "A good charm bag am make of red flannel with frog bones. . . . Dat bag protect you from your enemy."[67] The idea that red flannel was a source of protection against evil can be found elsewhere. For example, ninety-one-year-old Jerry Eubanks of Mississippi testified that he knew "about de charms what was wore. Most of em wore dimes with a whole [*sic*] in it to keep off evil spirits, and red flannel bands around the wrist to keep from loosin de nerve."[68] The high regard for red flannel as a spiritual prophylactic can also be detected in the statement of a Florida planter who purchased nine of the slaves illegally brought into Georgia in 1858 aboard the *Wanderer*: "For a considerable time it was difficult to make them wear clothing, though if red flannel were given them, they would wear that more readily than anything else."[69] It should be noted that the objection was not so much to wearing clothes as to wearing foreign apparel symbolic of their degradation.

Patsy Moses, in discussing the red flannel bag, provides the basis for the proposal that red flannel had come to symbolize the deceit involved in the European slave trade: "Iffen dat bag left by de doorstep it make all kind misfortune and sicknesses and blindness and fits."[70] The matter of burying charms for purposes of "fixing" victims will be discussed in the next chapter. Suffice it here to say that, aside from the bag's ability to protect, it also has the potential to harm. In this aspect of its efficacy a close relationship between red flannel and the practice of conjuring can be viewed. In contemplating the methods by which they had been reduced to the level of chattel, the African-based community may have concluded that the whole process of enslavement had been guided by unseen, malevolent forces, and that they had been conjured by Europeans onto the slavers. Indeed, were not the Europeans themselves spirits? In fact, had not red flannel been left "by de doorstep" of Africa, and had it not left in its wake "all kind of misfortune and sicknesses and blindness and fits?"

Of course, all of these red cloth stories (and others related to them) require further explication, especially regarding their functionality. In the first place, it should be made clear that the African-based community was well aware of what actually happened with regard to the slave trade. As has been discussed in places throughout this study, the trade in African slaves usually required the consent and cooperation of African polities of varying types, from large empires to small homesteads. To be sure, there are important exceptions to this generalization; Benin is perhaps the most prominent among them, whose indifference and even hostility toward the slave trade rendered its economy more or less independent of it.[71] Various Muslim polities, including Bundu and Futa Jallon, pursued antislave trade policies at various times in their histories; the *tubenan* movement in Senegambia was precisely formulated to alter the direction of the trade. The previously mentioned Antonian movement of Dona Beatrice Kimpa Vita was also opposed to the slave trade in that it advocated the cessation of civil wars within Kongo. Certain groups were known for their opposition to the trade, including the Balanta, Djola, and Kru of Sierra Leone. Others could be added to the list.

Notwithstanding the existence of opposition, internal organization proved sufficient to facilitate the trade. The clear consensus is that the vast majority of Africans were procured for export via warfare and kidnapping, as the case of the Igbo so vividly demonstrates. Transported Africans and their progeny were intimately acquainted with these facts. The survivors of the *Wanderer*, for example, in responding to queries about life in their native land, volunteered that they were familiar with the institution of slavery.[72] They described the practice of pawning, whereby a child was initially given to a creditor to cover an adult's debt. Interestingly, the survivors were careful to mention that uncles were sometimes the ones who pawned the children. If the debt went unpaid, the children became the creditor's property and were subject to sale into the Atlantic trade. Otherwise, children were kidnapped "by other negroes" and transferred through successive owners to the coastal trade.

In addition to the foregoing testimony, there are also statements in the WPA materials that plainly indicate that the African-based community understood the actual dynamics of the trade. Centenarian Polly Turner Cancer of Mississippi, for example, synopsized the whole process very candidly: "I heard tell 'mong de niggers dat de way dey got to de United States wuz dat de Africans sol' dem to de white traders; dey bot dem wid red bandanna handkerchiefs."[73] The complicity of the African agent, then, was well understood.

Given that black folk appreciated the full dimensions of what physically transpired, how does one interpret their insistence upon a version of events that makes no mention of African complicity in the procurement of slaves? For by leaving out the role of the African mediator, there is no opportunity to assign this person an appropriate measure of culpability. The evidence leaves room for no alternative explanation except that Africans were aware of such culpability; indeed, their descendants made mention of it on occasion and under direct questioning. However, the stylized and sanctioned version of the initial capture, a well-known tale widely circulated throughout the South, excluded African agency and collusion. What can this mean?

The development of an initial capture account that points the finger exclusively at the European and excludes any mention of his African counterpart is highly significant, for it marks an important stage in the emergence of the African American aggregate identity and signals the fording of a major divide in the journey from ethnicity to race as the principal determinant of collective self-perception. For what the sanctioned version is fundamentally conveying is the idea that, notwithstanding the involvement and betrayal of African political and familial entities, the Atlantic trade in Africans was first and foremost the idea of Europeans; they initiated it, they had the ships, they made the voyage, they supplied the commodities, they transported the victims. It was the New World plantation complex that mercilessly drove the exchange. It was inescapable, therefore, that the overwhelming balance of blame and guilt belonged to white folk, for it appeared to the African that they all spoke with one voice in support of the trade. And indeed, many benefited from the trade, from towns and shipbuilders and merchants and collateral businesses in Europe, to planters and miners in America, to textile manufacturers everywhere.[74] For all of her alleged lack of sophistication, her red cloth tales reveal that the African definitely understood the bottom line.

The African-based community not only found white people responsible for the trade but also anticipated a debate that would become much more heated centuries later. By emphasizing the deceitfulness of Europeans, the African was in essence stating that, although Africans were involved in procuring individuals, they could not have been aware of the full dimensions of the trade, of what the passage would truly entail, of what life would be like on the other side. Further, by focusing on the notion that by various means Africans were tricked, the African was pronouncing judgment upon the European, who had a hidden agenda that he never fully revealed, having presented himself as a friend, as an associate in commerce, but all along was quite the villain. The European was not at all what he presented himself to be.

So then, the African and his progeny reviewed the facts as they knew them. They examined the role of the European and the white American and weighed them in the balance with that of their African colleagues. The African and his enslaved descendants considered all the evidence carefully and over the decades worked through all of the inconsistencies and contradictions. Versions were compared and edited by the "committee of the whole." Accounts passed from mouth to ear all the way from Virginia to Texas. White southerners, so engaged in managing the machinery of plantation agriculture and slavery as the principal means of social control (at least from 1830 on), were quite unaware that right beneath their noses their supposed chattel were engaged in a complicated process of analyzing, debating, and collating their experiences. It was a mammoth undertaking, this business of arriving at an evaluation that was truthful as well as didactic. From the waters along the Carolina coast, the call would go forth, containing in it the collective experiences of Africans taken to Charleston; and from the swamps and plantations of the lower Mississippi, the response would eventually come, having absorbed the vantage points of the Carolinas and merged them with their own. By way of the domestic trade here, through the pathways of escape there, slaves throughout the South exchanged data and created syntheses. Eventually, consensus was reached. A verdict was rendered. The white man was found guilty of guile, guilty of violence, guilty of horrors unimaginable. This is the fundamental truth that the African-born wanted their offspring to understand about the initial capture. This, the red cloth tales teach, is the underlying significance of the slave trade.

And in the process of collation and revision, something transformative took place. The collective perspective of the African-based population made a conscious decision concerning the question of group identity. They took a decisive step toward embracing race over ethnicity. Not that the decision was universally adopted everywhere, or that everyone gravitated to it with similar speed. But to the degree that African Americans concluded that white folks bore responsibility for the evils of slavery, and to the extent that African Americans agreed to leave out the slave trader's African analogue in the equation of culpability, African Americans were essentially saying that they saw white people, whether from America or Europe, whether French- or Spanish- or English-speaking, as one and the same. African Americans were saying that although there were differences in the details, the experiences of Africans of all backgrounds and regions were sufficiently similar to cast them all as a common ordeal. African Americans, whether their parents were Igbo or Akan, had begun to see the world in like manner. To the degree that all of the above is true, African Americans had taken a definitive turn toward viewing race as the great American divide.

To be sure, continuities that hearkened back to very specific ethnic heritages remained within the community. Without question, certain policies adopted by the slaveocracy that either used or exacerbated ethnic distinctions resulted in class and caste distinctions within the community. It is precisely the argument here that the reformulation of an African American identity was not at all thoroughgoing. Africans brought to North America did not conceive of human society in terms of race; however, by the end of legalized slavery, the concept of race had crystallized in the community. The transition was therefore made during slavery, notwithstanding its incomplete or unfinished quality. And this transition is implicit in the African American version of the initial capture.

Having said all that, the question becomes, What happened to all of the details about the initial capture that were ultimately considered extraneous? Were they somehow suppressed by the African-based community? Did black folks censure their cultural transmissions? More specifically, was the knowledge that Africans themselves were active in the enslaving of other Africans something that was considered, in the parlance of the 1990s, politically incorrect and therefore its conveyance discouraged? Did African Americans collectively engage in historical revisionism?

In response to these queries, it should be pointed out that black folk knew about African complicity in the slave trade—this has already been demonstrated. The red cloth accounts therefore represent the preferred version of the community, the version that was most efficacious in communicating the trade's implications. At the same time, however, it was not possible to eradicate from memory the role played by the African accomplices of the slave interests. Too much information had crisscrossed the South through the mouths of both young and old for their pivotal, even essential role to be forgotten. The African-based community therefore faced the question of

African involvement by separating it from that of the European's. In order to stress the latter, it was important to isolate it within a broadly distributed story of its own, in which European liability was featured exclusively. As for the African component, it would also receive some attention, but not as much as the former. It would also circulate through the medium of another, different tale, but not as widely. African Americans would address the issue, but within its proper context. It was therefore the decision of the community to fashion and designate tales such as the King Buzzard story as the vehicles by which posterity would learn of African complicity.

Stuckey has produced a very fine analysis of the King Buzzard tale as a part of his discourse on slave culture. His research suggests that the tradition is more representative of the Igbo experience in southeastern Nigeria, where native agency was particularly crucial to the procurement of human beings for export.[75] In addition to his observations on the meaning and implications of this tale, observations that merit revisiting, a few additional comments can be made relating to the initial capture. For reasons that will become manifest, the restatement of a substantial portion of the story will greatly assist the present inquiry. Tad, the principal character in the account, has been in the woods. When he returns to his friends, he is disheveled and upset, and upon being asked about his condition, he replies as follows:

I had been walkin' 'long de edge er Big Alligator Hole, an' de air been stink; an' I walk on an' I see sump'n riz up in front er me bigger 'an a man. An' he spread he whing out an' say, "Uuh!" He eye been red an' he de nastiest lookin' thing I ever see. He stink in my nostrils. He so stink, he stink to my eye an' my year. An' I look at him an' see he been eat a dead hog right dere in de night time. I ain' never see buzzard settin' on a carcass in de night 'fore dis. An' he look so vigus, he look like he ain' care ef he stay dere an' fight or no.

An' I been so oneasy an' frighten, till I ain' kin do nothin'; an' 'fore I knowed it, I jump at him. An' he riz up—makin' dat same dreadful sound—an' start flyin' all 'round me. Look like he tryin' to vomick on me. An' I dodge, an' dere in de moonlight dat ole thing circle 'round— look like he guh tackle me. An' he spewed he vomick every which er way, an' I see de leaf an' de grass wuh it fall on dry up. All de air seem like it were pizen.

An' I turned to leff, an' it keep on gittin' nigher an' nigher to me. An' I ain' know wuh would er happen, ef I ain' git in a canebrake wey he ain' kin fly. An' I crawl 'round for God knows how long, an' when I find myself, I been lost. Jesus know I ain' never wan' see no more buzzard like dat.

Cricket: "My God!"

Voice: "Wuh kind er buzzard dat?"

Tad: "God knows."

Tom: "Dat ain' no buzzard. I hear 'bout dat ole thing 'fore dis.

"My pa tell me dat 'way back in slavery time—'way back in Af'ica—dere been a nigger, an' he been a big nigger. He been de chief er he tribe, an' when dem white folks was ketchin' niggers for slavery, dat ole nigger nuse to entice 'em into trap. He'd git 'em on boat wey dem white folks could ketch 'em an' chain 'em. White folks nused to gee him money an' all kind er little thing, an' he'd betray 'em. An' one time atter he betray thousands into bondage, an' de white folks say dey ain' guh come to dat coast no more—dat was dey last trip—so dey knocked dat nigger down an' put chain on him an' bring him to dis country.

"An' when he dead, dere were no place in heaven for him an' he were not desired in hell. An' de Great Master decide dat he were lower dan all other mens or beasts; he punishment were to wander for eternal time over de face er de earth. Dat as he had kilt de sperrits of mens an' womens as well as dere bodies, he must wander on an' on. Dat his sperrit should always travel in de form of a great buzzard, an' dat carrion must be he food. . . . An' dey say he are known to all de sperrit world as de King Buzzard, an' dat forever he must travel alone."[76]

Tad's account of his encounter with King Buzzard is clearly a recapitulation of the ordeal of initial capture and is instructive in that it is concerned exclusively with the buzzard. Tad thinks he is escaping the creature by fleeing into a canebrake, but the fact that he is lost when he "finds" himself, that is, he is now in America, means that the canebrake was in reality the transport through the Middle Passage. That he could mistake a slave ship for a place of refuge is not inconsistent with the red cloth stories, for the latter stresses the slaver's false presentation as a vessel of trinket-filled wonder. But Tad's tale is not at all concerned with the canebrake; it focuses instead on the role the buzzard played in maneuvering him into the canebrake.

Tom's explanation of Tad's experience also reveals that the tale is not primarily concerned with Europeans. They are mentioned, but they are peripheral to the true focus, the African ruler. The deceit of the European trader, so prominent in the red cloth stories, is almost entirely absent here; it surfaces only in connection with the African sovereign, who himself was ultimately deceived and enslaved ("dey knocked dat nigger down an' put chain on him"). Rather, it is suggested here that it was the African ruler who was responsible for the deception of his African victims, for "he'd git 'em on boat," at which point Europeans took over. This is important, for the King

Buzzard tale probably developed concomitantly with the red cloth stories, meaning that the slave community made a conscious decision to create two folkloric traditions (rather than one), which incorporated the African perspective of both the European and the African trader. The creation of two traditions facilitated the need, in the minds of the community, to keep the questions of guilt and responsibility separate. Whites would receive their due in the one tradition. But African involvement in the trade required special treatment.

Although the black community placed ultimate blame on white folk for the institution of slavery, it reserved unique and specific condemnation for the African trader. Such was his crime that hell itself, the presumed destination of the European traders, would not grant him entry. By divine decree, the African accomplice had descended onto a subreptilian level. His activities were so wicked, so reprehensible, that he was sentenced to wander "on an' on" in the waste spaces of creation.

Why was the African trader's crime so despicable? What had he done that the European trader had not, or in what sense was his transgression any worse? Tom has supplied the answer, and like the red cloth tales, the reply carries within it evidence of a transformation in the collective self-perspective of the African-based population. For Tom states that the ruler had "betrayed" his people, selling "thousands into bondage." Now, Africans who were forced into the passage had been forced by various means, but the two principal avenues were warfare and kidnapping; that is, the majority of Africans captured for the trade had fallen into hostile, black hands. They therefore realized, within the context of ethnicity, that their African captors were their enemies, and that if the tables had been turned, they may have done the same thing. In what sense, then, were they betrayed?

The logical answer is that they had come to believe that Africans had a responsibility to one another by virtue of the fact that they were all Africans. Participation in the slave trade was therefore a violation of that responsibility. It was one thing for whites to enslave blacks, but for blacks to assist in the process was far more serious. The betrayal cut so deep that it resulted in not only physical death but also the death of "de sperrits of mens an' womens." The crux of the matter is plain: the transgression of the African ruler was so evil as to be nefarious, for he had sold his own.

Africans could not have felt betrayed so long as they held to the construct of an ethnically based identity. That they reached this point is undeniable evidence of movement along the continuum from ethnicity to race as the primary criterion of identification. That Africans of different ethnicities had fought wars resulting in captives was disregarded. That discordant religious communities had taken up arms in violent and death-dealing altercations had become immaterial. All that mattered, according to the King Buzzard tradition, was that the powerful had taken advantage of the weak and had sentenced them to life in cruel and fettered exile. Such behavior was inexcusable.[77]

To be condemned to eternal wandering, to be forever homeless and rootless, is an African concept in which time is cyclical. In the cosmology of the Kuba of Congo, for example, a good person who dies remains a spirit for a brief period before being reincarnated; the evil individual, however, remains in spiritual limbo.[78] Fredrika Bremer, in speaking with an older slave named Romeo in Charleston, was able to determine that the elder was African-born. Further into the discussion, Romeo informed Bremer that, according to "what the people in his native land believed respecting life after death," the "good would go to the God of heaven who made them." The bad "'go into the wind,' and he blew with his mouth around him on all sides."[79] It was this essentially African construction of eternal damnation that informed the beliefs of a former slave who in a WPA interview explained:

> But I'm a believer, and this here voodoo and hoodoo and spirits ain't nothing but a lot of folks outen Christ. Hants ain't nothing but somebody died outen Christ and his spirit ain't at rest, just in a wandering condition in the world.
>
> This is the evil spirit what the Bible tells about when it say a person has got two spirits, a good one and a evil one. The good spirit goes to a place of happiness and rest, and you don't see it no more, but the evil spirit ain't got no place to go. Its dwelling place done tore down when the body died, and it's just a-wandering and a-waiting for Gabriel to blow his trump, then the world gwine to come to an end.[80]

The foregoing is a wonderful illustration of the fitting of Christian teaching into an African template. The woman makes a confession of faith, taking a firm stand against voodoo and hoodoo, only to articulate a syncretic perspective that is consistent with the beliefs of a number of African ethnicities, including the Igbo and Bambara. The linear progression of the Christian faith, however, with its strong eschatological component, places a limitation on just how long the evil spirit will be required to wander.

The African–African American community therefore faced the question of white liability and black complicity by separating the two issues without denying their relatedness. By this method, the community sought to resolve the question of accountability with respect to Europeans without exculpating Africans for their assistance. The process generated two distinct traditions, both of which were intended to explain the passage. One focused on the more profound implications of the initial capture, but when taken together, the accounts constitute the experience in its entirety. At the same time, the development of these two approaches reveals a transformation of the African American collective identity.

. . . .

I have argued that relations between Africans and African Americans were better than worse, and that with the passing of time other considerations involving class served to stratify African-based society. The gargantuan process of generating normative traditions representing how people of African descent viewed their initial captivity is illustrative of the intensity of those relations. But in the process of creating traditions about the initial capture, discussion of Africa itself was unavoidable. It was necessarily the case that the African-born related not only the circumstances of their capture but also the conditions of their existence prior to their capture. African cultural forms and worldviews would have been communicated in many ways to American-born progeny in the normal course of performing activities such as care of children and the elderly, food preparation, religious worship, the pursuit of leisure, on so on. But there would have also been the need to actually talk about what it meant to live in Africa. The question then becomes, Given the overall esteem in which the native African was held, how was Africa itself viewed?

Stampp has written, in responding to the early debate over "Africanisms," that "if anything, most ante-bellum slaves showed a desire to forget their African past and to embrace as much of white civilization as they could."[81] At first glance, a sampling of the WPA interviews would appear to substantiate Stampp's assessment. Samuel Boulware, age eighty-two at the time of his interview in Columbia, South Carolina, exclaimed that "if white folks had drapped us long time ago, we would now be next to de rovin' beasts of de woods. Slavery was hard I knows but it had to be, it seem lak. They tells me they eats each other in Africa. Us don't do dat and you knows dat is a heap to us."[82] John Brown, already quoted on the subject of the red cloth stories, told his interviewer that his African-born grandmother was "a savage in Africa— a slave in America."[83] Frank Bell, eighty-six at the time of the statement and a native of New Orleans, fixed his face to say, "You know, the nigger was wild till the white man made what he has out of the nigger. He done ed'cate them real smart."[84]

The preceding statements are agreed that Africa was a place of barbarism, and that slavery was redemptive in providing the means through which the African could attain to the rudiments of civilization. Such a perspective could not have been reached, however, by a dialogue confined to the African-based community, for it evinces attitudes and assumptions of a larger, external white community ignorant of and hostile to Africa. Given the obvious and direct relationship between Africa and African Americans, it was unavoidable that the denigration of the former would have adverse implications for the self-esteem of the latter. Consider the language of Mary Johnson, age eighty-five in 1937, who said: "I think Abe Lincoln was a fine man, and Jeff Davis was good too. Slavery did good to nigger, made him careful and know how to work."[85] Or take the observation of James Johnson of Columbia, South Carolina, that "a heap of niggers is lak wild animals, in a way. He laks to eat a heap, sleep a heap, and move 'bout slow. . . . De black man is natchally lazy, you knows dat. De reason he talks lak he does, is 'cause he don't want to go to de trouble to 'nounce his words lak they ought to be. . . . I is sorry I has to say all dis 'bout my own color but it is de truth."[86] Like Africa itself, "niggers" were wild and lacking in attributes of industry. It must be pointed out, however, that much of this testimony is clearly affected by the circumstances surrounding the interview itself and the editing process, so much so that one wonders if the interviewer did not simply put his own stereotypic notions about "culluds" into the informant's mouth.

Whether or not such testimony has been compromised, there is no reason to discount the possibility that former slaves not only made such pronouncements but actually believed them. African Americans were relating to and dealing with whites at the same time they were struggling against them, so it was inevitable that some would begin to internalize bits and pieces of racist sentiment. This internalization had to begin somewhere; that it continued was obvious even to Herskovits: "For no group in the population of this country has been more completely convinced of the inferior nature of the African background than have the Negroes."[87] The promotion of savage Africa was clearly calculated to aid both the apology of slavery and the conditioning of the slaves; its success among some of the enslaved is demonstrated in the words of Mississippian Elmo Steele, who is estimated to have been born between 1822 and 1827.[88] He claimed that his African great-grandfather told him that Africans did not wear clothes in Africa, and that "de hair growed several inches long all over deir body." At death, there were no funeral rites of any kind; rather, "dey took 'em off an' throw 'em down an' dat wuz all dey wuz to it." His great-grandfather's people had no organized religion, "but dey had a feelin' dat some kind o' worship ought to be. . . . Dey would git up an' try to say some 'em, dey wouldn't even know what dey meant deir selves an' dey would sing an' dance an' knock bones together fer time."

Jabbo Rivers, who was ninety years old and living in Mobile in 1937, concurred with Steele's perspective:

God gave it [religion] to Adam and took it away from Adam and gave it to Noah, and you know, Miss, Noah had three sons, and when Noah got drunk on wine, one of his sons laughed at him, and the other two took a sheet and walked backwards and threw it over Noah. Noah told the one who laughed, "you children will be hewers of wood and drawers of water for the other's two children, and they will be known by their hair and their skin being dark," so, Miss, there we are, and that is the way God meant us to be. We have always had to follow the white folks and do what we saw them do, and that's all there is to it. You just can't get away from what the Lord said.[89]

The invocation of the Hamitic curse is proof positive of Western contamination. The leap from Africa to blackness as the principal cause of sorrow was both short and effortless, resulting in an enduring struggle for many with the color of their own skin. Witness the pure, unadulterated self-hatred exemplified in the conversation between Gold and Gene following a story entitled "How the Church Came to be Split Up":

Then Gold spoke up and said, "Now, lemme tell one. Ah know one about a man as black as Gene."

"What you always crackin' me for?" Gene wanted to know. "Ah ain't a bit blacker than you."

"Oh, yes you is, Gene. Youse a whole heap blacker than Ah is."

"Aw, go head on, Gold. Youse blacker than me. You jus' look my color cause youse fat. If you wasn't no fatter than me you'd be so black till lightnin' bugs would follow you at twelve o'clock in de day, thinkin' it's midnight."

"Dat's a lie, youse blacker than Ah ever dared to be. Youse lam' black. Youse so black till they have to throw a sheet over yo' head so de sun kin rise every mornin'. Ah know yo' ma cried when she seen *you*."[90]

Such dialogue, ostensibly humorous, is quite deadly in its effect.

Whatever views African Americans had of Africa or themselves, self-deprecation was not something they learned from those born in Africa, notwithstanding the account of Elmo Steele. The testimony is overwhelming that native Africans were enamored with and thought very highly of their homeland, as is evidenced by their various attempts to abscond to Africa. To be sure, Africans were eager to leave America for home, as is clear in the letter of Sessi, who with thirty-eight other Africans (mostly Mende) mutinied aboard the *Amistad* in 1839. In December 1840 Sessi wrote Lewis Tappan: "I tell you Something and you let we go our country and we want go and we tell thing about Jesus Christ who came down from heaven to Died on the cross for Sinners.”[91] Even those who remained in North America for a considerable length of time retained a burning desire to repatriate, as can be observed in the 1904 correspondence of Cilucangy, or Ward Lee, a survivor of the *Wanderer*:

To the Public:

Please help me. In 1859 I was brought to this country when I was a child. I cannot say just what age I was then but I have been aroused by the spirit—and I trust it was the spirit of God—on last May. One year ago it was revealed to me to go home back to Africa and I have been praying to know if it was God's will and the more I pray the more it presses on me to go and now I am trying to get ready if God be with me to go back to Africa as soon as I can get off to go. And now I beg every one who will please help me. I will be glad of whatever you will give me. I have been trying to make some arrangements to go over ever since it was revealed to me to go. I am bound for my old home if God be with me white or black or yellow or the red I am an old African.[92]

However, it was often the case that those who survived slavery did so by forming ties of family and friendship, so that although they still felt the connection to their homeland, they now had indissoluble relations of blood and fraternity in America. This conflict can be seen in the testimony of Kazoola (Cudjoe Lewis), a survivor of the *Clotilde*. At the end of the Civil War he and his fellow survivors desired to return to Africa but lacked the means. By 1914 it was still their custom to assemble on Sunday afternoons and reminisce: “Kazoola says that he often thinks that if he had wings he would fly back; then he remembers that all he has lies in American soil—the wife who came from his native land, who was his helpmate and companion through the many years, and all his children.”[93]

Kazoola was really in much more anguish than the 1914 interview suggests. He was again interviewed in 1934, when at the estimated age of ninety-four he lived at Plateau, four miles north of Mobile. Illiterate and working as the caretaker of the Negro Baptist Church, he received those interviewing him with the greeting, “God bless you, and sit down my masters.” The deference of these words suggested a bit of dissembling was forthcoming if the wrong questions were raised and, in fact, he was asked if he wished to return to Africa. “ ‘Cudjo,’ he said, ‘no want to go back. No fadder, no mudder, no sister, no brudder, no child to meet Cudjo. Cudjo not even know where his home was. . . . And now Cudjo stay here. Cudjo's wife she buried here. Cudjo's son buried here. Cudjo he be buried here. No more he go back to Africa.’ ” But Cudjo drew his next breath and betrayed how he truly felt by saying: “No more he see the beeg, beeg yam. No more he eat the beeg melon. No more he see his people. No more he see his people.”[94]

The inner turmoil Kazoola suffered over the bipolarity of his ultimate loyalties was apparently experienced by many, so much so that this form of suffering entered into the corpus of folklore describing the slave's sojourn. The story of Gullah Joe, previously employed in discussing the red cloth tradition, also includes an exchange between Tad and Joe that illustrates the African's agony over simultaneous connections to widely divergent lands. Having alluded to the Middle Passage and his subsequent sale to "ole Marster," Joe is queried as to whether or not he had succeeded in forgetting his African home:

Tad: "Is you satisfy?"
Joe: "It seem to me I would be satisfy ef I jes could see my tribe one more time. Den I would be willin' to come back here. I is a ole man now an' de folks here been good to me. Anything good atter dat vessel [reference to Middle Passage]."
Tad: "You reckon ef you was to go back to Af'ica you'd know any er dem people?"
Joe: "Ef dey would jes take me an' set me down on Af'ica shore, I could walk right to my tribe, for I know everybody. My daddy was a chief an' I got aunt an' heap er kin folk an' friend, an' I know dey'd be glad to see me.

"I is a ole man now, but I has a longin' to walk in de feenda [forest]. I wants to see it one more time. I has a wife an' chillun here, but when I thinks er my tribe an' my friend an' my daddy an' my mammy an' de great feenda, a feelin' rises up in my th'oat an' my eye well up wid tear."[95]

For reasons already presented, the WPA interview does not always represent the actual sentiment of the former slave. The interview's purpose was to collect data on slavery for public consumption, which meant white folks as far as the informants were concerned. Their responses were necessarily tailored by such considerations. But folklore was internally directed, intended for people of African descent. Joe's replies in the foregoing tale, therefore, are much more representative of the African's sentiment toward his native land. His was a painful predicament.

By virtue of the fact that such folklore is extant, it is the case that Africans were successful in communicating their very high regard of and deep yearning for Africa to their descendants. The external environment would wage cultural war against a favorable representation of Africa, so that African Americans would experience the conflict for decades to come. But it is also the case that many of African descent not only loved their ancestors but thought favorably of their homeland as well. The evidence for this is abundant and is essentially derived from the very notion of African continuity and transformation. It can also be found in the many claims by African Americans to royal lineage, a phenomenon better investigated within the context of class distinctions. It would be appropriate, however, to introduce here two examples that support the notion that many African Americans maintained a salutary view of Africa. The first is a statement by the aforementioned eighty-year-old Thomas Smith of Georgia concerning the supernatural feats of Moses and Pharaoh: "Dat happen in Africa duh Bible say. Ain dat show dat Africa wuz a lan uh magic powuh since duh beginnin uh history?"[96] Smith had found biblical support for his existing admiration for Africa, and his is but one of the many ways in which African Americans subverted an authoritative source in the Western cultural arsenal. But a second example of African American affection for Africa can be found in songs heard by William Brown, a fugitive slave who had earlier worked aboard a Mississippi steamboat carrying slaves to New Orleans. One of the songs he heard contained the following lines:

> See these poor souls from Africa
> Transported to America;
> We are stolen, and sold to Georgia . . .[97]

The verses are remarkable in that they reveal the slaves' identification with Africa and a clear understanding of the method by which their ancestors found themselves transplanted. The memory of Africa forms the epicenter of the song's pain.

The African-based community had a great deal to resolve. Questions of exploitation, betrayal, identity, and the like were worked out within and between generations throughout the course of North American slavery. African- and American-born slaves worked closely not only on physical fields but also on intellectual and cultural terrains. The traditions examined so far clearly required collaboration between African and African American. The available evidence tends to substantiate the existence of intimate, interdependent associations between these two groups, suggesting that they regarded each other as equals. This is not to say, however, that classism did not exist within black society—it most certainly did. The following section will examine stratification within black society with a view to determining the role of African ethnicity in its evolution.

. . . .

The emergence of a new, collective self-perception in the African-based community was largely in response to the challenge of a hostile environment. The embrace of race traversed the various spaces of cultural difference, providing a viable rationale for corporate resistance. Race as a unifying ideal was not imposed upon the community but was a concept suggested by the logic and reality of the servile condition and adopted and fashioned by those of African descent to suit their own purposes. That is, the creation of the African American identity was largely an internal process.

Obviously, however, external influences also had an impact on the development of the African American community. Although these influences reached beyond mere expressions of physical control, they were essentially a consequence of that control and helped shape the self-perception of Africans and their progeny in significant and enduring ways. For example, the manipulation of the symbols and substance of power contributed directly to the diminution of self-esteem among some of African descent.

The stratification of the African-based community, however, was achieved by way of a complex interplay of forces originating both within and without the community and resulting primarily from differentiation based upon the assignment of labor. To be sure, the vast majority of Africans were imported to work as cultivators, but both on the farms and plantations, and certainly in the towns and cities, there were numerous tasks requiring other kinds of talents. Many Africans, already possessed of skills in animal husbandry, fishing, hunting, food preservation, tanning, sewing and weaving, wood-working, carpentry, metallurgy, and handicraft manufacturing would have been recruited to help lay the nation's rural and urban foundations by working as coopers, cartwrights, boat and shipbuilders, stevedores, cart drivers, construction and drainage workers, sugar and indigo processors, butchers, and so on. The African contributed expertise as well as brawn.

It is therefore reasonable to surmise that representatives from all the various ethnicities would have been found working in all kinds of capacities. However, what is intriguing is that, based upon qualitative and limited quantitative evidence, ethnic representation in labor assignments was disproportionate and peculiar to each colony/state. This was largely due to the stereotyping of the slaveholders, for although they recruited for skilled positions based upon the perception of individual acumen and merit, they also characterized whole ethnicities. Thus some groups were viewed as better suited for agricultural labor, whereas others were believed to possess natural propensities for the crafts. The unavoidable conclusion is that labor differentiation within the African-based community was directly informed by the legacy of ethnicity.

The process by which slaveholders arrived at their assessments is not obvious but, by way of conjecture, must have represented the confluence of both experience and prejudice. Europeans working in West and West Central Africa reported on their host societies, emphasizing qualities of economic organization deemed unique. Similarly, planters in Central and South America and the Caribbean shared their observations with their North American colleagues via correspondence and publication. The information was filtered through notions of hierarchy, so that groups more closely approximating the European phenotype were believed to have greater propensities for certain tasks. Thus although all were seen as agriculturalists, none more so than those from Sierra Leone. Muslims from all over West Africa, if identified as such, were prized as drivers, domestics, and caretakers of livestock throughout the South. The Akan were universally acclaimed as industrious and were certainly well represented in the skilled positions of Virginia and Maryland, where they were numerous, as well as in South Carolina and Georgia, where they were not. The Igbo were equally treated in Virginia and Maryland, but not so in South Carolina and Georgia, where they were in the minority and probably relegated to the fields. The West Central Africans would have been heavily recruited for skilled labor in South Carolina and Georgia, where they were in such large numbers. In Louisiana, the Senegambians had a reputation as cultivators, but they would have also been recruited, along with those from the Bight of Benin, for skilled labor positions. Both of these groups, in turn, formed the foundation of the privileged through the Spanish regime and after, when the importation of the Fon-Ewe-Yoruba profoundly affected both free and enslaved cultures of the lower Mississippi. Planters from Haiti brought with them not only their slaves but also the Haitian servile hierarchy. Such privilege did not diminish once it settled on Louisiana soil; if anything, it flourished.

The use of class in this study therefore refers to this complex process of differentiation within the African-based community. Initially and throughout the colonial period, ethnicity played an important role in labor assignments. With the diminution of the African-born and the numerical increase of their progeny in the antebellum period, ethnicity would give way to other considerations, such as continent of birth and color gradation, as important indexes of labor distinction. Although blacks born on both continents and of all shades belonged to the lowest class of field laborers, the ranks of the skilled, as time progressed, became increasingly and disproportionately filled by blacks born in America, a significant percentage of whom were lighter-skinned. Even in the antebellum period, however, the vestiges of ethnicism continued to be felt.

Based upon the discussion of the African-based community in preceding chapters, and in view of what is known about contemporary African American society, it is clear that people of African descent living in North America never constituted a seamless, undifferentiated mass of individuals. To be sure, the shared African background, the experience of slavery, and the long, common struggle against racism have been the primary components that have combined to produce an aggregate of individuals whose existence is distinctive and unusual, thereby justifying the referent community. Nevertheless, this population is at the same time quite diverse, owing to regional differences, demographic dissimilarities, socioeconomic disparities, religious and cultural variations, and the like. These differences are neither novel nor of recent invention, but were apparent with the introduction of the African to America.

Rawick has written that slaves developed their "own class system based upon the division of labor on the plantation."[98] The context for the statement is the cultural autonomy and spiritual independence slaves exhibited in the creation of their own church, language, and so forth. Similarly, Berlin and Morgan have compiled studies that emphasize the "internal economies" of the slaves, within which the latter engaged in subsistence farming, marketing, and handicraft and tool manufacturing, and those skilled as carpenters, coopers, and blacksmiths often hired themselves out for their own profit.[99] I am in substantial agreement with these authors; however, in the attempt to recognize agency, care must be taken not to overemphasize the options of the slave, nor to exaggerate her ability to negotiate her life's parameters. For in the end, the land used for subsistence farming, the skills required for moonlighting, and the time to pursue either had to be sanctioned or provided by the slaveholder (and he often did so out of self-interest). Ultimately, slave participation in both the external and internal economies devolved upon the authority of the slaveholder; class differentiation was necessarily brokered through his office. It is difficult to avoid the fact that in the power disparities of slavery, the will of the enslaved was without authority and promotion therefore void of transferable meaning (outside of the slave community), unless and until the slaveholder approved.

Beginning with the colonial period, the qualitative evidence is consistent that the major ethnic and regional populations experienced unequal and discriminatory receptions in North America relative to the colony in question. This a priori determination of African ethnic aptitude continued throughout the colonial era, so that all newly arriving Africans were seen in the same light. As long as the African-born were the majority, slaveholders continued to state their preferences in terms of African ethnicities. In colonial Louisiana, for example, the Bambara and the Wolof were favored as drivers and domestics (respectively) over American-born slaves.[100] But as the colonial period progressed and the percentage of American-born slaves increased throughout the South, the emphasis on ethnicity began to decline. The country-born had to be differentiated by other criteria. Selection of certain American-born slaves for skilled positions over others, however, necessarily reflected to some degree slaveholder preferences for their African parents or grandparents, which brings us back to ethnicity.

Subsequent African importations through the late colonial and early ante-bellum periods continued to go directly into the field. These Africans would socially and sexually interact with older Africans and their American-born progeny, but the latter two categories would have for the most part been field laborers as well. At the same time, earlier African imports of certain eth-nicities and their country-born children, selected for domestic and voca-tional work, would have formed the basis of a privileged class within the African-based community. Among the consequences of such developments was that privileged Africans and African Americans tended to lack propor-tional representation of certain ethnic groups, whereas the ranks of the field laborers were filled with representatives from all ethnicities. It would there-fore have been at the level of the field worker, at the level of the folk, that race as a unifying concept would have been most persuasive, for it was on this plane that the question of identity could have been resolved with as little interference from white society (the coercive sphere) as possible. To put it another way, the largest portion of the African American composite identity was fashioned by rural folk deeply influenced by the African antecedent.

At this point, it is important to understand that divisions between the skilled/privileged and the unskilled/unprivileged were by no means rigid, nor did they always detract from the cohesion of the community. As will be demonstrated shortly, the evidence suggests that both house and field slaves, in some instances, saw their plight as one and the same and joined together for purposes of resistance. Nevertheless, it is just as clear that not all blacks experienced slavery in the same way, and that some had a much more difficult time of it. Relative to whites, blacks have often sought to present themselves as a single people. Those doing the presenting have usually been privileged. But once removed from the presence of whites, fissures within African American society along class lines become readily apparent. The fact that cleavages were recognizable in the immediate aftermath of slavery means that their roots are to be found in the soil of slavery. The stratification of African America began somewhere.

Some individuals from select ethnic and regional groupings, chosen to perform tasks which required either trade skills or some level of increased interaction with whites, gradually became more isolated from the main body of black slaves, experiencing a decrease in their ethnic consciousness over time and through generational change. In lieu of an African-informed frame of reference, those so isolated would have begun to take on the perspectives of their white patrons; they would have been the first to have experienced what Du Bois calls "double consciousness."[101] Moving into the nineteenth century, there would have emerged a definite association between vocational or domestic work and privilege. Indeed, by closer involvement with whites, some began to dissociate themselves from not only ethnic ties but from all things African. This decision to distance and disclaim, however, does not diminish one of the original and historical bases for privilege within the African-based community-ethnicity. By the early years of the nineteenth century, some elite slaves may well have looked down their noses at the masses, but the foundation for such presumption was in many cases ethnocentricity, whether conscious or subconscious, and that heightened by the machinations of the slaveocracy.

In the first few decades of the nineteenth century, late-arriving Africans found that the percentage of their fellow African-born had declined to about 20 percent of the total. By then, a class of American-born, previously ethnically differentiated elites would have been well established. Complicating the picture was the development of a free black population, initially very tiny in number but growing dramatically with the onset of the American Revolution and consequent, wide-scale manumissions as payment for military service rendered during the war. In Georgia, for example, the number of free blacks increased more than fourfold between 1790 and 1810, whereas South Carolina saw their ranks double. The American Revolution was followed by its Haitian counterpart, resulting in the immigration to North America of a number of white slaveholders and black slaves as well as light-skinned *gens de couleur*. The latter, constituting their own class-caste and at enmity with both whites and blacks in Haiti, came into the lower South in some numbers, particularly into the ports of New Orleans and Charleston. White southerners officially banned the immigration of West Indian free persons of color because they were viewed as potentially subversive. Their efforts were largely unsuccessful, however, and in the cities of the lower South the mixed race émigrés added to the number of free blacks. In New Orleans, for example, the number of free blacks, most of whom were West Indian, increased by 400 percent between 1803 and 1810.[102]

It therefore follows that in the lower South, especially in places such as New Orleans and Charleston, the presence of Haitian and other West Indian *gens de couleur* contributed to the exacerbation of color consciousness within the African-based community. That is, associations between free status, relative privilege, and lighter skin were more readily made in these places. In Charleston, for example, the establishment in the 1790s of the mulatto-only Brown Fellowship Society reflected the growth and self-consciousness of lighter-skinned Haitians. In fact, Berlin argues that the lower South as a whole would develop a relatively lighter-skinned free black population in contrast to a darker hued free population in the upper South.[103] He theorizes that the former characterization was to some extent the consequence of the West Indian presence, whereas conditions in the upper South were largely the product of "indiscriminate manumissions and the addition of many black fugitives." It is important to understand, however, that the vast majority of free blacks (more than 85 percent in 1860) lived in the upper South.[104] It is therefore the case that the West Indian impact was most keenly felt in the ports of New Orleans and Charleston, to a lesser extent in the rural areas of the lower South, and hardly at all in the upper South. Their influence therefore, although of consequence, should not be overemphasized.

In the urban areas, free blacks in the upper South tended to provide unskilled labor (common laborers, domestics, factory hands, and so on), although most free blacks throughout the South, like whites, lived in rural areas, were engaged in agriculture, and remained poor. It was in the cities and towns of the lower South, however, that free blacks were employed in skilled labor in much larger numbers, even though the majority remained unskilled. Although women were for the most part confined to such jobs as domestics and washerwomen, men were able to perform other tasks. Considered "nigger work," such labor included barbering, butchering, blacksmithing, brick-laying, plastering, shoemaking, catering, bathhouse keeping, tailoring, making deliveries, and driving coaches. Many of these professions required great skill, notwithstanding their stigma, and many were learned while in slavery, which in turn suggests relative privilege even then.[105]

In contrast to free blacks and those arriving from the West Indies, the vast majority of late-arriving Africans were pressed into the fields, where they would have mixed and mingled with the established lower society of slaves and with whom they would have exchanged cultural influences. References to such exchanges include the testimony of Ruby Andrew Moore, the daughter of a former slaveholder, who spoke of a certain group of West Central Africans imported in 1858, who "as soon as they could make themselves understood by a gibberish that was a mixture of our own language and theirs, their stories, fables, traditions, etc., began to be circulated among the other darkies."[106] Moore went on to recount that about six hundred "Congolese" were purchased shortly before the Civil War and brought to Ossabaw Island along the Georgia coast. There they lived as they had in their native land, with the "domesticated slaves watching the performance and naturally imbibing many ideas and habits demonstrated by the savages."[107]

There is little research on the relationship between ethnicity and labor assignments during the colonial and antebellum South. Littlefield has made an attempt and found that by the eighteenth century, the Spanish and Portuguese, as well as the French and the Dutch, had all more or less gravitated to the position of the English with regard to the correlation of ethnicity and aptitude.[108] The English had evaluated the various ethnic groups for their collective propensities and had determined that of all the groups, the "Coromantees" or Akan speakers and the "Whydahs" or the Dahomean Fon ("Papaws") were particularly equipped for field labor. The "Mandingos" of Gambia, on the other hand, were "physically more attractive," as they were "refined and possessed of a gentle nature." As for the "Ibos," "Congos," and "Angolas," they were supposedly weaker than the Akan and the Yoruba and were "said to be more effective as house servants."[109]

Littlefield's overall remarks are consistent with testimony previously considered that argues that planters were conscious of ethnic differences among Africans and registered very strong preferences for certain groups over others. He makes the important point that these characterizations "were taken seriously and acted upon" by the planters. His assessment becomes dubious, however, when it focuses on the question of what was done with ethnicities seen as unsuitable for agricultural tasks. The idea that the "weaker" groups were given domestic work is a conjecture for which there is little or no supporting documentation. Further, Little makes no differentiation between English planters' preferences in the Caribbean and those that existed in the North American mainland. This is problematic, because North American planters differed in their predilections depending upon the colony/state.

Based primarily upon the work of Phillips and (to a lesser extent) Rice, Holloway has taken a further step in the attempt to analyze the relationship between ethnicity and labor divisions.[110] It is his contention that

> North Americans preferred Senegambians (Mandingos, Fulani, Bambaras, and Malinkes) as house servants—butlers, maids, nurses (nannies), chambermaids, and cooks. They wanted slaves from the West African region—Whydahs (Fons), Pawpaws (Fantes), Yorubas (Nagoes), and the Coromantee (Asante-Fante)—to work as domestic servants and artisans. These groups were also employed as carriage drivers, gardeners, carpenters, barbers, stablemen, wheelwrights, wagoners, blacksmiths, sawyers, washers, and bricklayers. The North Americans imported Africans from the Windward or Grain Coast (Mande and Mano River groups) because of their familiarity with the cultivation of rice, indigo, and tobacco.[111]

The findings of the present study are consistent with the work of Holloway, although based upon different and independent sources. In contrast to Littlefield, this study also agrees with Holloway that those deemed unwanted and despised in the American South did not end up in the "big house" but in the fields. To have assigned domestic responsibilities to Africans who were disdained, responsibilities reserved for only a select few, would have been to reward them, an egregious contradiction. Rather, Holloway writes that the Igbo in South Carolina "were at the bottom of the preference list, imported primarily to be common field laborers."[112] Most groups from Sierra Leone were also imported expressly for the purpose of cultivation. The implication of such observations is clear: Parallel to the formation of the African American elite, some groups destined to work the soil also tended to come from specific ethnicities. The Igbo were dominant in Virginia and Maryland but would be joined in the fields there by West Central Africans. These same West Central Africans arrived late in Louisiana fields and comprised most of the agricultural force in South Carolina and Georgia, where their numbers were augmented by the minority Igbo. After the mid-eighteenth century, thousands of Sierra Leonians swelled the ranks of these "field negroes."

Social divisions within slave society are supported by numerous references in the literature. Ingraham, for example, wrote in 1835 that there were three "classes" of slaves: house slaves, field slaves, and town slaves, many of whom were "hired out."[113] Patterson, in analyzing Jamaican slave society, has postulated that the division of slaves into domestics, field hands, and skilled workers was essentially a vertical design accompanied by horizontal strata within each of the three divisions.[114] For the purposes of this study, however, domestics and vocational workers are placed into the same category, as it is difficult to determine how their respective tasks may have differentiated them. With regard to the matter of horizontal distinctions, they probably existed among North American slaves as well, but the absence of any effective means on the part of slaves to transform such distinctions into tangible, material differences meant that only those determined or sanctioned by the slaveholders resulted in recognizable class divisions.

It is highly likely that in the rural areas, the field-versus-house dichotomy is overly simplistic and exaggerated. As will be demonstrated from the runaway slave ads, there are numerous examples of cooperation between these two categories, and Herskovits has suggested that the life of a house servant was not greatly different from the experience of a field hand.[115] Sufficient testimony exists, however, to substantiate some basis for the dichotomy. Sydnor, in writing on Mississippi, flatly states that house servants lived better than did field servants, and that the former's lot improved with the size of the plantation.[116] The situation in Louisiana was similar, such that the "loyalty and fidelity of the household servant, in particular, were often unquestionable. The mammies, for instance, practically ruled the Big Houses. . . . Mammy was so integrally a part of the family that she was lifted far above the other servants."[117]

The solution to whether life for domestics was significantly different from that of field hands depends to a large degree on exactly which hands are being compared with which domestics. A comprehensive study is needed to answer the question as it relates to slavery in general, or to slavery in a given colony/state. However, it is more probable than not that when slaveholdings of similar size are compared, divergence between hands and domestics widens as the size of the estate increases. The experience of a domestic on a plantation of twenty would likely differ from his or her counterpart who is one of eighty or ninety others. The former may have shared more in the agricultural duties of the other slaves than did the latter, whose owner could have afforded to allow domestics to devote their time exclusively to non-agricultural tasks. By the same token, agricultural responsibilities on a farm with less than twenty slaves may have required that all work with the soil, including the slaveholders. But of course, there were other factors that influenced the relative lives of field hand and domestic, not the least of which were the idiosyncrasies of the slaveholder.

Austin Steward, a former slave in Virginia, worked on a larger plantation and served as an errand boy in the big house at the age of eight.[118] Class distinctions are very apparent in his discussion of a social gathering of slaves on another plantation. First to arrive at the "grand dance" were the "unpolished" slaves, after which came their "aristocratic" analogues. The latter were "dressed in the cast-off finery of their master and mistress, swelling out and putting on airs in imitation of those they were forced to obey from day to day."[119] These house slaves were observed by the field hands for "direction in etiquette and protocol," but they were also "sometimes greatly envied, while others are bitterly hated." This enmity was richly deserved, according to Steward, for "many of them are the most despicable tale-bearers and mischief-makers," whose betrayals of their fellow slaves often ended in punishment for the alleged offender and reward for the tattler. Another former slave agreed with Steward, testifying that owners "taught us [mulattoes and blacks] to be against one another and no matter where you go you would always find one that would be tattling and would have the white folks pecking on you. They would try to make it soft for themselves."[120] In this way, class distinctions were not only created by slaveholders but also aggravated by them.

As the nineteenth century progressed, class distinctions among slaves, having been initially premised upon labor divisions, eventually took on cultural markers that served to reinforce those differences. Specifically, religion became an emblem of divergence, concerning which more will be stated in the following chapter. What can be said here, however, is that Christian conversion was first more associated with domestics than field hands. Harrison, in his early study of slave religion, maintained that most blacks converted to Methodism, and that they tended to be "house negroes" whose frequent contact with slaveholders resulted in their participation in the family altar as well as Sunday service.[121] The vast majority of slaves, Harrison claimed, "were not thus favored." Luther Jackson, whose subsequent studies of slave religion remain significant, concurs with Harrison, writing that for a generation or more prior to 1830, those of African descent participating in the Christian religion were largely domestic servants or individuals hired out to the urban areas.[122] Interestingly, Patterson's examination of Jamaican society led to a parallel discovery, whereby Methodism chiefly appealed to "coloured" or mixed-race individuals, whereas darker-skinned blacks, although attracted in some numbers to Methodism, flocked in droves to the Baptist denomination.[123]

In addition to labor and religion, a third aspect of class divisions among the slave community was the degree of intimacy between slaveholders and domestics. Armstrong records, for example, that every plantation had "play children," or enslaved children carefully selected as playmates for the scions of the owners.[124] Robert Ellett, born in 1849, was such a play child: "I grew up with the young masters. I played with them, ate with them and sometimes slept with them. We were pals."[125] Ellett had apparently been selected as a play child by virtue of his parents' vaulted status: "We was favored slaves. My parents was the two best slaves on the plantation." Ophelia Settle Egypt, a member of Fisk's Social Science Institute and one who conducted interviews of former slaves in 1929 and 1930 in Tennessee and Kentucky, recorded a similar statement from an informant born in 1850:

> Yes, I was a house slave; I slept under the stairway in the closet. I was sorta mistress' pet, you know, he, he, he. We house slaves thought we was better'n the others what worked in the field. We really was raised a little different, you know; fact is, I kinda think I'm better'n most folks now, he, he, he, he.
>
> Yes'm, we was raised; they, that is, the field hands, wasn't.[126]

Harriet Gresham's experience concurs with both of the foregoing. Born in 1838 and having lived in Barnwell, South Carolina (but interviewed in Jacksonville, Florida), she was "one of a group of mulattoes" who belonged to Edmond Bellinger. Her mother was the plantation seamstress and her father was a driver, which allowed Harriet to live in the big house, where she "played with the children of her mistress and seldom mixed with the other slaves on the plantation." She told her interviewer: "Honey, I aint know I was any diffrunt fum de chillen o' me mistress twel atter de war."[127] From such testimonies as these, it is apparent that living in the big house as a child or working there as a youth created illusions in the malleable mind and maximized the acculturative process.

Of course, intimacy between slaveholder and house servant went far beyond play among children. As a result of sexual liaisons principally between white men and black women, the element of biraciality became an associated and important component of privilege within the slave community. Berlin, in his important contribution to the study of free blacks in the South, writes that during the colonial period "most mulattoes were the children of white indentured servant men and black women, and frequently . . . the offspring of black men and white servant women."[128] Braithwaite has identified a parallel phenomenon in Jamaica, where he found that the most salient feature of creolization was miscegenation.[129] While Fogel and Engerman have argued that the rate of miscegenation in North America was relatively insignificant, resulting in a mixed-race population of slightly less than 10 percent by 1860, it must be pointed out that the census upon which these authors base their assertions is notoriously faulty.[130] However, even if the census data were accurate, not every liaison ended with the birth and survival of a child.

The real issue here is not the size of the mixed-race population but its impact upon slave society. Lyell recorded that slaveholders preferred those of mixed race as house servants because "their appearance is more agreeable, and they are more intelligent," sentiments that echo and parallel planter preferences for Africans of certain ethnic types.[131] This is not to say that all house servants were therefore of mixed racial ancestry, but that a certain association had developed between lighter complexions and nonagricultural labor. Berlin's work supports this association, for he found that almost 40 percent of southern free blacks were of mixed race, and that free blacks were "generally more skilled, literate, and well connected with whites than the mass of slaves. Even before they were emancipated, most free Negroes enjoyed a privileged position within the slave hierarchy."[132] Not only was this association in the mind of the planter, as stated by Lyell, but it was also established in the mind of the slave. Willie McCullough's view of slave society, shared in a 1937 interview in North Carolina, reveals the perspective: "There were classes of slavery. Some of the half-white and beautiful young women who were used by the marster and his men friends or who was the sweetheart of the marster only, were given special privileges. Some of 'em worked very little."[133] Rebecca Hooks, age ninety when interviewed in 1937 in Lake City, Florida, echoed McCullough's sentiments in discussing her biracial mother and father in that she attributed their status directly to their skin color: "Because of this blood mixture Rebecca's parents were known as 'house niggers,' and lived on quarters located in the rear of the 'big house.'"[134]

The creation of mixed-race strata as intermediary stations between those of "pure" European and African ancestry is a well-known phenomenon throughout the various societies of the New World as well as parts of the

Old. From Brazil to Haiti to Senegal to South Africa, these formations have created layered societies in which power and entitlement filters down from the whitest to the blackest. Both Patterson and Braithwaite, for example, maintain that among house servants in Jamaica, skin color was more important than any other social marker.[135] The biracial daughter of a "colored" domestic was to be addressed as "Miss Polly" by the darker slaves. The association of skin color with status was such that it "was unusual for any of these household slaves to be pure Negro." Even "most of the tradesmen of the estates were coloured." Consistent with earlier testimony from North America, these Jamaican elites "dressed better than the field Negroes and were rarely punished. 'They considered themselves as a superior race to the blacks,' always referring contemptuously to the latter's colour whenever the two groups had a quarrel."[136] Patterson is quick to point out that the darker slaves did not internalize this racial paradigm but, rather, retained their deep sense of pride and self-worth. Consequently, the result of these two competing models of racial construction was often strong enmity, such that C. L. R. James wrote concerning Haiti: "The advantages of being white were so obvious, that race prejudice against the Negroes permeated the minds of the Mulattoes who so bitterly resented the same thing from the whites. Black slaves and Mulattoes hated each other."[137]

Although not without tensions, relations between mixed-race individuals and blacks in North America were not as acrid as what obtained in Haiti. Perhaps only the lower Mississippi, and specifically New Orleans, approached the more complex, multilayered societies of the Caribbean and South America as determined by specific admixtures of race. Blassingame's work on New Orleans reveals a social structure that has a number of mixed-race categories beyond simply black and white, within which existed bonds of recognition and responsibility between white fathers and biracial wives and their offspring.[138] Quadroons, the children of whites and mulattoes, were often sent by their fathers to study in Paris and were the major beneficiaries of the infamous quadroon balls.[139] Descendants of quadroons and whites, so-called octoroons, were even further elevated in status and were on the threshold of "passing." DeBow, based in New Orleans and therefore knowledgeable of such matters, set out to establish a delineation of the various racial classifications of the day which could be used in a court of law:

> The term negro is confined to slave Africans (the ancient Berbers) and their descendants. It does not embrace the free inhabitants of Africa, such as the Egyptians, Moors, or the negro Asiatics, such as the Lascars.
> Mulatto is the issue of the white and the negro.

When the mulatto ceases, and a party bearing some slight taint of the African blood ranks as white, is a question for the solution of a jury.

Whenever the African taint is so far removed, that upon inspection, a party may be fairly pronounced to be white, and such has been his or her previous reception into society, and enjoyment of the privileges usually enjoyed by white people, the jury may rate and regard the party as white.

No specific rule, as to the quantity of negro blood which will compel a jury to find one to be a mulatto, has ever been adopted. Between one quarter and one eighth seems to be debatable gronnd [*sic*]. When the blood is reduced to, or below one eighth, the jury ought always to find the party white. When the blood is one quarter or more African, the jury must find the party a mulatto.[140]

New Orleans represents the extreme to which implications of miscegenation were taken. What was generally true throughout North America, however, was that privilege and the "taint" tended toward mutual exclusivity.

It would therefore appear probable that house servants and vocational workers in North America, based upon what has preceded, were disproportionately made up of lighter-skinned blacks, who in turn were either from certain African ethnic groups and their descendants, or were of mixed racial ancestry, or both. Although such may have taken great pride in their color, the means by which they came to be were not so illustrious. In Jamaica, many "colored" domestics were mistresses of the planters.[141] The situation in North America was not radically different. One of many examples was Diana, a runaway African accompanied by both a nine-year-old daughter of "black complexion" and a ten-year-old daughter who was "a likely mulatto."[142] Henry Bibb's experience in Kentucky was certainly consistent with the circumstances resulting in the conception of Diana's first child. Bibb, born in 1815 in Shelby County, was technically a quadroon, the son of a white father and a mulatto mother. He recounts that slaveholders were guilty of keeping "houses of ill-fame" in that they entered "at night or day the lodging places of slaves," where they proceeded to "break up the bonds of affection in families" and "destroy all their domestic and social union of life." Bibb was forced to witness his own wife beaten, abused, and "exposed to the insults and licentious passions of wicked slavedrivers and overseers." Having separated from his wife in 1840 in his escape to freedom, he learned in 1845 that she had been "living in a state of adultery" with her owner for three years, having given up any hope of reuniting with Bibb.[143]

As a consequence of the emergence of mixed-race progeny, and the subsequent association of privilege with this group, darker-skinned members of the African-based community tended to be wary. Adeline Marshall, born a slave in South Carolina but living in Texas in the 1930s, had a very interesting view of interracial offspring. In commenting on her former owner, she stated that he did not have a wife, but that he did have a live-in black woman as a companion. "Dat de reason so many 'No Nation' niggers 'round. Some calls dem 'Bright' niggers, but I call dem 'No Nation' 'cause dat what dey is, ain't all black or all white, but mix."[144] There is more than a tinge of disparagement in her words, but it is a perceptive depiction nonetheless, and one that reveals a race-based consciousness. Similarly, in describing the desperate conditions and lack of choices many black women faced, another former slave made these comments: "Now mind you, all the colored women didn't have to have white men, some did it because they wanted to and some were forced. They had a horror of going to Mississippi and they would do anything to keep from it. A white woman would have a maid sometimes who was nice looking, and she would keep her and her son would have children by her. Of course the mixed blood, you couldn't expect much from them."[145] It would seem that "mixed bloods" or "no nation" blacks, due to their disproportionate recruitment into the ranks of the elite, were distrusted by many of darker skin. In turn, this distrust was fostered by a system in which the privileged were expected to help police the servile estate by way informing on its constituency. Domestics and vocational workers were by no means all tattlers, but you could never be certain.

Dissonance between the lighter- and darker-skinned components of the slave community was not without its consequences for the former. Indeed, many lighter-skinned blacks were neither house servants nor artisans; a lighter complexion only served as a helpful prerequisite to, but was by no means a guarantee of, a softer life. For those who remained in the fields with their darker colaborers, as well as for those who worked in the big house, there was significant psychological fallout. Branded a "no nation" black on the one hand, with the "taint" discernible to those on the other, the person of mixed race often had no place of refuge. The tragic mulatto theme of the late nineteenth (through twentieth) century had definite antecedents in the antebellum period.

From the same collection of African American traditions featuring the tale of King Buzzard comes another that just as equally reflects an internal dialogue within the black community. That is, it is the culmination of stories and anecdotes that circulated throughout significant portions of the slaveholding South and was finally codified in a version representing the consensus view. In fact, it is in the form of a conversation between "Yellow Jack" and "Tad." Entitled "A Yellow Bastard," it essentially concerns sociological questions raised by the emergence of mixed-race progeny.[146] It is important to understand that it also conveys an unfolding of the view of mixed-race individuals; that is, the perception of such people at the beginning of the dialogue has changed by its conclusion, so that the tradition is meant to depict how the African-based community gradually came to see people of mixed descent over time. The discussion begins with Tad asking Yellow Jack the essential questions: "Who is you an' wuh is you? I ain' 'member to axe you 'fore dis. Who is you an' wuh is you an' wey you come from?"

These queries reveal the philosophical difficulties that increasing numbers of mixed-race individuals began to pose for the larger black community. That their numbers were rising is indicated by Tad "not remembering" to ask the questions earlier. Because they had become more visible, it was the task of the larger community to comprehend the meaning of their existence. Yellow Jack answers by repeating the question, a classic example of call-and-response, and therefore conveys the message that he is fundamentally a member of the African American community, although that is not at all apparent:

> You axe me who I is an' wuh I is an' wey I come from. You axe a heap er question all in one, an' I guh axe you a question:
>
> Who business is it who I is an' wuh I is an' wey I come from? Is you care 'bout me? Is you my friend? I ain' think so. Is you my enemy? I ain' think dat neither. Is you axe me jes for talk an' compersation? Maybe you axe me who I is for laugh an' game makin'. Well, it do not matter. It ain't make no diff'ence wuh you' reason. I guh tell you who I is an' wuh I is. It ain't matter ef you laugh or cry.

Yellow Jack's response signifies the black community's early indifference to those of mixed race. It is an attempt to force the larger black society to come to terms with the latter's existence, to bring an end to the posture of ambivalence. There is pain in Yellow Jack's reply and a need to mask: "Laugh, ef you has a mind to. I ain' care. Grin, ef you wants to. I ain't to fault, an' I ain' care." The larger black community is reminded that miscegenation is one of the many consequences of living in a state of imposed violence ("I ain't to fault"), and that its issue is just as much a victim as everyone else. But there is also in these words an attempt to present a certain callousness, which in turn reveals that those of mixed ancestry had suffered a degree of ostracism. That this was the case is clear by what Yellow Jack says next: "I have thought an' dream, an' I dream beautiful dream, but it seem like I ain' kin tell my dream. I ain' seems rough enough. I ain' seems man enough to make my feelin's known. My dream ain' nothin' but for laughter for other folks, an' my dream is tear for me an' torment. But I dreams—dat's all dere is for me." Those of mixed ancestry who had not "made it" into the ranks of the elite—and this is precisely who Yellow Jack represents—desperately needed to belong to a community. Unfortunately, given the context of a racially polarized society, this need could only be fulfilled in an altered state of consciousness. The descendant of European and African lineage was truly in a quandary.

From this brief respite, during which Yellow Jack voices the introspection of the mixed-race contingent, he returns to the moment and faces his interrogator:

> You axe who I is an' wuh I is an' wey I come from.
> I come from wey de door is shet, an' I come to wey it still is closed. All I got is dreams, an' dey is drownded. I ain' kin make my feelin's known. Laughin' ain' make no diff'ence now. God has overlooked me. I is not strong enough. I ain' kin make my feelin's known.

"I come from wey de door is shet, an' I come to wey it still is closed." Yellow Jack, and those he speaks for, had been summarily rejected by whites and had yet to find full acceptance by blacks. Within a society literally founded upon race consciousness, Yellow Jack had an identity without location. He therefore "ain' kin make my feelin's known"; he had no frame of reference into which he could place himself and thereby understand himself. He makes this explicit by his next statements:

> You axe me wuh I is an' I guh tell you. I is wuh I is. I isn't wuh I mought er been. To my lonesome self I ain' nothin' but a yellow bastard—laugh, I ain' care—a yellow bastard wid no place—wid no place amongst de white folks an' a poorly place amongst de niggers. . . .
> I ain' kin make my feelin's known, for I ain' nothin'—nothin' but a yellow bastard to white an' black alike. I is wuh I is—nothin' but a yellow bastard—an' I ain' make my feelin's known. Laugh, I ain' care.
> Tad: I hear wuh you say. I ain' guh laugh an' I ain' guh cry. I ain' know wuh you is.

Tad's response, beyond simple indifference, is revealing. Over time, the larger black community came to understand the plight of mixed-race individuals. They did not despise them, for they only knew too well the truth of their origins. But neither did they feel sorry for them, for many had already exchanged their lighter skin for privilege and distance from the black community. At the point that this particular tradition was completed, therefore, the question of full acceptance of biracial persons by the black community is yet unresolved. What is important to remember, however, is the suffering of the mixed-race person.

In contrast to the black community's lighter-skinned members who worked in the fields, the assessment of those who moved into the big house could be very different. It really depended upon how the person of higher status acquitted herself. She could have opted to retain strong ties to those in the field, collaborating in resistance and helping to meet their needs by appropriating supplies from the master's quarters. Or she could have constricted her ties and occupied a niche between black and white. The latter strategy would have brought swift condemnation from the larger black community, suggesting that it fundamentally viewed mixed-race persons as belonging to them. This is implicit in a litany entitled "Brass Ankles":

Does you know 'em
Wid dey hungry dog look?
Calls dey self white.
Hates a nigger;
Calls he name
Wid a curl
Er dey lip.
Says "nigger" wid a snarl;
Puts a twis' on it;
Gits part er it
Through dey nose;
Twists an' turns it
An' put it on de air
As sump'n ain't fitten to hear.

Calls dey self white—
Brass ankles dey is—
White wid a little tech er yellow;
Niggers dat's passed on up,
Dey say,
Ain' have so far to go.
Better 'an a nigger,
Ain't nobody know it but dey;
Somebody tell 'em,
Find it out
When dey is grown.

Tryin' to prove it ever since
By insult an' murder—
Feared er dey standin'.
Some on 'em sets on de jury—
Turns dey kind loose;
Claims to be white—

Sets in judgment an' votes.
Bitter coffee drinkers,
Gall-berry eaters,
Brass ankles dat claim to be white.[147]

Black folk, although not clear on all things, have been consistently clear on one: the rejection of claims to superiority by those of mixed race. But an even greater offense is the hypocritical denial of blackness. In this way, Tad's earlier, seemingly noncommittal stance can be more fully understood. For the black community, the question of the reception of biracial persons did not ultimately rest with them but with those of mixed race. Some would cast their lot with the majority of blacks, and others would opt to do otherwise. Those who sought acceptance within the African American community would quickly find it, but they had to first answer the essential question: "Who is you an' wuh is you an' wey you come from?"

The black community's response to the bifocality of those of mixed race in the characters of Yellow Jack and Brass Ankles clearly diverges based upon how these people defined themselves. What is instructive, moreover, is that the emergence of mixed-race persons did not muddle or obfuscate the question of race but, in fact, clarified it. Moving away from ethnicity, the descendants of the African-born began to adopt a racial identity by avenues already discussed. The creation of racial dualities further assisted the process in that it helped those of African descent to see themselves in relationship to whites as opposed to one another. Skin color, from the whitest white to the blackest black, had clearly become the most important marker of social distinction.

Notwithstanding the tensions between those of lighter and darker hue, there is abundant evidence of cooperative ventures between the two, principally in the form of escape. What this means is that the larger black community always took the posture of receptivity pending the correct answer to Tad's query; a response confirming the bond of African ancestry was embraced and honored. In a spirit of camaraderie and fellowship, blacks both light and dark regularly braved the lash and stole away together. It was by such collaborative efforts that ancient and dusky ties were consecrated and covenants renewed.

In many instances of absconding, those of mixed race cast their lot not only with darker African Americans but also with Africans. Thus in 1774 John H. Cocke of Surry County, Virginia, reported the absence of Bob and Bristol, the former a mulatto and the latter "an outlandish Fellow . . . as ignorant as the other is artful."[148] Thomas Phepoe placed an ad in Charleston's *South-Carolina and American General Gazette* in November 1780 publicizing the escape of two women: Betty, a mulatto, and Molly, who was African-born, "her country marks on her face."[149] In July 1768, forty-year-old Carolina of "Guinea" ran away from a Georgia estate with Mulatto John.[150] Just three years earlier, twenty-two-year-old Boson had absconded with an eighteen-year-old biracial woman.[151] These examples of mixed race–African collaboration illustrate that bonds of loyalty could and did exist among the various components of the African-based community. In fact, identification with Africa could go very deep indeed; Robert Johnston of Charleston described one of his escaped slaves as a mulatto named "Will, about 22 years of age, with a very bushy head of hair, and a remarkable scar on each cheek and in his forehead," an apparent reference to country marks.[152]

Of course, those of mixed race also joined with darker-skinned, American-born blacks to flee the plantation. There are many references to such cooperation in the runaway advertisements. In Mississippi, forty-five-year-old Jim, described as a "small yellow fellow, with grey or blue eyes, and very smart and cunning," took flight in September 1839 along with forty-year-old Caro and their twenty-five-year-old accomplice Isaac; the latter two were depicted as "dark."[153] In June 1819, Isaac Wellborn of Madison County, Alabama, placed ads in various newspapers for the return of twenty-three-year-old Lawrence, described as a "large mulatto," and a "small black fellow" aged between thirty-five and forty named Jacob.[154] In Georgia, Adam and Jack, respectively called mulatto and dark, ran away in August 1817, as did Jack (mulatto) and Bob in 1811, both of whom could read.[155] In some instances abscondees even exploited their color differences to advantage. In March 1817, John Anderson of Nashville offered a $150 reward for Josiah, considered to be "very black, about twenty-five years of age," who had run away with a twenty-six-year-old "mulatto Slave named John, Very fair looking, so as to be almost white . . . speaks English, French, and Spanish." It was believed that they were headed for New Orleans, "and that the Mulatto will pass for a freeman and change his name, which he can do readily, and the other will pass as his servant."[156]

It was often the case that darker- and lighter-skinned blacks belonged to the same family. Thus it was that James, a mixed-race person, and his wife Harriet, "a black woman," took their leave of Thomas Jones in January 1806.[157] In October 1825, a twenty-two-year-old "bright mulatto" named John and native of Cuba excused himself along with his twenty-three-year-old wife Ann, described as "much darker."[158] Monday, a thirty-eight-year-old biracial man, and his thirty-year-old wife "Rachel . . . a black wench," stole away together in June 1802.[159] The gender-color relationship could be reversed as well, so that darker-skinned men married or otherwise joined lighter-skinned women. Randal, twenty-one years old and "black," accompanied twenty-two-year-old "Amy . . . a bright mulatto woman" in their escape from a Georgia establishment.[160] The progeny of such unions helped to solidify bonds and resolve lingering ambiguities.

Despite evidence of cooperation between darker- and lighter-skinned blacks, however, there is also indication that some mixed-race individuals saw themselves as a separate entity and resisted slavery in their own right, quite apart from other blacks. In 1838, for example, Charity and her husband John along with their two children, all mulattoes, took flight together.[161] In August 1819, two "bright mulattoes" named George and Charles escaped together from South Carolina.[162] A more intriguing example of this kind was recorded in 1813 and concerns the case of Fanny and "Betsey . . . two fair Mulatto Women carrying with them their two very fair Children," the implication being that their children were even "fairer" by way of white fathers (or father).[163] "Fanny is a tall, good-looking, stout made woman, with black hair and high cheek bones," whereas Betsey was a "rather short, stout made, lively woman, very fond of dress. . . . Both the women are about 20 years of age, and uncommonly smart." Relative privilege is implicit in these remarks; Fanny could even "write a little." The women apparently hitched their fortunes to a black couple who were "believed to be old runaways," but the arrangement was temporary; the women had their own agenda.

Class differences, however, were not the only indexes by which blacks distinguished themselves. Another method of stratification was by association with the relative worth and position of the slaveholder. Bremer explained that "one peculiarity in these so-called children of nature is their aristocratic tendency. . . . They pride themselves on belonging to rich masters, and consider a marriage with the servant of a poor master as a great misalliance."[164] How widespread this phenomenon was is unclear, but in essence it represents an extraneous influence in that slaves were reacting to circumstances determined beyond the slave quarters. At the same time, slaves were aware of their contributions to the plantation and knew that their labor was the source of the slaveholder's wealth. Consequently, the planter's standing was largely a measure of their industry.

But there was yet another means by which people of African descent determined social rank among themselves, a method that was much more autonomous than that premised upon labor divisions and planter status: stratification according to African ancestry. The various sources are filled with references to the exalted status of African forebears, which often meant claims to royal lineage of some type. It is unimportant that such claims are difficult to substantiate. What is critical is that black folk appealed at all to their African ancestry, for by so doing, they affirmed their identity and self-worth in a pernicious environment. By tracing their claims back to Africa, they were forging psychological weapons of resistance (as well as possibly telling the truth). For in appealing to Africa, they were resisting the imposition of class and status as dictated by whites. Something of this pride in African identity survived slavery, survived Reconstruction, survived Jim Crow. Something of this pride migrated to places such as New York in the early twentieth century, where it was rekindled by the call of Marcus Garvey's rhetoric. Indeed, Garvey's message would resonate rather than convert.

And so it was that Samuel Ringgold Ward would state in his biography that his "father, from what I can gather, was descended from an African prince. I ask no particular attention to this, as it comes to me simply free tradition—such tradition as poor slaves may maintain."[165] Consistent with this testimony were the words of Ralph Forster, who in 1780 placed an ad in the Annapolis *Maryland Gazette* seeking the return of Caesar, an "imported negro, but speaks very good English, boasts much of his family in his own country, it being a common saying with him, that he is no common negro."[166] Virginia Newman, about one hundred years old when interviewed in Texas in the 1930s, echoed the sentiments of Caesar: "My grandmudder, she an Africy woman. They brung her freeborn from Africy and some people what knowed things one time tol' us we too proud but us had reason to be proud. My grandmudder's fambly in Africy was a African prince of de rulin' people."[167] Interestingly, Newman went on to mention that her "udder grandmudder was a pure Indian woman" who raised Newman and her siblings. Although there is some suggestion of honor by association with her Native American grandmother, it is striking that greater stake was placed into the family's ties to African royalty. Indeed, it was the observation of Henry Ravenel, a slaveholder in nineteenth-century South Carolina, that native Africans always spoke "of 'royal blood' in their own country—princes, or some such thing—and many of them would show the 'tattoo' marks of royalty seared upon their faces and bodies."[168]

That people of African descent were proud of their ancestry is consistent with all that has been examined up to this point. Most Africans would have been proud, and would have passed this on to their progeny. Although such pride would have been principally informed by ethnicity and former status, it nevertheless directs the descendant back to Africa and away from privilege as defined by whites in America. Herskovits argued long ago that captives were not the dregs and rejects of their societies, constituting the weakest and the most depraved.[169] Rather, the data from the Dahomean area suggested that many were from the "upper socioeconomic strata," including a number of royal and priestly individuals. In fact, one priestly informant told him that "you have nearly all the people of this family in your country. They knew too much magic."

Of course, most slaves from Dahomey did not end up in North America, but the larger issue should not be lost. As the discussion of the Muslim experience demonstrates, no one in Africa was beyond the reach of the transatlantic trade, whether rich or poor, royal or common. As a consequence, victims were recruited from all walks of life. It is therefore not surprising to read that some who wound up in North America asserted direct ties to a noble past. Charles Ball's grandfather, in fact, "claimed kindred with some royal family in Africa, and had been a great warrior in his native country." As a result, his grandfather "always expressed great contempt for his fellow slaves, they being, as he said, a mean and vulgar race, quite beneath his rank, and the dignity of his former station."[170]

Although discriminatory and ethnocentric, Ball's grandfather at least took his source from Africa. And ultimately, as black corporate identity shifted from ethnicity to race, the pride that the descendants of the African-born would come to express would relate to Africa more as a unified, conceptual whole rather than as a collection of disparate entities. This is the form of "race pride" that Puckett witnessed throughout the South, having its demonstration in depictions of black angels in Bibles and on walls, its expression exemplified by the belief that "all men were at first made black, but that when Cain killed Abel he turned white from fear."[171] Ravenel also knew of this pride, and cautioned fellow slaveholders: "It must not be supposed that the negro is without pride. He has it as strongly as his white brother. . . . He is proud of his lineage, whether it dates from some African prince, or from some gray-headed patriarch who has served with fidelity in offices of trust and honor."[172] So strong was the pride of the African transported to America that attempts were made to pass on cultural material to those born on American soil. Examples of this phenomenon have been cited throughout this study, but the testimony of C. G. Samuel of Oklahoma, age sixty-seven in 1937, makes the connection lucid: "My father was a half African and my grandfather was a full blood African. My father had an African mark on his chest which was a circle with a small dot in the middle."[173] The country marks themselves had been passed on.

The weight of the African past was therefore considerable and often viewed very favorably by those descended from the continent. Distinctions were made within the slave community based not only upon ethnicity but also upon former rank in Africa, whether legitimate or fictive. Slaveholders were perceptive enough to detect and exploit some of these differences, so that throughout the colonial and into the antebellum period there were close associations between ethnicity and status as reflected in labor assignments. However, with the increase in the American-born slave population over time and the cessation of the legal transatlantic slave trade in the early nineteenth century, the African American community gradually began to see itself with reference to race. The ranks of privileged servility were joined by those of mixed race in disproportionate numbers. With the emergence of a Creole corpus of slaves who had undergone sufficient acculturation, later-arriving Africans tended to be placed in the fields, whatever their ethnic background. Thus Bancroft found that the domestic trade was "mainly in American-born negroes, who, as a rule, were the only slaves fit for house-servants or even partially skilled laborers."[174] Mullin concurs, writing that American-born blacks were educated and trained to some extent, but that native Africans were sent to the fields, as they were seen as "unsuitable" for "refinement."[175] The distinction between African- and American-born blacks became more rigid as the nineteenth century progressed, so that Phil Samuel, somewhere between 90 and 115 at the time of his interview, could clearly state: "Oh, we called dem what wuz born in Africa and bring over right to the fields Africans. Us as was born heah wuz diffrent."[176]

The implication of the foregoing has particular significance for places such as South Carolina, which received substantial cargoes of Sierra Leonians during the second half of the eighteenth century and into the nineteenth. What this suggests is that folk culture as developed in South Carolina and Georgia, especially along the coastal areas, was essentially Senegambian in origin and was subsequently developed, if not transformed, by groups from Sierra Leone. As alluded to earlier, the emergent Gullah and Geechee cultures and people have been associated with rural, unsophisticated lifestyles and seen by outsiders as backward. As one white observer put it, "The Negros [*sic*] that the coast refugees brought into the country, the rice niggers as the others called them was much inferior in intelligence, and in language, to the home Negros."[177] This is what Charlie Davis of Columbia, South Carolina, attempted to convey when he stated: "I come from de Guinea family of niggers, and dat is de reason I is so small and black. De Guinea nigger don't know nothin', 'cept hard work."[178]

From the colonial to the antebellum periods, Africans gradually underwent a process whereby the basis of their self-concept changed from ethnicity to race. To a certain degree this transformation was affected by white perceptions of the African, and was without question informed by the circumstance of a common servitude. But the way in which the transformation was approximated was largely determined by an internal dialogue. At the same time, the legacy of ethnicism militated against a thoroughgoing and complete reformulation of identity. Fissures within the black community followed the contours of divergent labor assignments and to a remarkable degree paralleled differences in skin pigmentation. As Berlin has so perceptively characterized it, the consequence was a process of creolization that "deeply divided" blacks in the South, in contrast to the North, where a "unified Afro-American population" emerged. A notable outcome of a minority of blacks living and working in close proximity to whites in the South was that the former became "increasingly light-skinned" and sought the approbation of the latter. In contrast, the "mass of black people . . . remained physically separated and psychologically estranged from the Anglo-American world and culturally closer to Africa than any other blacks on continental North America."[179]

The world of the physically separated and psychologically estranged, then, represents the heartland of the African American community. It is there that one must go to inquire further into the question of the metamorphosis of the African-based identity in North America. An important aspect of this process is obviously religion. In the following chapter I use sources both old and new to address a different set of queries relating to religion's role in the African's transformation.

9

TURNING DOWN THE POT

CHRISTIANITY AND THE AFRICAN-BASED COMMUNITY

As I have indicated in preceding chapters, the African enjoyed a comprehensive view of life that integrated the natural and the supernatural, the seen and the unseen. For her, the present time-space world was but a facet of a much greater reality, a much larger drama. The drama, having begun on African soil, was now unfolding upon a vastly different stage and under fundamentally altered circumstances. Indeed, she initially wondered if she had not passed out of temporality into timelessness; the violence and depravation of her condition, however, soon led her to conclude that America was all too real.

How to understand this new reality? What was she to make of her loss of status, her marginality? How was she to understand her identity in relationship to other Africans, especially those of different backgrounds? Who were these other black folk, born in America, some bearing the unmistakable mark of the master's licentiousness? These are only a few of the questions necessarily engendered by the experience of enslavement, and it was absolutely essential that they be answered. The replies to such queries, however, would change over time, as the enslaved population shifted from an African- to an American-born majority and as this population gained greater familiarity with their cultural and political surroundings. At the same time, the replies would to a significant degree be influenced by religion.

It is an unassailable fact that American Christianity is directly responsible for the psychological impairment of many within the African-based community. The white slaveholder's promotion of a white god aloft in white splendor, around whom stand the white heavenly host, was imagery sufficient to convey to the African a message of unmitigable disadvantage. The actual presentation of a gospel of apology, purporting to substantiate the immutability of the slave's condition, combined with such imagery to serve the African with notice of interminable servitude. Particularly insidious was the conflation of the white slaveholder as plantation father with an ethereal counterpart of identical visage. The white man's god was himself the ultimate slave master, having condemned by decree the African-as-Hamite to the servile estate.

In view of the foregoing, one would expect people of African descent to have eschewed Christianity, and that social, cultural, and psychological manipulation was behind those who embraced it. In fact, many did reject the religion, and others were most certainly victims of sustained enculturative efforts. Regarding those who converted, however, most were not coerced or maneuvered. Indeed, I argue that most did so of their own volition and by way of their own initiative. Furthermore, they understood the fundamentals of the religion as well as the implications of their own involvement with it. It becomes necessary, then, to explain this surprising turn of events.

There has been a great deal written on the subject of slave religion in the American South, particularly as it relates to the beginning of the black church. Although this chapter is concerned with more recent scholarship on the topic, it is appropriate to point out that much of what has been penned of late remains in large debt to the pioneers of such inquiries, including Du Bois, Woodson, and Frazier.[1] Understanding the ways in which their conclusions diverge, Raboteau and others have in essence fleshed out the general contours of their argument as opposed to fundamentally changing their basic conclusions.[2] This chapter develops the details a bit further.

The religion of the slave and the identity of the slave developed over time and in a relationship of mutual reciprocity. That is, the shift from an ethnically based to a race-premised collective personality was greatly influenced by the religious views of the African-based community. Simultaneously, the African American's religious beliefs were fundamentally affected by the transformation of the self-concept. This synchronous process, in turn, mirrored class distinctions within the black population, as the religion of the black elite was often at some distance removed from the faith and practices of the folk. As such, religion in enough instances reinforced color gradations and labor distinctions as markers of differentiated status.

African religions thrived in colonial North America, particularly in the South. This view is by no means universal. Stampp, after all, has written that most African religions imported during the slave trade were "lost within a generation."[3] In like manner, Genovese has contended that from "the moment the Africans lost the social basis of their religious community life, their religion itself had to disintegrate as a coherent system of belief."[4] Faced with the religion of the slaveholder, the African was more or less helpless, in Genovese's imagination, and could not resist the incursion of Christian thought and beliefs, so that by the late eighteenth and early nineteenth centuries, the "mass" of slaves were "apparently" Christian.[5] The functionalist model employed by Stampp and Genovese is premised upon twin notions of European religion as political appendage and African religion as emanation and instrumentation of social order. The imposition of European political will and consequent disruption of African society could therefore only lead to the eradication of African religious systems.

When the whole of the evidence is considered, however, an alternative conclusion is inescapable: Throughout the colonial period, the vast majority of African-born slaves and their progeny continued to practice various African religions. Rawick supports this finding, having concluded that the evidence "strongly suggests that there was sufficient time and opportunity for the establishment in North America of generalized West African religious forms."[6] Both Blassingame and Huggins hold similar views of the survivability of African religions in North America.[7] This perspective is informed by a countermodel of the relationship between African religion and society vis-à-vis Europe and argues for a resilience on the part of the former that was resourceful enough to withstand the exertions of the latter. As such, the countermodel is consistent with the view of African religions in the New World as "aggressive and imperialistic" as opposed to weak and ephemeral.[8]

Turning to the evidence itself, it was Edmund Ruffin who maintained that the African-born in Virginia rarely converted to Christianity, and that their American-born progeny were proselytized with greater success.[9] Marcus Jernegan took Ruffin's observations further and found that throughout the colonial period most slaves continued to practice African religions and were quite removed from the tenets of Christianity.[10] This in spite of the fact that organizations such as the Society for the Promotion of Christian Knowledge and the Society for the Propagation of the Gospel in Foreign Parts had been established by the Church of England. The latter was a missionary venture created in 1701 (ending in 1785, following the American secession) for the purpose of evangelizing Native Americans and Africans in North America and elsewhere. By its end, the society's efforts were largely unsuccessful.[11] Its correspondence consistently reflects the enormous difficulties involved in the attempt to convert the enslaved.[12]

According to one observer who wrote as late as 1698, native Africans in colonial Virginia were "not taught [Christianity] because the 'rudeness of manners, variety and strangeness of their language and shallowness and weak of mind [*sic*] made it impossible to make progress in their conversion.' "[13] The society's correspondence emphasizes the fact that the slaves were steeped in their "heathenish" customs and beliefs and acknowledges the difficulties in trying to persuade those "accustomed to the pagan rites and idolatries of their own country." In 1724 the society received the following response from the James City Parish in Virginia to its question concerning the condition of the "infidel" there: "My Lord, I can't say we have any freemen Infidels, but our Negroe Slaves imported daily, are, altogether ignorant of God and Religion, and in truth have so little Docility in them that they scarce ever become capable of Instruction."[14] Alexander Williamson, rector of St. Paul's in Kent County, responded similarly by dividing the slave population into three parts, "the first whereof are so grossly Ignorant, that there is no possibility of Instructing them in the principles of Christianity; the 2d are capable of instruction, and learn the answers to the questions of the church Catechism, but are so egregiously wicked as to render Baptism ineffectual. The 3rd are duly qualified, and of Exemplary Lives, some of whom are baptized, and others are soon to be Baptized."[15] The percentages of Africans falling into the second and third categories were relatively small, and after taking into consideration answers such as these, Jackson concluded that the "vast majority of Negroes in Virginia, as elsewhere in the colonies, 'lived and died strangers to Christianity.' "[16]

In addition to the challenge of language and the persistence of African religions, and despite the existence of such organizations as the Society for the Propagation of the Gospel, whites in North America also had to contend with their own decided apathy toward African conversion. Raboteau concludes that colonial America had little if any interest in slave conversion.[17] Jernegan wrote that in colonies in which slaves were numerous, "a vital interest in religion was lacking."[18] What is instructive is that this indifference to religion applied not only to slaves but also to whites. Jackson reminds us that only a small percentage of whites in any of the colonies were members of a church; not more than one out of twenty were members in 1700, a proportion that did not appreciably change until the 1730s.[19] Further, not only was there a shortage of ministers and missionaries, but those who were stationed in North America were notoriously decadent, many being alcoholics and/or "living in sin" with one or more African or Native American women.[20] Many Anglican clergymen were themselves slaveholders. As a result, the clergy of Wilmington Parish, Virginia, responded to the Society's question regarding the "state of infidelity" in the colonies by stating the following: "The Negroes who are slaves to the whites cannot, I think, be said to be of any Religion for as there is no law of the Colony obliging their Masters or Owners to instruct them in the principles of Christianity and so they are hardly to be persuaded by the Minister to take so much pains with them, by which means the poor creatures generally live and die without it."[21]

If whites were not indifferent to the conversion of their slaves, they were positively resistant to it.[22] Fears that slave conversion would ultimately undermine and weaken the slaveocracy fueled slaveholder opposition. Such was the resistance that Edmund London penned a letter in May 1727 to slaveholders in "English plantations abroad; Exhorting them to encourage and promote the Instruction of their Negroes in the Christian Faith."[23] London was specifically responding to the fact that little had been done to convert the slaves, and that even the feeble efforts of those who had made such an attempt had been "industriously discouraged and hindered." As a result of this combined indifference and hostility, only a few elite slaves could attend church services or receive religious instruction. "With comparatively few exceptions," Jernegan wrote, "the conversion of slaves was not seriously undertaken by their masters."[24]

It is clear, then, that at least through the first four decades of the eighteenth century, the overwhelming majority of slaves were strangers to the new covenant. And although some changes in slave religion took place as the eighteenth century progressed, Rawick has characterized efforts to convert slaves as "sporadic, and while they resulted in getting most slaves to adopt the outward forms of Christianity, the relative neglect also allowed the slaves to develop Christianity's interior meanings and practices in their own way."[25] Closer scrutiny of the evidence, however, strongly suggests that even Rawick's attempt to qualify the growth of Christianity among the slave population is overstated. The role of African religions was, it would appear, more pervasive than previously imagined and merits reconsideration.

"Little is known about the religious beliefs of the slaves during the seventeenth or most of the eighteenth century. Whites paid scant attention to them and did little to convert the slaves to Christianity."[26] It is statements such as these, made by one of the most influential scholars of the day, that point to the profound inconsistencies characterizing the Americanist approach to African American history. One cannot say that "little is known" about the religious beliefs of whites during the colonial period, for in addition to data on the subject emerging out of North America itself, the cultural precursor in Europe has been thoroughly assimilated by the scholarly community. The same is not true for the African background, yet such neglect is regularly excused, and such statements as the one above go uncontested. The African simply cannot get his due.

Contrary to such opinion, a great deal is known about the religious beliefs of the African American community during the colonial period. Many of their characteristics have already been discussed in preceding chapters. To appreciate the fact that Africans continued to practice their own beliefs in large numbers, one has only to afford them the same considerations and assumptions regularly afforded Europeans. That is, it should be expected that people from any given background would have strong propensities to preserve as much of their cultural patrimony as possible. As such expectations have been granted to non-African peoples as a matter of course, why should a leap of faith be required to accord the same to those of African descent?

As the earlier testimony has made clear, white slaveholders throughout the colonial period were either uninterested in or absolutely opposed to the religious indoctrination of their slaves. Thus slaves experienced little or no pressure to convert to Christianity. Despite the considerable disruption of enslavement, Africans would not have been forced to process or assimilate a competing, alternative worldview, and indeed, the challenge of enslavement may have caused the African to cling even more desperately to his existing religion and call even more fervently upon forces familiar to him. This is not to suggest that African religions did not suffer some loss of integrity in the fields of North America, for they surely did over time and in ways this chapter will examine more closely. During the colonial period, however, the cultural bonds between Africa and North American slaves were especially strong, so that enough of the core beliefs of African religions existed to fashion responses of defiance to the slaveocracy. That African religion served as a major reservoir of support for insurrection throughout the New World has been abundantly demonstrated in the literature, from South Carolina to Jamaica, from Louisiana to Haiti to Brazil.

In light of the foregoing observations, it is no surprise that Muslims continued to invoke the name of Allah in daily prayers upon prayer mats with prayer beads, both individually and collectively. Whether literate or limited to a few memorized *sūras* of the Qur'ān, these Africans observed the tenets of their religion and remained true to their faith. Islam would eventually recede, but not without leaving a legacy. In any event, the evidence is clear that the religion was practiced throughout both the colonial and antebellum periods.

The Bambara and other non-Muslim Senegambians in Louisiana and South Carolina–Georgia also continued to practice their religions. The Bambara retained their worldview as it relates to the spirit realm, confirmed by the prominent use of amulets. The Bambara cosmology was a tightly knit coherence, so that its manifestation at one level necessitated the comprehension of others. To be sure, this coherence was subject to corruption as time passed and as the percentage of native Africans decreased, but there is certainly no basis for the assumption of immediate depreciation. All the evidence points to the conclusion that throughout the colonial period, especially in Louisiana, the Bambara presence in all of its facets was imposing.

In the last quarter of the eighteenth and the first decade of the nineteenth century, Louisiana received a considerable infusion of Fon-Ewe-Yoruba and West Central African elements. Although the specific mechanisms by which Bambara, Fon-Ewe-Yoruba, and Congolese-Angolan religions converged is material for another study, there can be no question that the resulting synthesis is one of the better known examples of African cultural continuity in the United States. The subject of voodoo has received a great deal of attention, sufficient to make the case for religious continuity in Louisiana and elsewhere in the lower Mississippi.

With regard to various groups out of Sierra Leone, it must be remembered that a disproportionate number came during the second half of the eighteenth century and into the nineteenth century, that is, after the colonial period. Nevertheless, that the Sierra Leonian worldview continued in North America is confirmed by the activity of societies and related organizations clearly derivative of the Poro and Sande. Again, as was true of the Bambara, the Sierra Leonian society represented a core of closely connected values and beliefs that served to hold the various ethnicities together. Native Africans, initiated into the societies while in Sierra Leone, remembered their significance as they perpetuated the societies on North American soil.

The legacy of West Central African religion in the forms of mental healing, herbalism, and funeral practices is very pronounced in the southern United States. In particular, there has been remarkable and incisive discussion of practices such as the ring shout. These legacies are usually analyzed in relationship to their impact upon the African approach to Christianity, but there was necessarily an antecedent to the merger of Christian and West Central African elements. Some combination of these elements took place in Kongo, and Kongolese Catholicism may have in fact played a role in the development of African American Christianity.[27]

For the Akan and especially the Igbo, the removal of the land created a serious cosmological crisis, given its central role in their philosophies of life. The distortion in the physical immediately led to contradictions in the spiritual, resulting in the association of the Igbo with suicide and despondency. For the Igbo, then, the principal evidence for the retention of their beliefs is the startling correlation between their numbers and behavior strongly indicative of psychological distress.

Taken together, the foregoing is a composite of a colonial America in which Africans maintained beliefs inculcated prior to their capture and deportation. Although the evidence rarely details the African's religious activities in North America, partial glimpses of activities associated with a larger worldview are provided, and it is reasonable to conclude that what is only partially revealed was in reality more of a coherent whole than not.

Although the vast majority of the slave population remained unconverted to Christianity throughout the colonial period, some change began to occur around 1740. It was at this time that the Great Awakening stirred the religious life of the colonies. George Whitefield had come to Carolina in 1738, and although he initially found the South unresponsive, his movement eventually made an impact. Following Jackson's scholarship, the revival in Virginia lasted from 1740 to 1790, running in waves headed successively by Presbyterian, Baptist, and Methodist churches.[28] All of the revivals "brought in Negro converts by the thousands as well as the whites," particularly after the American secession from England. The Great Awakening ushered in the first of three periods in Jackson's scheme of black conversion to Christianity, lasting from 1760 to 1790. The next two periods, 1790 to 1830 and 1830 to 1860, coincide with major political developments in the South and are therefore reemployed here.

There were many reasons for the movement of the first noticeable, albeit small number of blacks into the church. To begin, there is the matter of manumission. Africans and their progeny may have been touched by Whitefield's avowed sincerity as he expressed interest in their spiritual welfare, novel for the time. But slaveholders were anxious, not because of Whitefield (who after all supported slavery and later became a slaveholder himself), but because of other exegetic forces exhorting slaveholders to manumit their slaves in view of their newly formed bonds of fellowship. Indeed, such fears were well founded, as Jackson relates: "On a whole, it can be said in conclusion that Negro slaves were emancipated in fairly large numbers by masters who had come under the influence of the revivals, or if not actually emancipated they were accorded a more humane treatment. Such really became the rule of the day in Virginia prior to 1790."[29] Many slaveholders who manumitted their slaves were responding to the problem of massive absconding.[30] But some were moved by both religious admonition and the lofty ideals of the American Revolution. Such high-mindedness would be effectively countered in the South with the dawn of a new militancy by 1830, wherein the same Bible would be employed to defend the enslavement of millions.

In contrast to Whitefield, a number of preachers called for the abolition of the institution, taking their stand at least through 1770, after which the period from 1785 to 1790 saw many reverse themselves.[31] John Leland and David Barrow were ministers who manumitted their slaves, as did Robert Carter, who over a number of years freed all of his several hundred servants, having become a Baptist.[32] This movement to emancipate the slaves, fed by economic expediency, religious contrition, and civic ideals, was certainly a factor in the number of free blacks in Virginia increasing tenfold from three thousand to thirty thousand between 1782 and 1810. The antislavery content of the revival, therefore, was a major draw for those of African descent.

Another reason for the attraction of revivalist activity was the sense of equality blacks experienced when worshiping with whites. This has been discussed by Sobel, who remarks that class divisions were a major feature of southern churches.[33] The revival, while affecting some slaveholders, was in effect directed toward lower-class whites and enslaved blacks. Discussing the revival in Virginia after 1750, Sobel writes:

> It began in response to the needs of the lower class, to their conflicts in values, and to their longings for coherence. Almost invariably, when it came, it came when and where whites were in extensive and intensive contact with blacks. Virtually all eighteenth-century Baptist and Methodist churches were mixed churches, in which blacks sometimes preached to whites and in which whites and blacks witnessed together, shouted together, and shared ecstatic experiences at "dry" and wet christenings, meetings, and burials.[34]

White and black coreligionists would diverge in nineteenth-century Virginia, but this experiment in religious diversity constitutes an important aperture into the understanding of those Africans and African Americans who began to drift into the Christian camp. Jackson writes that the "revivals of this period stood for equality in religion," and that the church was "open to all," especially among the Baptists and Methodists in whose congregations the idea of equality was "prominent."[35] Africans were treated with a quality of humanity of which they previously believed whites quite incapable. They were even allowed to assume leadership roles in this new experiment; included among preachers of African descent were "the Negro Lewis" and "Black Harry."[36] There was, therefore, no more powerful evidence of the efficacy of this new religion than that white folk underwent such marked change.

But a third factor, related to the second and possibly of greater significance, was that people of African descent were allowed to enter the revivalist experience on their own terms. That is, they were allowed to respond to the preaching of the Gospel in a fashion that was entirely consistent with their roots in indigenous African religion. They sang, they swayed, but more important, they danced and went into trance. Sobel, for example, writes that many of African descent were present at the revival meetings, during the peaks of which "mass hysteria was clearly reached."[37] White participants are described in these meetings as jerking, fainting, barking, shaking, running, chanting, laughing, shouting, and losing consciousness. Based upon the preceding testimony, certainly poor, but also affluent, whites were unschooled in the catechism and liturgy of the various churches, cut off as they were from clergy and edifice. The response of whites to the revivals, therefore, was not something they learned as children, and it probably was not brought over from England, Germany, Ireland, and so on. That is, there was very little in the way of their cultural patrimony that would have equipped them to jerk and shake and shout.

On the other hand, Africans were very familiar with dancing and shouting and "ecstatic" responses to the divine. Movement of all kinds, in particular dance, was the signature of the African worship experience, cutting across a number of ethnic and regional demarcations. Indeed, spirit possession was a fine art in many African societies. Jackson has written that the church prior to the Great Awakening lacked "emotionalism and a spirit to fire the masses."[38] This emotionalism was provided in the revivalist movement and is presumed to have been a major attraction for those of African descent. The position taken here is that what has been passed along as emotionalism was in fact a very typical, very African response to the divine. When in contact with the latter, the African tended to move. Whites did not teach her to respond in this way; quite the reverse, whites who jerked were attempting to mimic the behavior of the many blacks also in attendance at the revivals. "Blacks," Sobel writes, "no doubt influenced the emerging so-called white patterns."[39] To state it more accurately, Europeans may have provided the skeletal framework of Christianity, but it was the African who introduced the ways of the Holy Ghost.

The revival, then, was important because it afforded the African acceptance as an African. It is very possible that a considerable number of Africans participating in the revival had little or no idea of the substance of the message preached. But they were able to participate as themselves, so that many, no doubt, looked upon the new religion in an entirely different light. The direct implication of the revivalist movement is clear and unmistakable: rather than an imposition upon these early Africans, Christianity was something voluntarily embraced by the latter for reasons already explained as well as for others yet to be explored.

The decades between 1760 and 1790 clearly comprise an important beginning of the African American encounter with Christianity. Jackson has called the period "the hey-day for the Negro in Virginia and the country at large."[40] It was only a beginning, however, and a humble one at that. In fact, according to Jackson's own tabulations, only one out of twenty-three blacks in Virginia were church members by 1790.[41] This translates into only 4 percent of the African-based population, which is why Blassingame could claim that by the time of the American Revolution, "few slaves had had any contact with white ministers, and an overwhelming majority of them still believed in the religions of their African fathers."[42] It should be pointed out, though, that this estimated 4 percent reflects "official" church membership. There were undoubtedly Africans and African Americans who had converted to Christianity but failed to show up on the church rolls for any number of reasons. How to determine the size of this invisible church is problematic indeed. Perhaps another 4 percent should be added to the total, but this is pure speculation.

There are rare and (therefore) conspicuous references to Christian slaves in the runaway slave ads. In 1785, for example, Jack was one of four absconding slaves in Virginia who was "remarkable for affecting religious conversation."[43] In May 1778 one Nat, who "pretends to be very religious, and is a Baptist teacher," took flight from Turner Bynam of Brunswick County, Virginia, along with another man. John Gordon of Northumberland County, Virginia, reported in May 1778 the absence of two men, including Joe, said to be "fond of singing hymns, and exhorting his brethren of the Ethiopian tribe." Similarly, Samuel Hatcher of Virginia's Chesterfield County described two of the four runaways as "much given to singing hymns." Finally, one Frank, an absconded West Indian transferred to the ownership of Virginian James Davis, is simply described as a Baptist.[44] Based upon these few examples, Christianity was clearly having an effect opposite that of strengthening the established order.

Understanding that these examples represent such a small percentage of the black population, the question becomes, What about the remaining 92 to 96 percent? The evidence, though fragmentary, consistently supports the contention that either the vast majority continued to practice, or to at least believe in, the religions of Africa; or that this majority developed modifications, innovations, and syncretisms in African religious tradition on American soil. Among them would have been those who could not find points of correspondence with the Christian faith. For them there was no place of meeting.

Throughout the eighteenth century, men of the cloth regularly complained about the "idolatrous dances and revels" of the slaves. Writing in 1779, Alexander Hewatt's observations of slaves in Georgia and South Carolina led him to conclude that the slaves "are to this day as great strangers to Christianity and as much under the influence of Pagan darkness, idolatry and superstition, as they were at their first arrival from Africa."[45] Even when church services were held among blacks, there was suspicion that the ceremony was Christian in name only, and that other practices pertaining to the African past were the actual order of the day. This was certainly the sentiment of the Chatham County grand jury of Georgia, which in October 1788 presented "as a grievance, negroes, in different parts of this county, being permitted to assemble in large bodies, under pretence of religion, by which that holy institution is not only become a mockery, but a cloak for every species of blasphemy, theft, and debauchery."[46] By the end of this first phase, then, Christianity was the religion of very few of African descent.

Following Jackson's scheme, the second period from 1790 to 1830 was critical for the development of the black church, for it was during these four decades that the groundwork was laid for a class-based divergence among black churchgoers. Nevertheless, the numerical growth of the black church remained incremental, the overall percentage of Christians among the African-based community relatively small. Prior to the Great Awakening, the few blacks who became Christians were almost exclusively recruited from among the servile elite—the house servants and vocationally skilled. With the advance of the revivalist movement, the growing yet relatively modest number of blacks who participated included those who were field hands, consistent with the leveling effect and egalitarian emphasis of the phenomenon. However, the decade of the 1790s brought with it serious retrenchment on the part of whites from the grand ideals of both the revival and the American Revolution. As a result, the rural African-based community was denied further access into formal and officially recognized Christendom. At the same time, blacks living in urban areas were able to organize their own churches. The black church, therefore, began to develop in two different directions based upon class differences. One would progress in the fields along clandestine lines, and would be greatly informed by the African religious antecedent. The other, by virtue of its membership and its proximity to white paradigms, would seek to emulate those models and create as much distance from Africa as possible.

In 1789, the Baptist Church retreated from its earlier antislavery position.[47] The Methodists also retreated, signaling a decline of interest in black spiritual welfare. According to Jackson, the influx of "new aristocratic" members into the Methodist, Baptist, and Presbyterian Churches changed the overall perspectives of these institutions toward the African-based community.[48] Official black church membership in Virginia fell in the 1790s, rose between 1803 and 1810 with the introduction of the "camp meeting," only to fall again between 1810 and 1820. Evidence for the collective disinterest in proselytizing blacks led Jackson to declare that the great majority of blacks in Virginia were "neglected between 1790 and 1830."[49] If Virginia represents the South in general, it is logical to conclude that Christianity had yet to make serious inroads into the culture of the vast majority of rural Africans and African Americans. And even if it were true that the rapid replacement of the African-born by their American-born progeny occasioned a steady erosion in the coherence of African indigenous religions, it does not at all follow that, ipso facto, these people were becoming Christian. Genovese's speculation that most slaves had become Christian "in recognizable terms" by the late eighteenth and early nineteenth centuries has no basis in quantifiable data, and even the impressionistic data paint a contrary picture.[50] Raboteau is a bit closer to the reality when he states that the "majority of slaves . . . remained only minimally touched by Christianity by the second decade of the nineteenth century."[51] To take it a step further, it is much more likely that African religions were still practiced by a majority, with some transformation of meaning, along with the incorporation of a few tenets of the Christian faith.

In the urban areas, however, the situation was somewhat different. In these locations, blacks were busy organizing their own, independent assemblies.[52] This second period between 1790 and 1830, therefore, was characterized by the growth of the urban black church. Led by free blacks who reserved positions of authority for themselves, membership was open to all comers, including urban-based free blacks and privileged slaves, in addition to some of the rural slaves who visited town regularly. Yet this represented only a tiny fraction of a population that was overwhelmingly rural as well as enslaved. As a result, the growth of the urban, elite black church in Virginia, taken as a reflection of the South as a whole, only allowed for some thirty thousand blacks officially listed on church rolls by 1830. That translates into one out of every seventeen blacks, or some 6 percent. If another 6 percent is added to account for the invisible army of rural believers, that still leaves another 88 percent of the African American population. As late as 1830.

The growth of the urban black church in the South was concurrent with the development of a free black urban population. Although most free blacks lived in rural areas and engaged in agriculture (as did whites), they nevertheless settled disproportionately in urban areas. By 1860, more than one-third of the free black population in the South lived in towns and cities, compared with 15 percent of whites and 5 percent of slaves. Most free blacks involved in migratory activity never left the South—although there were those who did find their way to the North, to Canada, and even to Africa—instead settling in southern cities. There were many more free black women than men, and most of them also lived in urban areas. This is not unanticipated, for runaways could find the anonymity they sought in large communities, whereas those manumitted could reestablish familial and social ties in urban settings as well as ply their trades.[53] The urban black church, therefore, would have been central to the development of urban black culture.

The third period in the Christianization of the African-based population, from 1830 to 1860, saw a veritable sea change in the attitude of southern slaveholders. The political context in relation to the institution of slavery explains to a large extent this fundamental alteration. As the North grew increasingly hostile to the South's insistence upon preserving slavery, the South's response took on a similarly antagonistic tone. The region realized that its cherished way of life was very much threatened. In partial response, southern abolitionists were effectively silenced through either intimidation or pressure to relocate to northern, more hospitable climes, thereby denying the South the benefit of a loyal opposition. This purge reflected serious divisions within both the Baptist and Methodist denominations, culminating in the formation of the proslavery Southern Baptist Convention and the Methodist Church South in 1844.[54]

The religious debates were very much fueled by what was taking place in the South. Insurrections and rumors of insurrections filled the slaveholders' nights with anxiety and their days with increased vigilance. Then the dam burst. Denmark Vesey in 1822, followed by the prophet Nat Turner in 1831 and the concomitant publication of Garrison's *Liberator*, offered evidence of a widespread and sophisticated conspiracy to destroy the South and its beloved institution. Moreover, both Vesey and the prophet Nat were Christians, claiming to have been inspired by God to unleash a baptism of blood-letting and violence. That the Christian faith and the Bible could be used as tools of revolt was totally unacceptable to the slaveocracy; swift and decisive measures had to be taken to decouple Christianity from the just war.

The South's answer was to seize control of black religious life. Blacks, whether free or enslaved, could no longer lawfully assemble without the supervision of whites. They were to be instructed in the faith by white teachers and preachers, not black ones, and for the first time many slaveholders began to request that itinerant preachers include their plantations in their circuits. White pastors took over black congregations; missionary societies mounted valiant efforts to respond to the crisis "in the field." The plantation mission emerged, a movement aimed at the majority of slaves exiled in the rural backwaters.[55] Meeting houses were identified and used to promulgate a simple catechism: "Slaves, obey your masters as in the Lord! Cease, dark masses, from striving; look to God for heavenly reward!"

This about-face on the part of the planter class betrays a certain desperation, a need to reassert control. Implicit in the planter response is the fact that the horse was already out of the barn. To be clear, this turn of events strongly suggests that the planters' fear had come upon them, that their erstwhile subjects were now engaged in strategies of rebellion informed by holy writ. The implications of the Christian message, alternating between conservative and liberal interpretations, had touched a critical mass of blacks, who purposed to make good on the prophecy of the last becoming first. They identified with the Hebrew story of Egyptian bondage and internalized not only the suffering but the resurrection of Jesus.

What all of this means, among other things, is that whites were attempting to arrest and channel a force that had already captured the hearts and imaginations of a growing number of Africans and African Americans. It is clear that during the first two periods of this process, from 1760 through 1830, whites and slaveholders alike had little interest in converting blacks. Most needed converting themselves; Henry Bibb, for example, testified that the "poor and loafing class of whites, are about on a par in point of morals with the slaves at the South."[56] It was therefore the case that, as was true during the colonial era, blacks took it upon themselves to actively seek the new religion, and what they learned of it, they learned largely on their own. Most who converted did so voluntarily after a process in which the religion was first converted to the specifications of the African-based community. The "white man's religion," preached incessantly from 1830 on in an attempt to hold back the floodgates, was recognized for what it was, a message of political, social, and cultural containment. As it had not been converted, it was largely rejected, as shall be demonstrated shortly. Gramsci and Bourdieu could have learned something from these Africans.

The white man's religion was not only identifiable by its message, but also by its inherent hypocrisy. Joseph Smith, born in 1814 in Maryland, stated that the "professed Christians in the South didn't treat their slaves any better than other people, nor so well. I'd rather live with a card-player and a drunkard than with a Christian."[57] Mrs. Smith, Joseph's wife, concurred:

> The ministers used to preach—"Obey your masters and mistresses and be good servants"; I never heard anything else. I didn't hear any thing about obeying our Maker. Those who were Christians and held slaves were the hardest masters. A card-player and drunkard wouldn't flog you half to death. Well, it is something like this—the Christians will oppress you more. . . . I would rather be with a card-player or sportsman, by half, than a Christian.[58]

Virginia-born Susan Boggs, interviewed in Canada in 1863, confirms the tradition of white mendacity, rampant during the colonial period and faithfully maintained by their antebellum descendants:

> I didn't see any difference between the slaveholders who had religion and those who had not. The Protestants there are a great deal better than the Methodists and Baptists. They are more pure. The others are very deceptive. You know they carry a point out so neat, and are so very

religious, that they will deceive you. Why the man that baptized me had a colored woman tied up in his yard to whip when he got home, that very Sunday and her mother belonged to that same church. We had to sit and hear him preach, and her mother was in church hearing him preach. . . . And he had her tied up and whipped. That was our preacher! He preached, "You must obey your masters and be good servants." That is the greater part of the sermon, when they preach to colored folks. . . . I have learned more Scripture since I came away than I knew was in the Bible before, and now I begin to read a little.[59]

African Americans wanted nothing to do with this brand of religion, repulsed by its central message and the unprincipled lives of its professors. Some on these bases rejected Christianity altogether. As Bibb put it: "This kind of preaching has driven thousands into infidelity."[60]

In response to the attempted imposition of slaveholder religion, blacks continued to meet separately. They had customarily met separately since their arrival in North America, due to the fact that their principal liturgical vehicle, the ring shout, was originally devoted to the worship of African deities. Although slaveholders may have been vaguely aware of the slaves' religious activities, the latter labored to keep this aspect of their lives as discreet as possible. As time passed and they gradually began to convert to Christianity, it was still necessary to engage in the ring shout apart from whites due to the pivotal role of dance. As Stuckey puts it: "That whites considered dance sinful resulted in cultural polarization of the sharpest kind since dance was to the African a means of establishing contact with the ancestors and with the gods."[61] The only difference after 1830 was that they were forced to go underground with religious meetings that did not include the presence of whites, who in turn feared the slaves were actually plotting insurrection.

James Smith, a former slave, wrote that "when Nat Turner's insurrection broke out, the colored people were forbidden to hold meetings among themselves. . . . Notwithstanding our difficulties, we used to steal away to some of the quarters to have our meetings."[62] George Caulton remembered the need to steal away, as he reported that slaves would meet at night "in the sticks."[63] Another source who formerly lived on a Louisiana plantation with 150 other slaves echoed that "religious services among slaves were strictly forbidden. But the slaves would steal away into the woods at night and hold services. They would form a circle on their knees around the speaker who would also be on his knees."[64] These are only a few examples that make it abundantly clear that slaves frequently met in secrecy for the purpose of pursuing their own brand of religion, a manifest rejection of white cultural hegemony.

In order to secure the secrecy of the meeting, slaves would "turn down the pot." Explained Texan William Adams, a "spiritualist preacher and healer" who was ninety-three at the time of his statement, "De slaves didn' have no church den, but dey'd take a big sugar kettle and turn it top down on de groun' and put logs roun' it to kill de soun'. Dey'd pray to be free and sing and dance."[65] Cyrus Bellus, born in Mississippi in 1865, recounted that the slaves "had to take a kettle and turn it down bottom upward and then old master couldn't hear the singing and prayin'."[66] Kitty Hill, age seventy-seven in 1937, recalled her mother saying that "no prayer meetings wuz allowed de slaves in Virginia where she stayed. Dey turned pots down ter kill de noise an' held meetings at night."[67] Chana Littlejohn concurred, testifying that "when we sang we turned de washpots an' tubs in de doors, so dey would take up de noise so de white folks could not hear us."[68]

Rawick has attempted to explain the practice of turning down the pot by referring to the symbolism of the iron pot, "the original associations of which have been lost," and by suggesting a relationship between pots and drums and river spirits in Africa.[69] By his own admission, these are only tenuous associations, and more research is needed into the matter. However, there may be a purely functional as opposed to spiritual explanation that demystifies the procedure. For example, Louisiana-born William Mathews remarked that during the nightly prayer meetings in the cabins, each "one bring de pot and put dere head in it to keep de echoes from gittin' back. Den dey pray in de pot. Dat de Gawd's truth!"[70] Will Glass confirms the foregoing on the basis of his uncle's testimony, stating that the slaves "had to slip off and slide aside and hide around to pray. They knew what to do. People used to stick their heads under washpots to sing and pray."[71] Harriett Sanders, whose grandfather hailed from Georgia, stated that his generation "used to have to put de heds in a barrel to pray so de white folks couldn't hear em, case dey wasn't sposed to have religion!"[72] Whether turning down the pot operated mystically or practically or both, the reason for doing so is evident: people were serious about their religion, so much so that the slaveholder version of it was totally unacceptable.

Black professors of the faith, in rejecting planter religion and its accommodationist message, were motivated by an entirely different and separate ethic. By the close of legal slavery, however, they remained a numerical minority. According to Jackson, only one out of every nine blacks was on official church rosters in Virginia by 1860, which is slightly more than 11 percent.[73] Taking Virginia as representative of the South, this means that only 22 percent (including the invisible church) of the black community may have been Christian by the dawn of the Civil War. Until evidence is presented that substantially alters this picture, we can only conclude that approximately

78 percent of African Americans remained unconverted just prior to the South's secession. Blassingame supports this, estimating that by 1860 some 1 million slaves were regularly receiving instruction in the faith, or approximately one-fourth of the slave population.[74] For the majority of blacks, therefore, conversion to Christianity came relatively late in the history of their American sojourn.

To be sure, it does not necessarily follow that all who were not practicing Christianity by 1860 were necessarily practicing some form of African religion. Sufficient time had passed between the end of the legal transatlantic trade and the culmination of the antebellum period for a different tradition to have emerged both in the slave quarters and wherever else blacks lived. There is in the literature some evidence of nonreligious folk, individuals who made no claim whatsoever to any recognizable creed. We should therefore allow for the possibility of a secular tradition. As an example, Reuben Madison, interviewed in 1827 by the religious abolitionist and suffragette Abigail Mott, stated that although all except one of his siblings belonged to the Baptist Church, his own mother was "not a professor of religion."[75] In Lucy Skipwith's 1859 letter to John Cocke, she remarks that her daughter had just converted to Christianity after her recent arrival: "She came home a stranger to god and a stranger to me, but I thank the Lord that she is now able to say that she once was lossed, but now is found, was blind, but now she see."[76] The implication, of course, is that others remained "lossed." For his part, Bibb testified that "the Sabbath is not regarded by a large number of the slaves as a day of rest," and that those making "no profession of religion" customarily went into the woods in large numbers on Sundays to gamble, drink, and fight, all encouraged by slaveholders who viewed such activities (especially the fisticuffs) as a source of entertainment.[77]

On the other hand, there is sufficient indication that substantial fragments of African religion not only continued through the antebellum period but also extended beyond the Civil War. Charles Ball's African-born grandfather, for example, "never went to church or meeting, and held, that the religion of this country was altogether fake, and indeed, no religion at all; being the mere invention of priests and crafty men, who hoped thereby to profit through the ignorance and credulity of the multitude."[78] Ball's grandfather had his own African religion, which in some aspects resembled Islam but in others varied greatly. In addition to his grandfather, Ball, born around 1781, also encountered "a great many African slaves in the country. . . . I became intimately acquainted with some of these men. Many of them believed there were several gods; some of whom were good, and others evil, and they prayed as much to the latter as to the former." Even those who professed Christianity were thoroughly African in their totality of their lives:

There is, in general, very little sense of religious obligation, or duty, amongst the slaves on the cotton plantations; and Christianity cannot be, with propriety, called the religion of these people. They are universally subject to the grossest and most abject superstition; and uniformly believe in witchcraft, conjuration, and the agency of evil spirits in the affairs of human life. Far the greater part of them are either natives of Africa, or the descendants of those who have always, from generation to generation, lived in the south, since their superstition, for it does not deserve the name of religion, is no better, nor is it less ferocious, than that which oppresses the inhabitants of the wildest regions of Negro-land.[79]

Ball's assessment of black, rural Christianity was formed during the first quarter of the nineteenth century. It is remarkably similar, however, to the subsequent statements of Olmsted who, having traveled through Virginia, commented on the "almost heathenish condition of the slaves on many of the large plantations."[80] Although he had been informed that "a goodly proportion" of Virginia's blacks "profess religion," he could only conclude that "it is evident, of the greater part even of these, that their idea of religion . . . is very degraded." Having apparently witnessed a black worship service, Olmsted judged that the worshipers were "subject to intense excitements, often really maniacal, which they consider to be religious, is true; but as these are described, I cannot see that they indicate anything but a miserable system of superstition."[81] He was essentially saying the same thing about blacks in Mississippi and Louisiana when he stated that three-fourths of them were "thorough-bred Africans." Explains Stuckey: "He meant thorough-bred in culture, which suggests the continuing power of African culture when passed from one generation to another."[82] Olmsted's observations, as well as his condemnations, are consistent with those of Charles C. Jones, who wrote in the 1840s that although "heathenism" was on the decline, Georgian blacks persisted in believing in "second-sight, in apparitions, charms, witchcraft, and in a kind of Satanic influence."[83]

As the WPA interviews will make clear, much of what Jones and Olmsted observed and lamented continued through the end of legal slavery and into the postbellum period. Indeed, "Cheveux Gris" complained as late as 1875 that freedpersons were "relapsing" into African "paganism" while maintaining the outward appearance of Christianity.[84] Joseph LeConte, former slaveholder, likewise complained that in the postbellum black belt of Georgia, from which whites had migrated in large numbers, blacks "are either stationary or are gradually relapsing into fetishism and African rites and dances."[85] While factoring in the support of such views for southern redemption, the external evidence concurs that much of what LeConte bemoaned was in fact taking place. LeConte and Cheveux Gris did not err in reporting what they saw; they simply lacked the sophistication to contextualize it.

Africans and their descendants, then, were not immediately immersed in the tenets of Christianity upon arriving on North American shores. There were few whites qualified for or interested in such a mission. Rather, blacks throughout the eighteenth century arrived at an understanding of the religion via circuitous means and in small numbers, usually in contravention of the expressed wishes of slaveholders in general. In stark contrast to the model of coercion, those blacks who converted to the religion did so of their own volition. They did so, however, after the religion had itself undergone a conversion, by which it became useful to the slave's physical and psychological struggle to be fully human. This is what Huggins probably meant when he wrote: "Oddly though, the process of Christianizing the Afro-American was not one of abject surrender of Africa to the West. In the spirit of Afro-Americans, Christianity was converted to their needs as much as they were converted to its doctrine."[86]

After a drop in church membership at the turn of the nineteenth century, African American Christianity grew incrementally and along two separate tracks: one laid by the urban elite; its counterpart cleared in the woods and thickets and other clandestine places of the southern countryside. The growth of both the urban and the invisible black church was sufficient to cause planters to abruptly reverse themselves and take a proactive role in the religion of their slaves. By taking over positions of clerical authority and mandating the circumstances of assembly, whites sought to control the direction of black membership toward accommodation and away from confrontation. Notwithstanding their Johnny-come-lately efforts, the black church, and particularly that segment of it based in the rural areas, continued to insist upon preserving ways of thinking and modes of worship that were clearly derivative of African cultural norms, an insistence that transcended the boundaries of the antebellum period.

· · · · · · ·

The preceding discussion, while offering a chronology of black conversion to Christianity at some variance with perceptions both popular and scholarly, really begs two fundamental questions: How and why did Africans convert to Christianity, especially in the absence of any measurable pressure to do so well into the nineteenth century? In response, it will be necessary to revisit the ring shout. Other areas of exploration include the relationship of water baptism to conversion, as well as the role of funerary rites in both conversion and the movement toward a collective identity based upon race. Why Africans converted is obviously related to how they did so, and a reexamination of Howard Thurman's work will shed further light on this query. In addition, a recontextualization of the concept and practice of hoodoo in the colonial and antebellum South will not only help answer the basic questions but also assist in making the connection to the African antecedent more viable. Related to an examination of all these phenomena, of course, is the unfolding of social strata within the black community. What follows attempts to uncover the general contours of this relationship.

Stuckey effectively makes the case for cultural continuity and attendant transformation within the African-based community in his *Slave Culture*. Drawing upon folklore and contemporary accounts, he argues that the ring shout was one of the most important vehicles for the perpetuation of West and West Central African religious beliefs. In these regions, "an integral part of religion and culture was movement in a ring during ceremonies honoring the ancestors." Although the circle's "ancestral function" was important in West Africa, it was even more so in West Central Africa, where it was "so powerful in its elaboration of a religious vision that it contributed disproportionately to the centrality of the circle in slavery." In fact, the ring shout was of such significance that it is possible to posit that "it was what gave form and meaning to black religion and art."[87] The ring shout was observed in the 1940s and 1950s in places as widespread as Louisiana, Texas, South Carolina, and Georgia, and can still be observed.[88]

For all of its significance as a principal medium of cultural transfer, Stuckey is saying something more about the ring shout, something that goes to the core of the present inquiry. For when he writes that the "ring in which Africans danced and sang is the key to understanding the means by which they achieved oneness in America," he is addressing directly the question of the transition from ethnicity to race and the transformation of the African American identity.[89] That the ring shout could have been so instrumental in the process is intriguing and demanding of further investigation. In addition to the sources employed by Stuckey, the present effort is informed by a reexamination of the WPA interviews, especially those collected along the coast of Georgia.

Ring ceremonies associated with religion are commonplace wherever people of African descent are found in the Western Hemisphere. In a study of Haitian religion, for example, Deren points out that it is a composite of West and West Central African influences. Deren then goes on to make a subtle yet crucial comment: "At dances for the divinities . . . there is, to be sure, no ritual choreography apart from the general counterclockwise direction of the floor-movement around the center-post."[90] This reference to a counterclockwise ring ceremony in Haiti recalls Puckett's earlier discussion of the "slavery time 'shout'" of southern black culture, which "consisted of moving about in a ring, shuffling the feet along inch by inch, sometimes dancing silently, but more frequently singing spirituals." Puckett went on to make a conjecture consistent with Deren's findings: "It is possible that the whole ceremony is a relic of some native African dance."[91] The comments of these two independent investigations are so similar that it is possible to apply Deren's analysis to the American South and Puckett's to Haiti absent significant alterations. That is, the ceremonies were clearly derivative of the same origins.

Stuckey has cited numerous examples of how the ring shout functioned in the South.[92] One of the most vivid illustrations was provided in 1862 along the South Carolina coast, where and when Thomas Wentworth Higginson observed what he called "the monotonous sound of that strange festival, half pow-wow, half prayer-meeting, which they know only as a 'shout.'" Before actually describing the shout, Higginson re-creates the context by employing evocative language to refer to the place of meeting: "These fires are usually inclosed in a little booth, made neatly of palm leaves and covered in at top, a regular native African hut, in short, such as is pictured in books." Having established, wittingly or unwittingly, Africa as the source of the ceremony, Higginson proceeds to describe how black men filled the "tent" and sang "at the top of their voices, in one of their quaint, monotonous, endless, negro-Methodist chants . . . all accompanied with a regular drumming of the feet and clapping of the hands, like castanets." With this accomplished, the shout takes flight:

> Then the excitement spreads: inside and outside the inclosure men begin to quiver and dance, others join, a circle forms, winding monotonously round some one in the centre; some "heel and toe" simultaneously, others merely tremble and stagger on, others stoop and rise, others whirl, others caper sideways, all keep steadily circling like dervishes, spectators applaud special strokes of skill; my approach only enlivens the scene; the circle enlarges, louder grows the singing, rousing shouts of encouragement come in, half bacchanalian, half devout, "Wake 'em, brudder!" "Stan' up to 'em, brudder!" and still the ceaseless drumming and clapping, in perfect cadence, goes steadily on. Suddenly there comes a sort of snap, and the spell breaks, amid general sighing and laughter. And this not rarely and occasionally, but night after night.[93]

Higginson found the entire experience not only strange and amusing but also alarming. His allusion to the African hut reveals his assessment of the ritual's source, but beyond this boundary he does not cross. Ostensibly repulsed, he was clearly drawn to the overt and subliminal sensuality of the ceremony, as "night after night" the shout ended "suddenly" after a gradual increase in excitement.[94]

The testimony of those outside of the circle could only be approximate. Contrary to what Higginson believed, black folk were not at all interested in performing the shout for whites. For that matter, the African-based rural community was more closed than open to outsiders regarding most aspects of their lives. Lydia Parrish's reflections on this matter are insightful, and bear repeating:

> There are survivals of African songs on the coast of Georgia. But let no outsider imagine they can be heard for the asking. From experience I know this to be true. It took me three winters on St. Simon's to hear a single slave song, three times as many winters to see the religious dance called the ring-shout, still more winters to unearth the Buzzard Lope and similar solo dances, and the game songs known as ring-play. . . . The secretiveness of the Negro is, I believe, the fundamental reason for our ignorance of the race and its background, and this trait is in itself probably an African survival.[95]

The secretiveness of the African American is also apparent in the WPA interviews. Not many details are divulged, but a careful reading reveals a number of interesting applications of the ring ceremony. The aforementioned Silvia King, who claimed Moroccan ancestry, was quite familiar with the ring shout as employed in regular religious services: "De black folks gits off down in de bottom and shouts and sings and prays. Dey gits in de ring dance. It am jes' a kind of shuffle, den it git faster and faster and dey gits warmed up and moans and shouts and claps and dances."[96] In addition to the employment of a ring ceremony in an Africanized Christian worship service, there are frequent mentionings of "ring play," usually involving young children or young couples engaged in recreational activities.[97] But the ring was also used to celebrate the harvest. Katie Brown of Sapelo Island, the previously mentioned descendant of Bilali, related that "harves time wuz time fuh drums. Den dey hab big time. Wen hahves in, dey hab big gadderin. Dey beat drum, rattle dry goad wid seed in um, an beat big flat tin plates. Dey shout an moob roun in succle an look lak mahch goin tuh heabm. Hahves festival, dey call it."[98] Harvest in West and West Central Africa, particularly in the form of various yam festivals, is the basis for this North American merrymaking in which a ring ceremony was central. Shad Hall, another descendant of Bilali, also commented on the harvest festival: "Den dey staht tuh dance an tuh bow tuh duh sun as it riz in duh sky. Dey dance roun in a succle an sing an shout. Sho is a big time."[99] The ring ceremony as described by both Brown and Hall is one of the clearer cases for a syncretism between

African and Christian beliefs; this is not to say that syncretism was prevalent, but it is apparent in these instances. The various African gods would have been thanked for the harvest, and were still thanked until Christian dogma took firmer root. At such time, the old African celebration continued, but the name of the deity changed. Still, people continued to "bow tuh duh sun" to the rhythm of drums, normally banned during slavery. The syncretism becomes even more evident when the testimony of Catherine Wing (St. Simons) is considered: "We use tuh hab big times duh fus hahves, an duh fus ting wut growed we take tuh duh chuch so as ebrybody could have a piece ub it. We pray obuh it an shout. Wen we hab a dance, we use tuh shout in a ring."[100] In her account the harvest, the church, and the ring ceremony are all integrated into one celebratory experience.

Besides harvests and regular church services, a ring ceremony was also employed at funerals. Lawrence Baker remarked that "when we hab a few-nul, we all mahch roun duh grabe in a ring. We shout an pray."[101] The ring ceremony was believed to assist the deceased in her or his "homegoing." Home was originally Africa, as is suggested by the collection of flying African tales. When taken together, the beauty of the ring shout, whether engaged for ordinary worship services or for occasions such as funerals and harvests, represented a point of reconnection. In Africa, participants experienced the spirit realm by way of possession. But in North America, the spiritual dimension also represented a return to Africa. In Africa, the ring ceremony re-created that place in the timeless past when and where humans and gods were in perfect fellowship. In North America, the ring was "shouted" in an effort to re-create a time and place in which the African community was whole.

Although the focus of shout participants shifted over the years from the African gods to Jesus, and from Africa to heaven, the ring shout was performed throughout. Given the fact that it antedates the African's conversion to Christianity in North America, it is the Christian faith that was necessarily grafted onto the tree of African tradition. It is the Christian faith that had to undergo its own conversion prior to its acceptance by the African-based community. For some, that conversion began on African soil in Kongo; for the vast majority, however, the transition took place in America and to a significant extent by way of the ring shout. That the shout survived into the twentieth century is sure testimony to this observation. This is something of what Du Bois meant when he wrote of the black church:

It was not at first by any means a Christian church, but a mere adaptation of those rites of fetish which in America is termed obe worship, or "voodooism." Association and missionary effort soon gave these rites a veneer of Christianity and gradually, after two centuries, the church became Christian, with a simple Calvinistic creed, but with many of the old customs still clinging to the services. It is this historic fact, that the Negro church of to-day bases itself upon the sole surviving social institution of the African fatherland, that accounts for its extraordinary growth and vitality.[102]

It is the Africanization of the Christian faith, not its imposition by external forces, that accounts for its success in the African American community.

There are apparently no extant accounts of ring ceremonies from the colonial period, but given the low level of conversion to Christianity, the ceremonies necessarily had African deities as the foci. In this way, they may not have been very dissimilar from the account of Patsy Moses of Texas, born around 1863:

> My old grand-dad done told me all 'bout conjure and voodoo and luck charms and signs. . . . De old voodoo doctors was dem what had de most power, it seem, over de nigger befo' and after de war. Dey has meetin' places in secret and a voodoo kettle and nobody know what am put in it, maybe snakes and spiders and human blood, no tellin' what. Folks all come in de dark of de moon, old doctor wave he arms and de folks crowd up close. Dem what in de voodoo strips to waist and commence to dance while de drum beats. Dey dances faster and faster and chant and pray till dey falls down in a heap.[103]

This ceremony makes it clear that non-Christian, African religion was practiced. As time passed and black folk began converting, they did so largely on their own terms, largely absent formal instruction of any kind. They understood the basic tenets of the new religion, but they understood a great deal about religion in general. Christian thought was incorporated into a means of approaching and experiencing the divine that was totally African. In the camp meetings where whites and blacks gathered together, only bits and pieces of the African liturgical approach were shared with whites, and even that was enough to begin dramatically affecting the latter's mode of worship.[104] But the full force of African American worship could only be unleashed in a place of safety, in the community of the African-derived.

Over and over again, the sources repeat the fact that Africans and African Americans were cognizant of white ways of worship and consciously rejected them. As an example, Emily Dixon, born in 1829, testified that "on Sundays us would git tergether in de woods an' have worship. Us could go to de white folks' church but us wanted ter go whar we could sing all de way through an' hum 'long an' shout, yo' all know, just turn loose lak."[105] Minerva Grubbs echoed Dixon's sentiments regarding worship and also felt the need to sing all the way through: "Us went to de white folks' church, an' set on back seats, but didn't jine in de worship. You see, de white folks don't git in de spirit, dey don't shout, pray, hum, and sing all through de services lak us do."[106] To get in the Spirit required turning loose, and black folk could only do that within the security and familiarity of the shout. Dixon and Grubbs were witnesses, as was the aforementioned Virginian, James Smith, born Lindsey Payne sometime during the first quarter of the nineteenth century. Having converted at age eighteen, Smith went on to become an "exhorter." The power of the shout continues to reverberate through his testimony: "The way in which we worshiped is almost indescribable. The singing was accompanied by a certain ecstasy of motion, clapping of hands, tossing of heads, which would continue without cessation about half an hour; one would lead off in a kind of recitative style, others joining in the chorus. The old house partook of the ecstasy; it rang with their jubilant shouts, and shook in all its joints."[107] The shout was the sanctuary in every sense of the word.

Not all blacks, however, approved of the shout. For the elite, the ritual was a vivid and unmistakable reminder of their African heritage, an origin they earnestly sought to forget. Black clergymen in urban areas, whose congregations were substantially made up of free persons of color, were particularly sensitive to anything associated with "heathenism." In 1819, John F. Watson blasted "extravagant" practices in the Methodist church, especially the "shout and ring-dance practices (which he claimed had 'already visibly affected the religious manners of some whites') as particularly distasteful."[108] Richard Allen was equally critical of African retentions in the church and sought to replace the African-inspired rhythms of the church with more "decorous music." But it was the Reverend Daniel Alexander Payne, born in Charleston in 1811 to free parents, who epitomized the opposition to the shout. The first president of Wilberforce, Payne was ordained a bishop in the African Methodist Episcopal (AME) Church in 1852. Stuckey has already described Paynes's encounter with the shout, but it is an incident so crucial as to merit repeating. Payne experienced the shout as far north as Philadelphia and as late as 1878, where and when he "attended a 'bush meeting.'" He had gone there "to please the pastor whose circuit I was visiting. After the sermon they formed a ring, and with coats off sung, clapped their hands and stamped their feet in a most ridiculous and heathenish way." Payne, clearly offended by the Africanity of the ritual, brought it to a halt, taking its leader aside and demanding that the congregation sing "in a rational manner. I told him also that it was a heathenish way to worship and disgraceful to themselves, the race, and the Christian name."

The specifics of the bishop's rebuke reveal the ultimate source of his discomfort—a liturgical style with roots in a dubious and "uncivilized" past. The response of the congregation to this directive, along with the explanation of their leader, is most critical:

> In that instance they broke up their ring, but would not sit down, and walked sullenly away. After the sermon in the afternoon, having another opportunity of speaking alone to this young leader of the singing and clapping ring, he said: "Sinners won't get converted unless there is a ring." Said I: "You might sing till you fell down dead, and you would fail to convert a single sinner, because nothing but the Spirit of God and the word of God can convert sinners." He replied: "The Spirit of God works upon people in different ways. At campmeeting there must be a ring here, a ring there, and a ring over yonder, or sinners will not get converted."[109]

The young leader agreed that the Spirit must move for there to be a transforming work, but he disagreed that human beings were in position to proscribe such movement. In this way, he perhaps exhibited a more profound, but certainly more African, comprehension of limitless eternity.

So widespread was the phenomenon of the shout, and so concerned was the bishop with its potential, that he went on to call for "a host of Christian reformers like St. Paul, who will not only speak against these evils, but who will also resist them, even if excommunication be necessary. The time is at hand when the ministry of the A.M.E. Church must drive out this heathenish mode of worship or drive out all the intelligence, refinement, and practical Christians who may be in her bosom."[110] The bishop clearly had a dilemma on his hands, which he may or may not have appreciated. He was swimming upstream in wrestling with the concrete issue of class divisions within the African-based community, expressed in terms of religion. In the final analysis, there was little he or anyone else could do to alter the two trajectories. Each emerged out of specific socioeconomic conditions that called the classes into existence, historical forces that conspired against a monolithic community. Religion was an important marker of difference, of divergence, that neither side wanted to surrender. Consciously or unconsciously, the shout had become not only a means of worship but also an indicator of social rank and means of ancestral identification. Those who so worshiped had been forced to "get it" on their own—there had been no host of Christian reformers around during the formative period of African American Christianity, and those few who were around had not exhibited the slightest interest. Because they had gotten it on their own, they did not need the high and mighty to now come and show them how to proceed. From what they could see, they were not the ones in need of enlightenment.

The ring shout, then, had become a powerful symbol as well as effective vehicle for continuity. Stuckey sees it as a place and moment of transformation, out of which eventually emerges a unified African American community, previously fragmented by considerations of ethnicity and regional background. Because of the ubiquity of the ring ceremony throughout West and West Central Africa, native Africans from all walks of life could immediately identify with it. Speaking a number of different languages, positing faith in different gods based upon related yet unique cosmologies, these various Africans could all join in the ring ceremony. The beauty of it is that the ceremony conveyed different meanings to the assorted groups, but its form was universal as opposed to exclusionary. Everyone could participate, free to enjoy their own interpretations. Even though the process was not thoroughgoing, I concur that the shout was instrumental to the movement from ethnicity to race.

Given the evidence submitted earlier, those participating in the shout during the eighteenth century were overwhelmingly non-Christian. Although individuals were drawn to it out of their own understanding of the ring's significance, the fellowship resulting from corporate worship would have steadily eroded the parochiality of ethnicity, and a kind of pan-African religious synthesis would have been under way. It was within such contexts as the ring ceremony that Senegambians and Sierra Leonians compared notes concerning their vision of divinity. The embrace of the shout allowed the Igbo, the Akan, and the Mende to understand just how much they had in common with respect to their veneration of the ancestors and their connection to the land. The Akan distinction between the *ntoro* (spirit) and the *kra* (soul) would have found resonance in the Bambara division of *ni* (soul) and *dya* (double). Lesser deities, such as the *agbara* of the Igbo and the *abosom* of the Akan would have found reciprocity, while these same two groups merged with the Bambara and Sierra Leonians in their belief in reincarnation. The shout brought them together, transcending cultural barriers and hastening the creation of a pan-African cultural matrix with numerous points of intersection.

With the slow pace of conversion to Christianity, a new yet complementary understanding of the divine joined the circle; its adherents would have been welcomed. The shout would not have changed or altered its form with the addition of Christians. Unwelcome and unable to worship with whites in enough instances and well into the nineteenth century, converts to Christianity preferred the company of their own anyway. They understood the shout, and now that they were saved, they simply shouted a little louder. Every once in a while, such as during the Great Awakening and the subsequent camp meeting movement, whites saw flashes of Africanized worship and were deeply influenced by them. But the complete release of the Holy Spirit had to await the formation of the ring, from which whites were excluded. In this way and others, Christianity was converted to the needs of Africans, as it has remained in what is called the black church.

The shout, essentially African in origin and derivation, became associated with the masses, with the rural folk. But not all rural folk. While it is true that the shout was fairly widespread, it cannot be demonstrated that it was practiced by all. And even if it was, it is clear that certain social divisions, premised in ethnic divergence, continued to militate against achieving a culturally united community. To cite just two examples, the Gullah and Geechee of coastal Georgia and South Carolina suffered bias and recrimination by other blacks, many of whom were just as "country." The shout certainly went far in providing a meeting place, but not all made the rendezvous. The shout, together with other vehicles of unification, could not eliminate all vestiges of ethnicity.

There were other mechanisms by which the movement from ethnicity to race was facilitated, however. A ritual as widespread as the shout, if not more so, was water baptism. In his nineteenth century southern travels, Lyell was struck by the degree to which blacks were drawn to the outdoor baptismal ceremonies.[111] His impressions are substantiated by the testimonies of the participants and their descendants, who all agree that these ceremonies were most memorable. For July Ann of Halfen, Mississippi, the event was transformative: "I was baptised in the Tangipaho River right here in Osyka, an' all de folks wus shoutin' an' I went down in de water shoutin'—I tell yo' I neber wus so happy as I wus dat day, an' I is been a good Christian woman eber since I wus baptised." Far from a perfunctory ritual, the baptism generated a sense of purpose and power that transcended the moment: "I talks to de Lord an' his spirit tells me I am gwine to meet my Maker shoutin'—He tells us to shout fur joy."[112] July Ann's story is as classic a conversion as they come.

But July Ann was not baptized as an individual. She was baptized into a community of believers, along with a number of other individuals. That is to say, the African American baptismal tradition very early emphasized the value of the many; through baptism one became a integral part of the whole. Thus Anna Scott, born in 1846 in South Carolina, commented in 1937 that "when several persons were 'ready,' there would be a baptism in a nearby creek or river."[113] Louis Napoleon, born in 1857 in Tallahassee, was able to provide greater detail: "On the day of baptism, the candidates were attired in long white flowing robes, which had been made by one of the slaves. Amidst singing and praises they marched, being flanked on each side by other believers, to a pond or lake on the plantation and after the usual ceremony they were 'ducked' into the water. This was a day of much shouting and praying."[114] In other words, there was a living and corporate context into which individuals were immersed. Baptism was a means by which the community grew closer.

Often enough, these baptisms were grand, picturesque, almost panoramic events. Mack Mullen, born in 1857 in Georgia, lived on Dick Snellings's plantation along with some two hundred other slaves. In a 1936 interview, he vividly recalls how slaves from the Snellings place, along with those from other plantations, would gather at the river on baptismal day. "The slaves would be there in great numbers scattered about over the banks of the river. Much shouting and singing went on." The candidates for baptism would wait patiently, a striking ensemble of young and old, male and female outfitted in flowing robes of white. "Some of the 'sisters' and 'brothers' would get so 'happy' that they would lose control of themselves and 'fall out.'" The emphasis on the experiential, so prominent in the shout, was carried over into the baptismal ceremony; indeed, rites associated with baptism could be understood as a continuation of the shout. "It was said that the Holy Ghost had 'struck 'em.' The other slaves would view this phenomena [sic] with awe and reverence, and wait for them to 'come out of it.' 'Those were happy days and that was real religion,' Mack Mullen said."[115]

There are varying analyses of the African and African American predilection for water baptismal rites. The more sophisticated of them seek to establish a cosmological relationship to the African precursor, and as was true of the shout, water baptism contains the potential for both Christian and non-Christian interpretations. This is clearly the point of Sobel's discussion of the "Afro-Baptist" tradition of faith.[116] Stuckey, building upon Herskovits's earlier work concerning Yoruba, Fon, and Akan affinities for rivers, makes the point that the aforementioned Bakongo belief concerning their ancestors' habitation of a world below water "casts additional light on why water immersion has had such a hold on blacks in America and why counterclockwise dance is often associated with such water rites."[117] According to this view, the meaning of the cross was not Christian but Bakongo, in that it represented "a bridge that mystically put the dead and the living in perpetual communication." Even the white baptismal robes recalled the Bakongo conception of the *mpemba*, or netherworld, as a "land of all things white."

Again, periodization is a useful tool of organization. As such, it is perfectly reasonable to reconstruct a colonial and early antebellum South in which a majority of the few who underwent the rite of Christian baptism understood and participated in it from an African, "traditional" perspective. Like the shout, which may very well have been conjunctively performed, water baptism allowed for varying religious perspectives to engage in the ceremony simultaneously. With the incremental growth of Africanized Christianity, the

Christian interpretation of the ceremony would have begun to successfully compete with preceding notions. In some cases, it is possible that Christian and non-Christian beliefs became mutually supportive. In particular, the Bakongo association of water with the ancestral realm is not unlike the Christian imagery involving the Jordan River, the crossing of which represented death and the hereafter.[118] But independent of such syncretic possibilities, it is clear that the Christian ritual of baptism, although conforming to its fundamental purpose as defined by church dogma, was thoroughly Africanized by the manner in which it was carried out. It was, like the shout, simultaneously spiritual and communal.

Beyond its role in the Christianization of the African-based community, baptism was also an important medium by which the message of race consciousness was transmitted. Jackson has written that "the mode of baptism among the Baptists satisfied the desire of the Negro for the spectacular."[119] To be sure, the sight of numerous individuals congregating on the banks of a river and in a state of religious fervor was necessarily spectacular. But it was also an occasion of recreation, a time when friends and relatives from plantations and farms and towns and villages both near and far came together and formed a legal assembly. There they spent the day together and refreshed the bonds of fellowship. There, away from the gaze, they were renewed. Whether Igbo or Mandinka, whether of light or dark complexion, whether salt-water or country-born, all could come and reestablish the circle. Indeed, it was probably spectacular, but it was deeply instructive. Here was a community of persons from all ethnicities and backgrounds, tranquil and at rest, the unique circumstances of their assembly totally predicated upon a single common factor—their blackness.

The shout and water baptism were therefore important vehicles in both conversion and movement towards reconceptualization. But there was a third rite, a third factor that greatly accelerated both of these processes, perhaps even more so than the first two combined. The homegoing of the slave, as well as her freed counterpart, was truly a remarkable event. It was far more than marking the passing of an individual; it was a collective, salutary proclamation of resistance and defiance in a number of ways. Its efficacy in the cause of group cohesion was considerable, if for no other reason than its frequency.

Important research has gone into various aspects of black funerary rites. As was true of water baptism, the work tends to focus on the question of African influence and derivation. Probably the most provocative example of this approach is the work of Thompson, who maintains that "nowhere is Kongo-Angola influence on the New World more pronounced, more profound, than in black traditional cemeteries throughout the South of the United States."[120] Thompson proceeds to discuss the significance of artifacts adorning the grave site, such as personal effects last handled by the deceased, plates, cups, broken glassware, seashells, white pebbles, trees newly planted to mark the occasion, and flowerpots either deliberately turned upside down or placed upright with floral paper turned inside out.[121] He argues that such articles are in effect forms of *minkisi*, or sacred medicines, deployed to properly guide the deceased's spirit to the ancestral realm. The establishment of such an ethnically specific continuity is a major contribution to our understanding of African American culture and is consistent with the demographic evidence concerning the prominence of immigrants from West Central Africa in South Carolina, Georgia, and Louisiana.

Although significant, the focus here is not so much on cultural continuities as it is their impact on community relations. To begin, funerals were extremely important to people of African descent in America.[122] To be sure, there is former-slave testimony that appears to contradict this assertion, such as the statement of Georgia Smith of Georgia, age 87 at the time of her 1936 interview: "W'en slaves died dey jes' tuk 'em off an buried 'em. I doan' 'member 'em ever havin' a funeral."[123] Berry Smith of Mississippi (born in Alabama), purportedly 116 years old at the time of her statement in 1936, also maintained that slaves were not given funerals; rather, whites "jus' make a box an' put us in, way dey done us."[124]

The foregoing statements cannot be taken as evidence that death was inconsequential to black folk. Instead, they serve to illustrate Roediger's point that slaveholders did not "consistently demonstrate a commitment to provide a decent burial for slaves."[125] The fact that the African community was not always afforded the opportunity to observe the homegoing should not therefore be confused with their desire to do so. Their decided preference is reflected in the words of Ed McCree, age seventy-six in 1936, who related that "when folks died den, Niggers for miles and miles around went to de funeral. Now days dey got to know you mighty well if dey bothers to go a t'all."[126] Paul Smith, age seventy-four at the time, concurred: "When dere was a death 'round our neighborhood, everybody went and paid deir 'spects to de fambly of de dead."[127] In some instances the homegoing was extravagant, as was the case in Nashville, from where George H. Clark wrote his sweetheart Elizabeth in Fredricksburg, Virginia, to give her "some idea of the extremes and extravagances of the place—on last Sunday I saw a negro funeral, a slave too—at which there was twenty eight cariages [*sic*] and upwards of a hundred on horseback besides a long procession on foot."[128]

When a black person died, the body was washed and shrouded in white, tasks mainly performed by women and occasionally by an individual or group designated for such a responsibility. The shrouded body was then usually placed upon a "cooling board," a table also covered with a white cloth; sometimes, however, the body was placed directly into a coffin.[129] At this point, the "settin' up," or wake, began, which always lasted through the night.[130] Paul Smith recounted that "folkses sot up all night wid de corpse and sung and prayed. Dat settin' up was mostly to keep cats offen de corpse."[131] Smith's functional explanation of the all-night wake is certainly plausible, but an analysis of all the evidence reveals a much more powerful and spiritual principle involved in the wake. A strong sense of collective responsibility is reflected in seventy-eight-year-old Hamp Kennedy's memory of the rite: "When a nigger died, we had a wake an' dat was diffrunt too frum whut 'tis today. Dey neber lef' a dead nigger 'lone in de house, but all de neighbors was dere an' helped."[132] Reena Clark, age eighty-seven at the time of her 1936 interview, related that black folk "always 'set up' with their 'daid.' They have, she says, 'songs, prayers and mournin' all night'!"[133] That is, the wake was a sacred moment for black folk, in which elements of grief, despair, recollection, consolation, and consideration of the hereafter were all combined. Black folk needed time to accomplish all of this.

Roediger has summarized the meaning of the wake as a "highly personal bidding of farewell to the corpse in which each mourner paused at the coffin to say good-bye. That this intimate act, which was often coupled with an embrace of the corpse, was based upon African traditions is clear not only from the prevalence of such personal leave-taking among West African tribes but also from the testimony of ex-slaves."[134] That the wake is an African continuity is an important point and merits further study. The statement's reference to personal leave-taking, adequate for its purposes, requires elaboration at this point.

The passing of a fellow, whether enslaved or freed, was of great significance to black folk. As preceding testimony demonstrates, it was not necessary for the deceased to have been a relative or even a personal acquaintance. What mattered was that someone of like fate had passed on, and it was vitally important that she or he be remembered. It was important that the person be remembered by the community, because "the world" would not remember. It would not have mattered to most white folk that the deceased had ever lived; her life was of no special significance in the overall scheme of things. So it was critical that black folk pay respect to their own. It was essential that as many as possible come out, for in honoring the deceased, they validated their own worth.

No one knows what or how these sojourners felt at such times. The emotions may be incomparable to those of European immigrants who, for all of their sacrifice and suffering, nonetheless made the voyage voluntarily. For the African-born, the passing of a fellow was especially difficult, for as surely as death had come for the deceased, death would find him as well, away from family and familiar surroundings, away from all that could bring him solace. To stare into the death mask was to reflect upon his own certain mortality, and that on foreign soil. Perhaps the only consolation was in the sure knowledge that upon death, he would return to ancestral land.

The repose of the soul was also a time of bitter reflection for the descendant of the African-born. At least the latter belonged to some portion of the earth. The country-born could claim no such space. She was born and she would die without a home. The meaning of her life was difficult, her rootlessness fully exposed. Further, she would have been disturbed that her spirit would remain in the land of her birth. If the deceased was Bambara and related, how could the *dya* and *ni* make their way back to her child; or if Akan, by what means could the *mogya* and *ntoro* return to this place of sojourn? She and her progeny would be cut off forever from her African-born relatives, condemned to dwell in troubled terrain. In such moments, the Christian call to heaven would have been of great appeal, an answer to the conundrum, a way out of no way.

Both the African- and the American-born mourned, and that together. They surely reflected not only upon their individual plights but also upon the circumstances visited upon them collectively. The source of lamentation was the suffering and mistreatment of the slave and his freed cousin. But beyond all of this, they mourned the waste and destruction of potential and creativity. The deceased would never know what could have been. This was, and remains, the greatest tragedy of the African American. We do not bemoan death. Rather, we grieve that the African experience in America is preemptive of life.

The homegoing was an intense period of transition. Consequently, the relatively lighter atmosphere characterizing the postburial period should be construed as evidence not of frivolity but rather of a tremendous capacity to collect oneself and move on, to make the best of a difficult situation. When the totality of the record is considered, from the work songs to the sorrow songs to the folklore to the blues, it becomes clear that the slave's passing deeply wounded those surviving.

Notwithstanding the pain of the homegoing, the experience further aided the movement of black folk toward a corporate identity. Roediger estimates that the average funeral procession ranged from three hundred to seven hundred people; obviously all of these people were not related, nor could they have all known one another.[135] But they all came together anyway, and in their coming together they made the collective statement that they belonged to and were affirming each other. They were becoming a single community.

The transformative function of the shout, water baptism, and the home-going Africanized North American Christianity, an important and necessary precursor to the Christian conversion of Africans and African Americans. But although a discussion of the shout and water baptism speaks to the process or means of conversion, it does not address directly the more fundamental question of the reasons for African American conversion. That is, why would black folk embrace Christianity of their own volition? What did Christianity have to offer that could not be found in other African religions?

In contrast to what a number of scholars have suggested, it is my position that when people of African descent converted, they understood what they were doing.[136] To be sure, the missionary literature dating from the colonial period repeatedly refers to the difficulties of communicating with the African-born, so that absent a common language, it was unlikely that conversions took place. However, as the nineteenth century progressed the barrier of language was steadily surmounted and the meanings of words became communicable, including those emanating from the Bible.

The argument here is that those who converted were able to understand and appreciate the basic tenets of Christianity. This was primarily because the underlying concepts of the new religion, as opposed to the language through which they were conveyed, were not as foreign as some would like to believe. In fact, there are many points of correspondence with African religions, a discovery made by many while still in Kongo. The notion of a high god is nearly universal. That this high god would have a son was also consistent with beliefs regarding a multiplicity of divine beings (although the absence of a divine mother was a source of perplexity). That this son would die and rise again could not have shocked the Igbo, the Akan, the Bambara, and others who were very familiar with the concept of reincarnation. Ritual death and rebirth, the basis of water baptism, were conventional concepts to those from Sierra Leone who had participated in the activities of the Sande and Poro societies. Blood sacrifice was certainly familiar. Informed by the essentials of the Gospel, those who converted aspired to transcend nominalism. As one contemporary observed, "Whatever may be thought of the religious professions of the slave-holders, there can be no question that many of the slaves were sincere believers in the Christian religion, and endeavored to obey the precepts according to their light."[137]

Christianity also has an ecstatic legacy and component, whether it is owned up to or not. The Bible speaks of miracles on earth and signs in heaven. The prophets dreamed dreams and saw visions while in trance. Holy men and women heard God speak, and they in turn spoke in tongues. The sick were healed, the deaf talked, the lame walked, and the dead were brought back to life. And with regard to dance, who worked it better than King David? In other words, black folk and poor whites did not invent all of this on their own. There is a record of such phenomena in the Bible itself. Africans chose the literal interpretation and made the transition from imploring the lesser divinities and the ancestors to calling upon the Holy Ghost. After all, was not the role of the Spirit to intervene in the everyday lives of women and men?

From initial associations between tenets of African beliefs and those pertaining to Christianity, Africans and their progeny went on to an appreciation of the latter on its own terms. That is, although there was certainly some degree of reinterpretation, so that the Holy Ghost was the facade and Legba (for example) the reality, reinterpretation gradually gave way to a form of religion in which the fundamental beliefs of Christianity were embraced (although the liturgy was Africanized). In addition, into those cultural and social interstices about which the Bible was either silent or had yet to be communicated were placed certain African practices, about which more will be stated shortly. As long as these practices did not violate what was understood to be the central message and teachings of the Bible, they were pursued.

In addition to correspondences between African religions and Christianity, there were also opportunities, particularly in the Baptist denomination, for Africans to realize certain social and cultural continuities. Returning to the subject of water baptism, it has been alleged that immersion is the main reason for the inordinate attraction of blacks to the Baptist Church. It has also been argued that blacks saw in the baptismal rite an equivalency with African rites relating to river cults. Frazier rejected this association, pointing out that blacks flocked to the Baptist and Methodist Churches primarily because these two denominations made concerted efforts at proselytization.[138] Frazier went on to point out that the level of self-government in the Baptist Church was an added attraction for blacks.

Whatever the truth about African river cults and the Baptist rite of water immersion, Frazier, in the attempt to divert attention away from the possibility of cultural retentions, in fact unwittingly achieved the opposite. Indeed, the Baptist Church is known for decentralization, local autonomy, democratic tendencies, and granting clerical recognition to those without formal education yet called to preach.[139] This denomination was ideal for people accustomed to such liberties, whose society mirrored similar privileges. In fact, the correspondences between Baptist and Igbo governmental structures are remarkable; it is no wonder that blacks in Virginia, many of whom were Igbo or descendants thereof, flocked to the Baptist articulation of Christianity.

Viewing the black Baptist Church as an extension of Igbo culture yields fascinating results. Instead of the minister or preacher as the focus of the congregation, it is the deacons who are preeminent, in the same manner as the elders of the Igbo village were. Indeed, the authority of the Baptist deacon is legendary, as real and final power in a given local assembly is often vested in the deacon board, not the minister. Raymond noted as early as 1863 that "Negro deacons" were very powerful and influential, functioning as intercessors between their congregations and white ministers.[140] Via the freedom allowed in the Baptist faith, those of Igbo descent could continue their part-time, proscribed responsibilities of oversight within their communities. The Baptist deacon, in this way, is in all probability an example of a relatively unchanged and specific ethnic retention.

With regard to the black preacher, the current study finds the that the prevailing scholarship has overlooked an important clue to this individual's African origins. Proceeding under the debatable assumption of the historicity and ubiquity of the West African priest-king, scholars since Du Bois have posited that the black minister in North America was formerly the African priest or priest-king who transferred and recast his skills in the new setting.[141] Although there must be some evidence for this, it has proven to be highly elusive. There seems to be some relationship in the minds of scholars between the African priest and what came to be known as conjuring in North America. Yet the evidence establishing strong links between black ministers and conjuring is tenuous at best, premised more so on conjecture than anything else.

Rather than looking to the African priest or diviner, it may be more beneficial to consider the role of the West African *griot*. After all, words were his (and at times her) province, and their use in recalling the past for panegyric purposes a very high art. It fell to the *griot* to re-create the past, or whatever the subject of his dissertation, in such a way as to make the past present, to make it palpable, to place the listener within the framework of the text. A *griot*'s reputation rose or fell commensurate with his ability to make the story come alive.

As with representatives from all other caste groups, *griots* would have also found themselves exported to North America. There they would have gravitated toward those responsibilities with which they had greater facility, just as some of the Fulbe came to be more associated with the care of livestock than rice. The *griots* and their progeny would have certainly been involved in the fashioning of folklore in America, but they would have also taken advantage of the opportunities presented by Christianity, and especially the Baptists, to learn new words and master their delivery. Black preachers, as was true of the *griot*, established reputations based upon their ability to tell and retell "the story." That is, the telling became the vehicle of transformation, renewal, and reimagination. In order to facilitate the telling of the message, the black preacher, particularly in the Baptist tradition, developed a unique style of delivery, a kind of "sing-song" sermon that was part speech, part exhortation, part ballad, all performance. The lyrical, indeed musical, quality of the traditional black preacher's style is proverbial, and is another indication of *griot* origins, as the latter often told his stories through song and by way of musical accompaniment. The potential connection between the black preacher and the African *griot*, then, deserves further exploration.

Of course, *griots* did not lead their societies. During slavery, however, ministers became leaders of their congregations and the larger communities, if for no other reason than the lack of alternative options for leadership. Thus although the black preacher may be the spiritual descendant of the *griot*, he had to transcend that role, blending the oratorical skills of the latter with the responsibility of interfacing with whites. The black preacher, were he to minister openly, experienced the pressures of being an advocate for the concerns of his constituency at the same time that he was expected to communicate the sentiment and perspective of the planter class. Given these contradictory roles, the black preacher often chose to cast his lot with the aggrieved, so that prior to 1830, it was not unusual to read of ministers operating in prophetic office and in resistance to the slaveocracy, tied more closely as they were to their African forebears. With the advent of the militant South, however, white ministers were conscripted to lead the religious services and instruction of black folk, while a different kind of Negro preacher, described by Blassingame as "obsequious to a fault," was recruited and trained to do the bidding of the planters.[142] In this way, and perhaps others, the tradition of the black minister developed along two divagating lines: one externally funded and driven by directives to keep the disaffected under control; the other sustained by the congregation and led by a basic vision of redress, with hybrids and permutations in between. To this day the black clerical community continues to reflect the conflicting models of Uncle Tom on the one hand and Nat Turner on the other.

The foregoing certainly suggests areas of resonance between African and Christian religions, but the heart of the matter remains untouched. Based upon the preceding discussion, there is still no clear, compelling reason for converting to Christianity. Resonance is just that. Why did not the Africans develop a pan-African religion, composed of those elements shared by the various ethnicities, or simply continue to adhere to the religion of their ancestors, as opposed to adopting a different religion? Of course, the answer is that many, if not most, did just that well into the nineteenth century. Others rejected religion of any kind. The concern here, however, is with those who elected to convert. Why did they do so?

In addition to factors relating to social mobility and assimilation, Thurman's ideas are critical to answering this question.[143] What emerges from his work is the perspective that for the slave, Christianity provided an explanation for large-scale suffering that could not be found in African religions. Tremendous upheaval had taken place in the lives of millions of Africans and their descendants as a consequence of enslavement, and the religions of the ancestors were unable to satisfactorily explain it. Although Sobel is accurate in stating that black folk needed to achieve a "new coherence" in their worldview, the coherence was required not simply because African religions were dissipating.[144] Even more, the sufferers had a deep-seated need to recontextualize the meaning of their lives in such a way that their past could be reconciled to their present. Christianity, for its part, offered a rationale of inhumanity and evil that was at once empathetic of those who suffer and critical of those who bring suffering. Floridian and former slave Isabel Barnwell, born around 1854, related a song that captures the essence the slave's growing identification with a God acquainted with suffering and certain to render justice. Transcribed under the title "We Hab a Jest Gawd," it is a powerful and moving statement of faith:

> We hab a jest Gawd ter plead our cause,
> —Plead our cause.
> We hab a jest Gawd ter plead our cause,
> Fur we are de chillun of Gawd.
>
> Come along, I tell yuh, dontcha be afeared,
> —Dontcha be afeared.
> Come along, my people, dontcha be shamed,
> Fur we are de chillun of Gawd.
>
> O-o-h We hab a jest Gawd ter plead our cause,
> —Plead our cause,
> We hab a jest Gawd to plead our cause,
> Fur we are de chillun of Gawd.[145]

With its roots deep in the story of the Hebrew children, Christianity presented front and center the passion of Jesus. God's chosen, in both instances, underwent injustice and hardship for divine, redemptive purposes. To identify with either was to locate oneself within a context of destiny. It was to forge both a political ideology and a philosophical premise. As such, it constituted the antithesis of the white man's religion.

. . . .

Notwithstanding, and indeed in conjunction with the embrace of Christianity, the ways of the ancestors continued to reverberate throughout the African-based community. Those who converted went on to worship the Father as they had worshiped the high god in Africa. And many were quite sincere in what they professed and practiced. Even so, a perspective deeply African yet not without parallel in Native American and European societies absolutely pervaded the African-based community. Whether Christian or not, whether a believer or not, the essentially African perspective of an all-encompassing dual reality permeated the cultural and social fabric of African Americans of all walks of life. The unmistakable evidence for this perspective was the widespread practice of healing and intercessory procedures collectively and alternately known as voodoo, hoodoo, conjuration, working roots, and so on. These terms have been used interchangeably, but they can represent separate albeit related practices. As was stated earlier, for the purposes of this investigation, the term *voodoo* has been used to refer to those African-based religiocultural expressions largely Fon-Ewe-Yoruba in origin and usually associated with the lower Mississippi. *Hoodoo*, although very much connected to the foregoing, consisted of mechanisms of intervention that evolved out of the religions of ethnicities from places other than the Bight of Benin. There are numerous areas in which the two systems overlap, although in others they are essentially the same. The purpose of distinguishing between them, however, is to further underscore the diverse origins of the African-based community.

In the 1860s, a white observer of southern blacks commented that "in all instances which I remember to have noticed with reference to such fact, I have found among the religious slaves of the South traces, more or less distinct, of a blending of superstition and fetishism, modifying their impressions of Christianity."[146] This was a reference to the existence of hoodoo. Some thirty years later, at the close of the century, Lenora Herron explained that conjuring in the South was "very probably a relic of African days," and given the unavailability of justice and equality before the law, it was not surprising that "the Negro . . . brought up in ignorance, and trained in superstition . . . should invoke secret and supernatural powers to redress his wrongs and afford him vengeance."[147]

In order to fully appreciate the practice of hoodoo in America, it is required that some reference be made to the African background. Throughout premodern Africa, it was commonly believed that causality lay in unseen realms. That is, phenomena manifested in the temporal world have their origins in the spiritual universe.[148] It therefore follows that in order to influence events in the physical, it is necessary to first negotiate with the incorporeal. The means and methods by which one negotiates with unseen forces is the practice of traditional intercession, alternatively called magic, sorcery, witchcraft, voodoo, or hoodoo, as it has been so named in North America. Such power can be used for good or evil and is inextricably interwoven into the other components of African religions.

In places such as Brazil, Haiti, and other parts of the Antilles, African religious specificity was better able to survive the vicissitudes of slavery than they were in North America, where with the possible exception of the lower Mississippi, African gods and the sacrificial rites associated with their adoration became increasingly unspecified. What remained, however, were two critical continuities: the African perspective of causality and the techniques of traditional intercession. Thus hoodoo represents the legacy of the African worldview divorced from its proper religious context. Some worshiped Jesus and others did not, but they all tended to see the physical world in the same way. It was therefore not necessarily problematic for black churchgoers to consult with "hoodoo men" and women to resolve their everyday problems.

The principal manifestation of traditional intercession in Africa was the amulet or charm. Across the vast expanse of the continent, women and men have protected themselves against dangers foreseen and unforeseen by wearing amulets on their persons. Whether making war, love, or warding off disease, impoverishment, and famine, amulets were everywhere in Africa. Thompson emphasizes the *minkisi*, or charms, of the West Central African Bakongo and argues their preeminence in African America, a point reiterated by Washington Creel.[149] These charms typically involved a "spirit-embodying" receptacle such as graveyard dirt wrapped in a protective medium of some sort. Without question, the Bakongo *minkisi* had an impact upon North America, but they were by no means the only type of amulet. Virtually all who were imported via the transatlantic, including Muslims, were familiar with the amulet, or "gris-gris." Once in America, these amulets took on other names, such as "jacks," "hands," "mojos," and "tobes," the latter a Bakongo term.

References to charms in the literature are abundant. Bibb, born in 1815, recalled that "there is much superstition among the slaves. Many of them believe in what they call 'conjuration,' tricking, and witchcraft."[150] Louis Hughes, born a slave in 1832 in Virginia, wrote that "it was the custom in those days for slaves to carry voo-doo bags. It was handed down from generation to generation; and, though it was one of the superstitions of a barbarous ancestry, it was still very generally and tenaciously held to by all classes."[151] And in Georgia, as early as 1788, an ad was placed for the return of "Long Hercules, otherwise known as Doctor Hercules, from his remarkable conjurations of pigs feet, rattlesnakes teeth, and from the feet and legs of several sick people, many of whom still believe him in reality to have performed miracles."[152]

Doctor Hercules, in his adherence to the power of amulets, had nothing on George Boddison of Tin City, Georgia, who as late as the 1930s presented himself to an interviewer with his arms and wrists wrapped with copper wire strung with amulets, his fingers covered with several large rings, and his head encircled with copper wire to which were attached two pieces of broken mirror at each temple, reflecting out.[153] In fact, the residents of coastal Georgia all understood hoodoo and discussed (to a degree) their knowledge of amulets or charms, along with their experiences in the supernatural. They shared, for example, their struggles with witches or "hags," living individuals who visited the innocent in the dead of night in order to "ride" or torture them. Dye Williams of Old Fort (Savannah), whose mother was a slave, talked about witches who "rides folks." The witch, she explained, "come lak a nightmeah tuh duh folks wile dey sleepin. But ef yuh puts duh bruhm cross duh doe, yuh kin keep any witch out duh ruhm at night."[154] Brooms, salt, and pages of newspaper were believed to be effective against witches because the latter would have to stop and count the strands, grains, or letters before continuing, a task that would take the balance of the night. As Josephine Anderson of Florida explained: "One thing bout witches, dey gotta count everything fore dey can git acrosst it. You put a broom acrosst your door at night an old witches gotta count ever straw in dat broom fore she can come in."[155]

The evidence of such nocturnal visits was the sensation of strangling or smothering during sleep. S. B. Holmes, also of Tin City, recalls that a neighbor's wife once had this problem. Her husband went about laying a "trap," so that when "he heah his wife strugglin, he git a axe an begin frailin roun in duh dark till he hit sumpm. It let out a screech an a cat run out duh winduh an down duh paat. So duh nex mawnin duh man git his dog an put im on duh cat's trail. Well, suh, bout half a mile down duh road in duh fence cawnuh wuz ole Malinda Edmonde wid tree rib broke. She beg im not tuh kill uh, but dat broke up duh witch ridin."[156] The interviews from coastal Georgia are filled with these kinds of stories, including references to spirits or ghosts or "haints," who populate the world and intervene in the affairs of human beings on a regular basis. Taken together, they are powerful testimony that the prevailing worldview of the African-based community in America was one essentially informed by what had been learned in Africa.

The literature on hoodoo in North America treats a wide variety of subjects, including specific remedies and incantations, the ingredients required to "fix" a person (for example, the hair or nails of the intended victim), the meanings of certain signs, the different kinds of spirits and their purposes (such as "Raw Head and Bloody Bones"), as well as how one becomes qualified to practice hoodoo (for example, being born the seventh son of a seventh son, or emerging from the birth canal with a "caul" or membrane covering the face).[157] The properties of specific roots such as Golden Seal, Blood Root, High John the Conqueror, Black Snake Root, and Lady Slipper are all discussed. The WPA interviews in particular are saturated with references to these subjects. Although they cannot be recounted here, there are some examples which are especially noteworthy.

As was true of the Bambara and, for that matter, most other groups, the world of the African-based community was dense with spirits. Tom Pimpton of Louisiana, a "spirit controller," explained that "there's land spirits and there's water spirits, and you gotta know how to talk to both kinds. The land spirits is bad and the water spirits is good. They got seven kinds of land spirits; that's part of the trouble. There is bulls, lions, dogs, babies, snakes, persons and pearls."[158] South Carolinian M. E. Abrams was told by her uncle that although some could see spirits, others could not: "Dats zactly how it is wid de spirits. De mout (might) sho de'self to you and not to me. De acts raal queer all de way round."[159] Henry Cheatam of Alabama, born in 1851, held similar views on the reality of the spirit realm: "Sum folks say dere ain't no sich thing as ghosts but I knoes dere is, 'cayse dere is good sperits an' bad sperits."[160] In two interesting examples of how Christianity had an impact on the view of the spirit world, one informant stated that he "used to see haunts so much I prayed to God that I might not see any more. And I don't see them now like I did then since I become an elect in the House of God. He has taken fear out of me."[161] In the other instance, Phillip Evans of South Carolina, whose grandfather was African, remarked: "Yes sir, dere is haunts, plenty of them. De devil is de daddy and they is hatched out in de swamps."[162] What is instructive is that although both comments are antagonistic, both fully accept the existence of the spirit realm.

In addition to witches and spirits, there were specialists in aspects of hoodoo and root working. Hoodoo men and women, referred to as "two-head niggers" (one head in this world and one in the next), were people who usually employed methods of intercession for good.[163] At the same time, there was the root worker, whose expertise was in the realm of medicinal herbs and plants and who may or may not have practiced hoodoo. Some of the Christians who were interviewed, while totally rejecting hoodooism as either fraudulent or satanic, were very comfortable with root working. These same Christians, while disavowing the efficacy of amulets, nevertheless believed in various kinds of signs.

On the other hand, there is the matter of evil. Whether the existence of the devil was posited or not, evil, as was true in Africa, was believed to emanate from a living person—a witch or sorcerer. The casting of evil was usually associated with conjuration; however, protecting against evil was also referred to as conjuration at times. Given the view of evil, people tended to agree with Addie Vinson's summation: "Everytime somebody gets sick it ain't natchel sickness."[164] Underscoring this insight, Sallie Layton Keenan of South Carolina related that "when my paw, 'Obie' was a courtin, a nigger put a spell on him kaise he was a wantin' my maw too. De nigger got a conjure bag and drapped it in de spring what my paw drunk water from. He wuz laid up on a bed o' rheumatiz fer six weeks."[165] Fellow South Carolinian Govan Littlejohn of Spartanburg also claimed that he had been conjured in a contest with another man over the affections of a woman. After his left foot swelled and forced him to remain in bed for three months, his "mother found the 'conjuration' right in the front yard at the door-steps. I must have stepped over it, or got my foot caught in it some way. The 'conjuration' was, pins, feathers, and something else all tied up in a bag."[166]

The technique of burying a conjuration bag under the doorstep, in the front yard, or in some location over which the intended victim was sure to pass is a direct African retention. As Anna Grant explained, "Anudder way dey conjures you is to get some of your hair and some roots and a little of your wine and put it all in a bottle and den cork it up real tight and bury it under your doorstep; and believe me you is fixed."[167] For all of its notoriety, however, not all black folk believed in conjuration. Said Hannah Irwin, who was twelve years old when "freedom declared": "No, Honey, I dont bleve in no ghosts, dese cunger wimmin say dey make my broken hip well if I giv em haf my rations, dey aint nuthen but low down niggers."[168] Or as Mississippian Mary Jane Jones put it even more poignantly, "No indeed, Hoodoo ain't no count; hit is just a poisoned mind, dat's all. Won't nothing help but prayer and money, and I got plenty prayer."[169]

The perspective of some black Christians toward conjuration was consistent with that of Mary Jane Jones—it was a total hoax. At the same time, they displayed receptive attitudes toward other components of what was essentially an African worldview. James Southall of Oklahoma City, to cite one case, stated that he "learned a long time ago dat dey was nothing to charms. How could a rabbit's foot bring me good luck? De Bible teaches me better'n dat. I believes in dreams though."[170] In a similar fashion, another informant said he did not believe in conjurers because he "asked God to show me such things—if they existed—and He came to me in person while I was in a trance and said, 'There ain't no such thing as conjurers.' I believe in root-doctors because, after all, we must depend upon some form of root or weed to cure the sick."[171] Although both Southall and the anonymous source rejected conjuring, they accepted dreams, visions, and herbal or root medicinal practices. The reference to the slaves' dependency on roots and herbs to defend against disease suggests a practical rather then supernatural approach to healing and warrants further inquiry.

As for other Christianized blacks, their perspective of conjuration was equivalent to their view of spirits: they exist, but they are satanic in origin. Willis Easter of Texas shared a song taught to him by his mother, in which the association between conjuring and the devil is hard and fast:

> Keep 'way from me, hoodoo and witch,
> Lead my path from de porehouse gate;
> I pines for golden harps and sich,
> Lawd, I'll jes' set down and wait.
> Old Satan am a liar and conjurer, too—
> If you don't watch out, he'll conjure you.[172]

Mom Sara Brown of Marion, South Carolina, also testified that conjuration was demonic: "O Lord, baby, I don' know a thing bout none of dat thing call conjurin. Don' know nothin bout it. Dat de devil work en I ain' bother wid it. Dey say some people can kill you, but dey ain' bother me. Some put dey trust in it, but not me."[173] Texan William Adams, ninety-three years old in 1937, was a fatalist in his explanation: "There is some born to sing, some born to preach, and some born to know de signs. There is some born under de power of de devil and have de power to put injury and misery on people, and some born under de power of de Lawd for to do good and overcome de evil power."[174] This view, then, rather than rejecting the validity of conjuring, simply reclassified it.

There are many other aspects and a tremendous amount of detail pertaining to African religious retentions in the form of intercession. The above is sufficient to demonstrate the kinds of issues connected with this intercession and is presented to give an idea of just how prevalent such beliefs were. Given the relative absence of Christianity within the slave quarters during the colonial and antebellum periods, and keeping in mind the evidence of continued African religious practices, it must be that methods of mediation later known as hoodoo were very widespread during these periods. With the advance of the nineteenth century and the rise of Africanized Christianity, the evidence suggests that hoodoo continued on somewhat unabated, as some Christians rejected it outright and others came to terms with it. Hoodoo, incorporating as it did practices from all of the various ethnicities and, to be sure, from Native Americans as well, was a force of cohesion within the black community. It was practiced everywhere, suggesting a collective, spiritual viewpoint among those of African descent.

The reactions of Christians to hoodoo have been discussed. What has not been considered is the response of those who rejected hoodoo, and by implication much of the African-derived perspective, on the basis of logic and analysis. That is, there were those who took the claims of hoodoo at face value and waited for results. When those results were not forthcoming, disbelief and cynicism set in. Of course, results were most desultory when the conjure man turned his attention to the slaveholder.

The failure of conjuration to effect change in slave-slaveholder relations was a major source of consternation for those who initially believed. For example, Horace Overstreet, born in 1856 in Texas, related the story of a "jack" being administered to a woman to prevent the slaveholder from beating her. "Dat same day she git too uppity and sass de massa, 'cause she feel safe. Dat massa, he whip dat nigger so hard he cut dat bag of sand [the jack] plumb in two. Dat ruint de conjure man business."[175] Another anonymous source, born in 1843, also rejected the claims of hoodoo based upon its inability to effect social and political change: "They had in those days a Hoodoo nigger who could hoodoo niggers, but couldn't hoodoo masters. He couldn't make ole master stop whipping him, with the hoodooism, but they could make Negroes crawl to them."[176] Silvia Witherspoon of Alabama, about ninety years of age when interviewed in 1937, wondered aloud about the power of the local conjurer Monroe King:

> You know dat ole nigger would putt a conjure on somebody for jus' a little sum of money. He sold conjure bags to keep de sickness away. He could conjure de grass an' de birds, an' anything he wanted to. De niggers 'roun' useta give him chickens an' things so's he wouldn't conjure 'em, but its a funny thing, Mistis, I ain't never understood it, he got tuk off to jail for stealin' a mule, an' us niggers waited 'roun' many a day for him to conjure hisself out, but he never did. I guess he jus' didn't have quite enough conjurin' material to git hisself th'ough dat stone wall. I ain't never understood it, dough.[177]

Witherspoon represents many others who, for all their perplexity, were yet unwilling to abandon hoodoo. Hattie Matthews's grandmother, on the other hand, had an explanation for this deficiency. According to her, "negroes couldn't hoodoo white peoples cause dey had strait hair. It wuz somethin' bout de oil in de hair. White folks habe to wash dere hair ta get de oil out, but negroes habe to put oil on deir hair."[178] Although plausible for those who thought along such lines, such rationalization was unacceptable for people like Louis Hughes, who had put the power of conjuration to the empirical test and found it wanting: "The claim that it would prevent the folks from whipping me so much, I found, was not sustained by my experience—my whippings came just the same."[179]

The implications behind the claim to control unseen forces went far beyond granting the ability to evade abuse. The obvious question was, If conjuring was so effective, why did not its practitioners conjure away slavery itself (and white folk with it)? That this had not been accomplished made hoodoo highly suspect. Whether a complete or partial fraud, it was viewed as a waste a time for many concerned with the destruction of the slaveocracy. As the nineteenth century progressed, there would be a "falling away" of those who formerly believed in the power of conjuring, consistent with those within the black community who all along condemned it as so much superstition.

· · · · · · ·

The shout and hoodoo were both clear and unmistakable continuities of African customs and beliefs, modified for the use of Africans and their descendants as they passed through the great tribulation. Throughout the eighteenth century, those who practiced the shout probably believed in hoodoo as well, as the African-based community was largely non-Christian and no more than one or two generations removed from African soil. With the progression of the nineteenth century, however, those who converted to Christianity split along class lines, and the urban elite developed a distinct distaste for the African ritual of the shout. They also maintained their distance from hoodoo, at least publicly.

10

....

THE LEAST OF THESE

....

The development of African American society through 1830 was very much the product of contributions made by specific ethnic groups. Africans did not all experience American slavery in the same way. Rather, varying mixes of ethnicities in each colony/state resulted in communities and cultural forms that were distinctive though related. A more meaningful explication of the African American experience therefore necessitates a reconsideration of the African antecedent.

The 1822 insurrection of Denmark Vesey represents the transitioning of the African American identity. By 1830, the shift had registered substantial progress. Its chief nemesis, classism, had also emerged as the vehicle by which all such movement could be arrested, or at least controlled. By the first quarter of the nineteenth century, then, at least two distinct and divergent visions of the African presence in America had achieved sufficient articulation and were in competition. One, drawing from the promise of the American liberal ideal and nurtured by faith in an expansive understanding of Christianity's potential, would engage in any number of strategies to become a partner in the American venture. The other, cognizant of the glaring inconsistencies between American prayers and practice, and dubious of ever becoming full participants in the American political experiment, placed their trust in that which transcended temporal powers and in ways which were familiar and reassuring, bringing them as close to the bosom of Africa as they could get.

Those who would comprise the black elite struck out along lines that held the best promise of inclusion. From the beginning of the nineteenth century into the final decade of the twentieth, their primary objective would be admission into the club. They would seek nothing less than equal status and privilege in the land of their birth. They would want nothing less than full acceptance.

Having determined the objective of full American citizenship and incorporation into the American body politic, many in the black elite proceeded to identify those obstacles that prevented or in other ways hindered their progress. Their analysis of "the problem" was very much a function of their class aspirations. The problem was initially slavery, and many heroic and indispensable campaigns were mounted to end this episode in human exploitation. With the abolition of slavery and the waning of Reconstruction, attention shifted to discrimination in the urban North and Jim Crow in the urban and rural South, a focus maintained through two world wars and into the 1950s and 1960s. People from all walks of life joined hands to march, sit, stand, and ride for freedom. Protests and threats of all kinds were issued—all noble and necessary efforts, whose objectives included the gradual dismantling of the discriminatory apparatus of the state. With the granting of civil rights and equal opportunities, freedom was at hand. And yet, after all the sacrifice and struggle, many remain poised on the precipice.

In contrast to the elite, the majority of the African-based community, beginning as early as 1830, defined the problem very differently. They saw slavery, sharecropping, Jim Crow, and related discrimination as symptoms of a much deeper and intractable generative source. The problem, as they saw it and experienced it and knew it intuitively, was the fundamental and unequivocal rejection of Africa as equal, otherwise known as racism. The majority certainly fought for civil rights and equal opportunities, but they always understood the primary issue to be more insidious.

The black elite manage to stay afloat with great difficulty. In any event, their condition is not so critical as those relegated to the category of underclass, the least of these, who continue to represent Africa to America.

APPENDIX

CENSUS ESTIMATES FOR 1790, 1800, 1810, 1820, AND 1830

CENSUS OF 1790

State	Slaves	Free	Whites
New York	21,193	4,682	314,142
New Jersey	11,423	2,762	169,954
Delaware	8,887	3,899	46,310
Maryland	103,036	8,043	208,649
Virginia	292,627	12,866	442,115
North Carolina	100,783	5,041	288,204
South Carolina	107,094	1,801	140,178
Georgia	29,264	398	52,886
Kentucky	12,430	114	61,133
Tennessee	3,417	361	31,913

CENSUS OF 1800

State	Slaves	Free	Whites
New York	20,903	10,417	557,731
New Jersey	12,422	4,402	194,325
Delaware	6,153	8,268	49,852
Maryland	105,635	19,587	216,326
Virginia	345,796	20,124	514,280
North Carolina	133,296	7,043	337,764
South Carolina	146,151	3,185	196,255
Georgia	59,406	1,019	102,261
Kentucky	40,343	739	179,873
Tennessee	13,584	309	91,709
Washington, D.C.	3,244	783	10,066
Mississippi	3,489	182	5,179

CENSUS OF 1810

State	Slaves	Free	Whites
New York	15,017	25,333	918,699
New Jersey	10,851	7,843	226,868
Delaware	4,177	13,136	55,361
Maryland	111,502	33,927	235,117
Virginia	392,516	30,570	551,514
North Carolina	168,824	10,266	376,410
South Carolina	196,365	4,554	214,196
Georgia	105,218	1,801	145,414
Kentucky	80,561	1,713	324,237
Tennessee	44,535	1,317	215,875
Washington, D.C.	5,395	2,549	16,079
Mississippi	17,088	240	23,024
Louisiana	34,660	7,585	34,311

CENSUS OF 1820

State	Slaves	Free	Whites
New York	10,088	29,279	1,333,445
New Jersey	7,557	12,460	257,558
Delaware	4,509	12,958	55,282
Maryland	107,397	39,730	260,223
Virginia	425,148	36,883	603,335
North Carolina	204,917	14,712	419,200
South Carolina	258,475	6,826	237,440
Georgia	149,656	1,763	189,570
Kentucky	126,732	2,759	434,826
Tennessee	80,107	2,737	339,979
Washington, D.C.	6,377	4,048	22,614
Mississippi	32,814	458	42,176
Louisiana	69,064	10,476	73,867
Missouri Territory	10,222	347	56,017
Alabama Territory	41,879	571	85,451
Arkansas Territory	1,617	59	12,597

State	Slaves	Free	Whites
New York	75	44,870	1,873,663
New Jersey	2254	18,303	300,266
Delaware	3292	15,855	57,601
Maryland	102,994	52,938	291,108
Virginia	469,757	47,348	694,300
North Carolina	245,601	19,543	472,843
South Carolina	315,401	7,921	257,863
Georgia	217,531	2,486	296,806
Kentucky	165,213	4,917	517,787
Tennessee	141,603	4,555	535,746
Washington, D.C.	6,119	6,152	27,563
Mississippi	65,659	519	70,443
Louisiana	109,588	16,710	89,441
Missouri	25,091	569	114,795
Alabama	117,549	1,572	190,406
Arkansas Territory	4,576	141	25,671
Florida Territory	15,501	844	18,385

Source: U.S. Department of Commerce, Bureau of the Census, *Negro Population, 1790–1915* (Washington, D.C., 1918), 45, 57. Compare with James D. B. DeBow, *The Industrial Resources, Statistics, Etc., of the United States and More Particularly of the Southern and Western States*, 3d ed. (New York, 1854), 2:404–25.

· · · · · · · · · · · · · · · · · ·

NOTES

· · · · · · · · · · · · · · · · ·

CHAPTER 1

1. For details on the Denmark Vesey insurrection, see John Oliver Killens, *The Trial Record of Denmark Vesey* (Boston, 1970); Robert S. Starobin, *Denmark Vesey: The Slave Conspiracy of 1882* (Engelwood Cliffs, N.J., 1970); John Lofton, *Denmark Vesey's Revolt* (Kent, Ohio, 1964; reprint, Kent, Ohio, 1983); Sterling Stuckey, *Slave Culture: Nationalist Theory and the Foundations of Black America* (Oxford, 1987), 43−52.

2. Killens, *Trial Record of Denmark Vesey*, 41−42.

3. Ibid., 62.

4. Starobin, *Denmark Vesey*, 21−22.

5. Killens, *Trial Record of Denmark Vesey*, 61.

6. Ibid., 63.

7. Ibid., 52.

8. Ibid., 78.

9. Ibid., 62.

10. Ibid., 45−46.

11. Starobin, *Denmark Vesey*, 29.

12. Criticisms of slave and former-slave narratives/interviews such as the WPA interviews of the 1930s have been duly registered; historians have questioned their value as sources. Regarding the slave narrative, there is difficulty dissociating its historical accuracy from its use as an abolitionist propaganda tool. There are often questions of authorship, as many narratives were dictated to white writers or editors. There are questions of representation, because the accounts apparently reflect the more educated and privileged of the slave population. Further, accounts from women and the lower South are in the decided minority. Similarly, the WPA interviews are geographically incongruent in that the large slaveholding state of Virginia is underrepresented, whereas Texas and Arkansas supply 45 percent of the 2,194 interviews. These interviews were only 2 percent of the total former-slave population at the time of the project. Some 66 percent of the informants were eighty years old and older, meaning that only 16 percent were fifteen years of age or older by the beginning of the Civil War. Further, since many of the interviewers were white, their biases and relationships with the informants (who were in instances acquainted with the interviewers), together with the political climate at the time, must be taken into consideration. The issue of reliability, therefore, is as central to a careful exploitation of these sources as is the matter of representation. See John W. Blassingame, "Using the Testimony of Ex-Slaves: Approaches and Problems," *Journal of Southern History* 41 (1975): 473−92; Norman R.

Yetman, "The Background of the Slave Narrative Collection," *American Quarterly* 19 (1967): 534–53. Much of the analysis is revisited in Charles T. Davis and Henry Louis Gates Jr., eds., *The Slave's Narrative* (Oxford, 1985).

The foregoing observations necessarily mean that these sources must be approached with great care. It is not always clear that a statement attributed to an informant was precisely what was said, nor if it was said in the manner so described, as editing usually took place at the conclusion of the interview. These considerations have a bearing on such issues as re-creating the dialect. It is also problematic that a former slave would respond candidly to a white interviewer in the Jim Crow South about conditions under slavery. Similarly, it is doubtful that former slaves, interested in the inclusion of their offspring and relations into the American mainstream, would be very forthcoming about matters relating to their African ancestry. Such individuals would understandably be reticent about discussing certain cultural or social conventions at variance with what they knew to be the acceptable American patterns. What can be reasonably expected, therefore, are muted and unspecific responses to questions regarding such matters. In this context, the relative absence of specificity is consistent with the thesis of African cultural continuity, rather than evidence for its rejection.

In conjunction with the probable reluctance of the informants to speak candidly for the aforementioned reasons, the methodology of the WPA interviewers themselves probably contributed to the absence of detail regarding the African background. The following excerpt from a typical WPA questionnaire reveals a rather parochial contextual approach as well as poor method, complete with leading questions:

> Were you superstitious? Did you believe that a screeching of an owl was the sign of death? That the bellowing of a cow after dark is a sign of death? That sneezing while eating, or if a dog howls after dark it is a sign of death. [*sic*] Did you believe that if there is a death in the house, the ticking of the clock must be discontinued at once and a white cloth hung over a mirror?
>
> Do you believe in signs? As if a dish cloth falls on the floor while washing dishes some one will come in hungry, or if the new moon is first seen through the trees it is a sign of the coming of a stranger, or if there is itching under the bottom of the foot it is a sign you are going to a strange land? (George P. Rawick, ed., *The American Slave: A Composite Autobiography* [Westport, Conn., 1972–77], Supplement Series, 4:567–68)

Because the interviewers were not sufficiently knowledgeable to ask appropriate questions about either the African background or the consequent cultural forms and their meanings, they had to rely upon widely held misconceptions and vague notions about such matters, and this is evident in their questions. The constraints of the queries themselves, therefore, necessarily conditioned the responses of the informants. Again, such circumstances do not constitute an argument against the continuity thesis, but in fact strengthen its claims, since a remarkable amount of information regarding the African influence can be gleaned from the interviews, the limitations of the project design notwithstanding. This information, however, tends to be nonspecific.

Given the lack of detail, the generalities engaged by the narratives and interviews must be used together to discern overall patterns in the testimony. From such patterns of agreement, inferences can be drawn and supported by what is known about the African antecedent and by those details which do exist. Such nodal points of consensus are very instructive and render high levels of probability when used in conjunction with the collaborative data.

13. Jan Vansina, *Paths in the Rainforests: Toward a History of Political Tradition in Equatorial Africa* (Madison, 1990), esp. 19–20.

14. See ʿAbd al-Raḥmān al-Saʿdī's *Taʾrīkh al-Sūdān* (Paris, 1900); Ibn al-Mukhtār, *Taʾrīkh al-Fattāsh* (Paris, 1913); Nehemia Levtzion and J. F. P. Hopkins, eds., *Corpus of Early Arabic Sources for West Africa* (Cambridge, 1981); Bernard Barbour and Michelle Jacobs, "The Miʾraj: A Legal Treatise on Slavery by Ahmad Baba," in *Slaves and Slavery in Muslim Africa*, ed. John Ralph Willis (London, 1985), esp. 158/translation 137; John O. Hunwick, "Songhay, Borno and the Hausa States, 1450–1600," in *History of West Africa*, 3d ed., ed. J. F. Ade Ajayi and Michael Crowder (New York, 1985). Furthermore, the groups referred to in Usuman dan Fodio's *Bayān wujūb al-hijra ʿalā al-ʿibād* (Oxford and Khartoum, 1978), and in other works associated with Sokoto as well, do not appear to be derivative of contact with Europeans, but rather a continuation of a dialogue already under way as early as the fourteenth century as to what groups could or could not be enslaved. See also John O. Hunwick's *Sharīʿa in Songhay: The Replies of al-Maghīlī to the Questions of Askia al-Ḥājj Muḥammad* (Oxford, 1985) for insight into *Sunni* Ali's comportment, around which controversy concerning potential servile populations was generated. Finally, see Charles Monteil, "La légende du Ouagadou et l'origine des Soninkés," *Mélanges Ethnologiques* (Dakar, 1953), and compare with *Taʾrīkh al-Sūdān* 9/translation 18–19 ("Wa hum baydān fī al-Asl") and *Taʾrīkh al-Fattāsh* 42/translation 78.

15. Sidney W. Mintz and Richard Price, *An Anthropological Approach to the Afro-American Past: A Caribbean Perspective* (Philadelphia, 1976), 12.

16. Melville Herskovits, *The Myth of the Negro Past* (New York, 1941), 110–13.

17. Ibid., 122.

18. The concept of volitive versus coercive spheres of culture is not unlike James C. Scott's discussion of "hidden" versus "public" transcripts in his *Domination and the Arts of Resistance: Hidden Transcripts* (New Haven, Conn., 1990). Although there are similarities, Scott's language and conceptual organization are not be employed here because the concept of slave discourse, either apart from whites/slaveholders or disguised in the latter's very presence, long antedates Scott in the anthropological literature. The discussion of the multiple ways in which slaves resist (Scott's "infrapolitics") is also well established in the scholarship on North American slavery, so that the present work draws upon these two branches of inquiry for its conceptual framework rather than Scott (as the references clearly demonstrate) and was largely completed prior to consulting Scott's work. Although I consider Scott's contribution valuable, I remain unconvinced that his broader argument is an effective rejoinder to the ideas of "ideological hegemony" and "cultural violence." It may be possible, however, to reconcile these conflicting interpretations by paying closer attention to class and periodization. At any rate, see Antonio Gramsci, *Selections from the Prison Notebooks*, ed. and trans. Quinten Hoare and Geoffrey Nowell Smith (London, 1971); Pierre Bourdieu, *Distinction: A Social Critique of the Judgement of Taste*, trans. Richard Nice (Cambridge, 1984); Pierre Bourdieu, *Outline of a Theory of Practice*, trans. Richard Nice (Cambridge, 1977).

19. Melville Herskovits, "Problem, Method and Theory in Afroamerican Studies," *Phylon* 7 (1946): 337–54.

20. From Lawrence W. Levine, *Black Culture and Black Consciousness* (London, 1978), xiii.

21. Ibid., 6.

22. See, for example, W. E. B. Du Bois, *Dusk of Dawn: An Essay toward an Autobiography of a Race Concept* (New York, 1940); Oliver C. Cox, *Caste, Class and Race: A Study in Social Dynamics* (New York, 1948); Ivan Hannaford, *Race: The History of an Idea in the West* (Baltimore, 1996); Henry Louis Gates Jr., ed., *"Race," Writing, and Difference* (Chicago, 1986); and Houston Baker, *Afro-American Poetics* (Madison, 1988).

23. To begin the discussion of the creation of the American identity, consult the following: Clarence L. Ver Steeg, *The Formative Years, 1607–1763* (New York, 1964); Edmund S.

Morgan, *The Birth of the Republic, 1763–89* (Chicago, 1977); Bernard Bailyn, *The Origins of American Politics* (New York, 1968); Bernard Bailyn, *The Ideological Origins of the American Revolution* (Cambridge, Mass., 1967); and David Potter, *People of Plenty: Economic Abundance and the American Character* (Chicago, 1954).

24. Toni Morrison, *Playing in the Dark: Whiteness and the Literary Imagination* (New York, 1992); Orlando Patterson, *Freedom in the Modern World* (New York, 1992), vol. 1.

For a discussion of the social construction of "whiteness," one should include David R. Roediger, *The Wages of Whiteness: Race and the Making of the American Working Class* (London, 1991); David R. Roediger, *Towards the Abolition of Whiteness: Essays on Race, Politics, and Working Class History* (London, 1994); Vron Ware, *Beyond the Pale: White Women, Racism and History* (London, 1992); Alexander Saxton, *The Rise and Fall of the White Republic: Class Politics and Mass Culture in Nineteenth-Century America* (London, 1991); Werner Sollors, *Beyond Ethnicity: Consent and Descent in American Culture* (New York, 1986); Ruth Frankenberg, *White Women, Race Matters: The Social Construction of Whiteness* (Minneapolis, 1993); Ward Churchill, *Fantasies of the Master Race: Literature, Cinema and the Colonization of American Indians* (Monroe, Maine, 1992); Robert Young, *White Mythologies: Writing History and the West* (London, 1990); Virginia Dominguez, *White by Definition: Social Classification in Creole Louisiana* (New Brunswick, N.J., 1986); George M. Fredrickson, *White Supremacy: A Comparative Study in American and South African History* (New York, 1981); and Michael Omi and Howard Winant, *Racial Formation in the United States, from the 1960s to the 1990s*, 2d ed. (New York, 1994).

CHAPTER 2

1. On the matter of implications for both Africa and the West, see Eric Williams, *Capitalism and Slavery* (New York, 1944), a classic whose central thesis is once again a focus of discussion after years of dismissal; Walter Rodney, *How Europe Underdeveloped Africa* (London, 1972); Walter Rodney, *A History of the Upper Guinea Coast* (Oxford, 1970); Andre Gunder Frank, *Capitalism and Underdevelopment in Latin America* (New York, 1969); Immanuel Wallerstein, *The Modern World System*, 2 vols. to date (New York, 1974–80); Paul Lovejoy, *Transformations in Slavery: A History of Slavery in Africa* (Cambridge, 1983); J. E. Inikori, *Forced Migration: The Impact of the Export Slave Trade on African Societies* (New York, 1980); David Eltis, *Economic Growth and the Ending of the Transatlantic Slave Trade* (Cambridge, 1987); Suzanne Miers and Richard Roberts, eds., *The End of Slavery in Africa* (Madison, 1988); Patrick Manning, *Slavery and African Life: Occidental, Oriental, and African Slave Trades* (Cambridge, 1990). For a most provocative examination of these matters, see John Thornton, *Africa and Africans in the Making of the Atlantic World, 1400–1680* (Cambridge, 1992), 43–125.

2. Representative of regional foci are Joseph C. Miller's *Way of Death: Merchant Capitalism and the Angolan Slave Trade, 1730–1830* (Madison, 1988); Roger E. Conrad's *World of Sorrow* (Baton Rouge, 1986); Charles Becker, "La Sénégambie à l'époque de la traite des esclaves. À propos d'un ouvrage recent de Philip D. Curtin," *Revue française d'histoire d'outre-mer* 64 (1977): 203–44; David Richardson, "The Eighteenth-Century British Slave Trade: New Estimates of Its Volume and Distribution," *Research in Economic History* 12 (1988); Jean Mettas, *Répertoire des expéditions négrières françaises au XVIIIe siècle*, 2 vols. (Paris, 1978–84); Serge Daget, *Répertoire des expéditions négrières françaises à la traite illegale (1814–1850)* (Nantes, 1988); Colin Palmer, *Human Cargoes: The British Slave Trade to Spanish America, 1700–1739* (Chicago, 1981); Daniel R. Mannix and Malcolm Cowley, *Black Cargoes: A History of the Atlantic Slave Trade, 1518–1865* (New York, 1962). For reviews of the trade as a whole, see David Henige, "Measuring the Immeasurable: The Atlantic Slave Trade, West African Population and the Pyrrhonian Critic," *Journal of African History* 27 (1986): 295–313; David

Richardson, "Slave Exports from West and West-Central Africa, 1700–1810: New Estimates of Volume and Distribution," *Journal of African History* 30 (1989): 1–22; Roger Anstey, *The Atlantic Slave Trade and British Abolition, 1760–1810* (London, 1975); Stanley Engerman and Eugene Genovese, eds., *Race and Slavery in the Western Hemisphere: Quantitative Studies* (Princeton, N.J., 1975); James A. Rawley, *The Transatlantic Slave Trade: A History* (New York, 1981); Paul E. Lovejoy, "The Impact of the Atlantic Slave Trade on Africa: A Review of the Literature," *Journal of African History* 30 (1989): 363–94. For the row between Curtin and Inikori, see J. E. Inikori, "Measuring the Atlantic Slave Trade: An Assessment of Curtin and Anstey," *Journal of African History* 17 (1976): 197–223; Philip D. Curtin, "Measuring the Atlantic Slave Trade Once Again," *Journal of African History* 17 (1976): 595–605; and R. Anstey, "The British Slave Trade 1751–1807: A Comment," *Journal of African History* 17 (1976): 606–7.

Of course, most of the preceding work either rests upon or grapples with the pioneering research of Philip D. Curtin's *Atlantic Slave Trade: A Census* (Madison, 1969).

3. See Lovejoy, "Impact of the Atlantic Slave Trade," 368; Curtin, *Atlantic Slave Trade*; Richardson, "Slave Exports"; Mettas, *Répertoire*; Anstey, *Atlantic Slave Trade*; Rawley, *Transatlantic Slave Trade*; Henige, "Measuring the Immeasurable"; Inikori, *Forced Migration*.

4. Attenuation of the import estimates for North America is appropriate. Curtin's estimate of 399,000 for British North America, plus 28,300 for Louisiana give a total of 427,300 (Curtin, *Atlantic Slave Trade*, 74–91). The numbers on Louisiana are very tentative and conservative. Anstey contends that Curtin's figures for the British slave trade between 1761 and 1807 should be revised upward by 10.3 percent (a revision accepted by Curtin); if we also assume that imports into the United States were similarly higher by the same proportion, this would mean that an additional 18,272 Africans should be added to the North American total, rendering a sum of 445,572 (Roger Anstey, "The Volume and Profitability of the British Slave Trade, 1761–1807," in Engerman and Genovese, *Race and Slavery*, 3–31). To this figure must be added Rawley's calculation that between 1626 and 1700 some 28,500 Africans were imported into British North America, a period not included in Curtin's estimates for North America. The new total becomes 474,072 (Rawley, *Transatlantic Slave Trade*, 167).

The estimate for the trade to Louisiana is calculated as follows: from 1719 to 1763, 18,928 Africans were imported, assuming 7,000 arrivals by 1735 and an annual import rate of 426 between 1735 and 1763 (Curtin, *Atlantic Slave Trade*, 82–83, 216). The trade was actually cut off for many of these years.

Along with an illegal British trade from West Florida beginning in the 1750s, the Spanish period saw a brisk trade in slaves from 1763 to 1788 (although the Spanish did not actually take control until 1769), estimated at 10,650 (ibid., 82–83, 216; Gwendolyn Midlo Hall, *Africans in Colonial Louisiana: The Development of Afro-Creole Culture in the Eighteenth Century* [Baton Rouge, 1992], 277–80). The next period, 1788 to 1803, saw the trade drop in the first half of the 1790s, reopen in 1795, and close again until 1800, when slaves entered until the U.S. takeover in 1803. In the absence of quantifiable data, however, a conservative estimate of 100 per annum yields a total of 1,500 (Paul Lachance, "The Politics of Fear: French Louisianians and the Slave Trade, 1786–1809," *Plantation Society in the Americas* 1 [1979]: 162–97; Curtin, *Atlantic Slave Trade*, 83).

The estimate for 1804 to 1808 is based upon Lachance's argument that the 1810 slave population of 34,660 is to an extent derived from imports in 1806 and 1807 (Lachance, "Politics of Fear," 167, 180–81, 186–87). The 1810 figure includes some 3,226 slaves imported between 1809 and 1810. If these years are excluded, it means the slave population increased by 6,634 between 1806 and 1808, or an annual increase of 13.4 percent for two years. When adjusted for a natural increase of 2 percent per year (Lachance argues for a 1.6

percent natural increase per annum from 1788–1806 in "Politics of Fear," 167, whereas Midlo Hall believes there was a slight natural decrease), it means that the remaining 11.4 percent increase is directly attributable to slave imports. Thus for 1806 some 2,827 slaves were imported, while 3,149 were brought in during 1807. Assuming a modest increase of 200 African slaves per annum for the years 1804 and 1805, and that at least 40 percent of those imported in 1806 and 1807 were born in Africa, the total number of African imports for the period 1804 to 1808 was around 2,790 (the 40 percent calculation is based upon table 4 of Paul Lachance's "'Ties That Can Be Called Familial': Saint-Domingue Refugees in New Orleans and Their Families" [paper presented at the International Conference on Family and Slavery in the Americas, University of Montreal, October 1994]; by permission of the author).

From 1809 to 1810, some 3,226 slaves entered New Orleans from Saint Domingue via Cuba, along with 5,883 whites or free persons of color. Assuming 40 percent were African-born renders a total of 1,290. It must be remembered that after 1803, there were substantial reshipments of Africans from Charleston until well after 1808. Midlo Hall is looking into this.

The total from all five periods is 35,158, which is substituted for Curtin's estimate of 28,300 for Louisiana. This gives a new total for the trade to British North America at 445,772. The new, low total for the whole of the trade to North America is therefore 480,930.

5. One problem with calculating the North American share of the trade is the relationship to the Caribbean and potential double-counting; it would appear, however, that no more than 10 percent of those imported into North America came by way of the West Indies. See Susan Westbury, "Slaves of Colonial Virginia: Where They Came From," *William and Mary Quarterly* 42 (1985): 228–37; Peter H. Wood, *Black Majority: Negroes in Colonial South Carolina* (New York, 1974), 43–45; W. Robert Higgins, "Charleston: Terminus and Entrepot of the Colonial Trade," in *The African Diaspora: Interpretive Essays*, ed. Martin L. Kilson and Robert I. Rotberg (Cambridge, Mass., 1976), 115; Frederic Bancroft, *Slave-Trading in the Old South* (Baltimore, 1931), 2–4; and Darold D. Wax, "Preferences for Slaves in Colonial America," *Journal of Negro History* 58 (1973): 374–75.

Much more difficult is the challenge of accounting for slaves imported illegally. Given its clandestine nature, research has yet to establish any credible quantification for the post-1807 enterprise. Indeed, slave ships were arriving on American shores as late as 1858; the *Clotilde* and the *Wanderer* disembarked on the coasts of Alabama and Georgia respectively in 1858 with hundreds of Africans. Such anecdotal information, however, does not lend itself to empirical study. Curtin's suggestion of 54,000 may be too conservative, whereas the 270,000 figure originally offered by Du Bois is supported by McClelland and Zeckhauser. See Curtin, *Atlantic Slave Trade*, 15–23, 74–75 (on the illegal trade from 1808 to 1861, Curtin is entirely arbitrary and states: "Only a shot in the dark is possible: a figure of perhaps 1,000 a year is not unreasonable."); John Hope Franklin and Alfred A. Moss Jr., *From Slavery to Freedom: A History of African Americans*, 7th ed. (New York, 1994), 120–21. On the illegal trade in Louisiana and the Bowie brothers, see Joe Gray Taylor, "The Foreign Slave Trade in Louisiana after 1808," *Louisiana History* 1 (1960): 36–43; and James Paisley Hendrix Jr., "The Efforts to Reopen the African Slave Trade in Louisiana," *Louisiana History* 10 (1969): 97–123. For an account of illegal activity near Mobile, see the *Alabama Republican*, 18 May 1821; Charles J. Montgomery, "Survivors from the Cargo of the Negro Slave Yacht *Wanderer*," *American Anthropology* 10 (October 1908): 611–23; and Zora Neale Hurston, "Cudjo's Own Story of the Last African Slaver," *Journal of Negro History* 12 (1967): 648–63. Finally, on overall estimates, see W. E. B. Du Bois, *The Suppression of the African Slave Trade to the United States of America, 1638–1870* (New York, 1904), 112–30;

and Peter D. McClelland and Richard J. Zeckhauser, *Demographic Dimensions of the New Republic: American Interregional Migration, Vital Statistics, and Manumissions, 1800–1860* (New York, 1982), 20–21, 44–49, 135–37. See also Michael Tadman, *Speculators and Slaves: Masters, Traders, and Slaves in the Old South* (Madison, 1989), 238–40.

6. Rawley, *Transatlantic Slave Trade*, 17.

7. Richardson, "Slave Exports," 8–11. The figure of 6.5 million takes into account Lovejoy's assessment that Richardson's estimate of 6,686,000 for the British eighteenth-century trade is 156,000 too high (Lovejoy, "Impact of the Atlantic Slave Trade," 370–73).

8. Curtin, *Atlantic Slave Trade*, 265.

9. According to Richardson, the fluctuations in the import rates were not as great as Lovejoy had suggested. See Richardson, "Slave Exports," 8–11; and Lovejoy, "Impact of the Atlantic Slave Trade," 365–72.

10. Richardson's estimates remain very useful, notwithstanding Lovejoy's contention that the former's estimates are about 156,000 too high (Lovejoy, "Impact of the Atlantic Slave Trade," 370–71).

11. Rawley upwardly adjusts Curtin's original estimates for the years prior to 1701. However, these figures do not take into account the illegal slave trade nor the Louisiana contingent.

12. See table 2.1. Richardson's contribution does not call into question that some 150,800 were imported between 1720 and 1760, but rather that there were probably substantially more imported between 1720 and 1740, and correspondingly less between 1740 and 1760, than table 2.2 indicates.

13. According to Stetson, as quoted by Curtin in *Atlantic Slave Trade*, 158.

14. Franklin and Moss, *Slavery to Freedom*, 57.

15. Westbury has examined the question of whether these Africans brought to Virginia were of West Indian or African origin. For the 1,300 arriving between 1670 and 1698 the question is difficult to answer, but for 1699–1726 the majority of the 22,897 imported into Virginia were from Africa. The quantitative picture becomes much clearer for the period between 1727 and 1775: about 91 percent (or 41,000) came directly from Africa, the remaining 9 percent (4,000) arriving from the West Indies. Even so, it is likely that of the 9 percent West Indian figure, most were also African-born, so that Sobel's claim that more than 60,000 Africans were brought to Virginia is plausible. See Westbury, "Slaves of Colonial Virginia," 228–37; Mechal Sobel, *The World They Made Together: Black and White Values in Eighteenth-Century Virginia* (Princeton, N.J., 1987), 5–6. One of the arresting aspects of this estimate is its claim that most of the more than 60,000 came before 1740 and that only 13,000 arrived after 1750.

16. Franklin and Moss, *Slavery to Freedom*, 58.

17. Ibid.

18. Peter H. Wood, *Black Majority: Negroes in Colonial South Carolina* (New York, 1974), 3–6.

19. Franklin and Moss, *Slavery to Freedom*, 60–61.

20. Wax, "Preferences for Slaves," 371–401.

21. Wood, *Black Majority*, 36–48; Rawley, *Transatlantic Slave Trade*, 332–33; Margaret Washington Creel, *"A Peculiar People": Slave Religion and Community-Culture among the Gullahs* (New York, 1988), 34–35; Charles Joyner, *Down by the Riverside: A South Carolina Slave Community* (Urbana, 1984), 13.

22. Higgins, "Charleston," 116–17.

23. Ibid., 118.

24. Bancroft, *Slave-Trading*, 3–4.

25. Franklin and Moss, *Slavery to Freedom*, 62; Higgins, "Charleston," 130.

26. Franklin and Moss, *Slavery to Freedom*, 62.

27. Higgins, "Charleston," 129–30.

28. Midlo Hall, *Africans in Colonial Louisiana*, 10, 34–35, 60.

29. Louisiana would be returned to France in 1800, although actual retrocession did not take place until 1 December 1803. By that time, events in Haiti (Saint Domingue) necessitated the sale of Louisiana to the United States in late December 1803.

30. Based upon Curtin's estimates. See note 4 in this chapter.

31. See Wood, *Black Majority*, 4–6; Julia Floyd Smith, *Slavery and Plantation Growth in Antebellum Florida, 1821–1860* (Gainesville, 1973), 9–27; Charles Loch Mowat, *East Florida as a British Province, 1763–1784* (Gainesville, 1943); James Pope-Hennessy, *Sins of the Fathers: A Study of the Atlantic Slave Traders (1441–1807)* (New York, 1968), 3; and Robert L. Hall, "African Religious Retentions in Florida," in *Africanisms in American Culture*, ed. Joseph E. Holloway (Bloomington, 1990), 98–118.

32. Rawley, *Transatlantic Slave Trade*, 332.

33. Washington Creel, *"Peculiar People,"* 33–34.

34. Sobel, *World They Made Together*, 3–5.

35. Herskovits, *Myth of the Negro Past*, 120.

36. Ibid., 122.

37. Franklin and Moss, *Slavery to Freedom*, 123–24.

38. Eugene Genovese, *Roll, Jordan, Roll: The World the Slaves Made* (New York, 1971), 7–10.

39. Sobel, *World They Made Together*, 3. Mullin, while acknowledging that his generalizations are based upon the investigation of a single Virginian county (Carolina), proposes that "small slave owners . . . provided the market for Africans"; he also refers to large slaveholders as "patriarchs" whose family included the slaves and about whom he knew a great deal. See Gerald W. Mullin, *Flight and Rebellion: Slave Resistance in Eighteenth-Century Virginia* (New York, 1972), 13–15, 19–30.

40. Kenneth M. Stampp, *The Peculiar Institution* (New York, 1956), 31–32.

41. William D. Piersen, *Black Yankees: The Development of an Afro-American Subculture in Eighteenth Century New England* (Amherst, 1988).

42. Ibid., 26.

43. Ibid., 18.

44. Stampp, *Peculiar Institution*, 31–33.

45. Curtin separates Sierra Leone from the Windward Coast (essentially Liberia and the Ivory Coast), whereas Richardson combines them for two reasons: Inikori's criticism of the Windward Coast construction (Inikori, "Measuring the Atlantic Slave Trade," 197–223, 607–27); and the objection that Curtin's export estimates for the Windward Coast are too high, and that a "large" (but unquantified) number of slaves he initially assigned to the Windward Coast actually came from the area he calls Sierra Leone (see Adam Jones and Marion Johnson, "Slaves from the Windward Coast," *Journal of African History* 21 [1980]: 17–34).

46. Curtin's estimates (*Atlantic Slave Trade*, 156–58) are based upon data from Virginia, South Carolina, and the British trade as a whole, with each component weighted at one-third: Senegambia, 13.3 percent; Sierra Leone, 5.5 percent; Windward Coast, 11.4 percent; Gold Coast, 15.9 percent; Bight of Benin, 4.3 percent; Bight of Biafra, 23.3 percent; Angola, 24.5 percent; Mozambique-Madagascar, 1.6 percent; and unknown, .2 percent. Richardson's estimates ("Slave Exports," 12–14) are derived from the coastal distribution of the British export trade from 1700 to 1807: Senegambia, 6.2 percent; Sierra Leone, 15.5 percent; Gold Coast, 13.1 percent; Bight of Benin, 7.5 percent; Bight of Biafra, 37.1 percent; and West Central Africa, 20.5 percent (for a total of 99.9 percent). The composite estimate

was created by substituting Richardson's relative totals for the British trade for Curtin's; these totals together with the Virginia and South Carolina estimates cited by Curtin were then each weighted at one-third. The remaining .1 percent of the total can be accounted for by both the Mozambique-Madagascar contribution and by the unknown factor.

See also Mettas, *Répertoire*, passim; David Geggus, "Sex Ratio, Age and Ethnicity in the Atlantic Trade: Data from French Shipping and Plantation Records," *Journal of African History* 30 (1989): 23–44. This research focuses on French participation in the trade and does not directly concern us here.

47. For example, see Lovejoy, "Impact of the Atlantic Slave Trade," 374.

48. Gwendolyn Midlo Hall, *Slavery and Race Relations in French, Spanish, and Early American Louisiana: A Comparative Study* (Chapel Hill, forthcoming). These new estimates were rough calculations at the time of this writing, but they compare favorably with her figures in *Africans in Colonial Louisiana*, app. C, table 2, 402–4. Consider the following:

	Slavery and Race	*Africans in Colonial Louisiana*
Senegambia	27.6%	27.1%
Bight of Benin	20.4%	28.7%
Bight of Biafra	8.6%	11.5%
Central Africa	35.8%	23.8%
Upper Guinea	5.3%	1.8% (Sierra Leone)
		3.9% (Windward Coast)
Gold Coast	1.1%	1.3%
Mozambique	1.2%	2.0%

While tentative, it is interesting to note that the percentages representing the Bight of Benin, the Bight of Biafra, and Central Africa are fairly consistent with the data on French and Saint Domingue plantations (see Lovejoy, "Impact of the Atlantic Slave Trade," 376–78).

49. Curtin, *Atlantic Slave Trade*, 125.

50. Elizabeth Donnan, *Documents Illustrative of the History of the Slave Trade to America* (Washington, D.C., 1930), 1:94.

51. Curtin, *Atlantic Slave Trade*, 96–126; Lovejoy, *Transformations in Slavery*, 35–37.

52. Curtin, *Atlantic Slave Trade*, 122.

53. Ibid.

54. Ibid.

55. Lovejoy, "Impact of the Atlantic Slave Trade," 381–86; Manning, *Slavery and African Life*, 97–98.

56. Tadman, *Speculators and Slaves*, 238 n. 3. Such a picture is incomplete, however, given the fact that children under fourteen years of age, who comprised a significant proportion of the import population, are not included in the profiles.

57. John W. Blassingame, *The Slave Community: Plantation Life in the Antebellum South* (New York, 1972), 149–50.

58. David Eltis and Stanley L. Engerman, "Was the Slave Trade Dominated by Men?," *Journal of Interdisciplinary History* 23 (1992): 251; Lovejoy, "Impact of the Atlantic Slave Trade," 382–83.

59. Manning, *Slavery and African Life*, 98–99. These figures are entirely consistent with Eltis and Engerman's estimates of children exported from the Bight of Biafra. According to them, the figure rises from 30 percent in 1775 to 44 percent by 1835 ("Was the Slave Trade Dominated by Men?," 252).

60. Eltis and Engerman, "Was the Slave Trade Dominated by Men?," 254.

61. Lovejoy, "Impact of the Atlantic Slave Trade," 384–85.

62. Eltis and Engerman maintain that although the export estimates of children from the Bight of Biafra and Angola are high, their importation into British America, which includes North America, rose and fell to only 9 percent between 1675 and 1800, with a high point of 20 percent in 1735 ("Was the Slave Trade Dominated by Men?," 252–53). Their explanation for this apparent discrepancy, which includes a reference to the Dolben Act of 1788 within the context of British abolitionist activity, does not necessarily apply to the United States. Further, British America would include the West Indies, into which considerable numbers of Africans were being imported. The area that would become the United States had unique tastes, as this investigation seeks to demonstrate. Given the U.S. focus on the Bight of Biafra and Angola, it seems fair to conclude that those exported from such areas found their way into the United States in sex and age ratios similar (if not identical) to those of their departure.

CHAPTER 3

1. Lathan Windley, comp., *Runaway Slave Advertisements: A Documentary History from the 1730s to 1790* (Westport, Conn., 1983), 3:31.

2. Ibid., 27.

3. Ibid., 45.

4. Ibid., 51–53.

5. Ibid., 108.

6. Ibid., 151–52.

7. Ibid., 4:38.

8. Ibid., 3:440–41.

9. Ibid., 4:32–33.

10. Ibid., 3:624–25.

11. Ibid., 224, 244–45.

12. Guion G. Johnson, *A Social History of the Sea Islands, with Special Reference to St. Helena Island, South Carolina* (Chapel Hill, 1930), 33.

13. Darold D. Wax, "Preferences for Slaves in Colonial America," *Journal of Negro History* 58 (1973): 391–93.

14. James A. Rawley, *The Transatlantic Slave Trade: A History* (New York, 1981), 334.

15. *Gazette of the State of Georgia*, 2 April 1795.

16. Peter H. Wood, *Black Majority: Negroes in Colonial South Carolina* (New York, 1974), 36–37, 58–62.

17. Richard Jobson, *The Golden Trade, or a Discovery of the River Gambra, and the Trade of the Aethiopians* (London, 1623; reprint, London, 1968), 49; Michel Adanson, *Voyage to Senegal* (London, 1759), 166; J. P. L. Durand, *A Voyage to Senegal* (London, 1806), 102; Joseph Corry, *Observations upon the Windward Coast of Africa* (London, 1807; reprint, London, 1967), 37. Mollien, traveling in Futa Toro, stated that he saw "the environs of Senopale, chiefly covered with fields of rice, the quality of which I will venture to say, equals that of Carolina." G. Mollien, *Travels in the Interior of Africa to the Sources of the Senegal and Gambia* (London, 1820), 124.

18. Charles Joyner, *Down by the Riverside: A South Carolina Slave Community* (Urbana and Chicago, 1984), 13.

19. *Virginia Gazette* (Williamsburg), 29 October–5 November 1736.

20. Ibid., 24 February–1 March 1737.

21. Ibid., 14–21 July 1738.

22. Ibid., 10–17 August 1739.

23. Ibid., 30 May–6 June 1745.

24. George P. Rawick, *The American Slave: A Composite Autobiography* (Westport, Conn., 1972–77), 4:42.

25. Joyner, *Down by the Riverside*, 14–15, 57–59.

26. Ibid., 57–59.

27. Windley, *Runaway Slave Advertisements*, 1:14–15; *Virginia Gazette*, 17–24 October 1745.

28. *Virginia Gazette*, 14–21 April 1738.

29. Windley, *Runaway Slave Advertisements*, 2:381.

30. Curtin, *Atlantic Slave Trade*, 156–57.

31. Patrick Manning, *Slavery and African Life: Occidental, Oriental, and African Slave Trades* (Cambridge, 1990), 98; David Geggus, "Sex Ratio, Age and Ethnicity in the Atlantic Trade: Data from French Shipping and Plantation Records," *Journal of African History* 30 (1989): 23–44. However, see Peter Caron, " 'Of a nation which the others do not Understand': Bambara Slaves and African Ethnicity in Colonial Louisiana, 1718–60," *Slavery and Abolition* 18 (1997): 98–121, who questions whether those described as Bambara actually were so.

32. Windley, *Runaway Slave Advertisements*, 3:203.

33. Ibid., 462–63.

34. *Gazette of the State of Georgia*, 27 November 1787.

35. *Louisiana Gazette*, 14 June 1810.

36. *Moniteur de la Louisiane*, 11 October 1806.

37. Gwendolyn Midlo Hall, *Africans in Colonial Louisiana: The Development of Afro-Creole Culture in the Eighteenth Century* (Baton Rouge, 1992), 41–55, 284–91.

38. Gwendolyn Midlo Hall, *Slavery and Race Relations in French, Spanish, and Early American Louisiana: A Comparative Study* (Chapel Hill, forthcoming); by Midlo Hall's earlier calculations (*Africans in Colonial Louisiana*, 403–4), Senegambians comprised 27.1 percent of the African population in Louisiana in 1771–1802, so the two estimates are consistent.

39. Geggus, "Sex Ratio, Age and Ethnicity"; Manning, *Slavery and African Life*, 97–98.

40. Midlo Hall, *Slavery and Race Relations*, and *Africans in Colonial Louisiana*, 294–301.

41. M. Saugnier and M. Brisson, *Voyages to the Coast of Africa* (London, 1792; reprint, London, 1969), 335.

42. *Moniteur de la Louisiane*, 18 July 1807.

43. *Louisiana Gazette*, 19 June 1819.

44. *Moniteur de la Louisiane*, 22 October 1808.

45. Ibid., 25 July 1807.

46. Ibid., 8 July 1807.

47. Midlo Hall, *Africans in Colonial Louisiana*, 10, 122–24.

48. Daniel H. Usner Jr., "From African Captivity to American Slavery: The Introduction of Black Louisiana to Colonial Louisiana," *Louisiana History* 20 (1979): 25–48.

49. Ibid., 34.

50. Jobson, *Golden Trade*, 34–44; Jean Barbot, *Description of the Gold Coast of Guinea* (London, 1732; reprint, London, 1992), 1:48; Frances Moore, *Travels into the Inland Parts of Africa* (London, 1738), 26–30; Mungo Park, *Travels in the Interior Districts of Africa* (London, 1799; reprint, New York, 1971), 34–59.

51. Boubacar Barry, *La Sénégambie du XVe au XIXe siècle: Traite négrière, Islam et conquête* (Paris, 1988), 25–26. See also Abdoulaye Bathily, *Les portes de l'or: Le royaume de Galam (Sénégal), de l'ère musulmane au temps des négriers (VIIe–XVIIIe siècle)* (Paris, 1989); Richard Roberts, *Warriors, Merchants, and Slaves: The State and the Economy in the Middle Niger Valley, 1700–1914* (Stanford, Calif., 1987); James Searing, *West African Slavery and Atlantic Commerce: The Senegal River Valley, 1700–1860* (Cambridge, 1993).

52. For a discussion of the upper Senegal in general and Bundu in particular, see Mi-

chael A. Gomez, *Pragmatism in the Age of Jihad: The Precolonial State of Bundu* (Cambridge, 1992). See also Charlotte A. Quinn, *Mandingo Kingdoms of the Senegambia* (Evanston, Ill., 1972); Jean Boulègue, "Contribution à la chronologie du royaume du Saloum," *Bulletin de l'Institut Fondamental d'Afrique Noire* 28 (1966): 657–62.

53. See Abdoulaye Bathily, "La traite atlantique des esclaves et ses effets économique et sociaux en Afrique: La cas du Galam, royaume de l'hinterland sénégambien au dix-huitième siècle," *Journal of African History* 27 (1986): 269–93; compare with Philip D. Curtin, *Economic Change in Precolonial Africa* (Madison, 1975).

54. For Bambara history and society, see the following works: Pascal James Imperato, *African Folk Medicine: Practices and Beliefs of the Bambara and Other Peoples* (Baltimore, 1971); Dominique Zahan, *Sociétés d'initiation Bambara* (Paris, 1960); Charles Monteil, *Les Bambara de Segou et du Kaarta* (Paris, 1924); Louis Tauxier, *La religion Bambara* (Paris, 1927); Louis Tauxier, *Histoire des Bambara* (Paris, 1942); Z. Ligers, *Les Sorko (Bozo), maîtres du Niger*, 3 vols. (Paris, 1966); André Blime, *Ségou, vieille capitale* (Angoulème, 1952); M. Delafosse, *Haut-Sénégal-Niger*, 3 vols. (Paris, 1912); Robert Pageard, *Notes sur l'histoire de Bambara de Ségou* (Clichy, 1957); and G. Dieterlen, *Essai sur la religion Bambara* (Paris, 1951).

55. Monteil, *Bambara*, 289–97, 324; Tauxier, *Histoire des Bambara*, 72–79; John Ralph Willis, "The Western Sudan from the Moroccan Invasion (1591) to the Death of al-Mukhtar al-Kunti (1811)," in *History of West Africa*, 3d ed., ed. J. F. Ade Ajayi and Michael Crowder (New York, 1985), 1:545–49.

56. Tauxier, *Histoire des Bambara*, 121–28; Willis, "Western Sudan," 1:549–51.

57. Barry, *Sénégambie*, 27.

58. Thus, the Wolof referred to the three social categories of free, caste, and slave as *baadoolo*, *neeno*, and *jam*; whereas the Malinke called the same groups the *foro*, the *namaxala*, and the *joon*. The Fulbe used the terms *riimbe*, *neenbe*, and *maacube*; while the Bambara employed the words *horon*, *namaxala*, and *jon* to describe the same social distinctions. See Hubert Deschamps, *Le Sénégal et la Gambie* (Paris, 1964); Yaya Wane, *Les Toucouleurs du Fouta Toro* (Dakar, 1969), 9; Curtin, *Economic Change*, 29–37; Barry, *Sénégambie*, 41–44, 52–53, 62; Nicholas Hopkins, "Maninka Social Organization," in *Papers on the Manding*, ed. Carleton T. Hodge (Bloomington, 1971); Paul Marty, *Etudes sénégalaises* (Paris, 1926); Paul Riesman, *Société et liberté* (Paris, 1974); and Louis Tauxier, *Moeurs et histoire des Peuls* (Paris, 1937). Domestic slavery in Africa has also become an important topic of investigation. In Senegambia, it could be divided into three parts: trade slaves, either purchased or captured and possessed no rights whatsoever; slaves "born in the house," that is, into captivity and enjoying fictive ties to the owning family; and royal slaves, usually individuals entrusted with positions of responsibility within government or the military. Although domestic slavery may antedate the transatlantic trade, the latter's commencement makes it difficult to separate the two processes; as the trade continued, these processes became indistinguishable. See Suzanne Miers and Ivor Kopytoff, eds., *Slavery in Africa: Historical and Anthropological Perspectives* (Madison, 1977); Suzanne Miers and Richard Roberts, eds., *The End of Slavery in Africa* (Madison, 1988); Claude Meillassoux, *Esclavage en Afrique précoloniale* (Paris, 1975); Claire Robertson and Martin Klein, *Women and Slavery in Africa* (Madison, 1983); Boubacar Barry, *Le royaume de Waalo: le Sénégal avant le conquête* (Paris, 1985); Frederick Cooper, "The Problem of Slavery in African Studies," *Journal of African History* 20 (1979): 103–25; Frederick Cooper, *Plantation Slavery on the East Coast of Africa* (New Haven, Conn., 1977); J. Grace, *Domestic Slavery in West Africa* (New York, 1975); H. Gemery and J. Hogendorn, eds., *The Uncommon Market: Essays in the Economic History of the Atlantic Slave Trade* (New York, 1979); J. R. Willis, ed., *Slaves and Slavery in Muslim Africa: Islam and the Ideology of Slavery*, 2 vols. (London, 1985); M. D. E. Nwulia, *The History of Slavery in Mauritius and the Seychelles, 1810–1875*

(Rutherford, N.J., 1981); and J. Watson, *Asian and African Systems of Slavery* (Berkeley and Los Angeles, 1980).

59. Michelle Gilbert, "Sources of Power in Akuropon-Akuapem: Ambiguity in Classification," in *Creativity and Power*, ed. W. Arens and Ivan Karp (Washington, D.C., 1989). Gilbert's interpretation deserves greater attention.

60. Barry, *Sénégambie*, 36; Gomez, *Pragmatism in the Age of Jihad*, 21.

61. Anne Raffenel, *Voyage dans l'Afrique occidentale . . . exécuté, en 1843 et 1844* (Paris, 1846); Anne Raffenel, *Nouveau voyage dans le pays des nègres*, 2 vols. (Paris, 1856), 1:380–84; Monteil, *Bambara*, 158, 161; Imperato, *African Folk Medicine*, 39–41. See also Willis, "Western Sudan," 1:531–76.

62. Imperato, *African Folk Medicine*, 11.

63. Speaking of accretions, Raffenel's second mid-nineteenth-century journey found Islam making rapid inroads into Bambara culture (for example, see Raffenel, *Nouveau voyage*, 1: 395–96). But only several years earlier, he claimed that "the religion of Mahomet is followed by very few of the Bambara" (*Voyage dans l'Afrique occidentale*, 299). Whatever the rapidity of Islamization, the question becomes: What was the pre-Islamic content of Bambara religion? Absent sufficient data from other contemporary sources, the anthropological record, used in ways which avoid the "ethnographic present," becomes indispensable.

64. Imperato, *African Folk Medicine*, 45–47. Raffenel says that the supreme being's name was Nallah ("evidently Allah"). Although possibly evidence of Islamic influence, *Nallah* and *Ngala* are very similar in sound to the western ear. Raffenel, *Nouveau voyage*, 1:396.

65. Raffenel, *Nouveau voyage*, 1:236–40; Tauxier, *Religion Bambara*, 1–14.

66. Tauxier, *Religion Bambara*, 15–25; Imperato, *African Folk Medicine*, 30–37.

67. See Tauxier, *Religion Bambara*, 4–13, for a discussion of spiritual categories.

68. Raffenel, *Voyage dans l'Afrique occidentale*, 299–300.

69. Midlo Hall, *Africans in Colonial Louisiana*, 9–10, 277–80.

70. Ibid., 9. Compare Midlo Hall's findings with those of Usner, "From African Captivity to American Slavery," 25–36.

71. Midlo Hall, *Africans in Colonial Louisiana*, 5–6.

72. Ibid., 162–64.

73. Ibid., 41.

74. Ibid., 187–88.

75. Ibid., 193.

76. Ibid., 168.

77. Ibid., 112.

78. Ibid., 97–98, 112, 162–63.

79. Ibid., 202–36.

80. Ibid., 206.

81. Ibid., 202.

82. Ibid., 203.

83. Ibid., 42.

84. Ibid., 317–36.

85. Ibid., 345. See also Jack D. Holmes, "The Abortive Slave Revolt at Pointe Coupee, Louisiana, 1795," *Louisiana History* 11 (1970): 341–62.

86. Midlo Hall, *Africans in Colonial Louisiana*, 362.

87. See Robin Law, *The Slave Coast of West Africa, 1550–1750* (Oxford, 1991); Patrick Manning, *Slavery, Colonialism, and Economic Growth in Dahomey, 1640–1960* (New York, 1982); Melville Herskovits, *Dahomey: An Ancient West African Kingdom*, 2 vols. (Evanston, Ill., 1938); C. W. Newbury, *The Western Slave Coast and Its Rulers* (Oxford, 1961); G. I. Jones, *The*

Trading States of the Oil Rivers (London, 1963); Daryll Forde and P. M. Kaberry, eds., *West African Kingdoms in the Nineteenth Century* (Oxford, 1967); Alan Ryder, *Benin and the Europeans, 1485–1897* (New York, 1969); Robert Smith, *Kingdoms of the Yoruba* (London, 1969).

88. A. I. Asiwaju and Robin Law, "From the Volta to the Niger, c. 1600–1800," in Ajayi and Crowder, *History of West Africa*, 1:412–64.

89. See William Snelgrave, *A New Account of Some Parts of Guinea and the Slave-Trade* (London, 1734; reprint, London, 1971), for an eyewitness account of some of these events. Compare with Paul Erdmann Isert's later perspective in *Journey to Guinea and the Caribbean Islands in Columbia (1788)*, trans. Selena Axelrod Winses (Oxford, 1992).

90. As an example of this process, see Mieko Nishida, "Manumission and Ethnicity in Urban Slavery: Salvador, Brazil, 1808–1880," *Hispanic American Historical Review* 73 (1993): 361–91. Regarding the Oyo and Ife-centered cosmology, all Yoruba believe that these two towns are at the center of creation; all Yoruba trace their ancestry back to Oyo and Ife.

91. Midlo Hall, *Slavery and Race Relations*; compare with the 28.7 percent estimate in her *Africans in Colonial Louisiana*, 284–94.

92. Paul Lachance, "The Politics of Fear: French Louisianians and the Slave Trade, 1786–1809," *Plantation Society in the Americas* 1 (1979): 187; Robert Tallant, *Voodoo in New Orleans* (London, 1962), 19–22; Lyle Saxon, Edward Dreyer, and Robert Tallant, *Gumbo Ya-Ya* (Cambridge, 1945), 225.

93. John W. Blassingame, *Black New Orleans: 1860–1880* (Chicago, 1973), 5–16.

94. For a discussion of the African background, see, for example, the following: J. O. Awolalu and P. A. Dopamu, *Yoruba Beliefs and Sacrificial Rites* (London, 1979); E. B. Idowu, *Olodumare, God in Yoruba Beliefs* (London, 1962); M. Oduyoye, *The Vocabulary of Yoruba Religious Discourse* (Ibadan, Nigeria, 1971); Julien Alapini, *Les initiés* (Avignon, 1953); Julien Alapini, *Les noix sacrées: Etude complete de Fa-Ahidegoun* (Monte Carlo, 1950); E. M. McClelland, *The Cult of Ifa among the Yoruba* (London, 1982); Robert Cornevin, *Histoire du Dahomey* (Paris, 1962); Herskovits, *Dahomey*; Karl Polanyi, *Dahomey and the Slave Trade* (Seattle, 1966); Paul Mercier, "The Fon of Dahomey," in *African Worlds: Studies in the Cosmological Ideas and Social Values of African Peoples*, ed. Darryl Forde (London, 1954); Pierre Saulnier, *Le vodun Sakpata: Recherche sur le vodûn Sakpata* (Porto-Novo, 1974); Maurice A. Glele, *Le danxome: Du pouvoir Aja à la nation Fon* (Paris, 1974); A. Akindele and C. Aguessy, "Contribution à l'étude de l'histoire de l'ancien royaume de Porto-Novo," *Mémoires de l'Institut Français d'Afrique Noire* (Dakar, 1953), 25; and W. D. Hambly, *Serpent Worship in Africa* (Chicago, 1931).

Regarding the Haitian component, review as examples the following: C. L. R. James, *Black Jacobins* (New York, 1963); Alfred Metraux, *Le vaudou Haitien* (Paris, 1958); Maya Deren, *Divine Horseman: Voodoo Gods of Haiti* (New York, 1970); Melville J. Herskovits, *Life in a Haitian Valley* (Garden City, N.Y., 1971); Jean Price-Mars, "Lemba-Petro: Un culte secret," *Revue de la société d'histoire et de géographie d'Haiti* 28 (1938); Harold Courlander, *The Drum and the Hoe: Life and Lore of the Haitian People* (Berkeley and Los Angeles, 1960); Henry Gilfond, *Voodoo: Its Origins and Practices* (New York, 1976); and Kyle Kristos, *Voodoo* (Philadelphia, 1976).

Finally, consult with the following as examples of the literature on the lower Mississippi: Blassingame, *Black New Orleans*; Saxon, Dreyer, and Tallant, *Gumbo Ya-Ya*; Tallant, *Voodoo in New Orleans*; Norman Whitten and John Szwed, eds., *Afro-American Anthropology: Contemporary Perspectives* (New York, 1970); Sidney W. Mintz and Richard Price, *An Anthropological Approach to the Afro-American Past: A Caribbean Perspective* (Philadelphia, 1976); Zora Neale Hurston, "Hoodoo in America," *Journal of American Folklore* 44 (1931); James Haskins, *Voodoo and Hoodoo* (New York, 1978); James Haskins, *Witchcraft, Mysticism, and Magic in the Black World* (Garden City, N.Y., 1974); Harold Courlander, *A Treasury of African Folklore* (New York, 1975); Robert Farris Thompson, *Flash of the Spirit* (New York, 1983); Jessie

Gaston Mulira, "The Case of Voodoo in New Orleans," in *Africanisms in American Culture*, ed. Joseph E. Holloway (Bloomington, 1990).

95. For this discussion, see Mercier, "Fon of Dahomey," 212–14; Thompson, *Flash of the Spirit*, 165–67.

96. Snelgrave (*New Account*, 10–11) states that a snake is Dahomey's "principal God." Isert concurs: "The most eminent of the temples is dedicated to the snake, which is the superior godhead here" (*Journey to Guinea*, 105).

97. Thompson, *Flash of the Spirit*, 164–91.

CHAPTER 4

1. With regard to North America itself, compare the discussion of African cultural transfer in William D. Pierson's *Black Yankees: The Development of an Afro-American Subculture in Eighteenth Century New England* (Amherst, 1988) with that found in Mecham Sobel's *World They Made Together: Black and White Values in Eighteenth-Century Virginia* (Princeton, N.J., 1987) or her earlier work *Trabelin' On: The Slave Journey to an Afro-Baptist Faith* (Princeton, N.J., 1979; reprint, Princeton, N.J., 1988). Margaret Washington Creel, *"A Peculiar People": Slave Religion and Community-Culture among the Gullahs* (New York, 1988), is an equally important contribution within this framework. Finally, Michael Mullin's *Africa in America: Slave Acculturation and Resistance in the American South and the British Caribbean, 1736–1831* (Urbana, 1992) provides an examination of the relationship between "spatial peculiarities" and slave revolts, among other things.

2. Consider William S. McFeely's speculations in *Frederick Douglass* (New York, 1991), 3–5.

3. For example, see Peter H. Wood, *Black Majority: Negroes in Colonial South Carolina* (New York, 1974), and Daniel C. Littlefield, *Rice and Slaves: Ethnicity and the Slave Trade in Colonial South Carolina* (Baton Rouge, 1981).

4. Concerning sources, one of the more useful is Allan D. Austin, *African Muslims in Antebellum America: A Sourcebook* (New York, 1984). For North America, it focuses on the following seven individuals: Umar b. Said (ca. 1770–1864), Lamine Kaba (ca. 1780–?), Salih Bilali (ca. 1765–?), Bilali (contemporary of Salih Bilali), Abd al-Rahman (ca. 1762–1829), Ayuba b. Sulayman (ca. 1702–73), and Yarrow Mahmud (elderly when portrait made in 1819).

Biographical accounts include Douglas Grant's condescending *The Fortunate Slave: An Illustration of African Slavery in the Early Eighteenth Century* (London, 1968); Terry Alford's very fine *Prince Among Slaves* (New York, 1977); and Ivor Wilks's "Abu Bakr al-Siddiq of Timbuktu," and "Salih Bilali of Massina," in *Africa Remembered: Narratives of West Africans from the Era of the Slave Trade*, ed. Philip D. Curtin (Madison, 1967).

I also interviewed Cornelia Walker Bailey in July 1992 on Sapelo Island, Georgia. She was born in Bell Marsh on 12 June 1945. Bilali is her great-great-great-grandfather through his daughter Bentoo (Arabic "Binta"). Bailey presently lives in Hog Hammock Community on Sapelo with her husband and family. The interview was taped, and notes were taken during the interview. Both the tapes and the notes are in the author's possession.

Concerning Muslim names, there is no standard method of transliteration into English. For example, just as the word *muslim* is often anglicized as *moslem*, so names such as "Sulayman" may appear as "Sulaiman" and "Muhammad" as "Mohammed." The approach used here is to employ a scheme of vowelization that most closely approximates standard Arabic. However, it must be kept in mind that Arabic names often underwent changes in West Africa, and in such cases, it is the African appellation that will be transliterated. That is, because it is common in West Africa to encounter "Mamadu" as opposed to "Mahmud" or "Ahmad," "Mamadu" will be used here.

Finally, the names of some individuals are rendered slightly different in English due to corruption and/or a lack of familiarity with the meaning and functions of the components of the name. For example, Ayuba b. Sulayman belongs to the Jallo clan of the Fulbe, and sometimes Jallo will be attached to the end of his name. In many instances "Jallo" will be written as "Diallo," owing to the French influence. The anglicizing of African and Arab names is problematic, to be sure. For the purposes of this study, care will be taken to make a full identification of the individual in question.

5. Jean Suret-Canale and Boubacar Barry, "The Western Atlantic Coast to 1800," in *History of West Africa*, 2d ed., ed. J. F. Ade Ajayi and Michael Crowder (New York, 1976), 1:466; Paul Lovejoy, *Transformations in Slavery: A History of Slavery in Africa* (Cambridge, 1983), 58.

6. G. R. Crone, ed. and trans., *The Voyages of Cadamosto* (London, 1937), 31.

7. G. Mollien, *Travels in the Interior of Africa to the Sources of the Senegal and Gambia* (London, 1820), 61.

8. Jean Boulègue and Jean Suret-Canale, "The Western Atlantic Coast," in *History of West Africa*, 3d ed., ed. J. F. Ade Ajayi and Michael Crowder (New York, 1985), 1:519.

9. Richard Jobson, *The Golden Trade, or a Discovery of the River Gambra, and the Trade of the Aethiopians* (London, 1623; reprint, London, 1968), 78–99; Frances Moore, *Travels into the Inland Parts of Africa* (London, 1738), 12–26; Mungo Park, *Travels in the Interior Districts of Africa* (London, 1799), 15–35; William Smith, *A New Voyage to Guinea* (London, 1744; reprint, London, 1967), 26–27.

10. M. Saugnier and M. Brisson, *Voyages to the Coast of Africa* (London, 1792; reprint, London, 1969), 220; Major William Gray and Surgeon Dochard, *Travels in Western Africa, in the Years 1818, 19, 20, and 21* (London, 1825), 266.

11. Lovejoy, *Transformations in Slavery*, 72–73.

12. Philip D. Curtin, *The Atlantic Slave Trade: A Census* (Madison, 1969), 96–126; Lovejoy, *Transformations in Slavery*, 35–37.

13. The term *tubenan* is from the Arabic *tawba*, or "to repent"; the Wolof word *tub* essentially carries the same meaning. For more on the *tubenan*, or "guerre des marabouts," see Philip D. Curtin, "Jihad in West Africa: Early Phases and Inter-Relations in Mauritania and Senegal," *Journal of African History* 12 (1971): 11–24; Boubacar Barry, "La guerre des marabouts dans la region du fleuve Sénégal de 1673 à 1677," *Bulletin de l'Institut Fondamental* (formerly *Français*) *d'Afrique Noire* 33 (1971): 564–89.

14. Suret-Canale and Barry, "Western Atlantic Coast," 1:470.

15. P. Cultru, *Premier voyage du Sieur de la Courbe fait à la Coste d'Afrique en 1685* (Paris, 1913), 30.

16. David Robinson, "The Islamic Revolution of Futa Toro," *International Journal of African Historical Studies* 8 (1975): 185–221.

17. Michael A. Gomez, *Pragmatism in the Age of Jihad: The Precolonial State of Bundu* (Cambridge, 1992); Abdoulaye Bathily, "La traite atlantique des esclaves et ses effets économiques et sociaux en Afrique: La cas du Galam, royaume de l'hinterland sénégambien au dix-huitième siècle," *Journal of African History* 27 (1986): 269–93; compare with Philip D. Curtin, *Economic Change in Precolonial Africa* (Madison, 1975).

18. Anne Raffenel, *Voyage dans l'Afrique occidentale . . . executé, en 1843 et 1844* (Paris, 1846), 299.

19. John Matthews, *A Voyage to the River Sierra-Leone* (London, 1788; reprint, London, 1966), 17–18; compare with Joseph Corry, *Observations upon the Windward Coast of Africa* (London, 1807; reprint, London, 1967), 41–44.

20. Walter Rodney, *A History of the Upper Guinea Coast* (Oxford, 1970), 95–113 (quoted phrase on 112).

21. Ibid., 244–55.

22. Ibid., 272; Thierno Diallo, *Les institutions politiques du Foûta Djalon au XIXe siècle* (Dakar, 1972), 20–34.

23. See the following for a discussion of causal possibilities: Boubacar Barry, *Le royaume du Waalo: Le Sénégal avant le conquête* (Paris, 1985); Suret-Canale and Barry, "Western Atlantic Coast"; William Derman and Louise Derman, *Serfs, Peasants, and Socialists: A Former Serf Village in the Republic of Guinea* (Berkeley and Los Angeles, 1973); Joye Bowman Hawkins, "Conflict, Interaction, and Change in Guinea-Bissau: Fulbe Expansion and Its Impact, 1850–1900" (Ph.D. diss., UCLA, 1980); and Joseph Earl Harris, "The Kingdom of Fouta Diallon" (Ph.D. diss., Northwestern University, 1965).

24. Gray and Dochard, *Travels in Western Africa*, 39–40; René Callié, *Travels through Central Africa to Timbuctoo* (London, 1830), 222.

25. Suret-Canale and Barry, "Western Atlantic Coast," 1:493–95; Alfa Ibrahim Sow, *Chroniques et récits du Foûta Djalon . . .* (Paris, 1968), 15.

26. Lovejoy, *Transformations in Slavery*, 59.

27. Ibid., 56.

28. See Ivor Wilks, *Asante in the 19th Century: The Structure and Evolution of a Political Order* (London, 1975); Lovejoy, *Transformations in Slavery*, 56.

29. Wilks, *Asante in the 19th Century*; Peter B. Clarke, *West Africa and Islam* (London, 1982), 50–60; Melville Herskovits, *The Myth of the Negro Past* (New York, 1941); and Melville Herskovits, *The New World Negro* (Bloomington, 1966), 90–93.

30. Lovejoy, *Transformations in Slavery*, 56–57 (quotation on 57).

31. João José Reis, *Slave Rebellion in Brazil: The Muslim Uprising of 1835 in Bahia*, trans. Arthur Brakel (Baltimore, 1993). Most of these "Hausas" were actually Yoruba Muslims.

32. Charles Sackett Sydnor, *Slavery in Mississippi* (New York, 1933), 141.

33. Lovejoy, *Transformations in Slavery*, 57–58; see also Paul Lovejoy, ed., *Africans in Bondage: Studies in Slavery and the Slave Trade* (Madison, 1986). Some Muslims from the wars in Adamawa also began to show up at the Cameroon coast after 1800. See Patrick Manning, *Slavery, Colonialism, and Economic Growth in Dahomey, 1640–1960* (New York, 1982).

34. Curtin, *Atlantic Slave Trade*, 157.

35. See Paul Lovejoy, "The Impact of the Atlantic Slave Trade on Africa: A Review of the Literature," *Journal of African History* 30 (1989): 363–94; James A. Rawley, *The Transatlantic Slave Trade: A History* (New York, 1981), 428; Curtin, *Atlantic Slave Trade*, 83–91.

36. For example, see the unsubstantiated estimates of Austin that 10–15 percent of all imported Africans were Muslims. Austin, *African Muslims*, 32–36.

37. For more on the Juula, see Timothy F. Garrard, *Akan Weights and the Gold Trade* (London, 1980); Ivor Wilks, "Wangara, Akan and Portuguese in the Fifteenth and Sixteenth Centuries," *Journal of African History* 23 (1982): 333–49 (pt. 1); 463–72 (pt. 2).

38. Regarding the role of clerics and amulets, see Jack Goody, ed., *Literacy in Traditional Societies* (Cambridge, 1968), and Mervyn Hiskett, *The Development of Islam in West Africa* (New York, 1984).

39. For an introductory discussion of this, see I. M. Lewis, ed., *Islam in Tropical Africa* (London, 1966), or Nehemiah Levtzion, ed., *Conversion to Islam* (New York, 1979).

40. Jane Landers, "Gracia Real de Santa Teresa de Mose: A Free Black Town in Spanish Colonial Florida," *American Historical Review* 95 (1990): 9–30.

41. Jane Landers, "Black Society in Spanish St. Augustine, 1784–1821" (Ph.D. diss., University of Florida, 1988), 27–28.

42. Gwendolyn Midlo Hall, *Africans in Colonial Louisiana: The Development of Afro-Creole*

Culture in the Eighteenth Century (Baton Rouge, 1992), 10–35; also Rawley, *Transatlantic Slave Trade*, 114–15.

43. For example, see *Moniteur de la Louisiane*, 11 September 1802, 30 July 1806.

44. Midlo Hall, *Africans in Colonial Louisiana*, 166. She goes on to say, "Some slaves with French names had Baraca, an Islamic religious title, as a second name." This is based upon the apparent use of the term *baraka* as an appellation in Louisiana; in fact, *baraka* is Arabic and means "communicable spiritual power." For more on *baraka*, see E. Westermarck, *Pagan Survivals in Mohammedan Civilization* (London, 1933), 87–144; J. O. Hunwick, "Religion and State in the Songhay Empire, 1464–1591," in I. M. Lewis, ed., *Islam in Tropical Africa* (London, 1980).

45. *Moniteur de la Louisiane*, 10 October 1807.

46. Ibid., 17 September 1808.

47. Ibid., 19 October 1808.

48. Ibid., 25 February 1809.

49. See Curtin, *Atlantic Slave Trade*, 156–57; Ulrich Bonnell Phillips, *American Negro Slavery* (Baton Rouge, 1918), 42–44; Darold D. Wax, "Preferences for Slaves in Colonial Louisiana," *Journal of Negro History* 58 (1973): 390–97; Herskovits, *Myth of the Negro Past*, 50; Marguerite B. Hamer, "A Century before Manumission: Sidelights on Slavery in Mid-Eighteenth Century South Carolina," *North Carolina Historical Review* 17 (1940): 232–36; Rawley, *Transatlantic Slave Trade*, 272–73; Elizabeth Donnan, "The Slave Trade into South Carolina before the Revolution," *American Historical Review* 33 (1928): 816–17.

50. For example, see David Duncan Wallace, *The Life of Henry Laurens* (New York, 1915), 76–77; Austin, *African Muslims*, 29.

51. Austin, *African Muslims*, 21. Midlo Hall, of course, argues that these terms were synonymous as early as the eighteenth century in Louisiana (*Africans in Colonial Louisiana*, 41–42).

52. David Richardson, "Slave Exports from West and West-Central Africa, 1700–1810," *Journal of African History* 30 (1989): 16; Lovejoy, "Impact of the Atlantic Slave Trade," 374.

53. For examples of names that probably have African origins, see Charles Lyell, *A Second Visit to the United States of America*, 2 vols. (New York, 1849), 1:263. For discussions of names as ethnic markers, see John C. Inscoe, "Carolina Slave Names: An Index to Acculturation," *Journal of Southern History* 49 (1983): 527–54; Cheryll Ann Cody, "There Was No 'Absalom' on the Ball Plantations: Slave-Naming Practices in the South Carolina Low Country, 1720–1865," *American Historical Review* 92 (1987): 563–96.

54. Lathan Windley, comp., *Runaway Slave Advertisements: A Documentary History from the 1730s to 1790*, 4 vols. (Westport, Conn., 1983); Inscoe, "Carolina Slave Names," 533–35.

55. In Hausa, "Sambo" is not a corruption of "Samba," and it means second son. However, in Mende and Vai, the name implies disgrace. See Lorenzo Dow Turner, *Africanisms in the Gullah Dialect* (Chicago, 1949; reprint, Chicago, 1974); Keith E. Baird and Mary A. Twining, "Names and Naming in the Sea Islands," in *The Crucible of Carolina: Essays in the Development of Gullah Language and Culture*, ed. Michael Montgomery (Athens, 1994).

56. Windley, *Runaway Slave Advertisements*, 4:64.

57. The evidence for Moors in America comes from Midlo Hall's research, in which the appellation "Nar," a Wolof term for "Moor," is used to characterize a number of slaves in Louisiana (*Slavery and Race*).

58. Windley, *Runaway Slave Advertisements*, 3:593.

59. Ibid., 605.

60. *Charleston Courier*, 1 May 1809.

61. The author has only partially examined early Mississippi and Louisiana newspapers. This assessment is therefore subject to revision.

62. Charles Joyner, *Down by the Riverside: A South Carolina Slave Community* (Urbana, 1984), 14–15; Wood, *Black Majority*, 58–62; Littlefield, *Rice and Slaves*, 76–98.

63. See Curtin, *Atlantic Slave Trade*, 156–58; Rawley, *Transatlantic Slave Trade*, 334–35. Littlefield (*Rice and Slaves*, 31–32) disagrees with the view that Virginian planters were unconcerned about ethnic origins. To the contrary, Littlefield maintains (based upon Wax's article "Preferences for Slaves") not only that Virginians were concerned but also that they preferred the Igbo and others from the Niger delta. Rawley, in turn, states that Virginians preferred those from the Gold Coast and Windward Coast, accepted the Igbo in large numbers, and disliked those from Angola.

64. *South Carolina Gazette*, 19 October 1738, in Windley, *Runaway Slave Advertisements*, 3:35.

65. *South Carolina Gazette*, 23 June 1757 and 1 March 1773, in Windley, *Runaway Slave Advertisements*, 3:155, 320.

66. *Georgia Gazette*, 7 September 1774, 15 March 1781, and 17 August 1774, in Windley, *Runaway Slave Advertisements*, 3:56, 89, 54–55.

67. *Edenton Gazette and North Carolina Advertiser*, 23 June 1808.

68. *Charleston Courier*, 19 June 1808.

69. *Gazette of the State of Georgia*, 7 June 1792.

70. *Royal Georgia Gazette*, 4 October 1781.

71. *Georgia Gazette*, 31 August 1774.

72. *Gazette of the State of Georgia*, 8 December 1791.

73. Austin, *African Muslims*, vii.

74. "Autobiography of Omar ibn Said, Slave in North Carolina, 1831," *American Historical Review* 30 (1925): 787–95; Dr. Bedell, "Prince Moro," *Christian Advocate* (1825): 306–7; Austin, *African Muslims*, 445–59.

75. Austin, *African Muslims*, 409–11; see also Theodore Dwight Jr., "Condition and Character of Negroes in Africa," *Methodist Quarterly Review* (January 1864): 77–90.

76. Theodore Dwight Jr., "Remarks on the Sereculehs, an African Nation Accompanied by a Vocabulary of the Language," *American Annals of Education and Instruction* 5 (1835): 451–56.

77. See Wilks, "Salih Bilali of Massina"; Austin, *African Muslims*, 309–16.

78. Lydia Parrish, *Slave Songs of the Georgia Sea Islands* (New York, 1942), 27–28; Austin, *African Muslims*, 265–68.

79. The manuscript is entitled the "Ben-Ali Diary," in the holdings of the Georgia State Law Library. See also Joseph H. Greenberg, "The Decipherment of the 'Ben-Ali Diary,' a Preliminary Statement," *Journal of Negro History* 25 (1940): 372–75; B. G. Martin, "Sapelo Island's Arabic Document: The 'Bilali' Diary in Context," *Georgia Historical Quarterly* 78 (1994): 589–601.

80. Joel Chandler Harris, *The Story of Aaron (so named), the Son of Ben Ali* (Boston, 1896).

81. See Alford, *Prince Among Slaves*; Cyrus Griffin, "The Unfortunate Moor," *African Repository* (February 1828): 364–67; Austin, *African Muslims*, 121–32.

82. See Thomas Bluett, *Some Memoirs on the Life of Job* (London, 1734); Moore, *Travels into the Inland Parts*; Philip D. Curtin, "Ayuba Suleiman Diallo of Bondu," in Curtin, *Africa Remembered*; Grant, *Fortunate Slave*.

83. Austin, *African Muslims*, 68–70. Austin includes Peale's comments on Yarrow Mahmud in this account.

84. J. M. Gray, *A History of the Gambia* (Cambridge, 1940), 211–12.

85. "Autobiography of Omar ibn Said," 792–93 (quotation on 793). Austin estimates that Umar arrived in Charleston in 1807, which means that the "large army" is probably a reference to the combined armies of Bundu, Kaarta, and Khasso, who invaded Futa Toro in 1806–7. See David Robinson, *Chiefs and Clerics: Abdul Bokar Kan and Futa Toro (1853–1891)*

(Oxford, 1975), 15–18; Robinson, "Islamic Revolution of Futa Toro"; Austin, *African Muslims*, 450.

86. Alford, *Prince Among Slaves*, 3–28.

87. Austin, *African Muslims*, 268. Interestingly, Cornelia Bailey says that Bilali's ethnicity was never discussed in her family, so that the Fulbe connection was not an issue (interview, July 1992).

88. Dwight, "Remarks on the Sereculehs," 451–52. For more on the Jakhanke, see Lamin O. Sanneh, *The Jakhanke: The History of an Islamic Clerical People of the Senegambia* (London, 1979), and Thomas Hunter, "The Development of an Islamic Tradition of Learning among the Jahanka of West Africa" (Ph.D. diss., University of Chicago, 1977).

89. Wilks, "Abu Bakr al-Siddiq of Timbuktu," 152–69.

90. Wilks, "Salih Bilali of Massina," 309–16.

91. Curtin, *Economic Change*, 159–68.

92. Austin, *African Muslims*, 68–70.

93. Grant, *Fortunate Slave*, 82–84.

94. Ibid.

95. Alford, *Prince Among Slaves*, 57–58; Austin, *African Muslims*, 6–7.

96. Austin, *African Muslims*, 265, 321.

97. Charles Ball, *Slavery in the United States* (New York, 1837; reprint, New York, 1969), 164–65.

98. John W. Blassingame, *The Slave Community: Plantation Life in the Antebellum South* (New York, 1979), 130–46; George P. Rawick, ed., *The American Slave: A Composite Autobiography* (Westport, Conn., 1972–77), 1:32–45.

99. Austin, *African Muslims*, 268, 313, 324–25.

100. Alford, *Prince Among Slaves*, 43–44, 77.

101. *Augusta Herald*, 11 November 1813.

102. John Stapleton Papers (South Caroliniana Library, University of South Carolina, Columbia), microfilmed on reels 6 and 7, series A, pt. 2, *Records of Ante-Bellum Southern Plantations from the Revolution through the Civil War*, Kenneth M. Stampp, gen. ed.

103. Dr. Collins, *Practical Rules for the Management and Medical Treatment of Negro Slaves* (1811), quoted in Grant, *Fortunate Slave*, 81.

104. William Dallam Armes, ed., *The Autobiography of Joseph LeConte* (New York, 1903), 29–30.

105. Austin, *African Muslims*, 129; see note 64.

106. Ibid., 265, 272–75. Cornelia Bailey maintains that Arabic was not taught but that "some African" was spoken.

107. Alford, *Prince Among Slaves*, 77–78. Two of the sons were named "Sulimina" (but called "Solomon" and "Samba").

108. *State Gazette of South Carolina*, 31 July 1786, in Windley, *Runaway Slave Advertisements*, 3:400.

109. *Runaway Slave Ads*, passim.

110. *Columbia Museum and Savannah Advertiser*, 11 May 1802.

111. Ibid., 27 March 1807.

112. State of Georgia Archives, GRG2-009 and GRG2-029 (Georgia Department of Archives and History, Atlanta).

113. Austin, *African Muslims*, 321.

114. Georgia Writers' Project, *Drums and Shadows: Survival Studies among the Georgia Coastal Negroes* (Athens, Ga., 1940), 178–83.

115. Ibid., 179–80.

116. Cornelia Bailey interview, July 1993. For more on Sapelo Island, see William S. McFeely, *Sapelo's People: A Memory of Slavery, an Appointment with Freedom* (New York, 1994).

117. Parrish, *Slave Songs*, 28 n. 22.

118. Georgia Writers' Project, *Drums and Shadows*, 158–60.

119. Ibid., 161.

120. Ibid.

121. Cornelia Bailey interview, July 1992.

122. Although Bilali was African-born, his wife and children may not have been. According to Bailey, his wife Phoebe was "from the islands" (the West Indies), meaning that she was either Caribbean-born or "seasoned" there. Because Bilali came with his entire family to Sapelo, this would mean that he also spent some time in "the islands." This, in turn, allows for the possibility that the family developed in the West Indies, rather than in Africa (Cornelia Bailey interview, July 1992).

123. Georgia Writers' Project, *Drums and Shadows*, 165–68.

124. Ibid., 164.

125. Ibid.

126. In response to a direct question about this, Bailey responded that Calina and Hannah were indeed Muslims, and that they came to Sapelo via the West Indies. Thus they could have converted to Islam while in the Caribbean (Cornelia Bailey interview, July 1992).

127. Georgia Writers' Project, *Drums and Shadows*, 120–21, 144–45, 154–56.

128. McFeely, *Frederick Douglass*, 3–5.

129. Greenberg, "Ben-Ali Diary."

130. Austin, *African Muslims*, 321.

131. Cornelia Bailey interview, July 1992.

132. Indeed, in the Georgia coastal area none of the descendants of African-born Muslims claim to be Muslim themselves in the WPA interviews.

133. For example, Rosanna Williams of Tatemville, Georgia, became so alarmed at the questions of the interviewers that she asked: "Wut yuh doin? Is yuh gonuh sen me back tuh Liberia?" (Georgia Writers' Project, *Drums and Shadows*, 71).

134. Ibid., 169–70.

135. Charles C. Jones, *The Religious Instruction of the Negroes* (Savannah, Ga., 1842), 125.

136. Cornelia Bailey interview, July 1922.

137. Newbell N. Puckett, *Folk Beliefs of the Southern Negro* (Chapel Hill, 1926), 528–29; Lyell, *Second Visit*, 1:266.

138. Phillips, *Negro Slavery*, 42.

139. Sydnor, *Slavery in Mississippi*, 141.

140. Puckett, *Folk Beliefs*, 528–29; Lyell, *Second Visit*, 1:266.

141. Collins, *Practical Rules*, 37; Austin, *African Muslims*, 81.

142. Gray and Dochard, *Travels in Western Africa*, 40; Callié, *Travels through Central Africa*, 222; Jobson, *Golden Trade*, 42.

143. Alford, *Prince Among Slaves*, 56.

144. Zephaniah Kingsley, *Treatise on the Patriarchal or Co-operative System of Society as it Exists in some Governments, and Colonies in America and in the United States under the Name of Slavery, with Its Necessity and Advantages* (1829; reprint, Freeport, N.Y., 1940), 13–14. See also Parrish, *Slave Songs*, 25; Austin, *African Muslims*, 268.

145. Ella May Thornton, "Bilali—His Book," *Law Library Journal* 48 (1955): 228–29. Cornelia Bailey disagrees with the idea that the Muslims of Sapelo enjoyed advantages over non-Muslim slaves and maintains that slaveholders treated both groups the same (Cornelia Bailey interview, July 1992).

146. For example, see Puckett, *Folk Beliefs*, 528–29.

147. See Blassingame, *Slave Community*, 73.

148. Austin, *African Muslims*, 316, 321.

149. See Austin, *African Muslims*, 448. Umar b. Said continued to implore the help of Allah and the prophet Muhammad with invocations found even within the margins of his Christian Bible.

150. Griffin, "Unfortunate Moor," 365–67.

151. Georgia Bryan Conrad, *Reminiscences of a Southern Woman* (Hampton, Va., n.d.), 13.

152. Cornelia Bailey interview, July 1992.

153. Arthur Ramos, *Negro in Brazil*, trans. Richard Pattee (Philadelphia, 1939; reprint, Philadelphia, 1980), 26.

154. For the Fulbe in West Africa, see Paul Riesman, *Freedom in Fulani Social Life* (Chicago, 1977); Victor Azarya, *Aristocrats Facing Change: The Fulbe in Guinea, Nigeria, and Cameroon* (Chicago, 1978); Marguerite Dupire, *Organisation sociale des Peul* (Paris, 1970); Maguerite Dupire, *Peuls nomades* (Paris, 1962); Paul Marty, *L'Islam en Guinée: Foûta-Diallon* (Paris, 1921); G. Vieillard, *Notes sur les coutumes des Peuls au Foûta Djallon* (Paris, 1939); Claude Rivière, *Mutations sociales en Guinée* (Paris, 1971); M. Z. Njeuma, *Fulani Hegemony in Yola (Adamawa), 1809–1902* (Yaoundé, Cameroon 1978).

155. Paul Irwin, *Liptako Speaks: History from Oral Tradition in Africa* (Princeton, N.J., 1971), 46–77.

156. Park, *Travels in the Interior Districts*, 59.

157. Bertram Wyatt-Brown, "The Mask of Obedience: Male Slave Psychology in the Old South," *American Historical Review* 93 (1988): 1228–52 (quotations on 1232).

158. Wilks, "Abu Bakr al-Siddiq," 162–63.

159. Marty, *L'Islam en Guinée*, 108–47; Jean Suret-Canale, "Touba in Guinea: Holy Place of Islam," in *African Perspectives*, ed. Christopher Allen and R. W. Johnson (Cambridge, 1870); and Gomez, *Pragmatism in the Age of Jihad*, 26–28. Curtin refers to literacy among Muslim slaves in Jamaica. See Philip D. Curtin, *Two Jamaicas: The Role of Ideas in a Tropical Colony, 1830–1865* (Cambridge, Mass., 1955), 24–25.

160. Grant, *Fortunate Slave*, 81.

161. Collins, *Practical Rules*, 81.

162. Griffin, "Unfortunate Moor," 365–67.

163. Rawick, *American Slave*, 4:290.

164. Austin, *African Muslims*, 127–31; Ball, *Slavery in the United States*, 164–65, 167, 186; see also Charles Ball, *Fifty Years in Chains, or the Life of an American Slave* (New York, 1859).

165. Robert Farris Thompson, *Flash of the Spirit* (New York, 1983), 218–23.

166. Theresa A. Singleton, "The Archaeology of the Plantation South: A Review of Approaches and Goals," *Historical Archaeology* 24, no. 4 (1990): 75.

167. Cornelia Bailey interview, July 1992.

168. See Washington Creel's *"Peculiar People,"* 320. Washington Creel maintains that the Gullah buried their dead so that the body faced the east; the practice may not, therefore, reflect a Muslim influence but a West Central African one. Little has been written on the subject, however, and additional research is warranted.

CHAPTER 5

1. Margaret Washington Creel, *"A Peculiar People": Slave Religion and Community-Culture among the Gullahs* (New York, 1988), breaks new ground in the history of African Americans by demonstrating linkages between the Sierra Leonian precursor and cultural develop-

ments among the Gullah of South Carolina. Although focused, her work has significant implications for all investigation into the cultural interplay between Africa and African Americans. As such, her contribution informs the present work in ways similar to Gwendolyn Midlo Hall's treatment of colonial Louisiana (*Africans in Colonial Louisiana: The Development of Afro-Creole Culture in the Eighteenth Century* [Baton Rouge, 1992]).

2. See Walter Rodney, *A History of the Upper Guinea Coast* (Oxford, 1970), for the definitive work on this area for the years covered. Also see Kenneth C. Wylie, *Political Kingdoms of the Temne* (New York, 1977); Kenneth Little, *The Mende of Sierra Leone* (London, 1969); Akintola J. G. Wise, *The Krio of Sierra Leone: An Interpretive History* (Freetown, Sierra Leone, 1989); Michael Jackson, *The Kuranko* (London, 1977); Christopher Fyfe, *A Short History of Sierra Leone* (London, 1979); C. Magbaily Fyle, *History and Socio-Economic Development in Sierra Leone* (Freetown, Sierra Leone, 1988); Christopher Fyfe, *A History of Sierra Leone* (Oxford, 1962); Arthur Abrahams, *The Amistad Revolt: An Historical Legacy of Sierra Leone and the United States* (Freetown, Sierra Leone, 1988); Merran McCulloch, *Peoples of Sierra Leone* (London, 1950); F. Harrison Rankin, *The White Man's Grave: A Visit to Sierra Leone in 1834* (London, 1836); H. Sawyer and W. T. Harris, *The Springs of Mende Belief and Conduct* (Freetown, Sierra Leone, 1968).

3. McCulloch, *Peoples of Sierra Leone*, 1.

4. John Matthews, *A Voyage to the River Sierra-Leone* (London, 1788; reprint, London, 1966), 18, 92–94.

5. Thomas Winterbottom, *An Account of the Native Africans in the Neighbourhood of Sierra Leone* (London, 1803; reprint, London, 1969), 2–10; Joseph Corry, *Observations upon the Windward Coast of Africa* (London, 1807; reprint, London, 1967), 134–39.

6. Fyfe, *History of Sierra Leone*, 1–2.

7. Wylie, *Political Kingdoms of the Temne*, 3.

8. Fyfe, *History of Sierra Leone*, 2; Rodney, *Upper Guinea Coast*, 102–3, 30–31.

9. Rodney, *History of the Upper Guinea Coast*, 41.

10. Ibid., 102–3, 112–13.

11. Fyfe, *History of Sierra Leone*, 2–3.

12. Ibid., 4–7; Rodney, *History of the Upper Guinea Coast*, 244–55; Fyfe, *Short History of Sierra Leone*, 12–13.

13. James A. Rawley, *The Transatlantic Slave Trade: A History* (New York, 1981), 273–74.

14. To begin the discussion of creolized African and European languages, see A. Valdman, ed., *Pidgin and Creole Linguistics* (Bloomington, 1977); R. Day, ed., *Issues in English Creoles: Papers from the 1975 Hawaiian Conference* (Heidelberg, 1980); Joseph H. Greenberg, *The Languages of Africa*, 3d ed. (Bloomington, 1970); David Dalby, *Language and History in Africa* (New York, 1970); David DeCamp and Ian F. Hancock, eds., *Pidgins and Creoles: Current Trends and Prospects* (Washington, D.C., 1974); D. Hymes, *Pidginization and Creolization of Languages* (Cambridge, 1971); and John Holm, *Pidgins and Creoles: Theory and Structure*, 2 vols. (Cambridge, 1988).

15. Fyfe, *History of Sierra Leone*, 8–9. The procedure was also called "panyarring."

16. Ibid., 112.

17. Wylie, *Political Kingdoms of the Temne*, 4–6, 15–16; Fyfe, *History of Sierra Leone*, 2–3.

18. Wylie, *Political Kingdoms of the Temne*, 15–16.

19. For an interesting discussion of trade by the Juula merchants in the southwestern Ivory Coast, which in our scheme qualifies as a part of Sierra Leone, see Robert Launay, *Traders Without Trade: Responses to Change in Two Dyula Communities* (Cambridge, 1982).

20. Little, *Mende of Sierra Leone*, 96–108; McCulloch, *Sierra Leone*, 11–21; Wylie, *Political Kingdoms of the Temne*, 6–8.

21. McCulloch (*Peoples of Sierra Leone*, 11) only includes unmarried daughters within the *mawe*; presumably, married daughters belong to the *mawe* of their husbands.

22. McCulloch, *Peoples of Sierra Leone*, 54–93.

23. Fyfe, *History of Sierra Leone*, 3.

24. Little, *Mende of Sierra Leone*, 195–96.

25. McCulloch, *History of Sierra Leone*, 9, 47–93; Fyfe, *Short History of Sierra Leone*, 3–4; Fyfe, *History of Sierra Leone*, 4; Little, *Mende of Sierra Leone*, 77–79; Daniel C. Littlefield, *Rice and Slaves: Ethnicity and the Slave Trade in Colonial South Carolina* (Baton Rouge, 1981), 76–98.

26. Littlefield, *Rice and Slaves*, 76–98.

27. See, for example, Mary A. Twining and Keith Baird, eds., *Sea Island Roots: African Presence in the Carolinas and Georgia* (Trenton, N.J., 1991); Dale Rosengarten, "Spirits of Our Ancestors: Basket Traditions in the Carolinas," in *The Crucible of Carolina: Essays in the Development of Gullah Language and Culture*, ed. Michael Montgomery (Athens, 1994); and Doris A. Derby, "Black Women Basket Makers: A Study of Domestic Economy in Charleston County, South Carolina" (Ph.D. diss., University of Illinois, Urbana, 1980).

28. For the Temne, this entity is referred to as Kuru; for the Limba, the name is Kanu or Masala or Masaranka. The Sherbro refer to this deity as Hobatoke, regarded as the father of the Sherbro who lives in the sky while married to his wife, the earth. As for the Mende, the supreme being is called Ngewo, Gewo, or Leve, and he is the creator of all. Jean Barbot, *Description of the Gold Coast of Guinea* (London, 1732; reprint, London, 1992), 221; Matthews, *Voyage to the River Sierra-Leone*, 65; J. P. L. Durand, *A Voyage to Senegal* (London, 1806), 94. McCulloch, *Peoples of Sierra Leone*, 39–40, 70–93; Little, *Mende of Sierra Leone*, 217–26; H. U. Hall, *The Sherbro of Sierra Leone* (Philadelphia, 1938), 9–11.

29. Little, *Mende of Sierra Leone*, 87.

30. Kenneth Little, "The Mende in Sierra Leone," in *African Worlds: Studies in the Cosmological Ideas and Social Values of African Peoples*, ed. Darryl Forde (London, 1954), 115–16.

31. Fyfe, *History of Sierra Leone*, 3; Winterbottom, *Account of the Native Africans*, 135–37; Corry, *Observations*, 134–39; Matthews, *Voyage to the River Sierra-Leone*, 83–85; Durand, *Voyage to Senegal*, 97–98. Durand "lifts" his discussion of the societies from Matthews.

32. Rankin, *White Man's Grave*, 2:215, 83.

33. Beryl L. Bellman, *The Language of Secrecy: Symbols and Metaphors in Poro Ritual* (New Brunswick, N.J., 1984), 3,9.

34. For example, see Edward Said's *Orientalism* (New York, 1978).

35. Fyfe, *Short History of Sierra Leone*, 3; Fyfe, *History of Sierra Leone*, 10–11; McCulloch, *Peoples of Sierra Leone*, 29–34.

36. Little, *Mende of Sierra Leone*, 243–47.

37. Ibid., 117; Hall, *Sherbro of Sierra Leone*, 6–7.

38. T. J. Alldridge, *The Sherbro and Its Hinterland* (London, 1901), 136–42.

39. Anita J. Glaze, *Art and Death in a Senufo Village* (Bloomington, 1981), 6–12, 46–73. See also B. Holas, *L'art sacré sénoufo: Ses différentes expressions dans la vie sociale* (Abidjan, Ivory Coast, 1978).

40. Glaze, *Art and Death*, 12.

41. Ibid., 12, 60–61.

42. For example, see Corry, *Observations*, 137.

43. Winterbottom, *Account of the Native Africans*, 139.

44. Glaze, *Art and Death*, 12.

45. Ibid., 46.

46. Ibid., 50–51. This is notwithstanding the fact that she cannot perform sacrifices or play the Poro drums.

47. Ibid., 48.

48. Little, *Mende of Sierra Leone*, 118–19, 244–47. Winterbottom states that males were "admitted" at age seven or eight or "rather serve a novitiate until they arrive at a proper age" (*Account of the Native Africans*, 135–36). Both Matthews (*Voyage to the River Sierra-Leone*, 83) and Corry (*Observations*, 135) say that males joined at age thirty.

49. Alldridge, *Sherbro and Its Hinterland*, 127–28; Hull, *Sherbro of Sierra Leone*, 7.

50. Corry, *Observations*, 134.

51. Alldridge, *Sherbro and Its Hinterland*, 125; Winterbottom, *Account of the Native Africans*, 135–36; see also Hall, *Sherbro of Sierra Leone*, 6.

52. Glaze, *Art and Death*, 11.

53. Ibid. In addition to the Poro and Sande were other organizations similarly structured, specializing in certain life experiences. Among the Mende, for example, the Humui was concerned with regulating sexual behavior; the Njayei sought to promote fertility of the land and was consulted in cases of mental illness, while the Wunde administered military training. The Humui and the Njayei also provided health care; for minor physical ailments, however, such as toothaches, it was common for the Mende to turn to the Kpa society, which was open to all. As was the case with the Mende, the Sherbro also had a number of societies complementing the Poro (called "Po" by the Sherbro) and the Bundu (referred to as the "Bondo"), including the Pok, the Yambo or Jambo, the Humoi (probably the equivalent of the Mende Humui), the Mane, the Ntuntung, and the Thoma. The last society, for example, admitted both women and men. See Little, *Mende of Sierra Leone*, 240, 247–53; Hall, *Sherbro of Sierra Leone*, 4–9.

54. Matthews, *Voyage to the River Sierra-Leone*, 83–85.

55. Ibid.; see Corry, *Observations*, 135–36, for a similar account.

56. Winterbottom, *Account of the Native Africans*, 135–36.

57. Kenneth Little, "The Mende Chiefdoms of Sierra Leone," in *West African Kingdoms in the Nineteenth Century*, ed. Darryl Forde and P. M. Kaberry (Oxford, 1967), 249.

58. Wylie, *Kingdoms of the Temne*, 5.

59. Little, *Mende of Sierra Leone*, 183–84.

60. Carter G. Woodson, *The African Background Outlined, or, Handbook for the Study of the Negro* (Washington, D.C., 1936), 169–70.

61. Washington Creel, *"Peculiar People,"* 2.

62. Ibid., 181.

63. Ibid., 182.

64. Ibid., 181–82.

65. George P. Rawick, *The American Slave: A Composite Autobiography* (Westport, Conn., 1972–77), 9:1459.

66. Matthews, *Voyage to the River Sierra-Leone*, 83; Winterbottom, *Account of the Native Africans*, 135–36; Rankin, *White Man's Grave*, 216.

67. Alldridge, *Sherbro and Its Hinterland*, 125.

68. Glaze, *Art and Death*, 11.

69. Washington Creel, *"Peculiar People,"* 286–97.

70. Ibid., 3.

71. Ibid., 15–19.

72. Rodney, *History of the Upper Guinea Coast*, 255.

73. Fyfe, *History of Sierra Leone*, 8–9.

74. Little, *Mende of Sierra Leone*, 73.

75. Lathan Windley, comp., *Runaway Slave Advertisements: A Documentary History from the 1730s to 1790* (Westport, Conn., 1983), 3:297.

76. Ibid., 319.

77. Ibid., 527.

78. Ibid., 4:117.

79. *South-Carolina Gazette and Country Journal*, 30 November 1773.

80. Windley, *Runaway Slave Advertisements*, 3:717.

81. Ibid., 4:53–54.

82. *Columbian Museum and Savannah Advertiser*, 12 May 1804.

83. *Republican and Savannah Evening Ledger*, 22 May 1810.

84. *South-Carolina Gazette and General Advertiser*, 22 June 1785.

85. Windley, *Runaway Slave Advertisements*, 3:670–71, 742.

86. *Georgia Gazette*, 2 September 1767.

87. *South Carolina Gazette*, 22 March 1773.

88. Marcus W. Jernegan, *Laboring and Dependent Classes in Colonial America, 1607–1783* (Chicago, 1931), 37.

89. For examples from only two newspapers, see the *Georgia Gazette*, 6 August 1766, 6 July 1768, 23 May 1770, 23 March, 1 June, 30 November 1774; and the *South Carolina Gazette*, 2 May, 6 June 1771, 23 April, 18 June 1772, 31 May 1773, 1 February 1806, 3 January 1807, 7 January, 4 March 1808.

90. *Georgia Gazette*, 30 November 1774.

91. Washington Creel, *"Peculiar People,"* 18.

92. Little, *Mende of Sierra Leone*, 73.

93. Ivor Wilks, *Forests of Gold: Essays on the Akan and the Kingdom of Asante* (Athens, Ohio, 1993), 91.

94. Madeline Manoukian, *Akan and Ga-Adangme Peoples* (London, 1950), 9–10; see also R. S. Rattray, *The Tribes of the Ashanti Hinterland*, 2 vols. (Oxford, 1923); Launay, *Traders Without Trade*.

95. Paul Lovejoy, "The Impact of the Atlantic Slave Trade on Africa: A Review of the Literature," *Journal of African History* 30 (1989): 375; Paul Lovejoy, *Transformations in Slavery: History of Slavery in Africa* (Cambridge, 1987), 55–56; Melville Herskovits, *The Myth of the Negro Past* (New York, 1941), 35. Patrick Manning states that the rise of Asante after 1700 resulted in a marked increase in the number of slaves from the region, but that they were taken from the "periphery" of the Akan population as opposed to being removed "from its core as before" (*Slavery and African Life: Occidental, Oriental, and African Slave Trades* [Cambridge, 1990], 65–66).

96. Lovejoy, *Transformations in Slavery*, 55–57; Manning, *Slavery and African Life*, 65–68.

97. Lovejoy, *Transformations in Slavery*, 56. Lovejoy argues that the surge took place in the 1780s; however, the Richardson data reveal that the only discernible surge took place in the 1790s.

98. Lovejoy, *Transformations in Slavery*, 56–57. This estimate does not include North American, Danish, or "other" carriers.

99. See Ivor Wilks, *Asante in the 19th Century: The Structure and Evolution of a Political Order* (London, 1975).

100. See Marguerite B. Hamer, "A Century before Manumission: Sidelights on Slavery in Mid-Eighteenth Century South Carolina," *North Carolina Historical Review* 17 (1940): 232–36; Elizabeth Donnan, "The Slave Trade into South Carolina before the Revolution," *American Historical Review* 33 (1927–28): 804–28; David D. Wallace, *The Life of Henry Laurens* (New York, 1915), 76–77.

101. Darold D. Wax, "Preferences for Slaves in Colonial America," *Journal of Negro History* 58 (1973): 391–94.

102. Washington Creel, *"Peculiar People,"* 30.

103. Ibid. See also Guion G. Johnson, *A Social History of the Sea Islands, with Special Reference*

to *St. Helena Island, South Carolina* (Chapel Hill, 1930), 33; Rawley, *Transatlantic Slave Trade*, 333–34.

104. Philip D. Curtin, *The Atlantic Slave Trade: A Census* (Madison, 1969), 161.

105. Philip D. Curtin, *Two Jamaicas: The Role of Ideas in a Tropical Colony, 1830–1865* (Cambridge, Mass., 1955), 24.

106. W. Robert Higgins, "Charleston: Terminus and Entrepot of the Colonial Slave Trade," in *The African Diaspora: Interpretive Essays*, ed. Martin L. Kilson and Robert I. Rotberg (Cambridge, Mass., 1976), 125. In fact, Higgins counted only three consignments arriving in Charleston from the Gold Coast.

107. Wax, "Preferences for Slaves," 395.

108. Workers of the Writers' Program of the Work Projects Administration in the State of Virginia, *The Negro in Virginia* (New York, 1940), 6–7.

109. Curtin, *Two Jamaicas*, 24.

110. Washington Creel, *"Peculiar People,"* 30.

111. Littlefield, *Rice and Slaves*, 11–14.

112. Wax, "Preferences for Slaves," 391–92.

113. Ivor Wilks, "The Mossi and the Akan States, 1400 to 1800," in *History of West Africa*, 3d ed., ed. J. F. Ade Ajayi and Michael Crowder (New York, 1985), 1:465–502.

114. See Timothy F. Garrard, *Akan Weights and the Gold Trade* (London, 1980); E. W. Bovill, *Caravans of the Old Sahara* (London, 1933); A. G. Hopkins, *An Economic History of West Africa* (New York, 1973); and Ivor Wilks, "Wangara, Akan and Portuguese in the Fifteenth and Sixteenth Centuries," *Journal of African History* 23 (1982): 333–49 (pt. 1), 463–72 (pt. 2).

115. Ivor Wilks, "The Mossi and the Akan States, 1500–1600," in *History of West Africa*, 2d ed., ed. J. F. Ade Ajayi and Michael Crowder (New York, 1976), 1:476–84.

116. See Robin Law, *The Horse in West African History* (Oxford, 1980), 13–15; Jack Goody, *Technology, Tradition, and the State in Africa* (Oxford, 1971); E. P. Skinner, *The Mossi of Upper Volta* (Oxford, 1964); and M. Izard, "Traditions historiques des villages du Yatenga: Cercle de Gourcy," *Recherches Voltaiques* (1965): 1:72–75, 129. For documents relating to Gonja, see Ivor Wilks, Nehemiah Levtzion, and Bruce Haight, eds., *Chronicles from Gonja: A Tradition of West African Muslim Historiography* (New York, 1986).

117. Wilks, *Asante in the 19th Century*, 176–77.

118. Manoukian, *Akan and Ga-Adangme*, 13–14.

119. Ibid; Wilks, "Mossi and the Akan," 3d ed., 1:491–93; L. F. Romer, *Tilforladelig Efterretning om Kysten Guinea* (Copenhagen, 1760), 185. See also Ray A. Kea, *Settlements, Trade, and Politics on the Seventeenth-Century Gold Coast* (Baltimore, 1982).

120. T. Edward Bowdich, *Mission from Cape Coast Castle to Ashantee* (London, 1819; reprint, London, 1966), 4–25; William Bosman, *A New and Accurate Description of the Coast of Guinea* (New York, 1704; reprint, New York, 1967), 1–69. Bosman in fact does not mention Asante, focusing instead on the kingdoms of "Accra, Axim, Dinkira, Akim, Acanny, Adom," and so on.

121. Christine Oppong, *Marriage Among a Matrilineal Elite* (Cambridge, 1974), 35–36.

122. Wilks, "Mossi and the Akan," 2d ed., 1:439–40; Wilks, *Asante in the 19th Century*, 61, 75, 81, 117, 137, 145.

123. Wilks, *Forests of Gold*, 66–72; T. C. McCaskie, *State and Society in Pre-colonial Asante* (Cambridge, 1995), 2.

124. I am following Wilks, *Asante in the 19th Century*, in describing the state in this way. McCaskie, however, critiques Wilks's emphasis on bureaucracy and superstructure without paying adequate attention to Asante society. McCaskie employs a Gramscian paradigm to

explain the state's ability to impose its ideology absent sufficient powers of coercion. See McCaskie, *State and Society*, 3–17, 82–90, 135.

125. Manoukian, *Akan and Ga-Adangme*, 18–21; McCaskie, *State and Society*, 26–33; K. A. Busia, "The Ashanti," in Forde, *African Worlds*, 202; M. J. Field, *Akim-Kotoku: An Oman of the Gold Coast* (London, 1970).

126. Emmanuel Akyeampong and Pashington Obeng, "Spirituality, Gender, and Power in Asante History," *International Journal of African Historical Studies* 28 (1995): 486–88.

127. McCaskie, *State and Society*, 75.

128. Manoukian, *Akan and Ga-Adangme*, 18–53; Oppong, *Marriage Among a Matrilineal Elite*, 28–29.

129. Timothy C. Weiskel, *French Colonial Rule and the Baule Peoples: Resistance and Collaboration, 1889–1911* (Oxford, 1980), 17–19.

130. So stated "Aunt Ella" regarding the capture and export of her African-born grandmother in Orland Armstrong's *Old Massa's People* (Indianapolis, 1931), 44–45. Support for Aunt Ella's statement can be found in a nineteenth-century European's observation that "the acknowledged head of a family possesses the unquestionable right to dispose of his descendants, and collateral relations, in any way that he may think fit; that they are in fact so much property, which he can sell, pawn, or give away at his pleasure." Brodie Cruickshank, *Eighteen Years on the Gold Coast of Africa* (London, 1853; reprint, London, 1966), 1:313–14.

131. Bosman, *New and Accurate Account*, 146–55. Bosman also recorded that "a great part of the Negroes believe that Man was made by Anansie, that is, a great Spider," whereas others believe in God as creator. Barbot had a similar view: "The natives of Mina . . . all live in an abominable state of idolatry and profound ignorance" (*Description of the Gold Coast*, 381). See also Cruickshank, *Eighteen Years on the Gold Coast*, 2:128–53, for another European perspective on Akan religion.

132. Michelle Gilbert, "Sources of Power in Akuropon-Akuapem: Ambiguity in Classification," in *Creativity and Power*, ed. W. Arens and Ivan Karp (Washington, D.C., 1989), 60–65.

133. Busia, "Ashanti," 192–93; McCaskie, *State and Society*, 117.

134. Gilbert, "Sources of Power," 68–71.

135. Kofi Appiah-Kubi, *Man Cures, God Heals* (Totowa, N.J., 1981), 10–11; Manoukian, *Akan and Ga-Adangme*, 58–59.

136. Manoukian, *Akan and Ga-Adangme*, 47.

137. Appiah-Kubi, *Man Cures, God Heals*, 17. See also P. Sarpong, *The Sacred Stools of the Akan* (Tema, Ghana, 1971; reprint, Tema, Ghana, 1991).

138. Gilbert, "Sources of Power," 66.

139. Manoukian, *Akan and Ga-Adangme*, 47.

140. Appiah-Kubi, *Man Cures, God Heals*, 8.

CHAPTER 6

1. Donnan, in Philip D. Curtin, *The Atlantic Slave Trade: A Census* (Madison, 1969), 156–57; Elizabeth Donnan, "The Slave Trade into South Carolina before the Revolution," *American Historical Review* 33 (1927–28): 816–17.

2. Daniel C. Littlefield, *Rice and Slaves: Ethnicity and the Slave Trade in Colonial South Carolina* (Baton Rouge, 1981), 10.

3. Ibid., 8.

4. Darold D. Wax, "Preferences for Slaves in Colonial America," *Journal of Negro History* 58 (1973): 391–94.

5. James A. Rawley, *The Transatlantic Slave Trade: A History* (New York, 1981), 334–35.

6. Ibid., 335.

7. Michael Mullin, *Africa in America: Slave Acculturation and Resistance in the American South and the British Caribbean, 1736–1831* (Urbana, 1992), 24; Mechal Sobel, *The World They Made Together: Black and White Values in Eighteenth-Century Virginia* (Princeton, N.J., 1987), 5.

8. Rawley, *Transatlantic Slave Trade*, 335; Sobel, *World They Made Together*, 5.

9. Mullin, *Africa in America*, 24.

10. Ibid., 13–14.

11. Littlefield, *Rice and Slaves*, 31–32.

12. Melville Herskovits, *The Myth of the Negro Past* (New York, 1941), 36–37.

13. Philip D. Curtin, *Two Jamaicas: The Role of Ideas in a Tropical Colony, 1830–1865* (Cambridge, Mass., 1955), 24.

14. Elizabeth Donnan, *Documents Illustrative of the History of the Slave Trade to America* (Washington, D.C., 1930), 2:15.

15. Mullin, *Africa in America*, 23–24.

16. U. B. Phillips, *American Negro Slavery* (Baton Rouge, 1969), 43.

17. Littlefield, *Rice and Slaves*, 11–14.

18. Georgia Writers' Project, *Drums and Shadows: Survival Studies among the Georgia Coastal Negroes* (Athens, Ga., 1940), 6.

19. Ibid., 15.

20. Ibid., 16.

21. Ibid., 18.

22. Ibid., 31.

23. Ibid., 48.

24. Ibid., 25. For additional references to flying Africans, see 53–54, 74–76, 100, 136–37, 149, 169.

25. Ibid., 143.

26. Ibid., 146.

27. See Sterling Stuckey, *Slave Culture: Nationalist Theory and the Foundations of Black America* (Oxford, 1987), passim.

28. Georgia Writers' Project, *Drums and Shadows*, 160.

29. Ibid., 175.

30. This incident may have taken place in 1803, when Igbo slaves transported from Savannah arrived in St. Simons. See Malcolm Bell Jr., *Major Butler's Legacy* (Athens, Ga., 1987), 132, 557. In his work on black New Englanders, William D. Piersen concurs that suicide by drowning was viewed as a "supernatural method for returning to Africa" (*Black Yankees: The Development of an Afro-American Subculture in Eighteenth Century New England* [Amherst, 1988], 75).

31. John S. Bassett, *Slavery in the State of North Carolina* (Baltimore, 1899), 92–93.

32. Charles Ball, *Slavery in the United States* (New York, 1837; reprint, New York, 1969), 219.

33. Littlefield, *Rice and Slaves*, 143–44.

34. Lathan Windley, comp., *Runaway Slave Advertisements: A Documentary History from the 1730s to 1790* (Westport, Conn., 1983), 3:254–55.

35. Ibid., 328.

36. *South-Carolina Gazette and General Advertiser*, 20–22 July 1784.

37. Windley, *Runaway Slave Advertisements*, 3:710.

38. Ibid., 372.

39. Ibid., 637.

40. Ibid., 649.

41. Ibid., 651.

42. Ibid., 79.

43. Ibid., 81.

44. Ibid., 185.

45. *South Carolina Gazette*, 21 March 1771.

46. Windley, *Runaway Slave Advertisements*, 3:348–49.

47. *Royal Georgia Gazette*, 4 January 1781.

48. Gwendolyn Midlo Hall, *Slavery and Race Relations in French, Spanish, and Early American Louisiana: A Comparative Study* (Chapel Hill, forthcoming).

49. *Moniteur de la Louisiane*, 2 December 1807 and 6 January 1808.

50. Ibid., 25 October 1806.

51. Ibid., 14 January 1809.

52. Ibid., 9 April 1808.

53. Windley, *Runaway Slave Advertisements*, 3:16.

54. Ibid., 538.

55. *Carolina Gazette*, 13 July 1804.

56. *South Carolina Weekly Gazette*, 26 July 1785.

57. Windley, *Runaway Slave Advertisements*, 3:124. However, because the name "Quamina" is Fante, it is very possible that the individual has been misidentified as Igbo.

58. David Northrup, "The Ideological Context of Slavery in Southeastern Nigeria in the 19th Century," in *Asian and African Systems of Slavery*, ed. James L. Watson (Berkeley and Los Angeles, 1980), 101–8.

59. Paul Lovejoy, "The Impact of the Atlantic Slave Trade on Africa: A Review of the Literature," *Journal of African History* 30 (1989): 375.

60. Paul Lovejoy, *Transformations in Slavery: A History of Slavery in Africa* (Cambridge, 1983), 143.

61. David Northrup, "The Growth of Trade among the Igbo before 1800," *Journal of African History* 13 (1972): 232.

62. Patrick Manning, *Slavery and African Life: Occidental, Oriental, and African Slave Trades* (Cambridge, 1990), 69.

63. E. J. Alagoa, "The Slave Trade in Niger Delta Oral Tradition and History," in *Africans in Bondage: Studies in Slavery and the Slave Trade*, ed. Paul Lovejoy (Madison, 1986), 127; Elizabeth Isichei, *The Ibo People and the Europeans* (New York, 1973), 46. See also A. J. H. Latham, *Old Calabar, 1600–1891* (Oxford, 1973); Daryll Forde, *Efik Traders of Old Calabar* (London, 1956).

64. A. E. Afigbo, *Ropes of Sand: Studies in Igbo History and Culture* (Nsukka, Nigeria, 1981), 16–17.

65. A. E. Afigbo, *The Warrant Chiefs: Indirect Rule in Southeastern Nigeria, 1891–1929* (New York, 1972), 9–12.

66. Isichei, *The Ibo People*, 17–19; Afigbo, *Ropes of Sand*, 6–7; Afigbo, *Warrant Chiefs*, 8–11; Victor Uchendu, *The Igbo of Southeastern Nigeria* (New York, 1965), 1–4.

67. S. J. S. Cookey, "An Ethnohistorical Reconstruction of Traditional Igbo Society," in *West African Culture Dynamics: Archaeological and Historical Perspectives*, ed. B. K. Swartz Jr. and Raymond E. Dumett (New York, 1980), 329–31.

68. See Timothy Shaw, *Igbo-Ukwu*, 2 vols. (Evanston, Ill., 1970); Timothy Shaw, *Unearthing Igbo-Ukwu* (Oxford, 1977).

69. Robert J. Allison, ed., *The Interesting Narrative of the Life of Olaudah Equiano, or Gustavus*

Vassa, The African. Written by Himself (London, 1789; reprint, Boston, 1995). For more on Equiano, see Catherine Obianuju Acholonu, *The Igbo Roots of Olaudah Equiano: An Anthropological Research* (Owerri, Nigeria, 1989); Folarin Shyllon, *Black People in Britain, 1555–1833* (London, 1977); S. E. Ogude, "Facts into Fiction: Equiano's *Narrative* Revisited," *Research in African Literatures* 13 (1982); G. I. Jones, "Olaudah Equiano of the Niger Ibo," in *Africa Remembered: Narratives of West Africans from the Era of the Slave Trade*, ed. Philip D. Curtin (Madison, 1967); Richard A. Coates, "Anna Maria Equiano's Epitaph," *Notes and Queries* (July/August 1977).

70. Allison, *Interesting Narrative*, 48.

71. Ibid., 52.

72. W. B. Baikie, "Summary of an Exploring Trip up the Rivers Kwora and Chadda," *Journal of the Royal Geographical Society* 25 (1855): 111.

73. John Nwachimereze Oriji, *Traditions of Igbo Origin: A Study of Pre-Colonial Population Movements in Africa* (New York, 1994), 3–20.

74. Cookey, "Ethnohistorical Reconstruction," 336–38. Cookey divides the Igbo into the western Igbo, the northern or Onitsha Igbo, the southern or Owerri Igbo, the eastern or Cross River Igbo, and the northeastern Igbo. Although the Igbo at the extremes of their territory speak dialects which are mutually unintelligible, they otherwise understand each other (Uchendu, *Igbo of Southeastern Nigeria*, 3–4).

75. Cookey, "Ethnohistorical Reconstruction," 336–39; Uchendu, *Igbo of Southeastern Nigeria*, 40–44; Philip Adigwe Oguagha and Ikechukwu Okpoko, *History and Ethnoarchaeology in Eastern Nigeria* (Oxford, 1984), 10–12.

76. Cookey, "Ethnohistorical Reconstruction," 337; Uchendu, *Igbo of Southeastern Nigeria*, 40.

77. Ambrose M. Chukwudum, *The Ancient City of Azia: A Typical Ibo Community of Old* (Ikeja, Nigeria, 1986), 172–73; Uchendu, *Igbo of Southeastern Nigeria*, 49.

78. Chukwudum, *Ancient City of Azia*; Igwebuike Romeo Okeke, *The "Osu" Concept in Igboland* (Enugu, Nigeria, 1986). Also see John E. Eberegbulam Njoku, *The Igbos of Nigeria* (New York, 1990), 27–33.

79. Oguagha and Okpoko, *History and Ethnoarchaeology*, 200.

80. C. K. Meek, *Law and Authority in a Nigerian Tribe* (New York, 1937), 18–19, 202–3.

81. Simon Ottenberg, *Masked Rituals of Afikpo: The Context of African Art* (Seattle, 1975), 9.

82. Allison, *Interesting Narrative*, 40.

83. Uchendu, *Igbo of Southeastern Nigeria*, 18; Chukwudum, *Ancient City of Azia*, 64–66.

84. Meek, *Law and Authority*, 202–3.

85. Ibid.

86. Uchendu, *Igbo of Southeastern Nigeria*, 50.

87. Meek has described it as the "almost complete absence of any higher political or social unit than the commune or small group of contiguous villages" (*Law and Authority*, 3).

88. Afigbo, *Warrant Chiefs*, 7, 16–22.

89. A. E. Afigbo, "Prolegomena to the Study of the Culture History of the Igbo-Speaking Peoples of Nigeria," in Swartz and Dumett, *West African Culture Dynamics*, 319–20; see also Ikenna Nzimiro, *Studies in Ibo Political Systems* (Berkeley and Los Angeles, 1972).

90. Afigbo, "Prolegomena," 316.

91. Ibid.

92. Uchendu, *Igbo of Southeastern Nigeria*, 22–25.

93. Cookey, "Ethnohistorical Reconstruction," 337; Oguagha and Okpoko, *History and Ethnoarchaeology*, 11–12; Uchendu, *Igbo of Southeastern Nigeria*, 40–41; C. L. Ejzu, *Ofo, Igbo Ritual Symbol* (Enugu, Nigeria, 1986).

94. Meek, *Law and Authority*, 16–17; Uchendu, *Igbo of Southeastern Nigeria*, 24–25; Oguagha and Okpoko, *History and Ethnoarchaeology*, 14, 198–99.

95. Oguagha and Okpoko, *History and Ethnoarchaeology*, 199.

96. Herbert M. Cole, *Mbari: Art and Life among the Owerri Igbo* (Bloomington, 1982), 57–58.

97. Afigbo, "Prolegomena," 316–17.

98. Oguagha and Okpoko, *History and Ethnoarchaeology*, 199, 203–4; Meek, *Law and Authority*, 25.

99. Afigbo writes: "In this way *omenala* came to be the highest law. It was distinguished from, and superior to, *iwu*, rules made by man, the transgression of which involved no offense to *ala* and the ancestors and implied no moral lapse. *Ala* was thus the guardian of Igbo morality" ("Prolegomena," 316–17).

100. Cole, *Mbari*, 53–58; Uchendu, *Igbo of Southeastern Nigeria*, 94–95; Meek, *Law and Authority*, 20–25; Afigbo, "Prolegomena," 317; Elizabeth Isichei, *A History of the Igbo People* (London, 1976), 24–28; E. E. Onyenyeli, *The Concept of God in Ibo Traditional Philosophy* (Rome, 1984); F. A. Arinze, *Sacrifice in Ibo Religion* (Ibadan, Nigeria, 1970); A. O. Chegwe, "Re-Incarnation: A Socio-Religious Phenomenon among the Ibo-Speaking Riverines of the Lower Niger," *Cahier des religions africaines* 7, no. 13 (1973): 113–35; E. Ilogu, "Worship in Igbo Traditional Religion," *Numen* 20 (1973): 230–38; C. N. Uba, "Divinities and Ancestors in Igbo Traditional Religion," *Africa* (1982): 90–105; M. C. Obiagwu, *Our Praying Fathers* (Rome, 1983); E. I. Ifesieh, "The Concept of Chineke as Reflected in Igbo Names and Proverbs," *Communio Viatorum* 25 (1983): 109–27.

101. Cole writes: "In contrast to 'dark Ala,' Amadioha is considered fair-skinned, an attitude that puts him in charge of all the light-skinned Igbo people." It is not clear whether such color consciousness developed among the Igbo prior to contact with Europeans or following it. If the former, it would add an interesting twist to the conceptualization of race in North America in a way reminiscent of the earlier discussion of the islamized Fulbe (*Mbari*, 58).

102. Ibid., 53–55.

103. John Boston, *Ikenga Figures among the North-West Igbo and the Igala* (Lagos, 1977), 16–18; Ottenberg, *Masked Rituals*, 11–12. There is either disagreement between Ottenberg and Boston or a lack of clarity. Whereas the latter claims that the masqueraders depict anonymous ancestors, the former writes that the masqueraders "are not considered to be representations of ancestors, though they, like departed persons, represent tradition" (12). If Ottenberg means by this something other than what Boston has conveyed, we have an apparent conflict of interpretation.

104. Richard Henderson, *King in Every Man* (New Haven, Conn., 1972), 107.

105. Ibid., 106–7.

106. Ibid., 107.

107. Allison, *Interesting Narrative*, 41; Isichei, *History of the Igbo People*, 25–26.

108. Uchendu, *Igbo of Southeastern Nigeria*, 16–17.

109. Ibid., 19.

110. Ibid., 19–20.

111. Henderson, *King in Every Man*, 112–20.

112. Meek, *Law and Authority*, 39.

113. Boston, *Ikenga Figures*, 14.

114. Uchendu, *Igbo of Southeastern Nigeria*, 14–17.

115. Oguagha and Okpoko, *History and Ethnoarchaeology*, 15.

116. Henderson, *King in Every Man*, 112.

117. Meek, *Law and Authority*, 165–70.

118. Uchendu, *Igbo of Southeastern Nigeria*, 16.

119. M. Angulu Onwuejeogwu, *An Igbo Civilization: Nri Kingdom and Hegemony* (London, 1981), 11; Meek, *Law and Authority*, 165–70; Henderson, *King in Every Man*, 264–65.

120. Allison, *Interesting Narrative*, 34–35; Acholonu, *Igbo Roots*, 10–12, 29–30.

121. David Northrup, "The Ideological Context of Slavery in Southeastern Nigeria in the 19th Century," in *The Ideology of Slavery in Africa*, ed. Paul E. Lovejoy (London, 1981), 101–22.

122. Alagoa, "Slave Trade in Niger Delta Oral Tradition," 125–27. The slave trade did not actually end until the 1830s, with the British naval blockade.

123. Isichei, *Ibo People*, 44–45.

124. Cookey, "Ethnohistorical Reconstruction," 335.

125. Isichei, *Ibo People*, 45–46.

126. Ibid., 47; Lovejoy, *Transformations in Slavery*, 57–58.

127. Alagoa, "Slave Trade in Niger Delta Oral Tradition," 126–27.

128. Lovejoy, *Transformations in Slavery*, 57–58; see also Latham, *Old Calabar*.

129. Afigbo, *Ropes of Sand*, 26–27.

130. Allison, *Interesting Narrative*, 47–53.

131. Cookey, "Ethnohistorical Reconstruction," 335, 340–43.

132. Northrup, "Growth of Trade," 234–35.

133. Cookey, "Ethnohistorical Reconstruction," 340–41.

134. Alagoa, "Slave Trade in Niger Delta Oral Tradition," 127. Floyd argues that, as a result of controlling the trade routes, the Aro dominated Igboland itself. Barry Floyd, *Eastern Nigeria* (London, 1969), 29–30.

135. Northrup, "Growth of Trade," 234–35.

136. Chukwudum, *Ancient City of Azia*, 17; Cookey, "Ethnohistorical Reconstruction," 341.

137. Elechi Amadi, *Ethics in Nigerian Culture* (Ibadan, Nigeria, 1982), 44–45.

138. Alagoa, "Slave Trade in Niger Delta Oral Tradition," 127; Cookey, "Ethnohistorical Reconstruction," 341.

139. Isichei, *Ibo People*, 47, 53.

140. Uchendu, *Igbo of Southeastern Nigeria*, 45; Amadi, *Ethics in Nigerian Culture*, 44–45.

141. Amadi, *Ethics in Nigerian Culture*, 45.

142. *Mma*, the Afikpo term for "spirit," is also used to refer to Europeans (Ottenberg, *Masked Rituals*, 12).

143. Uchendu, *Igbo of Southeastern Nigeria*, 96, 102.

144. Isichei, *History of the Igbo People*, 26.

145. Lovejoy, "Impact of the Atlantic Slave Trade," 374; Joseph C. Miller, "The Slave Trade in Congo and Angola," in *The African Diaspora: Interpretive Essays*, ed. Martin L. Kilson and Robert I. Rotberg (Cambridge, Mass., 1976), 75.

146. Mario Azevedo, "Diversity of Cultural Setting," and Dennis Mitchell, James Brooks, Alpha Morris, and Adrienne Phillips, "Time and Space: The History of Cameroon and Chad," in *Cameroon and Chad in Historical and Contemporary Perspectives*, ed. Mario Azevedo (Lewiston, N.Y., 1988).

147. Tambi Eyongetah and Robert Brain, *A History of the Cameroon* (London, 1974), 1–55; Martin Njeuma, "The Lamidates of Northern Cameroon, 1800–1894," in *Introduction to the History of Cameroon, Nineteenth and Twentieth Centuries*, ed. Martin Njeuma (New York, 1989); René Gouellain, *Douala: Ville et Histoire* (Paris, 1975), 19–36, 54, 94–95.

148. Herskovits, *Myth of the Negro Past*, 36–37.

149. Ronald K. Engard, "Dance and Power in Bafut (Cameroon)," in *Creativity and Power*, ed. W. Arens and Ivan Karp (Washington, D.C., 1989), 129–56.

150. Ibid., 145.

151. See K. David Patterson, *The Northern Gabon Coast to 1875* (Oxford, 1975); Herskovits, *Myth of the Negro Past*, 36–37; and Thomas O'Toole, *The Central African Republic* (Boulder, Colo., 1986).

152. Curtin, *Atlantic Slave Trade*, 156–57; Mullin, *Africa in America*, 24; Sobel, *World They Made Together*, 5–6, 244–45; Wax, "Preferences for Slaves," 390.

153. Peter H. Wood, " 'More Like a Negro Country': Demographic Patterns in Colonial South Carolina," in *Race and Slavery in the Western Hemisphere: Quantitative Studies*, ed. Stanley Engerman and Eugene Genovese (Princeton, N.J., 1975), 151–53.

154. W. Robert Higgins, "Charleston: Terminus and Entrepot of the Colonial Trade," in Kilson and Rotberg, *African Diaspora*, 119–20; Wax, "Preferences for Slaves," 395; Phillips, *American Negro Slavery*, 44.

155. Rawley, *Transatlantic Slave Trade*, 334–35.

156. Herskovits's statistics anticipate this pattern by showing that from 1710 to 1769, only 8.5 percent of those imported into Virginia from Africa came from Angola, whereas South Carolina absorbed 34.2 percent of its African imports from Congo and Angola from 1733 to 1785 (*Myth of the Negro Past*, 46–48). Regarding Virginia, it should be noted that Herskovits has no "Congo" category as he does for South Carolina; hence, the 8.5 percent figure would in all probability increase with the inclusion of data for this area.

157. John K. Thornton, "African Dimensions of the Stono Rebellion," *American Historical Review* 96 (1991): 1101–13. Also see John K. Thornton, "On the Trail of Voodoo: African Christianity in Africa and the Americas," *Americas* 44 (1988): 261–78.

158. Wood, *Black Majority*; Margaret Washington Creel, *"A Peculiar People": Slave Religion and Community-Culture among the Gullahs* (New York, 1988), 30–37.

159. Mullin, *Africa in America*, 24.

160. Littlefield, *Rice and Slaves*, 11–14.

161. Herskovits, *Myth of the Negro Past*, 52. This image of the Kongolese is very much in conflict with Thornton's thesis that Kongolese political ideology greatly influenced the Haitian revolution. See John K. Thornton, " 'I Am the Subject of the King of Congo': African Political Ideology and the Haitian Revolution," *Journal of World History* 4 (1993): 181–214.

162. Midlo Hall, *Slavery and Race*.

163. See John W. Blassingame, *Black New Orleans: 1860–1880* (Chicago, 1973), 3–5; James R. Creecy, *Scenes in the South* (Philadelphia, 1860), 20–21.

164. Jerah Johnson maintains that the name "Congo Square" derived from Signore Gaetano's seasonal "Congo Circus"; but why did Gaetano choose this name? See Jerah Johnson, "New Orleans' Congo Square: An Urban Setting for Early Afro-American Culture Formation," *Louisiana History* 32 (1991): 117–57.

165. Gwendolyn Midlo Hall, *Africans in Colonial Louisiana: The Development of Afro-Creole Culture in the Eighteenth Century* (Baton Rouge, 1992), 404.

166. Windley, *Runaway Slave Advertisements*, 3:17.

167. Ibid., 109.

168. Ibid., 199.

169. *Georgia Gazette*, 25 January 1769.

170. *South-Carolina and American General Gazette*, 12–19 February 1768.

171. *Gazette of the State of Georgia*, 4 June 1789.

172. Ibid., 20 September 1792.

173. Windley, *Runaway Slave Advertisements*, 3:125–26.

174. *Georgia Gazette*, 19 July 1764.

175. Windley, *Runaway Slave Advertisements*, 3:243.

176. Ibid., 498.

177. Ibid., 218.

178. Ibid., 227–28.

179. Ibid., 239.

180. Ibid., 303.

181. *South-Carolina Gazette and General Advertiser*, 5–7 August 1784.

182. Windley, *Runaway Slave Advertisements*, 3:186.

183. Ibid., 195.

184. Ibid., 29.

185. *Georgia Gazette*, 8 November 1769.

186. *Columbian Museum and Savannah Advertiser*, 8 August 1804.

187. *Gazette of the State of South Carolina*, 6 October 1779.

188. Windley, *Runaway Slave Advertisements*, 3:21.

189. Ibid., 42.

190. Ibid., 87.

191. Ibid., 549.

192. Ibid., 36.

193. Ibid., 163.

194. *City Gazette and Daily Advertiser* (Charleston), 26 September 1789.

195. Robert W. Harms, *River of Wealth, River of Sorrow: The Central Zaire Basin in the Era of the Slave and Ivory Trade, 1500–1891* (New Haven, Conn., 1981).

196. Ibid., 24–30.

197. John K. Thornton, *Kingdom of Kongo: Civil War and Transition, 1614–1718* (Madison, 1983), introduction; see also Anne Hilton, *The Kingdom of Kongo* (Oxford, 1985).

198. David Birmingham, *Trade and Conflict in Angola: The Mbundu and Their Neighbours under the Influence of the Portuguese, 1483–1790* (Oxford, 1966), 1–4.

199. Ibid., 25–26, 42–64.

200. Ibid., 78–79, 104–27.

201. Joseph C. Miller, *Kings and Kinsmen: Early Mbundu States in Angola* (Oxford, 1976), 151–61. See also Gerald Bender, *Angola under the Portuguese: The Myth and the Reality* (Berkeley and Los Angeles, 1978).

202. Birmingham, *Trade and Conflict*, 8–9.

203. Donnan, *Documents Illustrative*, 2:572.

204. Phyllis M. Martin, *The External Trade of the Loango Coast* (Oxford, 1972), 97–99.

205. Rawley, *Transatlantic Slave Trade*, 277.

206. Martin, *External Trade of the Loango Coast*, 117–18.

207. Jan Vansina, *The Children of Woot: A History of the Kuba Peoples* (Madison, 1978), 5; Anita Jacobson-Widding, *Red-White-Black as a Mode of Thought: A Study of Triadic Classification by Colours in the Ritual Symbolism and Cognitive Thought of the Peoples of the Congo* (Uppsala, 1979), 23.

208. Joseph C. Miller, *Way of Death: Merchant Capitalism and the Angolan Slave Trade, 1730–1830* (Madison, 1988), 8.

209. Miller, "Slave Trade in Congo and Angola," 76; Jacobson-Widding, *Red-White-Black*, 24–25; Hilton, *Kingdom of Kongo*, 5–7; Alvin W. Wolfe, *In the Ngombe Tradition: Continuity and Change in the Congo* (Evanston, Ill., 1961), 54–55; Daniel Biebuyck, *Lega Culture: Art, Initiation, and Moral Philosophy among a Central African People* (Berkeley and Los

Angeles, 1973), 29–46; Thomas Q. Reefe, *The Rainbow and the Kings: A History of the Luba Empire to 1891* (Berkeley and Los Angeles, 1981), 3–12; George Balandier, *Daily Life in the Kingdom of the Kongo* (London, 1968), 153–55.

210. Biebuyck, *Lega Culture*, 29.

211. Jacobson-Widding, *Red-White-Black*, 24–25; Miller, *Kings and Kinsmen*, 43–44.

212. Hilton, *Kingdom of Kongo*, 7–9, 19–24.

213. Biebuyck, *Lega Culture*, 46–47.

214. Miller, *Kings and Kinsmen*, 50–51; Biebuyck, *Lega Culture*, 48–50; Jacobson-Widding, *Red-White-Black*, 24–25.

215. Luca da Caltanisetta, *Diaire Congolais (1690–1701)*, trans. François Bontinck (Paris, 1970), employs the term *libata*. See Thornton, *Kingdom of Kongo*, 15–45; Hilton, *Kingdom of Kongo*, 7–9.

216. Da Caltanisetta, *Diaire Congolais*, 25 and throughout; Lorenzo da Lucca, *Relations sur le Congo du Père Laurent du Lucques (1700–1717)*, trans. J. Cuvelier (Brussels, 1953), passim.

217. Jacobson-Widding, *Red-White-Black*, 25–26.

218. Biebuyck, *Lega Culture*, 52.

219. Thornton, " 'I Am the Subject,' " 188–89.

220. Thornton, "African Dimensions," 1103.

221. Da Caltanisetta, *Diaire Congolais*, 69. Thornton acknowledges this "war" against traditional religion (*Kingdom of Kongo*, 64).

222. Da Lucca, *Relations sur le Congo*, 101; see also 132–37.

223. Thornton, "African Dimensions," 1107.

224. Thornton, *Kingdom of Kongo*, 106–13; Thornton, " 'I Am the Subject,' " 192–98; Hilton, *Kingdom of Kongo*, 208–10.

225. Hilton, *Kingdom of Kong*, 9–26; also see Thornton, " 'I Am the Subject,' " 193.

226. Da Caltanisetta, *Diaire Congolais*, 95, 105, 112–13, 184.

227. Ibid., 154–56, for example, evinces da Catanisetta's preoccupation with destroying the "camp of the Kimpasi." Thornton (*Kingdom of Kongo*, 59–60) distinguishes between the *nganga* and the *kitomi* as follows: the former was a private figure concerned with rainmaking, curing epidemics, and making charms for hunting and cultivation; the *kitomi* functioned as a public official upon whom rain and soil fertility were dependent, and by whom marriages and the state were regulated and sanctioned.

228. Thornton, *Kingdom of Kongo*, 59, 107–10; Hilton, *Kingdom of Kongo*, 23–26.

229. Jacobson-Widding, *Red-White-Black*, 95.

230. Hilton, *Kingdom of Kongo*, 9; Wyatt MacGaffey, *Religion and Society in Central Africa: The Bakongo of Lower Zaire* (Chicago, 1986), 43. Also see Wyatt MacGaffey, *Custom and Government in the Lower Congo* (Berkeley and Los Angeles, 1970); MacGaffey, *Art and Healing of the Bakongo Commented by Themselves* (Stockholm, 1991).

231. Miller, *Way of Death*, 4–6; Harms, *River of Wealth*, 2–3.

232. Miller, *Way of Death*, 4.

233. Robert Farris Thompson, *Flash of the Spirit* (New York, 1983), xiv, introduction.

234. Ibid., 132.

235. Ibid., 104–5. Thompson also speculates that the Kikongo verb *dinza*, which refers to male ejaculation, was possibly corrupted in New Orleans and elsewhere into "jizz" and "jism," also used to refer to discharged semen, and could be the root of the term *jazz*.

236. MacGaffey, *Religion and Society*, 45.

237. Ibid., 106–14.

238. Ibid., 108–10.

239. Stuckey, *Slave Culture*, introduction, 8–99.

240. Rawley, *Transatlantic Slave Trade*, 335.

241. Midlo Hall, *Slavery and Race*.

CHAPTER 7

1. Orlando Patterson, *Slavery and Social Death* (Cambridge, Mass., 1982).

2. For the various methods of procurement in the Atlantic trade, see the summary of Paul Lovejoy in *Transformations in Slavery: A History of Slavery in Africa* (Cambridge, 1983).

3. See Ralph Austen, *African Economic Slavery* (London, 1987).

4. Patrick Manning, *Slavery and African Life: Occidental, Oriental, and African Slave Trades* (Cambridge, 1990), 58, 62, 64–72.

5. Lovejoy, *Transformations in Slavery*, 60–62.

6. Mungo Park, *Travels in the Interior Districts of Africa* (London, 1799; reprint, New York, 1971), 18.

7. Ibid.

8. Joseph C. Miller, "Some Aspects of the Commercial Organization of Slaving at Luanda, Angola—1730–1830," in *The Uncommon Market: Essays in the Economic History of the Atlantic Slave Trade*, ed. Henry A. Gemery and Jan S. Hogendorn (New York, 1979), 95–96.

9. Roger E. Conrad, *World of Sorrow* (Baton Rouge, 1986), 41.

10. Elizabeth Donnan, *Documents Illustrative of the History of the Slave Trade to America* (Washington, D.C., 1930), 1:199–209.

11. Ibid., 141–45.

12. Ibid., 201.

13. Ibid., 227.

14. Ibid., 2:15.

15. Alexander Falconbridge, *An Account of the Slave Trade on the Coast of Africa* (London, 1788), 18. The western section of the Windward Coast was alternately referred to as the "grain coast" (much of Liberia), whereas the eastern section was also called the "ivory coast," hence the modern nation's name.

16. Falconbridge, *An Account of the Slave Trade*, 19–21; Donnan, *Documents Illustrative*, 1:406.

17. Donnan, *Documents Illustrative*, 1:130.

18. James A. Rawley, *The Transatlantic Slave Trade: A History* (New York, 1981), 298.

19. William Bosman, *Description of the Coast of Guinea, 1699*, in Donnan, *Documents Illustrative*, 1:441–43.

20. Ibid.

21. Brantz Mayer, *Captain Canot, or, Twenty Years of an African Slaver* (New York, 1854), 102.

22. Ibid., 102–3.

23. Donnan, *Documents Illustrative*, 1:402–3.

24. William Snelgrave, *A New Account of Some Parts of Guniea and the Slave-Trade* (London, 1734; reprint, London, 1971), 162–63.

25. Donnan, *Documents Illustrative*, 1:462.

26. Robert J. Allison, ed., *The Interesting Narrative of Olaudah Equiano, or Gustavus Vasa, the African* (London, 1789), in Philip D. Curtin, ed., *Africa Remembered* (Madison, 1967), 91–94.

27. Rawley, *Transatlantic Slave Trade*, 297–98; Falconbridge, *Account of the Slave Trade*, 19–21; Mayer, *Captain Canot*, 103. Bosman claims they were fed three times a day (Donnan, *Documents Illustrative*, 1:443).

28. Donnan, *Documents Illustrative*, 1:406, 463.

29. Ibid., 204.

30. Ibid., 406–7.

31. Ibid., 2:15. It was found that Indian corn made the captives ill.

32. "From Jungle to Slavery—and Freedom," *Birmingham News-Age-Herald*, 2 December 1934.

33. Rawley, *Transatlantic Slave Trade*, 294–97.

34. Donnan, *Documents Illustrative*, 1:463.

35. Rawley, *Transatlantic Slave Trade*, 290–94.

36. Ibid., 283–84.

37. Herbert S. Klein, *The Middle Passage* (Princeton, N.J., 1978), 234. However, subsequent scholarship begs to differ with Klein. See David W. Galenson, *Traders, Planters, and Slaves: Market Behavior in Early English America* (Cambridge, 1986), 40.

38. For examples of tight packing, see Donnan, *Documents Illustrative*, 1:272, 443, 460.

39. Lovejoy, *Transformations in Slavery*, 48, 60–62.

40. Rawley, *Transatlantic Slave Trade*, 288–89, 301–2.

41. Donnan, *Documents Illustrative*, 1:355–56.

42. Ibid., 246–48.

43. Ibid., 442.

44. Workers of the Writers' Program of the Work Projects Administration in the state of Virginia, *The Negro in Virginia* (New York, 1940), 7–8.

45. Ibid., 290–91.

46. Harvey Wish, "American Slave Insurrections before 1861," *Journal of Negro History* 22 (1937): 301.

47. Donnan, *Documents Illustrative*, 1:394.

48. Falconbridge, *Account of the Slave Trade*, 23.

49. Rawley, *Transatlantic Slave Trade*, 300; Wish, "American Slave Insurrections," 301.

50. Wish, "American Slave Insurrections," 301.

51. Mayer, *Captain Canot*, 103.

52. *An Abstract of the Evidence delivered before a Select Committee of the House of Commons in the Years 1790, and 1791* (London, 1791), 38–44; Donnan, *Documents Illustrative*, 1:203–5.

53. Rawley, *Transatlantic Slave Trade*, 299–300; Wish, "American Slave Insurrections," 303–6.

54. Orland Armstrong, *Old Massa's People* (Indianapolis, 1931), 52.

55. Elsa V. Goveia, *Slave Society in the British Leeward Islands at the End of the Eighteenth Century* (New Haven, Conn., 1965), 245.

56. Orlando Patterson, *The Sociology of Slavery* (London, 1967), 150.

57. Philip D. Curtin, *Two Jamaicas: The Role of Ideas in a Tropical Colony, 1830–1865* (Cambridge, 1955), 26.

58. Falconbridge, *Account of the Slave Trade*, 23.

59. Angela Davis, "Reflections on the Black Woman's Role in the Community of Slaves," *Black Scholar* (December 1971): 3–15.

60. Nicholas Cresswell, *The Journal of Nicholas Cresswell, 1774–1777* (London, 1925), 36.

61. Galenson, *Traders, Planters, and Slaves*, 29–30.

62. Gerald W. Mullin, *Flight and Rebellion: Slave Resistance in Eighteenth-Century Virginia* (New York, 1972), 15.

63. The earlier September observations of Cresswell are consistent with the preferred season for the importation of captives from Africa. The colonial and antebellum newspapers are filled with notices advertising the arrival and sale of human cargo from various points in Africa. A review of forty such notices from a variety of colonies / states, beginning

in 1764 and ending in 1808, reveals that 82.5 percent (thirty-three) of the cargoes entering North American ports did so between March and September; that figure increases to 87.5 percent (thirty-five) if the month of October is included.

64. Mullin, *Flight and Rebellion*, 13–15, 34–35.

65. Michael Mullin, *Africa in America: Slave Acculturation and Resistance in the American South and the British Caribbean, 1736–1831* (Urbana, 1992), 22–23.

66. Ibid., 51.

67. Guion G. Johnson, *A Social History of the Sea Islands, with Special Reference to St. Helena Island, South Carolina* (Chapel Hill, 1930), 77–78; Patterson, *Sociology of Slavery*, 98; John Hope Franklin and Alfred A. Moss Jr., *From Slavery to Freedom: A History of African Americans*, 5th ed. (New York, 1980), 49.

68. Mullin, *Flight and Rebellion*, 15.

69. Johnson, *Social History of the Sea Islands*, 77–78.

70. Ibid., 78.

71. E. Franklin Frazier, *The Negro in the United States* (New York, 1957), 8.

72. Ibid.

73. To review the literature on so-called black English, begin with the following: Joseph E. Holloway and Winifred K. Vass, *The African Heritage of American English* (Bloomington, 1993); Joseph E. Holloway, ed., *Africanisms in American Culture* (Bloomington, 1990); Geneva Smitherman, *Talkin and Testifyin: The Language of Black America* (Detroit, 1977); Joshua A. Fishman and J. L. Dillard, *Perspectives on Black English* (The Hague, 1975); J. L. Dillard, *Lexicon of Black English* (New York, 1977); J. L. Dillard, *Black English: Its History and Usage in the United States* (New York, 1972); Thomas Kochman, ed., *Rappin' and Stylin' Out: Communication in Urban Black America* (Urbana, 1972); William Labor, *The Study of Nonstandard English* (Champaign, Ill., 1970); and Roger D. Abrahams, *Rapping and Capping: Black Talk as an Art* (New York, 1970).

74. See Paulo Freire, *Pedagogy of the Oppressed* (New York, 1993).

75. For a discussion on the relationship between language and the colonial effect, see Ngugi wa Thiong'o, *Decolonising the Mind: The Politics of Language in African Literature* (London, 1986).

76. Melville Herskovits, *The Myth of the Negro Past* (New York, 1941), 80.

77. John W. Blassingame, *The Slave Community: Plantation Life in the Antebellum South* (New York, 1972), 24.

78. Nathan Irvin Huggins, *Black Odyssey: The Afro-American Ordeal in Slavery* (New York, 1977), 62–63.

79. Herskovits, *Myth of the Negro Past*, 1–2.

80. Gwendolyn Midlo Hall, *Africans in Colonial Louisiana: The Development of Afro-Creole Culture in the Eighteenth Century* (Baton Rouge, 1992), 168.

81. Blassingame, *Slave Community*, 25.

82. Georgia Writers' Project, *Drums and Shadows: Survival Studies among the Georgia Coastal Negroes* (Athens, Ga., 1940), 22.

83. Ibid., 29.

84. Ibid., 50–51.

85. See Emma Langdon Roche, *Historic Sketches of the South* (New York, 1914), 49–64; Charles J. Montgomery, "Survivors from the Cargo of the Negro Slave Yacht *Wanderer*," *American Anthropologist* 10 (1908): 611–23; and "From Jungle to Slavery—and Freedom."

86. Montgomery, "Survivors from the Cargo," 613–14.

87. William S. Perry, ed., *Historical Collections Relating to the American Colonial Church* (New York, 1870), 1:283.

88. J. F. D. Smyth, "Travels in Virginia in 1773," *Virginia Historical Register* (April 1853): 82.

89. Frederick Law Olmsted, *A Journey in the Seaboard Slave States* (New York, 1856), 433–34.

90. William B. Poe, "Negro Life in Two Generations," *Outlook* 75 (1903): 493–98.

91. George P. Rawick, ed., *The American Slave: A Composite Autobiography* (Westport, Conn., 1972–77), 2:25.

92. J. Ralph Jones, "Portraits of Georgia Slaves," *Georgia Review* 21 (1967): 126–32. The interview of Gladdy was conducted by Jones in 1936.

93. Rawick, *American Slave*, 3:65.

94. Ibid., 113–14.

95. Charles Johnson, *Shadow of the Plantation* (Chicago, 1934), 22–23.

96. Lathan Windley, *Runaway Slave Advertisements: A Documentary History from the 1730s to 1790* (Westport, Conn., 1983), 4:134–35.

97. *Republican and Savannah Evening Ledger*, 2 August 1808.

98. Blassingame, *Slave Community*, 26.

99. Melville Herskovits, *The New World Negro* (Bloomington, 1966), 170–71.

100. *Gazette of the State of Georgia*, 4 February 1790.

101. *Georgia Gazette*, 22 November 1769.

102. Windley, *Runaway Slave Advertisements*, 3:207.

103. Ibid., 30.

104. Ibid., 459.

105. Ibid., 53.

106. Ibid., 643.

107. *Moniteur de la Louisiane*, 11 October 1806.

108. *Columbian Museum and Savannah Advertiser*, 28 December 1803.

109. *Augusta Herald*, 11 November 1813.

110. Zora Neale Hurston, "The Negro in Florida, 1528–1940" (unpublished manuscript, Federal Writers' Project in Florida, University of Florida, n.d.), 5–12.

111. Ibid., 9.

112. *Georgia State Gazette or Independent Register*, 28 October 1786.

113. Ibid., 19 May 1787.

114. Windley, *Runaway Slave Advertisements*, 2:42–43.

115. Ibid., 3:650–51.

116. Ibid., 466.

CHAPTER 8

1. Charles Ball, *Slavery in the United States* (New York, 1837; reprint, New York, 1969), 219.

2. *Gazette of the State of Georgia*, 23 April 1789.

3. Ball, *Slavery in the United States*, 219.

4. Charles Lyell, *A Second Visit to the United States of America* (New York, 1849), 1:267.

5. Newbell N. Puckett, *Folk Beliefs of the Southern Negro* (Chapel Hill, 1926), 528–29.

6. Kenneth M. Stampp, *The Peculiar Institution* (New York, 1956), 363–65.

7. Orlando Patterson, *The Sociology of Slavery* (London, 1967), 100, 146.

8. Charles Johnson, *Shadow of the Plantation* (Chicago, 1934), 22–23.

9. E. Franklin Frazier, *The Negro in the United States* (New York, 1957), 8.

10. Ibid., 8 n. 15.

11. Melville Herskovits, *The Myth of the Negro Past* (New York, 1941), 131–32.

12. John W. Blassingame, *The Slave Community: Plantation Life in the Antebellum South* (New York, 1972), 39–40.

13. Joseph B. Cobb, *Mississippi Scenes* (Philadelphia, 1851), 173.

14. Ibid., 174–75.

15. George P. Rawick, *The American Slave: A Composite Autobiography* (Westport, Conn., 1972–77), 12:89.

16. Joseph LeConte, *The Autobiography of Joseph LeConte* (New York, 1903), 29–30.

17. Rawick, *American Slave*, 8:807–9.

18. Bryan Edwards, in Edward Braithwaite, *The Development of Creole Society in Jamaica, 1770–1820* (Oxford, 1971), 166.

19. M. G. Smith, "The African Heritage in the Caribbean," in *Caribbean Studies: A Symposium*, ed. Vera Rubin (Seattle, 1960), 47.

20. Patterson, *Sociology of Slavery*, 145–46.

21. Eliza J. Kendrick (Lewis) Walker, "Other Days," 1924, in the Alabama State Archives, Montgomery, SPR 208.

22. Ibid.

23. *Virginia Gazette or the American Advertiser*, 21 December 1782.

24. *Georgia Republican and State Intelligencer*, 14 September 1811.

25. *Georgia Gazette*, 13 September 1764.

26. *Washington Republican and Natchez Intelligencer*, 14 May 1817.

27. *Louisiana Gazette*, 15 April 1819.

28. *Louisianian*, 2 October 1819.

29. *Georgia Gazette*, 3 January 1765.

30. Ibid., 17 August 1768.

31. *Winyaw Intelligencer*, 10 March 1819.

32. *Knoxville Register*, 21 January 1825.

33. *Royal Georgia Gazette*, 11 October 1781.

34. *Virginia Gazette or the American Advertiser*, 22 June 1782.

35. *City Gazette and Daily Advertiser*, 16 June 1788.

36. *Gazette of the State of South Carolina*, 2 September 1766.

37. *South Carolina Weekly Gazette*, 15 November 1785.

38. Lathan Windley, comp., *Runaway Slave Advertisements: A Documentary History from the 1730s to 1790* (Westport, Conn., 1983), 3:3.

39. *Charleston Courier*, 8 January 1825.

40. *Jacksonville Courier*, 6 August 1835.

41. *Royal Georgia Gazette*, 25 April 1782.

42. Rawick, *American Slave*, 3:14, 4:163.

43. Ibid., 9:139.

44. Ibid., 8:858–59.

45. Ibid., Supplement Series, 10:2003–12.

46. Ibid., 2:118.

47. Ibid., 13:37.

48. Ibid., 2:34.

49. Lee Haring, "A Characteristic African Folktale Pattern," in *African Folklore*, ed. Richard M. Dorson (Bloomington, 1972), 165–79. Also see Harold Courlander, *A Treasury of Afro-American Folklore* (New York, 1976); Isidore Okpewho, *African Oral Literature* (Bloomington, 1992); Claude-Helène Pérrot, *Sources orales de l'histoire* (Paris, 1989); Denise Paulme, *La statut du commandeur: essais d'ethnologie* (Paris, 1984); Denise Paulme, *La mere devorante: essai sur la morphologie des contes africains* (Paris, 1976); Denise Paulme, "The Impossible Imitation in African Trickster Tales," in *Forms of Folklore in Africa*, ed. Bernth Lindfors (Austin, 1977); Robert D. Pelton, *The Trickster in West Africa* (Berkeley and Los Angeles, 1980); François Tsoungui, *Clés pour le conte africain et créole* (Paris, 1986); Youssef Nacib,

Elements sur la tradition orale (Algiers, 1982); Ruth Finnegan, *Oral Literature in Africa* (Oxford, 1970); Ruth Finnegan, *Limba Stories and Story-Telling* (Oxford, 1967); Mary Augusta Klipple, *African Folktales with Foreign Analogues* (New York, 1992); Barbara K. Walker and Warren S. Walker, *Nigerian Folk Tales* (Hamden, Conn., 1980); Daniel J. Crowley, *African Folklore in the New World* (Austin, 1977); Jack Berry, *West African Folktales* (Evanston, Ill., 1961); and Robert H. Nassau, *Where Animals Talk: West African Folk Lore Tales* (New York, 1912).

50. Rawick, *American Slave*, 2:172.

51. Ibid., 4:163.

52. Ralph Austen, *African Economic History* (London, 1987), 99–100; Paul Lovejoy, *Transformations in Slavery: A History of Slavery in Africa* (Cambridge, 1983), 104–5; A. G. Hopkins, *An Economic History of West Africa* (New York, 1973), 110–12.

53. Rawick, *American Slave*, 2:63–64. See William D. Piersen, *Black Legacy: America's Hidden Heritage* (Amherst, Mass., 1993), 35–50, for a parallel yet independent discussion of the red cloth tales.

54. Rawick, *American Slave*, 7:24–25.

55. Ibid., 102.

56. Ibid., 169.

57. Ibid., 12:119, pt. 2.

58. Ibid., 14:190.

59. Ibid., Supplement Series, 12:268–69.

60. E. C. L. Adams, *Nigger to Nigger* (New York, 1928), 227–29.

61. *Slave Narratives of South Carolina* (St. Clair Shores, Mich., 1976), 2:64–65.

62. Lawrence W. Levine, *Black Culture and Black Consciousness* (London, 1978), xiii.

63. Rawick, *American Slave*, 13:330–31, pt. 3.

64. Georgia Writers' Project, *Drums and Shadows: Survival Studies among the Georgia Coastal Negroes* (New York, 1972), 156–57.

65. An invoice from the slaver *Arthur* operating off the West African coast in the late seventeenth century, for example, lists those goods in greatest demand at the Royal Company factory at "Oryshra in Arda." The list includes "Red Broad Cloth and fine Scarlett Cloth"; "Broad White Baftares [or "bafts," an inexpensive cotton fabric]"; "All Sorts Cuttanes [Indian linen] Red the best without Stripes or Flowers"; and "Rangoes [or "arrangoes," an English cloth] of a deepe Red Coller." Elizabeth Donnan, *Documents Illustrative of the History of the Slave Trade to America* (Washington, D.C., 1930), 4:237.

66. Anita Jacobson-Widding, *Red-White-Black as a Mode of Thought: A Study of Triadic Classification by Colours in the Ritual Symbolism and Cognitive Thought of the Peoples of the Congo* (Uppsala, 1979), 157–74.

67. Rawick, *American Slave*, 4:142–44, pt. 3.

68. Ibid., Supplement Series, 7:697.

69. Charles J. Montgomery, "Survivors from the Cargo of the Negro Slave Yacht *Wanderer*," *American Anthropologist* 10 (1908): 621.

70. Rawick, *American Slave*, 4:142–44, pt. 3.

71. See Winston McGowan, "African Resistance to the Atlantic Slave Trade in West Africa," *Slavery and Abolition* 11 (1990): 5–29; Richard Rathbone, "Some Thoughts on Resistance to Enslavement in Africa," *Slavery and Abolition* 6 (1985): 11–22; Alan Ryder, *Benin and the Europeans, 1485–1897* (New York, 1969), 45–65, 168–69, 198, 201, 233; Walter Rodney, *A History of the Upper Guinea Coast* (Oxford, 1970), 109–10, 256; John K. Thornton, *Kingdom of Kongo: Civil War and Transition, 1614–1718* (Madison, 1983), 106–13; and Anne Hilton, *The Kingdom of Kongo* (Oxford, 1985), 208–10.

72. Montgomery, "Survivors from the Cargo," 616–18.

73. Rawick, *American Slave*, Supplement Series, 7:349.

74. See Eric Williams, *Capitalism and Slavery* (New York, 1944), 51–84.

75. Sterling Stuckey, *Slave Culture: Nationalist Theory and the Foundations of Black America* (Oxford, 1987), 3–5. See also Douglas B. Chambers, " 'My own nation': Igbo Exiles in the Diaspora," *Slavery and Abolition* 18 (1997): 82; Francis Arinze, *Sacrifice in Igbo Religion* (Ibadan, Nigeria, 1970), 37; John E. E. Njoku, *A Dictionary of Igbo Names, Culture and Proverbs* (Washington, D.C., 1978), 78; Northcote W. Thomas, *Anthropological Report on Ibo-speaking Peoples of Nigeria*, Vol. 2, *English-Ibo and Ibo-English Dictionary* (1913; New York, 1969), 157, 382.

76. Adams, *Nigger to Nigger*, 12–15.

77. In addition to the African accomplice, "Ole Man Rogan" represents another tradition involving a similar punishment for slave traders. Although it borrows from African beliefs regarding eternal punishment, and although the parallels with the transatlantic trade are obvious, Ole Man Rogan does not seek to answer the same questions addressed by the other two traditions:

> He [Ole Man Rogan] always buy ooman wid chillun, and ooman wid husband, and ain't nobody can buy from Ole Man Rogan mother and chile or man and ooman. He great pleasure been to part. He always love to take er baby away from he ma and sell it, and he take he ma somewhere else and sell her, and ain't luh 'em see one another again. He love to part a man and he ooman, sell de man one place and sell de ooman another, and dat look like all Ole Man Rogan live for, and when he ain't 'casion 'stress dat er way, he been onrestless. He love to see a man wid he head bowed down in 'stress, and he love to see chillun holdin' out dey arms cryin' for dey mother, and he always looked satisfied when he see tear runnin' down de face of er ooman when she weepin' for her chile.
>
> And Ole Man Rogan die on Boggy Gut, and ever since den he sperrit wander and wander from Boggy Gut to de river and wander 'cross de big swamps to Congaree [in South Carolina]. Whether it be God or whether it be devil, de sperrit of Ole Man Rogan ain't got no res'. Some time in de night ef you'll set on Boggy Gut, you'll hear de rattle of chains, you hear a baby cry every which er way, and you hear a mother callin' for her chile in de dark night on Boggy Gut.
>
> And you kin set on de edge of Boggy Gut and you'll see mens in chains bent over wid dey head in dey hands—de signs of 'stress. While you sets you see de sperrit of Ole Man Rogan comin' 'cross de big swamps. You see him look at de womens and mens and chillun, and you see him laugh—laugh at de 'stress and de tears on Boogy Gut, and he laugh like he satisfied, but he ain't had no res'. And when he stayed a minute on Boggy Gut, to de river 'cross de big swamps and back again he wanders, on de edge of Boggy Gut. (E. C. L. Adams, *Congaree Sketches* [Chapel Hill, 1927], 49–51)

The enormity of the domestic trader's transgression lay in the fact that he separated families. His actions were therefore just as despicable as were those of the African operative.

78. Jan Vansina, *The Children of Woot: A History of the Kuba Peoples* (Madison, 1978), 6–7.

79. Fredrika Bremer, *The Homes of the New World* (New York, 1853), 1:394.

80. Benjamin Botkin, *Lay My Burden Down: A Folk History of Slavery* (Chicago, 1945), 39.

81. Stampp, *Peculiar Institution*, 363.

82. Rawick, *American Slave*, 2:67.

83. Ibid., 7:24.

84. Ibid., 4:61.

85. Ibid., 3:57.

86. Ibid., 43.

87. Herskovits, *Myth of the Negro Past*, 31.

88. Rawick, *American Slave*, Supplement Series, 10:2026–34.

89. Ibid., 6:335–36.

90. Zora Neale Hurston, *Mules and Men* (Philadelphia, 1935), 47.

91. John W. Blassingame, ed., *Slave Testimony* (Baton Rouge, 1977), 31.

92. In Montgomery, "Survivors from the Cargo," 621.

93. Emma Langdon Roche, *Historic Sketches of the South* (New York, 1914), 114, 121.

94. "From Jungle to Slavery—and Freedom," *Birmingham News-Age-Herald*, 2 December 1934, in the Papers of Samuel Anderson Weakley, box 6, folder 11, Manuscripts—Hard Copies, VI-F-2, Ac. No. 68-266, Tennessee State Archives, Nashville.

95. Adams, *Nigger to Nigger*, 227–29.

96. Georgia Writers' Project, *Drums and Shadows*, 25.

97. William W. Brown, *Narrative of William W. Brown, A Fugitive Slave* (Boston, 1847), 51.

98. Rawick, *American Slave*, 1:8.

99. For example, see the articles in Ira Berlin and Philip D. Morgan, eds., *Cultivation and Culture: Labor and the Shaping of Slave Life in the Americas* (Charlottesville, 1993); Berlin and Morgan, eds., *The Slaves' Economy: Independent Production by Slaves in the Americas* (London, 1991).

100. Gwendolyn Midlo Hall, personal correspondence, 16 October 1995. It should be pointed out here that while the Wolof may have been preferred over American-born blacks as drivers, this does not mean that Louisiana slaveholders were unconcerned with phenotype. On the contrary, the Wolof are a very distinctive-looking group of West Africans—though very dark, they are far from typical. Second, the use of Wolof as domestics further strengthens the argument that Muslims were promoted to such positions. See the names in Midlo Hall, *Africans in Colonial Louisiana: The Development of Afro-Creole Culture in the Eighteenth Century* (Baton Rouge, 1992), app. D, 407–12. Some of them, such as Fatima, are clearly Muslim.

101. W. E. B. Du Bois, *Souls of Black Folk* (Chicago, 1903).

102. Ira Berlin, *Slaves Without Masters: The Free Negro in the Antebellum South* (New York, 1976), 35–36, 48–49, 57–58, 108–16. Midlo Hall qualifies this increase by pointing out that Haitian free blacks arriving in New Orleans between 1809 and 1810 only doubled the free black population; the remainder of the free black increase is attributable to manumissions and so forth taking place in Louisiana (personal correspondence, 16 October 1995).

103. Ibid., 48–49, 58.

104. Ibid., 48–49, 179–80.

105. Ibid., 218–41.

106. Ruby Andrews Moore, "Superstitions from Georgia," *Journal of American Folklore* 7 (1894): 305–6.

107. Ibid.

108. Daniel C. Littlefield, *Rice and Slaves: Ethnicity and the Slave Trade in Colonial South Carolina* (Baton Rouge, 1981), 11–21.

109. Ibid.

110. Joseph E. Holloway, "The Origins of African-American Culture," in *Africanisms in American Culture*, ed. Joseph E. Holloway (Bloomington, 1990), esp. 11–18. Holloway relies upon U. B. Phillips, *American Negro Slavery* (New York, 1940), 42–44; and U. B. Phillips, *Life and Labor in the Old South* (Boston, 1929), 190.

111. Ibid., 12.

112. Ibid., 13.

113. J. H. Ingraham, *The Southwest by a Yankee*, 2 vols. (New York, 1835), 2:247–57.

114. Patterson, *Sociology of Slavery*, 61–62.

115. Herskovits, *Myth of the Negro Past*, 125–31.

116. Charles Sackett Sydnor, *Slavery in Mississippi* (New York, 1933), 4.

117. Lyle Saxon, Edward Dreyer, and Robert Tallant, *Gumbo Ya-Ya* (Cambridge, 1945), 245.

118. Austin Steward, *Twenty-Two Years a Slave, and Forty Years a Freeman* (1856; New York, 1968), 20–32.

119. Ibid., 30.

120. Ophelia Settle Egypt, *Unwritten History of Slavery* (Nashville, 1968), 1–2.

121. W. P. Harrison, *The Gospel among the Slaves* (Nashville, 1893), 96–97.

122. Luther P. Jackson, "Religious Instruction of Negroes, 1830 to 1860, with Special Reference to South Carolina," *Journal of Negro History* 15 (1930): 72–73.

123. Patterson, *Sociology of Slavery*, 210–14. Methodism in Jamaica represented for those of mixed race the only viable alternative between the unattainability of Anglicanism and the unacceptability of the Baptist faith.

124. Orland Armstrong, *Old Massa's People* (Indianapolis, 1931), 73–74.

125. James Redpath, *The Roving Editor: Or, Talks with Slaves in the Southern States* (New York, 1859), 84.

126. Egypt, *Unwritten History of Slavery*, 111–12.

127. "Slave Interviews," in Federal Writers' Project (Negro Writers' Unit), P. K. Yonge Library of Florida History, University of Florida, Gainesville.

128. Berlin, *Slaves Without Masters*, 6. Other important works on free blacks include Carter G. Woodson, *Free Negro Heads of Families in the United States in 1830* (Washington, D.C., 1925); E. Franklin Frazier, *The Free Negro Family* (Nashville, 1932); James Oliver Horton, *Free People of Color: Inside the African American Community* (Washington, D.C., 1993); John Hope Franklin, *The Free Negro in North Carolina, 1790–1860* (Chapel Hill, 1943); Larry Kroger, *Black Slaveowners: Free Black Slave Masters in South Carolina* (Jefferson, N.C., 1985); Loren Schweninger, *Black Property Owners in the South, 1790–1915* (Urbana, 1990); Michael P. Johnson and James L. Roark, *Black Masters: A Free Family of Color in the Old South* (New York, 1984); and Michael P. Johnson and James L. Roark, *No Chariot Let Down: Charleston's Free People of Color on the Eve of the Civil War* (Chapel Hill, 1984).

129. Braithwaite, *Development of Creole Society*, 303–4.

130. Robert William Fogel and Stanley L. Engerman, *Time on the Cross* (Boston, 1974), 129–35. There are a number of specious arguments employed by this study to support the notion that white-black, nonconsensual sexual contact was minimal, including an appeal to the Victorian principles of planters, dubious comparisons with white prostitutes in Nashville, and questionable references to source materials which are, in other parts of the study, taken to task for their reliability.

131. Lyell, *Second Visit*, 1:208.

132. Berlin, *Slaves Without Masters*, 178–79.

133. Rawick, *American Slave*, 15:78, pt. 2.

134. "Slave Interviews," in Federal Writers' Project (Negro Writers' Unit), P. K. Yonge Library of Florida History, University of Florida, Gainesville.

135. Patterson, *Sociology of Slavery*, 61–64; Braithwaite, *Development of Creole Society*, 167–75.

136. Patterson, *Sociology of Slavery*, 61–64.

137. C. L. R. James, *Black Jacobins* (New York, 1963), 31.

138. John W. Blassingame, *Black New Orleans: 1860–1880* (Chicago, 1973).

139. Ibid.; Lyell, *Second Visit*, 1:94.

140. James D. B. DeBow, *The Industrial Resources, Statistics, Etc., of the United States and More Particularly of the Southern and Western States*, 3d ed. (New York, 1854), 2:270.

141. Braithwaite, *Development of Creole Society*, 175.

142. *Georgia Gazette*, 14 August 1800.

143. Henry Bibb, *Narrative of the Life and Adventures of Henry Bibb* (New York, 1849), in Gilbert Osofsky, ed., *Puttin' on Ole Massa* (New York, 1969), 64–65, 77–80.

144. Rawick, *American Slave*, 4:46, pt. 3.

145. Egypt, *Unwritten History*, 1–2.

146. Adams, *Nigger to Nigger*, 33–35.

147. Ibid., 71–72.

148. Windley, *Runaway Slave Advertisements*, 1:146.

149. Ibid., 3:575.

150. Ibid., 4:31.

151. Ibid., 17–18.

152. Ibid., 3:581.

153. *Southern Reporter*, 7 September 1839.

154. *Town Gazette and Farmers Register*, 16 August 1819.

155. *Augusta Chronicle and Gazette of the State*, 20 August 1817 and 19 January 1811.

156. *Washington Republican and Natchez Intelligencer*, 19 March 1817.

157. *Virginia Argus*, 21 January 1806.

158. *Ariel*, 10 October 1825.

159. *Augusta Chronicle and Gazette of the State*, 3 June 1802.

160. *Columbus Enquirer*, 23 January 1835.

161. Ibid., 1 February 1838.

162. *Knoxville Register*, 31 August 1819.

163. *Charleston Courier*, 25 March 1813.

164. Bremer, *Homes of the New World*, 1:386.

165. Samuel Ringgold Ward, *Autobiography of a Fugitive Slave* (London, 1855), 5.

166. Windley, *Runaway Slave Advertisements*, 2:126–27.

167. Rawick, *American Slave*, 4:148, pt. 3.

168. Henry Ravenel, "Recollections of Southern Plantation Life," *Yale Review* 25 (1936): 750.

169. Herskovits, *Myth of the Negro Past*, 105–7; Melville Herskovits, *The New World Negro* (Bloomington, 1966), 87–88.

170. Ball, *Slavery in the United States*, 21.

171. Puckett, *Folk Beliefs*, 4–5.

172. Ravenel, "Recollections of Southern Plantation Life," 757.

173. Rawick, *American Slave*, 12:267.

174. Frederic Bancroft, *Slave-Trading in the Old South* (Baltimore, 1931), 19.

175. Gerald W. Mullin, *Flight and Rebellion: Slave Resistance in Eighteenth-Century Virginia* (New York, 1972), 17–18.

176. Rawick, *American Slave*, Supplement Series, 1:385.

177. Joshua Haget Frier II, "Reminiscences of the War between the States by a Boy in the Far South at Home in the Ranks of the Confederate Militia," Manuscript Collection, Florida State University, Tallahassee.

178. Rawick, *American Slave*, 2:252, pt. 1.

179. Ira Berlin, "Time, Space, and the Evolution of Afro-American Society on British Mainland North America," *American Historical Review* 85 (1980): 54.

CHAPTER 9

1. See, for example, Carter G. Woodson, *The History of the Negro Church* (Washington, D.C., 1921); E. Franklin Frazier, *The Negro Church in America* (New York, 1970); W. E. B.

Du Bois, *Black Folk, Then and Now* (New York, 1939); W. E. B. Du Bois, *The Negro* (New York, 1915); W. E. B. Du Bois, "The Religion of the American Negro," *New World* 9 (1900): 614–25.

2. A leading and important work on the colonial and antebellum black church is Albert J. Raboteau's *Slave Religion: The "Invisible Institution" in the Antebellum South* (Oxford, 1980).

3. Kenneth M. Stampp, *The Peculiar Institution* (New York, 1956), 371.

4. Eugene Genovese, *Roll, Jordan, Roll: The World the Slaves Made* (New York, 1971), 184.

5. Ibid.

6. George P. Rawick, *The American Slave: A Composite Autobiography* (Westport, Conn., 1972–77), 1:33.

7. John W. Blassingame, *The Slave Community: Plantation Life in the Antebellum South* (New York, 1972), 20–24; Nathan Irvin Huggins, *Black Odyssey: The Afro-American Ordeal in Slavery* (New York, 1977), 62–77.

8. William Shuttles, "African Religious Survivals as Factors in American Slave Revolts," *Journal of Negro History* 56 (1971): 98.

9. Genovese, *Roll, Jordan, Roll*, 183.

10. Marcus Jernegan, "Slavery and Conversion in the American Colonies," *American Historical Review* 21 (1916): 504–27; Marcus Jernegan, *Laboring and Dependent Classes in Colonial America, 1607–1783* (Chicago, 1931), 24–37.

11. Raboteau, *Slave Religion*, 120–21.

12. Charles C. Jones, *The Religious Instruction of the Negroes* (Savannah, Ga., 1842), 6–30; W. P. Harrison, *The Gospel among the Slaves* (Nashville, 1893).

13. Mary F. Goodwin, "Christianizing and Educating the Negro in Colonial Virginia," *Historical Magazine of the Protestant Episcopal Church* 1 (1932): 144.

14. In William S. Perry, ed., *Historical Collections Relating to the American Church* (n.p., 1840), 1:264–65.

15. Ibid., 4:305.

16. Luther P. Jackson, "Religious Development of the Negro in Virginia from 1760 to 1860," *Journal of Negro History* 16 (1931): 169.

17. Raboteau, *Slave Religion*, 98–120.

18. Jernegan, "Slavery and Conversion," 517.

19. Jackson, "Religious Development," 169–70.

20. Perry, *Historical Collections*, 1:346–48.

21. Ibid., 277–78.

22. Jackson, "Religious Development," 169–70; Jernegan, *Laboring and Dependent Classes*, 24–31.

23. In Frederick Dalcho, *An Historical Account of the Protestant Episcopal Church in South Carolina* (New York, 1820; reprint, New York, 1972), 104.

24. Jernegan, *Laboring and Dependent Classes*, 24.

25. Rawick, *American Slave*, 1:32–33.

26. Genovese, *Roll, Jordan, Roll*, 185.

27. Limited sources make it difficult to state anything more definitive beyond this. According to an eyewitness account of the Stono Rebellion, the "Angolan" (Kongolese) participants were Catholics. However, the remaining primary sources used for this study make no mention of "Angolan" Catholicism during this or any other period; some extrapolation is therefore required. See "An Account of the Negroe Insurrection in South Carolina," in *Colonial Records of the State of Georgia*, ed. Allen D. Candler and William J. Northern (New York, 1904–16, 1970), vol. 22, pt. 2:232–36; John K. Thornton, "African Dimensions of the Stono Rebellion," *American Historical Review* 96 (1991): 1102.

28. Jackson, "Religious Development," 170–71.

29. Ibid., 178–79.

30. See Sylvia Frey, *Water from the Rock* (Princeton, N.J., 1991).

31. Mechal Sobel, *Trabelin' On: The Slave Journey to an Afro-Baptist Faith* (Princeton, N.J., 1979, 1988), 85–89.

32. Jackson, "Religious Development," 179.

33. Mechal Sobel, *The World They Made Together: Black and White Values in Eighteenth-Century Virginia* (Princeton, N.J., 1987), 178–80.

34. Ibid., 180.

35. Jackson, "Religious Development," 172.

36. Ibid., 176.

37. Sobel, *Trabelin' On*, 97–98.

38. Jackson, "Religious Development," 170.

39. Sobel, *Trabelin' On*, 98.

40. Jackson, "Religious Development," 177.

41. Ibid., 180.

42. Blassingame, *Slave Community*, 72.

43. Lathan Windley, comp., *Runaway Slave Advertisements: A Documentary History from the 1730s to 1790* (Westport, Conn., 1983), 1:232.

44. Ibid., 269–70, 339, 392.

45. Blassingame, *Slave Community*, 36.

46. *Gazette of the State of Georgia*, 23 October 1788.

47. John Hope Franklin and Alfred A. Moss Jr., *From Slavery to Freedom: A History of African Americans*, 5th ed. (New York, 1980), 110–12.

48. Jackson, "Religious Development," 181–86.

49. Ibid., 187.

50. Genovese, *Roll, Jordan, Roll*, 184.

51. Raboteau, *Slave Religion*, 149.

52. Ibid., 187–203.

53. Ira Berlin, *Slaves Without Masters: The Free Negro in the Antebellum South* (New York, 1976), 135–77, 218.

54. See John Hope Franklin, *The Militant South 1800-1861* (Cambridge, Mass., 1956); Jackson, "Religious Development," 203–34.

55. Luther P. Jackson, "Religious Instruction of Negroes, 1830 to 1860, with Special Reference to South Carolina," *Journal of Negro History* 15 (1930): 72–79.

56. Henry Bibb, *Narrative of the Life and Adventures of Henry Bibb* (New York, 1849), in Gilbert Osofsky, ed., *Puttin' on Ole Massa* (New York, 1969), 69.

57. John W. Blassingame, ed., *Slave Testimony* (Baton Rouge, 1977), 411.

58. Ibid.

59. Ibid., 420.

60. Bibb, *Narrative*, in Osofsky, *Puttin' on Ole Massa*, 69.

61. Sterling Stuckey, *Slave Culture: Nationalist Theory and the Foundations of Black America* (Oxford, 1987), 25.

62. James L. Smith, *Autobiography of James L. Smith* (Norwich, Conn., 1881), 30.

63. Rawick, *American Slave*, Supplement Series, 3:170.

64. John B. Cade, "Out of the Mouths of Ex-Slaves," *Journal of Negro History* 20 (1935): 331.

65. Rawick, *American Slave*, 4:10, pt. 4.

66. Ibid., 8:142.

67. Ibid., 14:425, pt. 1.

68. Ibid., 15:56, pt. 2.

69. Ibid., 1:39–45.

70. Ibid., 4:69, pt. 3.

71. Ibid., 9:40, pt. 3.

72. Ibid., Supplement Series, 10:1912.

73. Jackson, "Religious Development," 232–34.

74. Blassingame, *Slave Community*, 97–98. Du Bois, in some contrast, related that some 468,000 southern blacks were church members in 1859 (*The Negro Church* [Atlanta, 1903], 29).

75. Blassingame, *Slave Testimony*, 185.

76. Ibid., 76.

77. Bibb, *Narrative*, in Osofsky, *Puttin' on Ole Massa*, 69.

78. Charles Ball, *Slavery in the United States* (New York, 1837; reprint, New York, 1969), 21.

79. Ibid., 164–65.

80. Frederick Law Olmsted, *Journey in the Seaboard Slave States* (New York, 1856), 124–25.

81. Ibid., 114.

82. Stuckey, *Slave Culture*, 60.

83. Genovese, *Roll, Jordan, Roll*, 215–26.

84. Cheveux Gris, "The Negro in His Religious Aspect," *Southern Magazine* 17 (1875): 498–502.

85. Joseph LeConte, *The Autobiography of Joseph LeConte* (New York, 1903), 234–35.

86. Huggins, *Black Odyssey*, 174.

87. Stuckey, *Slave Culture*, 11.

88. Ibid., 17. I am in contact with colleagues who have experienced the shout in Maryland. It can also be found in remote areas of Georgia and South Carolina, and it is presented as performance in coastal Georgia.

89. Ibid., 13.

90. Maya Deren, *Divine Horsemen: Voodoo Gods of Haiti* (New York, 1970), 240.

91. Newbell N. Puckett, *Folk Beliefs of the Southern Negro* (Chapel Hill, 1926), 532.

92. See also Charles Lyell, *A Second Visit to the United States of America* (New York, 1849), 1:270; Charlotte Forten, "Life on the Sea Islands," *Atlantic Monthly* 13 (1864): 593–94; Abigail M. Holmes Christensen, "Spirituals and 'Shouts' of Southern Negroes," *Journal of American Folklore* 7 (1894): 154–55; Edward Channing Gannett, "The Freedmen at Port Royal," *North American Review* 101 (1865): 10. Spaulding, who was also at Port Royal in 1863, provides an even more descriptive account of the shout: "After the praise meeting is over, there usually follows the very singular and impressive performance of the 'Shout,' or religious dance of the negroes. Three or four, standing still, clapping their hands and beating time with their feet, commence singing in unison one of the peculiar shout melodies, while the others walk in a ring, single file, joining also in the song. Soon those in the ring leave off their singing, the others keeping it up the while with increased vigor, and strike into the shout step, observing most accurate time with the music. This step is something halfway between a shuffle and a dance, as difficult for an uninitiated person to describe as to imitate. At the end of each stanza of the song the dancers stop short with a slight stamp on the last note, and then, putting the other foot forward, proceed through the next verse." Spaulding has also attempted to record the music itself in this article. See H. G. Spaulding, "Under the Palmetto," *Continental Monthly* 4 (1863): 197.

93. Thomas Wentworth Higginson, *Army Life in a Black Regiment* (Boston, 1900), 23–24.

94. The ring shout not only had implications for the worship style of the black (and white) church but also influenced secular music. Stearns, for example, argues that the shout was "of critical importance to jazz, because it means that an assortment of West African musical characteristics are preserved, more or less intact, in the United States." This

"shuffle in a counter-clockwise direction around and around, arms out and shoulders hunched," was, Stearns accurately determined, "actually a West African circle dance." The impact of the shout upon the development of jazz was not necessarily the result of collective historical memory but was often by way of tangible links: "Many jazzmen, even among the ultra-moderns, are familiar with all or part of it because they lived with or near one of the Sanctified Churches during childhood" (Marshall W. Stearns, *The Story of Jazz* [New York, 1956], 12–14).

95. Lydia Parrish, *Slave Songs of the Georgia Sea Islands* (Hatboro, Pa., 1942, 1965), 20.

96. Rawick, *American Slave*, 4:294, pt. 2.

97. Ibid., 10:161–62, pt. 5; 16:113; Supplement Series, 3:170; Supplement Series, 6:284, are examples.

98. Georgia Writers' Project, *Drums and Shadows: Survival Studies among the Georgia Coastal Negroes* (Athens, Ga., 1940), 152.

99. Ibid., 160.

100. Ibid., 166.

101. Ibid., 147.

102. Du Bois, *The Negro*, 188–89.

103. Rawick, *American Slave*, 4:142, pt. 3.

104. Compare, for example, the revivalist experiences of whites in Kentucky in 1800 with the salient features of the ring shout. Given the widespread incidents of shouting, jerking, leaping, and being "slain" (losing consciousness in an ecstatic context), the probability is high that these forerunners to the "holy rollers" had been influenced by a more ancient and African set of rites. See Frederick M. Davenport, *Primitive Traits in Religious Revivals* (New York, 1906), 66–79.

105. Rawick, *American Slave*, Supplement Series, 1:623.

106. Ibid., Supplement Series, 8:892–93.

107. Smith, *Autobiography*, 27.

108. Sobel, *Trabelin' On*, 143–44.

109. Daniel Alexander Payne, *Recollections of Seventy Years* (New York, 1888; reprint, New York, 1968), 253–54.

110. Ibid., 255–56.

111. Lyell, *Second Visit* 1:269.

112. July Ann in Rawick, *American Slave*, Supplement Series, 8:904.

113. Anna Scott, 11 January 1937, Jacksonville, "Slave Interviews," Federal Writers' Project—Negro Writers' Unit, P. K. Yonge Library of Florida History, University of Florida, Gainesville.

114. Louis Napoleon, 17 November 1936, Jacksonville, ibid.

115. Mack Mullen, 20 November 1936, Jacksonville, ibid..

116. See Sobel, *Trabelin' On*.

117. Stuckey, *Slave Culture*, 13–14, 34–35.

118. See Newbell N. Puckett, "Religious Folk Beliefs of Whites and Negroes," *Journal of Negro History* 16 (1931): 9–35, for a discussion of the role of the Jordan.

119. Jackson, "Religious Development," 199.

120. Robert Farris Thompson, *Flash of the Spirit* (New York, 1983), 132.

121. Ibid., 132–42. See also Sarah H. Torian, "Ante-Bellum and War Memories of Mrs. Telfair Hodgson," *Georgia Historical Quarterly* 27 (1943): 350–56; H. Carrington Bolton, "Decoration of Graves of Negroes in South Carolina," *Journal of American Folklore* 4 (1891): 214.

122. Puckett, *Folk Beliefs*, 87–88.

123. Rawick, *American Slave*, 13:282, pt. 3.

124. Ibid., Supplement Series, 10:1985.

125. David R. Roediger, "And Die in Dixie: Funerals in the Slave Community," *Massachusetts Review* 22 (1981): 164.

126. Rawick, *American Slave*, 13:61, pt. 3.

127. Ibid., 330, pt. 3.

128. George H. Clark, letter, 9 May 1847, Nashville, in "Slavery: Correspondence by Author," V-K-1, box 1, 67-116, Tennessee State Archives, Nashville.

129. Roediger, "And Die in Dixie," 168–69.

130. An example of a wake lasting for several nights can be found in an anonymous account from Arkansas. The author mistakenly believes he or she witnessed an attempt at a resurrection: "I was, in 1819, on a plantation on the banks of the Lower Mississippi, where, for three nights, the congregation of a colored church kept up fires and queer dances around the grave of their dead pastor, a negro elder, trying to bring him back to life by those same conjuring methods employed in the interior of Africa" (*Journal of American Folklore* 1 [1888]: 83).

131. Rawick, *American Slave*, 13:330, pt. 3.

132. Ibid., Supplement Series, 8:1273.

133. Ibid., Supplement Series, 7:411.

134. Roediger, "And Die in Dixie," 170.

135. Ibid., 169.

136. Margaret Washington Creel, for example, states that Gullah slaves had a poor understanding of Christian doctrines. *"A Peculiar People": Slave Religion and Community-Culture among the Gullahs* (New York, 1988), 261–63.

137. Louis Hughes, *Thirty Years a Slave* (n.p., 1897), 51–52.

138. E. Franklin Frazier, *The Negro in the United States* (New York, 1957), 16–17.

139. Jackson, "Religious Development," 198–200.

140. Charles A. Raymond, "The Religious Life of the Negro Slave," *Harper's Magazine* 27 (1863): 816.

141. For example, see Du Bois, *The Negro*, 188–89; Stuckey, *Slave Culture*, 37–39.

142. Blassingame, *Slave Community*, 132.

143. Howard Thurman, *Deep Rivers: Reflections on the Religious Insight of Certain of the Negro Spirituals* (New York, 1955); Howard Thurman, *Jesus and the Disinherited* (New York, 1949).

144. See Sobel, *Trabelin' On*, 99–104.

145. Mrs. Isabel Barnwell, "A Day at Nueva Esperanza (New Hope) Plantation," Nassau County, Florida, 30 July 1939, P. K. Yonge Library of Florida History, University of Florida.

146. Raymond, "Religious Life," 816.

147. Lenora Herron, "Conjuring and Conjure-Doctors," *Southern Workman* (July 1895): 117–18.

148. For example, see E. B. Idowu, *African Traditional Religion: A Definition* (London, 1973); M. Okediji, ed., *Principles of "Traditional" African Culture* (Ibadan, Nigeria, 1992); O. A. Iloanusi, *Myths of the Creation of Man and the Origin of Death in Africa* (Frankfurt, 1984); L. Mbefo, *The Reshaping of African Traditions* (Enugu, Nigeria, 1988); John S. Mbiti, *African Religions and Philosophy* (London, 1969); Benjamin Ray, *African Religions* (Englewood Cliffs, N.J., 1976); J. B. Danquah, *Akan Doctrine of God* (London, 1968); D. Zahan, *The Religion and Spirituality and Thought of Traditional Africa* (Chicago, 1979); E. I. Metuh, *Comparative Studies of African Traditional Religions* (Onitsha, 1987); E. I. Metuh, ed., *The Gods in Retreat: Continuity and Change in African Religions* (Enugu, Nigeria, 1985); P. E. Ofori, *Black African Traditional Religions and Philosophy* (Liechtenstein, 1975); R. Griaule, *Conversations with Ogotemmêli* (London, 1965); K. A. Opoku, *West African Traditional Religion* (Legon, Ghana, 1977); J. K. Olupona, ed., *African Traditional Religion in Contemporary Society* (New York, 1990); J. O.

Awolalu and P. A. Dopamu, *West African Traditional Religion* (Ibadan, Nigeria, 1979); J. O. Kayode, *Understanding African Traditional Religion* (Ile-Ife, Nigeria, 1984); W. van Binsbergen and M. Schoffleleers, eds., *Theoretical Explorations in African Religions* (London, 1985); N. S. Booth Jr., ed., *African Religions: A Symposium* (New York, 1977); P. M. Peek, ed., *African Divination Systems: Ways of Knowing* (Bloomington, 1991); T. N. O. Quarcoopome, *West African Traditional Religion* (Ibadan, Nigeria, 1987).

149. Thompson, *Flash of the Spirit*, 117–31; Washington Creel, *"Peculiar People,"* 153–54.

150. Bibb, *Narrative*, in Osofsky, *Puttin' on Ole Massa*, 70.

151. Hughes, *Thirty Years a Slave*, 108.

152. Windley, *Runaway Slave Advertisements*, 4:160.

153. Georgia Writers' Project, *Drums and Shadows*, 18–19.

154. Ibid., 3.

155. Rawick, *American Slave*, 17:3–4. See the testimony of Wash William concerning the role of newspapers in 4:199–200, pt. 4. Compare with Letha Golson in Supplement Series, 8:814.

156. Georgia Writers' Project, *Drums and Shadows*, 5–6.

157. For example, see Zora Neale Hurston, "Hoodoo in America" *Journal of American Folklore* 44 (1931); A. M. Bacon, "Conjuring and Conjure-Doctors," *Southern Workman* 24 (1895): 193–94, 209–11; Lyle Saxon, Edward Dreyer, and Robert Tallant, *Gumbo Ya-Ya* (Cambridge, 1945).

158. Saxon, Dreyer, and Tallant, *Gumbo Ya-Ya*, 259.

159. Rawick, *American Slave*, 2:8.

160. Ibid., Supplement Series, 1:93.

161. Ibid., 19:208.

162. Ibid., 2:37, pt. 2.

163. Ibid., 9:302.

164. Ibid., 13:276, pt. 4.

165. Ibid., 2:78–79, pt. 3.

166. Ibid., 106–7, pt. 3.

167. Ibid., Supplement Series, 3:326.

168. Ibid., Supplement Series, 1:206.

169. Ibid., Supplement Series, 8:1246.

170. Ibid., 7:309.

171. Ibid., 19:76.

172. Ibid., 4:3, pt. 2.

173. Ibid., 2:143.

174. Ibid., 4:4–5, pt. 1.

175. Ibid., 161, pt. 3.

176. Ibid., 18:100.

177. Ibid., 6:430–31.

178. Ibid., 11:251.

179. Hughes, *Thirty Years a Slave*, 108.

SELECTED BIBLIOGRAPHY

ARCHIVAL SOURCES

Alabama Department of Archives and History, Montgomery

Manuscripts, Diaries, and Correspondence

Zillah Haynie Brandon Diaries, 1823–71. EW7N SPR 262.
John Witherspoon DuBose, 1836–1918. EW7S, Box 44.
John Erwin Papers. EW7N.
John H. Evans, "Reminiscences of Olden Times." SPR 186.
Edward Hawthorne Moren Papers. LPR 55.
Rev. Murdoch Murphy Diary, 1813–33. SPR 301.
Solomon Palmer Papers, 1839–96. SPR 263.
John Dabney Terrell Papers. EWS7, Box 240.
James Monroe Torbert Journal, 1848–53. Macon County.
John G. Traylor Papers. SPR 302.
Eliza J. Kendrick (Lewis) Walker, "Other Days." SPR 208.

The Avery Institute, Charleston, South Carolina

African Burial Ground Plot, 1847. County Planning Board.
William and Jane Pease Collection of Research Notes (Free and Slave Negro Households in Charleston, 1828–42).

Florida Department of Archives, Tallahassee

Craigmiles Family Papers, 1802–99. M87-023.
Joshua Hoyet Frier Papers, 1859–65. M76-134.

University of Florida, P. K. Yonge Library, Gainesville

Manuscripts, Diaries, and Correspondence

Isabel (O'Neill) Barnwell Interviews, Florida Plantation Records.
Bellamy/Bailey Family Papers, 1825–94. Manuscript Collection, Box 77.
"Florida Folklore and Custom." Federal Writers' Program in Florida, n.d.

Ianthe (Bond) Hebel Papers. Manuscript Collection, Box 13.

Zora Neale Hurston, "The Negro in Florida, 1528–1940." Federal Writers' Program in Florida, n.d.

"Life Among the Seminoles." Federal Writers' Program in Florida, 1936.

James T. O'Neil Papers, 1815–74. Manuscript Collection.

Ormond Family Papers. Manuscript Collection.

Charles Seton Papers, 1812–73. Manuscript Collection, Box 85.

"Slave Interviews" from the Negro Writers' Unit. Federal Writers' Program in Florida, n.d.

Dissertations

James D. Glunt. "Plantation and Frontier Records of East and Middle Florida, 1789–1868." Ph.D. diss., University of Michigan, 1930.

Jane Landers. "Black Society in Spanish St. Augustine, 1784–1821." Ph.D. diss., University of Florida, 1988.

Georgia Department of Archives and History, Atlanta

Manuscripts, Diaries, Correspondence

Correspondence of John Couper. 223-9. GRG 2-009.
Correspondence of John Couper. 223-15. GRG 2-029.

Church Records

Abilene Baptist, Columbus County, 1820–59.
Americus First Baptist, Sumter County, 1832–1934.
Antioch Baptist, Morgan County, 1809–48.
Antioch Baptist, Oglethorpe County, 1813–83.
Antioch Baptist, Talbot County, 1829–72.
Antioch Baptist, Harris County, 1838–58.
Athens First Baptist, Clarke County, 1819.
Bark Camp Baptist, Burke County, 1790–1858.
Bethlehem Baptist, Washington County, 1791–1912.
Bethsaida Baptist, Fulton County, 1830–1913.
Big Sandy Baptist, Wilkinson County, 1809–1908.
Blakely Baptist, Early County, 1837–94.
Cabin Creek Baptist, Jackson County, 1829–66.

Tennessee Department of Archives, Nashville

Manuscripts, Diaries, Correspondence

James G. Carson, 1815–63. II-H-1. 719.
George H. Clark Letter, 1847. V-K-1. 67-116.
Duncan Brown Cooper Papers, 1838–1965. VIII-L-1-2. 72-153.
Henry Gray, "Mississippi Pioneers." IV-E-2. 68-239.
J. A. McKinstry Letters, 1913. IV-A-5. 455.
Samuel Anderson Weakley Papers, 1700–1968. VI-F-2. 68-266.

Records of Antebellum Southern Plantations from the Revolution through the Civil War (edited by Kenneth M. Stampp)

Series A: Selections from the South Caroliniana Library, University of South Carolina.

Glover Family Plantation Books, 1837–64, Colleton District, South Carolina. Part 2, Reel 3.

James Henry Hammond Papers, 1795–65, Silver Bluff, South Carolina. Part 1, Reels 1–14.

John Stapleton Papers, 1790–1839, Beaufort District, South Carolina. Part 2, Reels 6 and 7.

Series B: Selections from the South Carolina Historical Society.

Thomas Porcher Ravenel Papers, 1731–1899, Charleston District, South Carolina. Part 1, Reel 1.

Series C

Duncan Clinch Letterbook, 1834–36, Camden County, Georgia. Part 2, Reel 1.

Edward Frost Papers, 1817–65, Charleston and Georgetown Districts, South Carolina. Part 2, Reel 1.

Series F: Selections from the Manuscript Department, Duke University Library.

John Ball Sr. and John Ball Jr. Papers, 1773–1892, Charleston District, South Carolina. Part 2, Reel 2.

Haller Nutt Papers, 1846–60, and the Journal of Araby Plantation, 1843–50, Natchez (Adams County), Mississippi and Madison Parish, Louisiana. Part 1, Reel 1.

Series H: Selections from the Howard-Tilton Library, Tulane University and the Louisiana State Museum Archives.

Plantation Hospital Book, 1838–43, Butler's Island, McIntosh County, Georgia (Louisiana State Museum). Part 1, Reel 1.

NEWSPAPERS CONSULTED

Alabama

Advertiser and State Gazette, 1849–56.
Alabama Baptist, 1843–92.
Alabama Beacon, 1843–1911.
Alabama Courier, 1822.
Alabama Intelligencer and States Rights Expositor, 1835–36.
Alabama Journal, 1825–57.
Alabama Mercury, 1837.
Alabama Planter, 1848–49.
Alabama Reporter, 1844–73.
Alabama Republican, 1817–32.
Alabama Sentinel, 1836.
Alabama State Gazette, 1825.
American Citizen, 1855.
American Whig, 1826.
Cahaba Democrat, 1840.
Cahaba Press and Alabama Intelligencer, 1819–25.

Cahawba Democrat, 1839.
Chronicle, 1846.
Courtland Herald, 1827, 1830.
Crystal Fount, 1851–73.
Daily Alabama Journal, 1849–54.
Democrat, 1823–72.
Florence Enquirer, 1840–47.
Florence Register, 1826.
Herald and Tribune, 1845–46.
Huntsville Gazette, 1816.
Independent Monitor, 1841–79.
Loco-Foco, 1840.
Macon Republican, 1849–59.
Marion Herald, 1839–45.
Mobile Advertiser and Chronicle, 1840–41.
Mobile Centinel, 1812.
Mobile Commercial Register and Patriot, 1832–44.
Mobile Daily Advertiser, 1843–67.
Mobile Daily Advertiser and Chronicle, 1829–43.
Mobile Mercantile Advertiser for the County, 1823–39.
Mobile Register and Journal, 1843–49.
Mobile Weekly Register, 1853–71.
Montgomery Daily Advertiser, 1841–75.
Montgomery Republican, 1821–23.
Morning Herald, 1843.
Patriot, 1839–41.
Selma Courier, 1827–29.
Selma Free Press, 1835–41.
Semiweekly Dallas Gazette, 1845.
Southern Advocate and Huntsville Advertiser, 1825–60.
Southern Democrat, 1837–39.
Southern Parlor Magazine, 1851.
Spirit of the South, 1857–58, 1861.
Tuscaloosa Chronicle, 1827.
Tuscaloosa Inquirer, 1831.
Tuscumbia Telegraph, 1827–28.
Tuskegee Republican, 1856–59.
Voice of Sumter, 1836–38.
Weekly Atlas and Secession, 1851.
Weekly Chronicle, 1845–46.
Weekly Flag and Advertiser, 1848.
Western Arminian, 1823–24.

Florida

Apalachicola Courier, 1839.
Apalachicola Gazette, 1836–40.
East Florida Advocate (Jacksonville), 1839–40.
East Florida Gazette (St. Augustine), 1783.

East Florida Herald (St. Augustine), 1823–34.
Florida Sentinel (Tallahassee), 1841–43, 1845–53.
Florida Watchman (Tallahassee), 1838.
Floridian (Pensacola), 1821–24.
Floridian (Tallahassee), 1828–48.
Floridian and Advocate (Tallahassee), 1829–31.
Jacksonville Courier, 1835–37.
Magnolia Advertiser, 1828–30.
News (St. Augustine), 1838–45.
Pensacola Gazette, 1825–55.
Pensacola Gazette and West Florida Advertiser, 1824–29.

Georgia

Albany Patriot, 1845–61.
American Patriot (Savannah), 1812.
Augusta Chronicle and Gazette of the State, 1786–1818.
Augusta Herald, 1812–14.
Columbia Museum and Savannah Advertiser, 1796–1822.
Columbus Enquirer, 1832–60.
Daily Georgian, 1819.
Federal Union, 1830–56.
Gazette of the State of Georgia, 1783–96.
Georgia Gazette, 1763–93.
Georgia Gazette, 1797–1802.
Georgia Journal, 1827–36.
Georgia Journal and Independent Federal Register (Savannah), 1793–94.
Georgia Journal and Messenger, 1823–58.
Georgia Messenger (Ft. Hawkins and Macon), 1824–41.
Georgia Patriot, 1824–25.
Georgia Republican (Savannah), 1807.
Georgia Republican and State Intelligencer (Savannah), 1803–4.
Georgia State Gazette or Independent Register (Augusta), 1786–89.
Georgian (Savannah), 1818.
Louisville Gazette and Republican Trumpet, 1799–1803.
Macon Telegraph, 1826–42.
Milledgeville Republican and Reflector, 1816–19.
Patriot and Commercial Advertiser, 1806–7.
Public Intelligencer (Savannah), 1807–9.
Reflector (Milledgeville), 1818.
Republican and Savannah Evening Ledger, 1807–41.
Savannah Daily Georgia, 1818–56.
Savannah Republican, 1803–50.
Southern Banner, 1832–59.
Southern Centinel and Gazette of the State, 1793–99.
Southern Patriot and Commercial Advertiser (Savannah), 1806–7.
Southern Recorder, 1820–58.
Virginia Gazette (Williamsburg), 1736–41, 1745–51, 1763–77.

Louisiana

Abeille (New Orleans), 1827–30.
Ami des lois et journal du commerce (New Orleans), 1820–21.
Asylum (Saint Francisville), 1823–25.
Asylum and Feliciana Advertiser, 1821–23.
Attakapas Gazette (Saint Martinsville), 1824–26.
Baton-Rouge Gazette, 1819, 1827–35, 1837–53.
Courier de la Louisiane, 1808, 1810–14, 1816–33, 1837, 1839–59.
Louisiana Gazette (New Orleans), 1804–10, 1817–26.
Louisiana Gazette and New-Orleans Advertiser, 1812–15.
Louisiana Gazette and New-Orleans Daily Advertiser, 1810–12.
Louisiana Gazette and New-Orleans Mercantile Advertiser, 1815–17.
Louisiana Journal (St. Francisville), 1824–26, 1828.
Louisiana State Gazette (New Orleans), 1826.
Louisianian.
Moniteur de la Louisiane (New Orleans), 1802–19.
New Orleans Price-Current and Commercial Intelligencer, 1825–31.
Port-Gibson Correspondent, 1821–22.
Republic (Baton Rouge), 1822–23.
Télégraphe, et le commercial advertiser (New Orleans), 1803–4.
Télégraphe, et le commercial advertiser and New Orleans Price Current, 1806.
Télégraphe et le general advertiser, 1807–9.
Télégraphe louisianais and Mercantile Advertiser, 1811–12.
Time Piece (St. Francisville), 1811, 1813–15.
Union, Etc. (New Orleans), 1804.
Union, or, New Orleans Advertiser and Price Current, 1803–4.

Maryland

Dunlap's Maryland Gazette or the Baltimore General Advertiser, 1775–79.
Maryland Gazette or the Baltimore General Advertiser, 1783–91.

Mississippi

Ariel (Natchez), 1825–28.
Mississippi Free Trader (Natchez).
Mississippi Messenger (Natchez).
Mississippi Republican (Natchez), 1813–18.
Mississippian (Jackson).
Saturday Morning Herald (Grenada).
Southern Galaxy (Natchez).
Southern Planter (Woodville).
Southern Reporter (Grenada, Yalobusha County).
Washington Republican, 1813–15.
Washington Republican and Natchez Intelligencer, 1815–17.

North Carolina

Cape Fear Mercury (Wilmington), 1769–75.
Cape Fear Recorder (Wilmington), 1816–32.

Carolina Centinel (and Sentinel) (New Bern), 1818–24, 1825–37.
Carolina Federal Republican (New Bern), 1809–18.
Catawba Journal, 1824–28.
Edenton Gazette, 1806–31, 1880–81.
Edenton Intelligencer, 1788.
Elizabeth City Gazette, 1807–8.
Fayetteville Gazette, 1789, 1792–93, 1820–22.
Fayetteville Intelligencer, 1811.
Fayetteville Observer, 1816–19, 1823–65.
Hall's Wilmington Gazette, 1797–98.
Herald of Freedom (Edenton), 1799.
Newbern Gazette, 1798–1804.
North Carolina Centinel (Fayetteville), 1795.
North Carolina Chronicle (Fayetteville), 1790–91.
North Carolina Gazette (Edenton), 1787.
North Carolina Gazette (Hillsboro), 1785–86.
North Carolina Gazette (New Bern), 1751–59, 1784–98.
North Carolina Gazette (Wilmington), 1766.
North Carolina Intelligencer (Fayetteville), 1806–8.
North Carolina Journal (Fayetteville), 1826–35, 1836–38.
North Carolina Journal (Halifax), 1792–1810.
North Carolina Magazine (New Bern), 1764–65.
North Carolina Minerva and Fayetteville Advertiser, 1796–99.
Post-Angel (Edenton), 1800.
Raleigh Minerva, 1799–1821.
State Gazette of North Carolina (Edenton), 1788–99.
State Gazette of North Carolina (New Bern), 1787–88.

South Carolina

Camden Gazette, 1816–18.
Camden Gazette and Mercantile Advertiser, 1818–22.
Camden Journal, 1826–91.
Carolina Galaxy and Commercial Gazette (Hamburg), 1834.
Carolina Gazette (Charleston), 1798–1836.
Carolina Weekly Messenger (Charleston), 1807–9.
Carolinian (Edgefield), 1829–35.
Charleston Courier, 1803–73.
Charleston Evening Post and Commercial and Political Gazette, 1815–16.
Charleston Mercury, 1822–29.
Cheraw Gazette, 1835–37.
Cheraw Intelligencer and Southern Register, 1823–26.
City Gazette and Daily Advertiser (Charleston), 1787–89, 1795–1826.
Columbia Herald, 1786–91.
Columbia Hive, 1832–36.
Columbia Telescope, 1816–20, 1831–39.
Columbia Telescope and South Carolina State Journal, 1824–27.
Farmer's Gazette and Cheraw Advertiser, 1839–43.
Gazette (Charleston), 1815–16.
Gazette of the State of South Carolina, 1777–80.

Georgetown Chronicle and South Carolina Weekly Advertiser, 1796–97.
Georgetown Gazette, 1798–1816.
Georgetown Gazette and Commercial Advertiser, 1806–10.
Georgetown Gazette and Mercantile Advertiser, 1815–17.
Georgetown Union, 1837–39.
Greenville Republican, 1826–28.
Miller's Weekly Messenger (Pendleton), 1810–11.
Observer (Charleston), 1827–45.
Pendleton Messenger, 1813–14, 1818–51.
Royal Gazette, 1781–82.
Royal South Carolina Gazette, 1780–82.
South-Carolina and American General Gazette Weekly, 1764–81.
South Carolina Gazette (Charleston), 1730–90.
South-Carolina Gazette and County Journal, 1765–68, 1773–75.
South-Carolina Gazette and General Advertiser, 1783–85.
South Carolina Gazette and Public Advertiser (Charleston), 1784–86.
South Carolina Independent Gazette and Georgetown Chronicle, 1791–92.
South Carolina State Gazette and Columbian Advertiser, 1801–16.
South Carolina Weekly Gazette (Charleston), 1759–64, 1783–86.
South Carolinian (Columbia), 1838–49.
Southern Chronicle and Camden Gazette, 1822–25.
Southern Patriot and Commercial Advertiser, 1815–18.
State Gazette of South Carolina (Charleston), 1785–94.
Times (Charleston), 1800–1821.
Winjah Intelligencer (Georgetown), 1817–35.

Tennessee

Central Gazette, 1832–48.
Chattanooga Gazette, 1839–61.
Clarksville Chronicle, 1836.
Clarksville Gazette, 1819–20.
Columbia Observer, 1834–47.
Knoxville Gazette, 1792–1818.
Nashville Gazette, 1819–27.
Nashville Register, 1819–29.
Nashville Whig, 1812–26.
Tennessee Democrat, 1835–50.
Tennessee Weekly Chronicle, 1814–19.
Town Gazette and Farmers Register, 1819.
Washington Republican and Farmers Journal, 1832–36.
Wilson's Knoxville Gazette, 1807–16.

Virginia

Alexandria Advertiser, 1797–99.
Virginia Argus, 1793–1816.
Virginia Chronicle and Norfolk and Portsmouth General Advertiser, 1792–94.
Virginia Gazette, 1736–1836.
Virginia Gazette and General Advertiser (Richmond), 1790–1809.

Virginia Gazette and Petersburg Intelligencier, 1796–1805.
Virginia Gazette and Weekly Advertiser (Richmond), 1787–89, 1793, 1795.
Virginia Gazette or the American Advertiser, 1782–86.
Virginia Herald (Fredericksburg), 1792–1836.
Virginia Independent Chronicle (Richmond), 1786–90.
Virginia Journal and Alexandria Advertiser, 1784–88.

INDEX

Lega, the, 144, 145
Legba (Fon-Ewe), 57
Liberia, 27, 86, 88, 102, 103
Li Grand Zombi, 57
Loango, 141, 142, 143, 144
Loango Bay, 143
Loas, 56–57
Loko, the, 88, 89, 90, 97
Louisiana, 23–24, 27–28; Bambara in, 38,
    43, 87; from Bight of Benin, 54–58;
    Muslims in, 67–68; West Central
    Africans in, 137, 151; Akan in, 151;
    Fon-Ewe-Yoruba, 151; Igbo in, 151;
    Senegambians in, 151; Sierra Leonians
    in, 151; seasoning in, 170; ethnic mixing
    in, 173–74
Louisiana Creole, 51
Lozi, the, 143
Luanda, West Central Africa, 141, 156
Luba, the, 143
Lubata (plural *mabata*, Kikongo), 145
Lunda, the, 142, 143

Maasina, Senegambia, 63, 73
Madagascar, 27, 29, 41
Madrasa, 85
Mafuk, 143
Malagasy slaves, 41
Malebo Pool, 141, 143
Mali: imperial, 5, 7, 46, 108; modern,
    45–46, 96
Malinke, the, 7; preferred in Carolina, 42;
    in Senegambia, 45, 46
Mamprussi, kingdom of, 65, 108
Mande speakers, 38, 39; in Senegambians,
    45, 46, 64, 65, 68, 87; and Juula mer-
    chants, 48; terms, 50–51; descriptions
    of, 82; Muslims among, 86; in Sierra
    Leone, 88, 89, 90, 92, 102
Mandingo (or Mundingo), 39–40, 42, 64,
    65, 68
Mandinka, the, 60, 68, 74. *See also* Mende,
    the
Mane, the, 89–90, 92; wars of, 89–90
Mani (Kikongo), 145
Maroons: among Bambara, 52; in
    Louisiana, 52–53; in Florida, 182; in
    Georgia and South Carolina, 182–85.
    See also Runaway slave advertisements
Martinique, 55, 56

Maryland, 21, 24, 27, 41; Muslims in, 71;
    Charles Ball in, 74; Akan in, 107; Igbo
    in, 124, 150
Massachusetts, 26, 29
Massassi dynasty, Senegambia, 46–47
Matamba, 142
Mawe (plural *mawesia*, Mande), 93, 111
Mawu-Lisa (Fon-Ewe), 57
Mbanza Kongo, 141
Mbumba, 146
Mbundu, 141, 142
Mende, the, 88, 93, 94, 98–99, 102, 111;
    aboard the *Amistad*, 216–17. *See also*
    Mandinka, the
Methodist Church, 251–52, 255, 257, 279
Methodist Church South, 257
Middle Passage, the, 13, 14; and Igbo,
    116, 117, 119; and branding, 159; and
    denuding, 159; and white cannibalism,
    159–60; and diet, 160–61; and disease,
    161–62, 163–64; and tight packing,
    162–63; and "melancholy," 163–64; and
    mortality, 163–64; memory of, 164–65;
    and shipmates, 165–66; and sexual
    exploitation, 165–67; and Gullah Jack
    story, 202–4, 218
Militant South, the, 257–61, 281
Mina, the, 53
Minkisi (or *nkisi*), 146, 148, 152, 153, 250,
    275; and hoodoo, 283–90
Mississippi, 24, 27; voodoo in, 55, 57–58;
    Muslims in, 71; societies of men and
    women in, 100–101
Mitombo, Sierra Leone, 90
Mobile, Ala., 167, 175
Mogya (Akan), 111, 277
Monday Gell (Vesey codefendant), 3
Moors: and Nasir al-Din, 63, 64; identified
    in North America, 69, 70, 75, 86, 87–88
Morocco: as origin of slaves, 75, 86
Mossi, the, 108
Mozambique: and Islam, 66; and slave
    trade, 143
Mozambique-Madagascar, 27, 29
Mpemba, 147, 164, 273
Mpinda, West Central Africa, 141
Mulattoes: as runaways, 41; Marie Laveau,
    57; and social stratification, 224–25,
    230–43; definition of, 231–32
Music, African American, 4, 10–11

Population: in North America, 19–24; spatial arrangement of, 24–27
Poro society of men, 94–100. *See also* Societies of men
Portuguese, the: in Sierra Leone, 89–90; in Gold Coast, 105–6, 108; in Bight of Biafra, 131–32; in Angola, 135; in Congo and Angola, 141–44, 147
Pots: turning down the, 259–63
Poyas, Peter (Vesey codefendant), 2–3
Pra River, 105
Preacher Little, 81
Presbyterian Church, 251, 255
Protestantism, 10
Puerto Rico, 53
Pulaar language, 75–76, 77

Quadroon balls, 231
Qur'ān, 67, 75, 77, 79, 85, 249

Race, 3–5, 11–13, 15; influence on Muslims, 86; development in Middle Passage, 165–67; and language, 180–82; and folklore, 212–13; transition to, 221; mixed, 224–25, 230–43; and ring shout, 264–72; and water baptism, 272–74; and funerary rites, 277–78
Rada (voodoo tradition), 57
Ragbenle society of men. *See* Poro society of men
Red cloth tales, 199–209
Reincarnation, beliefs in: among Bambara, 49; in Sierra Leone, 94; among Akan, 111–12; among Igbo, 130–31, 133–34
Reinterpretation, 10
Religion, 1–4, 6, 10, 59
Revolt, slave, 1–4; among Bambara, 51–54
Rhode Island, 26–27
Rice cultivation, 24; from Sierra Leone, 40–41, 93; from Madagascar, 41; crucial to colonial economies, 44; in Georgia and South Carolina, 69–70; and contribution of women, 93, 96; in Bight of Biafra, 128
Ring ceremonies, 266–67
Ring shout, 4, 16; and flying Igbo, 118; among Bafut of Cameroon, 134–35; and Kongo cosmogram, 149; from West Central Africa, 250; in Haiti, 264–65; in

North America, 264–72; rejection by elite, 269–70
Rio Nunez, 91
Rio Pongas, 91
Risāla of Ibn Abī Zayd, 71, 79
Rolla (Vesey codefendant), 2–3
Royal African Company, 20, 31, 32, 71, 90, 157, 163
Royal blood: claims of, 239–40
Runaway slave advertisements, 5, 38–40; and Muslims, 67, 68–71, 76; and the Kissi and Gola, 102–3; from Angola, 103; from Guinea, 103; and the Igbo, 120–24; from West Central Africa, 137–40; and Africans and African Americans, 195–97; black and mixed race, 237–39; and Christians, 254

Sahara desert: trade in, 46, 108
St. Augustine, Fla., 23–24, 67
St. Helena Island, Ga., 75
St. Johns River, 175
Saint Mose (or Fort Mose), Fla., 24, 67
St. Simons Island, Ga., 71, 74, 76–87, 118
Salih Bilali, 71, 73, 74, 76–87
Salt-water Africans, 14, 168, 189
Sande society of women, 94–100, 250
Sandogo. *See* Bundu society of women; Sande society of women
Sando-Mother, 96. *See also* Bundu society of women; Sande society of women
Santo Domingo, 2–3, 21
São Salvador, 141
São Tome, 141
Sape, the, 89, 92
Sapelo Island, 71, 74, 76–87, 205, 266
Sapelo River, 138
Savannah, Ga., 23, 69, 70, 117, 167; Muslims near, 76; Igbo in, 133
Scarcies River, 89
Scarification patterns. *See* Country marks; Runaway slave advertisements
Seasoning, 14, 168–70, 190
Seminoles: and Africans, 182–85
Seminole Wars, 182
Senegal, 27, 28; Bambara from, 42; in Louisiana, 43, 44, 54; women from, 44; Muslims from, 75, 82
Senegal valleys, 46, 61, 62, 63, 64; Muslims from, 72, 73

Whydah, West Africa, 54, 67, 175
Windward Coast, 40, 103, 158. *See also* Sierra Leone
Wofa (Akan), 111
Wolof, the: in Louisiana, 43; women, 43, 44; description of, 44; in Senegambia, 45; and Islam, 62, 63, 64; and stratification, 222
Woman marriage, 127
Women, 22, 35–37; individual runaways, 40, 43–44, 68, 103, 196–97; Wolof, 43, 44; interethnic marriages, 43, 86; Igbo, 43, 120–23, 126–28; in workhouse, 44; of Creole families in Louisiana, 51; Muslim, 70, 74–75, 76, 77–87; and rice and cotton, 93; in Mende household, 93; societies of, 94–99; ancestresses of Akan, 105, 109; Akan, 110, 111; Igbo woman marriage, 127; Ala (or Ana, Igbo), 129; West Central African, 139–40; Lega, 144; and social stratification, 152–53; aboard slavers, 158–59; examined at barracoons, 161; exploitation of in Middle Passage, 166–67; African and African American, 196–97; African

mothers remembered, 198–99; biracial, 237–39; royal, 240–43; brutalized, 258–59
Working roots, 286–90. *See also* Amulets; Hoodoo; *Minkisi*; Voodoo
Worship, clandestine, 259–63
Wuli, Senegambia, 46
Wyemba, West Africa, 157

Yarrow, Mahmud, 72, 73
Yarse merchants, 67
Yatenga, kingdom of, 108
Yaws, 161
Yellow Bastard tale, 233–36
York Island, Sierra Leone, 90
Yoruba, the, 7, 114; in Louisiana, 54; and urbanity, 54–55; in Brazil, 55; and Islam, 65, 66
Yowa line, 148

Zaghawa, the, 7
Zaire. *See* Congo; Kongo, kingdom of; West Central Africa
Zinzin (Bambara), 50–51. *See also* Amulets; Hoodoo; *Minkisi*; Voodoo